Desire, Self, Mind,
and the Psychotherapies

New Imago: Series in Theoretical, Clinical, and Applied Psychoanalysis

Series Editor
Jon Mills, Canadian Psychological Association

New Imago: Series in Theoretical, Clinical, and Applied Psychoanalysis is a scholarly and professional publishing imprint devoted to all aspects of psychoanalytic inquiry and research in theoretical, clinical, philosophical, and applied psychoanalysis. It is inclusive in focus, hence fostering a spirit of plurality, respect, and tolerance across the psychoanalytic domain. The series aspires to promote open and thoughtful dialogue across disciplinary and interdisciplinary fields in mental health, the humanities, and the social and behavioral sciences. It furthermore wishes to advance psychoanalytic thought and extend its applications to serve greater society, diverse cultures, and the public at large. The editorial board is comprised of the most noted and celebrated analysts, scholars, and academics in the English speaking world and is representative of every major school in the history of psychoanalytic thought.

Titles in Series:

Desire, Self, Mind, and the Psychotherapies: Unifying Psychological Science and Psychoanalysis by R. Coleman Curtis.

Desire, Self, Mind, and the Psychotherapies

Unifying Psychological Science and Psychoanalysis

R. COLEMAN CURTIS

JASON ARONSON
Lanham • Boulder • New York • Toronto • Plymouth, UK

"Dream Boogie," from *The Collected Poems of Langston Hughes* by Langston Hughes, edited by Arnold Rampersad with David Roessel, Associate Editor, copyright © 1994 by The Estate of Langston Hughes. Used by permission of Alfred A. Knopf, a division of Random House, Inc.

Published in the United States of America
by Jason Aronson
An imprint of Rowman & Littlefield Publishers, Inc.

A wholly owned subsidary of
The Rowman & Littlefield Publishing Group, Inc.
4501 Forbes Boulevard, Suite 200, Lanham, Maryland 20706
www.rowmanlittlefield.com

Estover Road
Plymouth PL6 7PY
United Kingdom

Copyright © 2009 by Jason Aronson Publishers, Inc.

British Library Cataloguing in Publication Information Available

Library of Congress Cataloging-in-Publication Data

Curtis, R. Coleman, 1947–
  Desire, self, mind, and the psychotherapies : unifying psychological science and psychoanalysis / R. Coleman Curtis.
      p. cm.
  Includes bibliographical references and index.
  ISBN-13: 978-0-7657-0596-9 (cloth : alk. paper)
  ISBN-10: 0-7657-0596-6 (cloth : alk. paper)
  eISBN-13: 978-0-7657-0610-2
  eISBN-10: 0-7657-0610-5
  1. Psychology. 2. Psychoanalysis. I. Title.
  BF38.C925 2009
  150.1—dc22   2008034290

Printed in the United States of America

♾™ The paper used in this publication meets the minimum requirements of American National Standard for Information Sciences—Permanence of Paper for Printed Library Materials, ANSI/NISO Z39.48-1992.

Contents

Preface

The thinker who has a mortal fear of being wrong will give all that is valuable in himself to that little ambition.

— Walter Lippmann, 1914

Cognitive-affective science is now dominating the world of psychology. Although psychologists have now embraced the long-rejected idea of the influence of unconscious processes, with Malcolm Gladwell's best seller *Blink* even documenting these processes for the general public, Freud's psychoanalysis is considered by many scientists and much of the public to be dead. Yet cognitive-affective science fails to capture the imagination and its passions the way that the sex and aggression of psychoanalysis did. We now have cognitive, behavioral, and experiential therapists trying to change personality without a theory of desire, the self, or the mind that captures the role of unconscious passions. We have psychoanalysts engaged in a change process based upon a theory that is not always consistent with the data from scientific research. How can we have a theory of change if we don't have a satisfactory theory of desire, the self, and the mind? This book is an attempt to move towards an integrated theory.

R. C. C.
New York City
December, 2007

Acknowledgments

I would not have been able to write this book without the stimulating intellectual environments of the Derner Institute at Adelphi University, including the environments created by my colleagues involved with the Honors Program and the Core Curriculum, and the William Alanson White Institute. I am also indebted especially to colleagues of the Rapaport-Klein Study Group at the Austen-Riggs Institute, the Society for the Exploration of Psychotherapy Integration, the Society for Psychotherapy Research, and to all of the many colloquia, lectures, and conferences available through the American Psychological Association and in New York City by a variety of psychoanalytic institutes, universities, clubs, and other organizations. Participants in the research groups of the American Psychoanalytic Association, especially Robert Wallerstein, the International Federation of Psychoanalytic Societies, the Nags Head Conferences on Social-Personality Psychology, and the Neuro-Psychoanalysis have also been of enormous assistance, along with various anonymous journal reviewers. I would also like to thank my colleagues and friends from many walks of life who seemed to believe I had something worthwhile to contribute, including Mark Blechner, Joerg Bose, John Norcross, Jack Drescher, Morris Eagle, Mary Farrell, Herb Fensterheim, Mary Fitzpatrick, Tina Harrell, Denise Hien, Jonathan Jackson, Leopold Katz, Yvonne Korshak, Marylou Lionells, Raul Ludmer, Leigh McCullough, Paolo Migone, Stephen Mitchell, Stanley Riklin, Jane and Douglas Smith, Eugene Roth, Eleanor Shaw, Stanley Spiegel, Paul Wachtel, Drew Westen, participants in the various study groups I attended, and my graduate assistants Jay Crosby, Arianne Miller, Cristy Rasco, Anat Dgani-Ratsaby, Petra Amrani, and Kelly Rotella. The permission of my patients enabled me to include session material. Without my patients, the book could not have been written. I am also indebted to the great libraries of New York City, especially to Columbia, and also those of the Metropolitan Museum of Art and the Frick Museum and the very helpful ones in the Hamptons. I must also acknowledge the owners of book stores who exhibited their enticing titles and let me browse, especially Barnes and Noble, Bookhampton, and Canio's of Sag Harbor, Long Island, and to the developers of the Internet and Google!

None of this would have been possible without the financial and emotional support of my husband. I also thank my older brother Aubrey Coleman, and his wife Ann Coleman, for always being there when I needed them. I am grateful to my sons, patients, and students for giving me awareness on a daily basis of my limitations as well as my strengths, humility about my own capacities, and encouragement to continue thinking, acting, feeling, and living. And of course, I am thankful for my parents, both now deceased, who not only gave me love, but were thrilled by my curiosity, tolerated my eccentricities, and helped me pick up the pieces (or create some new ones) whenever I felt all I had worked toward was falling apart. I am grateful to my sons, patients, and students for giving me awareness on a daily basis of my limitations as well as my strengths, humility about my own capacities, and encouragement.

Chapter 1

Heteroclitics and Psychology

There is a worse kind of disorder than that of the *incongruous*. . . . I mean
the disorder in which a large number of possible orders glitter separately,
in the lawless and uncharted dimension of the *heteroclite*.

—Michel Foucault, 1970

It is in the nature of profound things to clash and combine, to evolve from
one another.

—Antonin Artaud, 1966

At approximately 12:15 AM on June 5, 1968, Sirhan Sirhan shot Robert F.
Kennedy. Apparently, Sirhan had attacked Kennedy in a very agitated state
and remembered nothing about the event afterward. Bernard L. Diamond
(Bower 1981), the forensic psychiatrist who examined Sirhan hypnotized him
and helped him reconstruct the memories of what had happened in the kitchen
of the Los Angeles hotel. "Under hypnosis, as Sirhan became more worked
up and excited, he recalled progressively more, the memories tumbling out
while his excitement built to crescendo leading to the shooting. At that point
Sirhan would scream out the death curses, 'fire' the shots, and then choke as
he reexperienced the secret service guard nearly throttling him after he was
caught" (129). Despite the fact that Sirhan would have liked to have felt that
he did the deed (in the cause of Arab nationalism), he was never able, through
conscious effort in a non-hypnotized state, to remember doing so.

How do we understand the differing self-states, the motivation, and the
mind of someone like Sirhan? For one hundred years psychology and psychoanalysis have differed in their conceptualizations of the basic mental processes
affecting Sirhan and the rest of humanity. Cognitive psychologists have now
rediscovered the unconscious processes so important to Freud but banned

1

from the study of mainstream psychology by its founder William James. So far, however, these rediscovered unconscious processes have been primarily the "adaptive ones" described in such popular books as Malcolm Gladwell's *Blink* and Timothy Wilson's *Strangers to Ourselves*. Not only have these two disciplines had different models of the mind, their models of the self and of desire have also been different. Is there any way now to develop a paradigm acceptable to both psychologists and psychoanalysts?

HETEROCLITICS

Foucault (1970) explains that, in the etymological sense, the state of the *heteroclite* is one in which "things are 'laid,' 'placed,' 'arranged' in sites so very different from one another that it is impossible to find a common place beneath them all" (48). Both in the humanities and sciences of the latter twentieth century the ideas of possible orders and parallel worlds (Halpern 2004; Kaku 2004) have permeated our views. In a multicultural world we are aware on a daily basis of people who live in different social orders from our own. But each of us in our own way can be a heteroclite. Our minds all glitter separately and can leave us with difficulty finding the common human experiences that we all share somewhere inside.

Heteroclites: Psychology and Psychoanalysis

In the domain of psychology multiple worlds have existed simultaneously with surprisingly little overlap. Psychoanalysis and psychology have had very little interconnection or dialogue, in spite of their concern with the same subject (Whittle 1999). Psychiatry is yet another world, but it is beyond the focus of this book. It often seems in psychology that we are in the state of the heteroclite that Foucault (1970) portrayed. I shall describe briefly the separate histories of psychology and psychoanalysis and then discuss some areas of convergence in recent years.

For a century psychoanalysis and psychology existed largely in "splendid isolation" (Freud 1914) from one another. Funder (1997) referred to the two disciplines as being in a state of "mutual myopia," with psychologists and psychoanalysts ignoring each other most of the time, and when they interact, attacking or at best lecturing each other "without listening to the other side" (273). Whittle (1991), referring to the gulf between psychoanalysis and experimental psychology stated: "The size of this split within what outsiders regard as a single subject is without parallel in any other academic discipline. Neither side reads the literature of the other" (235). The problem of the split of psychoanalysis from science was taken up in the *Journal of the American Psychoanalytic Association* by Shevrin (1995a) and seven respondents. In response to the commentaries, Shevrin (1995b) expressed hope that during the second century of psychoanalysis a concerted effort would be made toward developing a comprehensive science drawing from the strengths of clinical practice, psychotherapy research, and experiments investigating its fundamental propositions. The essays in this volume are part of such an effort.

The discipline of clinical psychology developed first in the United States. In the United States, however, only physicians, usually psychiatrists, were allowed training in most psychoanalytic institutes and acceptance into the American and International Psychoanalytic Associations. Psychologists were not allowed training to become practitioners of psychoanalysis. Psychologists, located in schools of arts and sciences in universities, had little connection to psychiatrists at medical schools who might have training in psychoanalysis. William James, considered by most people to be the founder of psychology in this country, had effectively banned the study of unconscious factors, the foundation of psychoanalytic thinking, from the domain of psychology by proclaiming the examination of unconscious processes to be the "tumbling ground of whimsies" (1890, 163). The psychiatrists in hospital consulting rooms and private offices had virtually no contact with psychologists in university research laboratories.

As psychologists turned their attention to the processes of learning, change, and eventually to psychotherapy, the ways of helping people by clinical psychologists developed independently of the Freudian thinking of most psychoanalysts. In recent years, however, psychologists have begun to investigate unconscious processes and psychoanalysis in the United States has become more and more dominated by a relational theory of psychoanalysis rather far removed in its theory of the mind from its Freudian roots. These developments allow for an integration of ideas from these two disparate disciplines about the self and identity, motivation—including sex and aggression—and conscious and unconscious processes.

As human beings have gained more knowledge about the world, their ability to predict and, in many ways control, what happens has increased. In the past century, people's confidence that they can shape their own consciousness has risen. Psychoanalysis and psychotherapy have contributed to this belief. The belief that people can shape their own lives has been spurred on by the ability for the first time to reliably separate reproduction from sexual behaviors. Enormous social change has occurred as people have asked whether sexuality needs to be regulated and differences between male and female roles have diminished. These changes have also affected people's psychology, that is, their consciousness.

With twentieth-century views derived from quantum physics emphasizing interconnectedness and mutual interactions, the vision of linear causality embedded in Aristotelian philosophy and Newtonian physics, which gave rise to the drive models in psychoanalysis and psychology, no longer captures our view of reality. Once Bohr (1934) proclaimed that physical entities possess no dynamic attributes of their own, it became difficult for scientifically oriented psychologists to hold onto theories positing innate drives of the organism. Instinct and drive theories withered away in both psychoanalysis and psychology, while the effects of our biological heritage are still being reckoned with. The findings of evolutionary psychologists, as well as the passions described by Freud and the great writers, must be taken into account while recognizing that the lives of human beings are determined less by their genes than the lives of any other species. The paradigm shift from drives to desires is one where people are now viewed as able to affect the forces, both external and internal, that are shaping their own consciousness. This revolution is as dramatic as the change that occurred when evolving human beings became aware that the voices they were hearing within were their own minds thinking. Still, we are often not aware of many of the factors affecting us.

The view of physical reality in recent years has also been jolted by the knowledge of the order that emerges out of disorder. Between order and chaos lies complexity. Between a settled, rigid system and a stormy, turbulent one is a boundary, an edge where a pattern begins to appear out of formlessness. Such is the image of reality from the new physics (cf. Gleick 1987; Lewin 1992; Waldrop 1992). And between the biological determinism of the past and total chaos within psychoanalytic psychology lies the complexity of contemporary theory in which the patterns of a new model are beginning to emerge from a long overdue interface with psychology and neuroscience.

PSYCHOLOGY AND ITS RELATION TO PSYCHOANALYSIS

Clinical psychology

Clinical psychology developed completely independently of psychoanalysis. Clinical psychology was largely a discipline dealing with intelligence testing and personality theory before World War II. The first training program in clinical psychology was begun at the University of Pennsylvania in 1897 (Routh 2000) where Witmer had started a clinic dealing basically with child guidance. The American Association of Clinical Psychology was formed in 1917 (Abt 1992).

Initially, there had been little sign that there would be hostilities between psychology and psychoanalysis (Hornstein 1992). There was some mild interest in the articles that appeared in psychology journals in the early 1900s (e.g., Putnam 1906; Scott 1908). G. Stanley Hall invited Freud to Clark University in 1909 to give the lectures that introduced Americans to psychoanalysis. Shakow and Rapaport (1964) wrote that by 1910, however, those who expressed strong opposition to Freud's ideas were almost a "Who's Who" of neurology and psychiatry in the United States. Morton Prince, the founder of the *Journal of Abnormal Psychology* expressed the point of view that psychoanalysts "fit the facts to the universal concepts which dominate the school" (1910, 349). Criticisms of psychoanalysis continued to increase in the young science, with Woodworth of Columbia calling psychoanalysis an "uncanny religion" in 1916 (396) and criticizing "Freudism" in 1917. In the 1920s a member of the American Psychological Association was rebuked for mentioning Freud's name at a gathering of scientists (Dallenbach, cited in Hornstein 1992). By 1927 Watson referred to it as "voodooism" (502) and Jastrow in 1932 called it "a delusion" (285). In the 1930s, however, "Freud was little known to many [psychologists]" (Abt 1992, 176).

Gordon Allport published nine articles in 1940 on psychoanalysis by analyzed psychologists in his *Journal of Abnormal and Social Psychology*. Psychologists began testing psychoanalytic concepts in the following decade making themselves the arbiters of which psychoanalytic concepts, if any, were valid scientifically. Psychotherapy began in earnest with the treatment of soldiers in World War II, and Rogers published *Counseling and Psychotherapy* in 1942. In 1950 Ellis published a paper entitled "An Introduction to the Principles of Scientific Psychoanalysis" with thirteen sections, nine of which were devoted to the dangers of psychoanalysis. In the same year Dollard and Miller published *Personality and Psychotherapy*, integrating learning theory and psychoanalysis. The effectiveness of psychoanalytic therapy was challenged, however, by Eysenck in 1952 and 1966. By 1973, Eysenck and Wilson found psychoanalysis lacking any scientific support whatsoever.

By the 1970s the behavioral view dominated the American psychological scene. The prominence of the behavioral orientation was soon surmounted by the cognitive revolution. Clinical psychology reflected these trends. Clinical psychology in the United States continues to be aligned more with social/cognitive and learning psychology than with psychoanalysis.

The Psychoanalytic World

Psychoanalysis was plagued by hostilities. In Europe Freud had ousted Jung and Adler from his fold because of their lack of acceptance of some of his basic ideas. In the United States in 1941 the New York Psychoanalytic Institute removed Karen Horney from the teaching faculty, declaring her views contrary to the principles of psychoanalysis, leading to an exodus of analysts and candidates from the New York Psychoanalytic Institute and to the founding of other institutes. Although psychoanalysis in Europe had been largely a pursuit of medical doctors, it was not exclusively so. In the United States, however, persons without a medical degree were excluded from training. The role of nonmedical analysts was complicated when they arrived in the United States from Europe. Horney had invited Erich Fromm, who was not a medical doctor, to Chicago in 1932. Later, in New York, Horney founded the American Institute of Psychoanalysis after her own exclusion from the teaching faculty at New York Psychoanalytic where she had been a member of the faculty since 1935. Horney deprived Fromm of faculty status at the American Institute, seemingly as their romantic relationship came to an end. In the United States, then, psychoanalysis was limited to medical doctors. Psychologists were rarely working in hospitals where they might have contact with psychoanalysts before World War II. Although the W. A. White Institute, established in 1943 by Fromm, Fromm-Reichmann, the Riochs, Sullivan, and Thompson, accepted psychologists for training, it was excluded from membership in the American and International Psychoanalytic Associations. Only recently, after settlement of a lawsuit (by psychologists) in 1988, were psychologists accepted for training in the institutes of the American Psychoanalytic Association.

Psychotherapy Integration

Ferenczi and Rank (1923) experimented with active and other techniques in the psychoanalysis of difficult patients, although they appeared to abandon these techniques as they moved on to other ideas about transference, regression, and, in Rank's case, separation anxiety. Later attempts at integrating psychoanalysis and behavior therapy have been described by Arkowitz (1984), Goldfried and Newman (1992), and Gold (1993, 1996). According to Arkowitz, Ischlondy (1930) published the first paper on psychotherapy integration in German. In 1932 French delivered an address at the meeting of the American Psychiatric Association commenting upon certain similarities in psychoanalysis and Pavlovian conditioning. The paper and the mixed comments from the audience were published the following year. Kubie (1934) then noted that Pavlov had suggested that certain associations might occur outside consciousness and that free association might allow such unconscious associations to emerge. The idea that common factors might affect therapeutic change more than theoretical principles was first articulated by Rosenzweig (1936). Watson (1940) argued that there was more agreement in what therapists did in practice than in theory. "Homework" assignments in the context of psychodynamic therapy were suggested by Herzberg (1945). Alexander and French (1946) stirred up considerable controversy in the psychoanalytic world by advocating that psychoanalysis be modified by using more active approaches. Eissler (1953) was quite critical of Alexander and French's ideas, as was most of the rest of the psychoanalytic world, and provided his own guidelines for modifications, as will be discussed in chapter 8. Woodworth (1948), in a book describing the various schools of psychology, wondered if synthesis might soon be possible.

Dollard and Miller (1950) wrote the aforementioned classic describing how psychoanalytic concepts could be understood in terms of learning theory. After this publication, the 1960s brought an increase in the writings dealing with rapprochement, most notably Frank's (1961) *Persuasion and Healing*. Frank described similar change processes in religious practices, brainwashing, placebo effects in medicine, and psychotherapy. The arousal of hope and common factors in the relationship were seen as major areas of overlap. In 1963 Alexander wrote an article arguing that psychoanalysis could be understood in terms of learning theory. His colleague Marmor (1964) published a chapter about the learning principles he believed underlay psychoanalytic therapy. Several authors, including Rogers (1963), London (1964), Wolf (1966) and Marks and Gelder (1966) discussed the limitations of specific orientations and the advantages of complementary approaches.

In 1967 Lazarus published his concept of "technical eclecticism." He maintained that therapists could effectively use techniques developed by therapists from other orientations without necessarily agreeing with the theories that originally led to their development. Bergin (1970) and others argued in favor of cognitive techniques being integrated into behavior therapy. The 1970s saw a burst of articles on psychotherapy integration, including an article by Wachtel in 1975 followed by his 1977 book, *Psychoanalysis and Behavior Therapy*. Psychologists were also writing about the integration of Gestalt and humanist approaches to behavior therapy and psychoanalysis. In addition, two papers were published on the overlap of Zen Buddhism and psychoanalysis (Mikulas, 1978; Shapiro, 1987). A panel on the compatibilities and incompatibilities of psychoanalysis and behavior therapy was organized at the Association for the Advancement of Behavior Therapy in 1978.

It is unclear how much impact these writings on integration had upon practicing psychoanalysts. Although psychologists continued to write articles about integration, Strupp (1976) criticized psychoanalysts for using therapeutic approaches based more upon faith than data. His article, along with Grinker's (1976) response, was one of the few articles on integration published in a psychoanalytic journal.

By the 1980s a number of therapists were writing about integrated treatments. In 1981 an informal two-day conference was held to determine if it were fruitful for clinicians of varying orientations to discuss clinical material. In 1982 the World Congress of the Adler Society for Individual Psychology held in Vienna was devoted to the exchange of views of representatives of divergent models of therapy. A collection of commentaries on psychotherapy integration was published in the *British Journal of Clinical Psychology* in 1983 and a volume of dialogues between supporters and opponents of psychotherapy integration was compiled by Arkowitz and Messer (1984).

The Society for the Exploration of Psychotherapy Integration was organized in 1983. This organization has now become international. In 1987 the *International Journal of Eclectic Psychotherapy* became the *Journal of Integrative and Eclectic Psychotherapy*. The *Journal of Psychotherapy Integration* was started in 1991. Two handbooks of psychotherapy integration were published in the 1990s (Goldfried and Norcross 1992, [also revised in 2005]; Stricker and Gold 1993a) and Gold (1996) and others published a number of integrative volumes. Although, theoretically, relational psychoanalysis is more compatible with other therapies than classical psychoanalysis is, few relational analysts (Curtis 1996b; Frank 1999; Gold 1996; and Wachtel 1977, 1997 are some exceptions) have written about integration, leaving most of the work toward integration to psychodynamically oriented and other therapists.

RECENT CONVERGENCES IN PSYCHOANALYSIS AND "MAINSTREAM" PSYCHOLOGY

The New Paradigm in Psychoanalysis

Psychoanalysis continued to evolve in the United States with completely new perspectives elaborated by Sullivan (1953) and Kohut (1971). Both theorists abandoned Freud's almost exclusive emphasis on sexual and aggressive drives and focused upon the development of the self. In Europe Fairbairn (1944), Klein (1976), and others had also begun to think about the formation of the self in terms of internalization of representations of others and had developed object relations theories of psychoanalysis. In recent years Greenberg and Mitchell (1983; Mitchell 1988) suggested a combination of elements of Sullivan's interpersonal theory, Kohut's self psychology, and object relations theories into a paradigm of relational psychoanalysis distinct from Freudian psychoanalysis. Relational psychoanalysis has since become an umbrella organization of psychoanalysis distinct from its Freudian forebear in some important ways (cf. Curtis and Hirsch 2004). First, the paradigm is focused upon desires, not sexual and aggressive drives. Desires include biological ones, but also socially constructed ones. A major desire is for relationships. Development is not viewed primarily according to sexual stages. Instead, early attachment experiences are considered important in their effect on later experiences. Second, the theory of the mind is not that of Freud's structural theory of id, ego, and superego, but rather a mind socially constructed from interactions with others and the external world in addition to subjective experiences related to biological and sensory processes. Third, repression is not the primary way of defending against threatening experiences, but rather a wide variety of types of dissociations of experiences consistent with the thinking of Sullivan and Fairbairn. Fourth, the philosophical underpinnings are not those of the objective science of Freud's time, but rather of the world of connectedness and uncertainty, ushered in by quantum theory and Heisenberg.

Two developments in psychology allow for integration. Psychology has now rediscovered unconscious processes. Although the processes examined in psychology are largely those of adaptive processes, the second development—that of an "affective" revolution—suggests that more researchers will begin to investigate the effects of anxiety on mental processes. When psychology was dominated by behaviorism, internal processes were eschewed. Social and cognitive psychologists continued to investigate such processes, however, and recently have conducted research on a wide variety of internalized representations of self, others, the world, and views of causality. Cognitive psychologists view representations (or prototypes) of people as being acquired in the same way as representations of other objects and changing in a similar manner through the processes of assimilation and accommodation. Unconscious cognitions have even been examined in an increasing number of research studies. The similarities in current thinking in psychoanalysis and psychology allows for an integration heretofore precluded (Curtis 1991a, 1991c; Westen 1992, 1997, 1998).

Although there is considerable overlap, there are, not surprisingly, still large differences in the approaches of the two disciplines. Psychoanalysis emphasizes unconscious processes, the effects of internal structures upon behavior, unique qualities of each individual, case studies as the source of data, psychopathology or problems in living, and views psychotherapy largely as an art. Psychology emphasizes conscious processes, the effects of external realities upon behavior or inner experiences as revealed by self-reports, nomothetic samples as the source of data, processes of normal people (nonclinical samples), and views psychotherapy largely as a science. When unconscious processes have been examined in experimental research, they generally have been in regard to perceptions of other people and not perceptions threatening to fundamental views about oneself or the world. The overlap between psychoanalysis and psychology at least makes it possible for each to complement the other, but, in addition, to critique each other from some sort of common framework. Although there are many minitheories within social/cognitive psychology, the discipline overall accepts a positivistic scientific approach which, according to Popper's (1983) criterion, allows only for propositions that can be falsifiable. This agreement leaves the minitheories falling within one overarching conceptual approach. Many psychoanalysts, howver, have rejected positivist science and embraced a hermeneutic approach that allows multiple interpretations of any phenomenon and no clear means for deciding upon the superiority of any.

Criticisms of Psychoanalysis by Psychologists and Philosophers of Science

In recent years a host of publications have declared the "death" of psychoanalysis (Prince 1999). Other psychotherapies have become more popular in the United States and are frequently preferred in Great Britain, Holland, and Germany. The "death" of psychoanalysis has been attributed to both problems in the theory and to the lack of appeal of a time-consuming, expensive enterprise. Bornstein (2001) attributed the impending death to seven deadly sins: insularity, inaccuracy, indifference, irrelevance, inefficiency, indeterminacy, and insolence. General psychology textbooks rarely refer to psychoanalysis except in a historical or critical context, similar to the way scientists refer to "creationism" in biology. A graduate of an Ivy League university told me recently that his psychology professors told him psychoanalysis was "disproven." Regardless of their actual words, this is the typical message that comes across from psychology professors. Popular writers, such as Gladwell (2005) point out that when they discuss unconscious processes, they are not talking about anything Freudian. Frederick Crews (1997), a critic of Freud and of "repressed memories," stated that I did not sound "psychoanalytic" when I discussed keeping ideas out of awareness and research supporting this view after publishing an article titled "The 'Death' of Freud and the Rebirth of Free Psychoanalytic Inquiry." (Curtis 1996a)

A close examination of the criticisms reveals that they often focus upon aspects of Freudian theory that have been questioned for decades within psychoanalysis itself. It is often as if the critics have read nothing in psychoanalysis since Freud's actual death. On the other hand, some of the criticisms seem valid and serious. Some criticisms of other therapies by psychoanalysts often have been equally out-of-date, yet others are not without merit. Many psychoanalysts are dismissive of the criticisms and continue to live in a world of "splendid isolation." Many psychoanalysts are simply not concerned with the general theory and only concerned with practice (cf. Holzman 1985).

A number of criticisms of psychoanalysis by psychologists (Eysenck 1990; Salter 1952) and by philosophers of science such as Grunbaum

(1984) are directed at Freudian psychoanalysis and have also been made by psychoanalysts. They are not applicable to contemporary relational psychoanalysis. Some of these outdated critiques relate to the following aspects of Freudian psychoanalysis: (1) the reductionism to sexuality, fear of castration, and the Oedipal conflict; (2) the death instinct; (3) the theory of repression; (4) the structural model of the mind—ego, id, and super-ego—; and (5) the theory of sexual developmental states—oral, anal, phallic, latency, and genital. There are many other criticisms of psychoanalysis or psychoanalytically oriented therapy that still apply to contemporary interpersonal/relational theories. Holt (1985) listed a number of problems with psychoanalytic "metapsychology" (the general psychological theory). Among the issues that still apply to non-Freudian theories are that the concepts are poorly defined, they overlap one another partly or completely, and are often reified.

Grunbaum (1983) stated that his criticisms apply equally to contemporary psychoanalytic theorists such as Kohut and the object relations school: He stated, ". . .the post-Freudian versions also deem the successful lifting of repressions to be the decisive agency in the postulated insight dynamic of the therapy" (47). Strenger (1991) responded that contemporary psychoanalysis is no longer concerned with making "causal claims between infantile events and present repressed memories" or interpreting "the causal nexus between symptoms" (73). Although Grunbaum's criticism regarding repression does not apply to contemporary relational theory's dissociative model of the mind (see chapter 4), his other criticisms do still largely apply (Curtis 1996a; Eagle 1984)—for example, the problem of the lack of validation of hypotheses outside the psychoanalytic situation which itself is contaminated by what others consider as similar to "experimenter expectancy effects." Flax (1981) responded to Grunbaum by saying that all data are contaminated by the observer's theory and interpretation. She misses the point that some data are more contaminated in their collection by suggestion and expectancy effects than other kinds of data. Several commentaries on Grunbaum's (1984) critique of psychoanalysis as it is related to relational psychoanalysis appeared in 1996 (*Psychoanalytic Dialogues*), although Grunbaum was not invited to respond. It should be pointed out that in his writings Grumbaum does not deal with interpersonal psychoanalysis at all.

Many psychoanalysts have responded to these criticisms largely by saying that psychoanalysis is not a science but an interpretive activity or an art. Although psychoanalysis is an interpretive activity and an art, many psychoanalysts and psychoanalytically oriented clinicians accept the idea that as a therapy, it is important to demonstrate that psychoanalytic therapy is as helpful as other forms of therapy and other interpretive (including religious) and artistic activities (Bader 1998; Curtis 1996a; Westen 2002b). Whereas a science makes hypotheses about the correlation of particular phenomena, in contrast some psychoanalysts still insist that each person is unique and that there are no general scientific principles that apply. If this is the case, it is unclear why so much theory is written in psychoanalysis and studied. There are probabilities of experiences that are believed to be more and less likely to co-occur. Another criticism is that many of the developmental theories still accepted in psychoanalysis are based largely on adult patients, philosophical arguments, or inadequate research. Most of the remaining criticisms apply largely to the theory of therapy: (1) looking for and interpreting intrapsychic (unconscious) factors as the major route to change; (2) the centrality of transference analysis as the major unconscious factor providing therapeutic traction; (3) the idea that the etiology of a problem is highly related to the way it will be overcome; (4) the lack of therapeutic success with many ordinary patients; and (5) the failure to use other techniques that have been demonstrated to be efficient or effective. These criticisms are serious and shall be dealt with more fully in a later chapter.

The lack of therapeutic success with many patients should be enough for psychoanalysts to question their method. Often one hears that the patient was not "analyzable." Many psychologists and social workers trained in a psychoanalytic orientation, if not psychoanalysts themselves, use a psychoanalytic therapy with all of their patients, however. Furthermore, in studies of training analyses with patients who are presumably analyzable, the percentage of successful cases leaves room for improvement. Shapiro's (1976) study of training analyses at Columbia University Psychoanalytic Center for Training and Research found that 82 percent of the cases reported improvement, although 28 percent reported severe difficulties in their analyses. Goldensohn's (1977) study at the W. A. White Institute found a 90 percent reported success rate and Curtis, Field, Knaan-Kostman, and Mannix, (2004) found 99 percent of the patients (psychoanalysts themselves) reporting improvement in a sample from the White Institute in New York and the Institute für Psykoterapi in Oslo, although the response rate was only 13 percent. In studies of the success of psychoanalysis among patients who were not analytic candidates but selected for this type of therapy, the Menninger (Wallerstein 1986) study found improvement in only 55 percent of the cases with a similar improvement rate (60 percent) in supportive therapy. Studies at psychoanalytic institutes found improvement in 78 percent (Columbia Psychoanalytic), 64 percent (Boston Psychoanalytic), and 55 percent (New York Psychoanalytic) of the patients (cf. Curtis and Qaiser 2005 for a review). Sandell et al. (2000), found that approximately 70 percent of their sample of seventy-four in psychoanalysis showed clinically significant improvement.

Criticisms of Psychological Theories and
Other Psychotherapies by Psychoanalysts

The major critiques of psychological theories and other forms of psycho-therapy by psychoanalysts are the following: (1) there is too much reliance on observable (conscious) factors; (2) the theories and therapies are too su-perficial—symptoms recur, transference cures are obtained, and no change occurs in unconscious affects and cognitions; (3) the theories of etiology are simplistic and insufficient; (4) what these theories say about human beings is boring and naive; (5) the techniques of change are already being incorporated by good analytic therapists; and (6) these therapies are not helpful with dis-orders of identity, when the patient is unclear about the problem, or when the patient has an erroneous view of the cause of the problem.

These areas of criticisms will be discussed more in the following chapters. Although some readers may be interested largely in clinical theory, the sta-tus of current psychoanalytic and psychological theories of motivation, the self, and mental processes is of importance before proceeding to the various theories and practice of therapy. Some readers may wonder what is psycho-analytic about a theory so far removed from Freud's theory. I maintain that a theory is psychoanalytic to the extent that it examines the possibilities of unconscious factors affecting current experiences, is thoughtful about the way such factors may be affecting the patient–therapist relationship, considers the potential usefulness of analyzing the patient–therapist relationship in the therapy, and considers conflict.

Frosh (1989), in his excellent book, *Psychoanalysis and Psychology: Minding the Gap*, points out that psychology has always been interested in accounting for the mental or interpersonal processes which are operating in a person in terms which are as objective as possible. Psychoanalysis, on the other hand, is interested in the subjective understanding of a person's intent and how each human is organized as an experiencing "subject." The differ-ent orientations produce completely different kinds of theories. Frosh's book, however, does not attempt to examine, the disparate theories of the self, mo-tivation, and change.

"No Frames, No Boundaries"

"When you go around the world in an hour and a half you begin to recognize that your identity is with that whole thing. And that makes a change. You look down and you can't imagine how many borders and boundaries you cross again and again. From where you see it, the earth is a whole . . . and it is so beautiful. There are no frames. There are no boundaries," stated the astronaut Richard Schweickard. It would be helpful if psychoanalysts and psychologists had an identity with the whole thing—the whole of the human being regardless whether knowledge is gleaned from the clinical situation, empirical studies, anthropologists, artists, biologists, criminals, or poets.

There are some of us who despair in the world of the heteroclite, the world described by Gergen (1991) as "multiphrenia." For some of us, there is a yearning to be inside the mind of another. There is also a longing, like that described by the physicist Bohm (1980), for a sense of wholeness, a unified theory, or a theory of everything. Wilson (1998) had this sort of goal in mind in his book *Consilience*. Sternberg and Grigorenko (2001) and others (Staats 1983a, 1983b, 1991) have recently pleaded for a unified psychology "which is the multiparadigmatic, multidisciplinary, and integrated study of psychological phenomena" (Sternberg and Grigornenko, 1,069) where problems rather than subdisciplines become the key basis for the study of psychology" (1,075). I shall describe what I think is an outline of one possible unified paradigm emerging in a psychoanalytic psychology, although the holes are still many.

Chapter 2

Desire (and Its Discontents)

Desire is the manifestation of life itself.

—Dostoevsky, 1864

Anxiety is the threat of non-being.

—Paul Tillich, 1986

"Its theory of motivation is at once the glory of psychoanalysis and its shame," Holt wrote in 1976 (158). Psychoanalysis has faced a crisis since the abandonment of drive theory. Drive theories have withered away in both psychoanalysis and psychology. Today psychoanalysts think more about desires, and psychologists think more about goals, standards, aspiration levels, and motivation, although the broader concepts are similar. "Any adequate social theory must first deal with the problem of desire," stated Alford (1991, 173). The same need holds for psychology and psychoanalysis.

Psychoanalysis has been described by Lacan (1988) as the science of desire. Desire has been a central concept far back in Western philosophy. In much of pre-Socratic thought there was a separation of psyche and soma. Desire, emanating from the body, was in conflict with reason. Plato made desire a part of the psyche, in conflict with other forces (see the following chapter on the self). For Plato, desire came from an emptiness or a lack, not from the body (*Philebus*, 34c–35d). Similar to ideas in Asian thought, for Plato, "It is the job of reason . . . to constantly thrust away the objects of desire, as well as desire itself" (Alford 1991, 68).

Outside of Western thought desire has also been central in Asian approaches to the understanding of the causes of human suffering—Brahminism, Jainism, and Buddhism—worldviews and ways of life predating psychoanalysis by at least fourteen hundred years. In these worldviews, "everything" is suffering and the origin of suffering is desire. After reviewing some major theories of motivation in psychoanalysis and psychology, I shall present what I believe is an accepted outline of a theory acceptable to both psychoanalysis and psychology—a dualistic theory derived from the ideas of Ernst Becker (1962, 1975).

MOTIVATION IN PSYCHOANALYSIS AND PSYCHOANALYTIC PSYCHOTHERAPY

Limitations of Freudian theory

The limitations of the Freudian theory of motivation have been noted by psychoanalysts for a long time. Good reviews of these problems can be found in Holt (1976), Greenberg (1991), and Westen (1997). I shall summarize some major difficulties.

Problems with the idea of the death instinct existed early on. It is difficult to reconcile this motive with the evolutionary motive of survival of the species, as organisms with less of a death instinct would be more likely to produce and nurture offspring. Freud's dual instinct theory failed to capture many motives that seemed important to humans, such as hunger, safety, attachment, self-esteem, and making meaning. Attempts to argue that these motives were derivatives of sexual and aggressive instincts have not been convincing to many analysts. Although a sexual "drive" seems to be accepted as a part of our biological heritage, aggression as a drive that must seek an object has not received support in the psychological literature (Baron and Richardson 1994; Berkowitz 1993; Geen 1990; Hollander and Stein 1995). Aggression, in the sense of hurting other people, appears to be more a capability and a behavior occurring under particular conditions, such as pain, frustration, relative deprivation, and situations of competition for scarce resources, than an innate drive, always present that must seek fulfillment. Other conceptual problems are summarized in the section on drives in psychology.

In the tradition of Fairbairn (1944) who proclaimed that people are "object-seeking," it has been accepted in psychoanalysis in both object relations and current relational theories that people are primarily oriented to seek out and maintain relationships. While there is recognition that there are plenty of other motivations, there has been no consensus on a theory among relational psychoanalysts. In the *Handbook of Interpersonal Psychoanalysis* (Lionells et al. 1995) there is no chapter on motivation.

Although George Klein (1967), Holt (1976) and Sandler (1985) attempted to revive Freud's original "wish" model of motivation, this model does not buy us much practically. "The wish model gives us great latitude of interpretive possibility; we are quite free to fill in the need which the wish is designed to satisfy" (Greenberg and Mitchell 1983, 29). This was the problem Freud encountered with this model and partly why he elaborated drive theory.

Greenberg (1991) proposed two primary motivations—safety and effectance. Lichtenberg (1989) proposed five basic motivations: (1) physiological, (2) attachment, (3) exploration/assertion, (4) withdrawal or antagonism in the presence of aversive events, and (5) sensory/sexual. Adler (1917) claimed that the motivation for self-esteem was primary, with Kohut (1971, 1977) adding on to ambitions and ideals the motivation for a cohesive sense of self. George Klein (1976) proposed reorienting psychoanalytic theory to the essential wisdom that we act to maximize pleasure and minimize unpleasure. He also stated there were six pleasures (or needs): (1) pleasure in reduction of unpleasant tension; (2) sensual pleasure; (3) pleasure in functioning; (4) pleasure in experiencing the self as an effective agent of change (effectance pleasure); (5) pleasure in pleasing; and (6) pleasure in synthesis. Stern (1985) noted a "plethora of motivation systems that operate early" (238) on in infants. Kernberg (1982) largely equated the pursuit of pleasure with libido and of displeasure with aggression, keeping Freudian drive theory while proposing affect as the major motivating force. Westen (1997), criticizing Kernberg, has argued that not all unpleasant emotions are aggressive (sadness and fear, for example) and, like Klein, has asserted that affect—seeking pleasure and avoiding pain—should be considered the major motivational force.

A problem with these alternative theories of motivation is that all of the specific motives suggested by different authors seem important yet hard to keep in mind. Although Lichtenberg provides the most extensive list in the psychoanalytic literature, it remains incomplete and unclear why these five motives are more important than, say self-esteem and self-cohesion. Self-cohesion seems to be yet another motive related in some way to the other five: "the clinical findings of any psychoanalytic theory should be explainable through the five motivational systems and the cohesiveness of the self" (Lichtenberg, Lachmann, and Fosshage 1992, 4).

Theories of Motivation in Psychology

Five major theories of motivation have existed in psychology: drive theory, reinforcement theory, evolutionary theory, expectancy value theories (achievement and attribution), and goal theory. In order to give readers some idea of what needs to be integrated, I shall describe very briefly the status of these theories and how they relate the various orientations to psychotherapy.

Drive theory

As exemplified by Hull (1952), a major problem with drive theory in psychology was that not all motivation stems from physical needs. Furthermore, sometimes partial need satisfaction leads to an increase in drive, as opposed to a decrease (e.g., hors d'oeuvres before dinner). Not all deprivation leads to an increase in a drive (e.g., vitamin deficiencies). Finally, people are motivated to engage in activities that increase rather than decrease tension.

Reinforcement theory

Behaviorism avoided the problem of motivation by declaring that any stimulus that increased the frequency of a response was reinforcing. Skinner's (1953) theory was based on the supposition that human behavior could be understood without reference to consciousness. This supposition was wrong (Binswanger 1991). According to Locke and Latham (1994), the consequences of behavior only affect action if the individual "(a) anticipates that the reinforcer will follow future actions; (b) desires or values the reinforcer; (c) understands what actions need to be taken to get it, and (d) believes that he or she can take the requisite actions" (14). Another major problem with reinforcement theory is that it tells us nothing about the general categories of stimuli that people will find reinforcing or pleasurable.

Evolutionary psychology

More recently, evolutionary theory (Buss 1995; McNally 2003) has become another of the major theories. Evolutionary theory assumes that characteristics that lead to the reproduction of the species are those most likely to be passed on, along with other characteristics that may be genetically linked with those adaptive qualities. Freud (1915a), early on, of course, had considered self-preservation to be a major motivation. Millon (1996) has suggested an evolutionary theory with two aspects of "the most basic of all motivations, that of existence" (242): that of life-preserving behaviors—"behaviors oriented to achieve security by repelling or avoiding events that are experientially characterized as 'painful'" (242–43) and life-enhancing behaviors "experientially recorded as 'pleasurable'" (242).

An example of a behavior selected in males was dominance. Dominance leads to more opportunities for mating. Evolutionary theories have often suggested that males try to inseminate as many females as possible. Today, however, behaviors leading to reproduction that were rewarded in the past have become problematic at a time when overpopulation is a major concern affecting the survival of the species. Now having fewer offspring may increase the chances that the offspring will have the resources to attract a mate and reproduce. Although this does not present a problem for ideas about evolutionary adaptation, the problems with overpopulation must be taken into account.

Expectancy value and goal theories

A model of partly unconscious motivation emerged from both the field theory and Gestalt traditions, focused primarily upon achievement motives (Atkinson 1957: McClelland et al. 1953), but also upon power and affiliation. According to Atkinson's model, the motivation to engage in an activity is a consequence of the motivation to succeed (a personality characteristic), the probability of success, and the value of the success minus the tendency to avoid failure, calculated by the motivation to avoid failure (anxiety), the probability of failure, and the value of the failure. These theories have been known more recently as expectancy value theories and have received considerable support experimentally (Feather 1982). Also, unconscious motives regarding achievement have been found to predict better over the long term than consciously reported motives (McClelland, Koestner, and Weinberger 1989). The probability of success and failure and their consequences are the major determinants of action. The model predicts that people who have a high need for achievement will choose tasks of moderate difficulty so that they can likely be successful and attribute their successes to their ability, as opposed to the difficulty of the task. People have been found to feel best if their goals consistently demand about 80 percent effort from them (Brim 1988).

A cognitive attribution model of motivation (Weiner and Kukla 1970) also came out of Gestalt theory. According to this model, the tendency to engage in actions depends not simply upon reinforcement and punishment, but the meanings people make of their successes and failures. If people attribute their successes to their ability and effort (internal causes), they will feel better about themselves than if they attribute their successes to luck and ease of the task (external causes). High achievers make such internal attributions for successes and external attributions for failure. Estimates of ability and task difficulty affect the judgments people make about engaging in future activities.

Locke and Latham (1994) have recently formulated a goal setting theory that they describe as based upon purely conscious goals. Some people perform better than others because they have different performance goals. They argue that behavior can be predicted based upon the specificity, difficulty, and intensity of goals. According to these authors, over four hundred studies have found that the harder the goal, the better the performance. Furthermore, specific, hard goals lead to higher performance than vague but challenging goals. The offering of incentives has been shown to have complex effects.

Incentives may improve performance but may lead to an undermining of intrinsic motivation when the incentives are removed (Deci, Koestner, and Ryan 1999). Goals and feedback are more effective together than either is alone. Because easy goals produce more satisfaction, they suggest setting moderately difficult goals that are constantly raised by small amounts.

Cognitive-behavioral psychology

Clinicians with a cognitive-behavioral orientation have generally accepted many of the various ideas about motivation proposed recently by learning theorists, cognitive psychologists, and social psychologists, such as reinforcement, expectancy value and goal theories. These models all offer some ideas that are complementary to those in psychoanalysis and are helpful in understanding the pursuit especially of conscious goals.

Humanistic psychology

Rogers (1951) suggested that psychological growth would occur, when conditions of worth were not communicated by the people in the environment. Maslow (1970) proposed five levels of motives organized in a hierarchy so that those at the lowest level must be at least partially satisfied before people can be motivated by the ones at the higher levels. These five levels of motives are as follows: (1) biological; (2) safety; (3) the need to belong and be loved; (4) esteem; and (5) self-actualization, meaning. Maslow's hierarchy of goals is usually included in general psychology texts and has considerable overlap with the motives described by Lichtenberg.

Limitations

Other than McClelland, Koestner, and Weinberger's formulations, these theories do not consider unconscious goals that are now accepted in psychology (Bargh 1990). Furthermore, they do not provide much assistance to clinicians regarding what sorts of unconscious goals might lead to self-defeating behaviors.

A Model of Motivation Integrating Psychoanalysis and Psychology

The Desire-affect model

There has been some consensus among a number of writers (Curtis 1991a; Migone and Liotti 1998; Westen 1997) who have attempted to unify psychoanalytic and psychological theories, that the basic model in academic psychology of goals, a comparison check to determine if the goal is attained, and a sequence of actions that is activated when the goal has not been attained originally articulated by Miller, Galanter, and Pribram (1960) and subsequently elaborated by Powers (1973) and Carver and Scheier (1981) is a useful one for understanding desires and their lack of fulfillment.

Relationship to therapy

Migone and Liotti have suggested that Weiss and Sampson's (1986) control-mastery theory has many similarities to Miller, Galanter, and Pribram's (1960) theory and can also be understood in terms of our knowledge of evolution and neuroscience. Although Weiss and Sampson did not relate their theory to the model of Miller, Galanter, and Pribram, their view of motivational processes is so similar that it even uses the same terms. These authors assume that patients have a plan, usually unconscious, that guides his or her strivings toward healing and self-righting. The patient acts in ways to recreate the old trauma or dilemma that was not mastered in the past in the hope of mastering it this time. The patient is hopeful, of course, that the therapist will not react in the way that was hurtful in the past, but will pass the "test" of reacting in a more beneficial way. Modell (2003) presents a similar theory, but not citing the Miller, Galanter, and Pribram model.

A model of motivation based upon affect (seeking pleasure, avoiding pain, and affect regulation) does not give us anything more than the wish model. It is accepted that organisms seek pleasure and avoid pain. The question then becomes one of what types of experiences lead to pleasure and pain. Given the unlimited nature of desires, there has not been a useful way of categorizing them that has captured the imagination to the extent that Freud's model did. Human desires are unlimited and, even if they were all fulfilled, new ones would be created in our current economic system. An exhaustive list of desires is impossible. This is the problem Freud had faced with the wish as the central concept of his motivational system prior to the drive model, and the problem with Sandler's and Holt's attempts to revive this model. The pain/pleasure or affect models leave us with the same latitude. It is possible, however, to categorize these unlimited desires into the biological and the psychological, noting that many behaviors involve both systems. To say this may seem so simplistic and obvious that it is not worth saying, but it opens up some possibilities that have received little attention in psychoanalysis. I shall discuss these more below. Another issue with a simple pleasure/pain model is that people often endure pain not simply in order to have greater pleasure in the future, but in order to survive. Although obviously survival could be considered as greater pleasure in the future, survival is likely a higher level motive.

A large number of people in the mental health fields probably have a model that dichotomizes desires into those with biological roots, including sex and aggression, and those relevant to "object relations"—self-cohesion, self-esteem, and relatedness—in other words, views of self, others, and views of the world. I wish to expand upon this dualism. Kohut accepted Freudian theory, but added on the motivation for self-cohesion and self-esteem. The proposed model accepts the biologically "driven" desires, and includes the socially constructed desires of self psychological and relational theories as part of an overarching desire for a meaning system. Two overarching types of desires arise: desire for survival and survival of the meaning system.

Desires for Survival and Survival of the Meaning System

Like Jay Greenberg, I think that positing a limited number of supraordinate motivations has its virtues. One of the criteria for a good theory is parsimony. The cultural anthropologist Ernst Becker (1962, 1969, 1975) suggested as the major motives the dualism of the motive to belong to something larger than oneself (transcendence of the self) and the motive still to be unique. A similar dualism was presented by Bakan's (1966) motives for agency and communion and Kohut's view of the bipolar self. I wish to offer a rubric dividing the major human desires into those for (1) physical survival (sometimes of the species) and (2) psychological survival—that is, survival of the meaning system or the meaning-making system itself. These ideas are derived largely from those of Becker. The motives of belonging and being unique Becker describes, or agency and communion in Bakan's terms, are both ways of making meaning. The dualistic model I am proposing is a basic and useful one that helps to remedy the abandonment of Freud's drive theory. Pleasure and pain occur to the extent the desires associated with these motives are satisfied, although the desire for pleasure may also exist on its own independent of these two categories.

Sometimes the desire to preserve the meaning system (or the worldview) is greater than the desire for self-preservation. This is seen among people who go to war to fight for their values and, of course, among suicide bombers who know they will die in the cause of their belief system. It is also seen among suicides who have the means of physical survival at their disposal, but cannot accept some way of living possibly devoid of a previous meaning system, such as the esteem of others. (The case comes to mind of the Pulitzer Prize–winner J. Anthony Lucas who killed himself before the reviews of a new book—raves, it turned out—appeared.)

Like other animals, humans are born with an instinct for self-preservation or preservation of their genes. The instinct for self-preservation was the basis of Schopenhauer's philosophy and Freud's initial theorizing. These biological instincts and their regulation comprise what Damasio (1999) has called the "proto-self." The primary differences between human beings and other animals are the profoundly advanced set of intellectual abilities through which humans regulate their behavior and the extent of the culture they have developed. The human mind develops cognitive representations of objects, other people, the self, the world, and causality. This cognitive complexity enables humans to be self-conscious and to be aware of their inevitable death.

As Greenberg, Solomon, and Pyszczynski (1997) have extended Becker's ideas, the awareness of the inevitability of death in an animal instinctively predisposed toward self-preservation creates the potential for terror. In an unpredictable, uncontrollable world filled with possibilities for premature death, the human species used its cognitive abilities to bring potential terror under control by developing and transmitting beliefs about the nature of reality. Cultural worldviews provide a buffer against this terror by providing an explanation for existence, a set of values that prescribe good and bad behavior, and a promise of safety and death transcendence to those who adhere to the standards of the worldview. People are willing to die in order to preserve their cultural worldviews. "Cultural worldviews ameliorate anxiety by imbuing the universe with order and meaning, by providing standards of value that are derived from that meaningful conception of reality, and by promising protection and death transcendence to those who meet those standards of value" (Greenberg, Solomon, and Pyszczynski 1997, 65). The cultural worldview makes it possible for people to feel significant, to have self-esteem. By participation in the culture one can potentially feel like a valuable member of a meaningful universe. The worldview provides knowledge about how desires can be satisfied, about how to obtain recognition from others, and a view of how people can do this fairly, so that desires can be socially regulated. (An excellent review of the psychology of worldviews was published recently by Koltko-Rivera [2004]).

The way human beings make meaning and seek a higher meaning can be summed up as follows: Human beings use their intelligence to make sense out of the world. Gradually, they see patterns and link the meanings together. Doing this helps with survival. "The myth of higher meaning is the general belief that everything makes sense and so can be understood" (Baumeister 1991, 73).

Survival

"All that a man has will he give for his life," the biblical figure Job had stated (Job 2:4). Although the United States provides welfare, to live on the income from welfare alone in New York City conjures up images of roach-infested, not always heated apartments, sometimes without running water and sometimes with leaks, flooding, and other states of disrepair in areas of the city with high crime rates. The small size of the apartment one is able to afford means cramped living space without a yard to sit in. The psychotherapy literature, especially the psychoanalytic literature takes a livelihood largely for granted. My patients in New York City are often afraid of losing their jobs and ending up "homeless." Although they probably would not be homeless, the dwelling they could afford seems more depressing aesthetically than dwellings in rural areas in the South, the Caribbean, or China surrounded by a yard. Of course, starvation is not usually an issue in this country. But homelessness is. I have one patient who ended up living in her car in Los Angeles. Several of my patients have been behind in their rent and facing eviction. Almost all of them talk about housing problems. Some of my patients talk a lot about how they are going to make a living. We have created a psychology that seems out of touch with the major concerns of most people of the world—food, housing, and making a living.

Death

All societies have rituals associated with death. Facing death can bring up many sources of stress, such as the inability to accomplish one's goals, the reminder that whatever we have accomplished may be forgotten, and perhaps meaningless. Kubler-Ross (1969) noted that people often engage in a bargaining process—"just let me finish this first"—when they are faced with their imminent death. To the extent people have placed value on the self, death is especially threatening because it also represents the destruction of the way meaning has been made. If people have no broader meaning, they may take comfort in the fact that their children will continue their life force. But children may not give a parent pleasure if they do not live up to the parent's standards, and people are increasingly choosing not to have children. Facing death is easier if one can see one's life as part of a broader whole—in the context of a broader meaning—an artistic or scientific creation or a religious or political cause that will endure for centuries.

For most of us death is usually something in the distant future. When it suddenly becomes an imminent possibility, as for those of us in New York on the morning of September 11, the importance of survival can suddenly rise to consciousness. With war on the horizon, Freud had noted the importance psychologically of the terror of death, stating, "Would it not be better to give death the place in actuality and in our thoughts which properly belongs to it, and to yield a little more prominence to that unconscious attitude towards death which we have hitherto so carefully suppressed" (1915a, 316–17). James, too, chimed in on the subject, "Let the sanguine healthy-mindedness do its best with its strange power of living in the moment and ignoring and forgetting, still the evil background is really there to be thought of, and the skull will grin in at the banquet" (1849/1958, 281). G. Stanley Hall (1915) saw the terror of death as the greatest evil and the source of the mystery cults of human resurrection in the Middle East, from which Christianity emerged victorious in the competition among them. Brown (1959) has suggested that the Freudian idea of the fear of castration be extended to the broader concern of the fear of death. Rank (1931, 1961) believed in the primacy of immortality striving: "Every conflict about truth is in the last analysis just the same old struggle over . . . immortality" (87). If your immortality system is fallible, then your life becomes fallible. For Rank, all cultural systems are sacred because they provide meaning to individual lives. Rank argued that taboos and laws were to further life and were voluntary acts rather than imposed by external authority. "As he [Rank] paradoxically put it, men seek to preserve their immortality rather than their lives" (Becker 1975, 65). Pleasure and the body are abandoned for cultural immortality. As Choron (1963) has noted, it is not possible to discern if the fear of death is the most basic anxiety, although Greenberg, Solomon, and Pyszczynski (1997) have claimed that their research results demonstrate that it is.

The importance of the desire to survive and the role of the meaning system in doing so are seen in the recent film The Pianist (2002). The protagonist is desperate to stay alive, but will not engage in acts hurtful to others in order to do so (his meaning system). Somehow, the meaning he finds in the arts and in his value system appear to carry him through years of hiding with nothing to do all day except hear music and thoughts in his head.

The desire to make meaning

Making meaning is integral to psychoanalysis. Psychoanalysis is a "psychology of meanings" (Klein 1976, 54). "Meaning (and intention) is . . . at the center of psychoanalytic work," stated Schafer (1976, 100). Gill (1976) commented that "clinical psychoanalysis is a 'pure psychology' which deals with intentionality and meaning" (85). Holt (1976) described Freud's work as dealing "always and almost exclusively with the patterns of meanings" (168). More recently, Lieberman stated that "psychoanalytic theory was built around the idea that mental organizations have meaning (2000, 324). Newirth (2003) has argued that there has been a change in focus in psychoanalysis from one of conflict to the creation of meaning.

People grow and change through new experiences and by making new meanings of experience. Singer (1988) stated, "Today we see humans as active explorers of their physical and social environment. We strive not primarily to reduce drives but rather to assign meanings, to form new schemas and scripts, to experience the excitement of confronting and investigating incongruities between our expectations and new situations, as well as to experience the joy of eventually assimilating novelty into the earlier clusters of schemas" (102). Suzanne Langer wrote that "The concept of meaning in all of its varieties is the dominant philosophical concept of our time" (cited in Gould 1993, 1).

Some psychoanalysts (e.g., Schafer 1992) have seen the creation of new narratives as the central therapeutic activity in psychoanalysis. Cognitive therapists quote Epitetus as saying, "It is not experiences but the meanings we make of them." For Gestalt psychologists, organizing perceptions of the environment into meaningful wholes is seen as basic to human life. They showed in experiment after experiment that people perceive meanings (e.g., motion in lights going on and off) that is not included in the sensory input. They found that we distinguish what is meaningful from the rest—that we see figure and background—and that figure is perceived by recognition of the identity of objects. "We select things that make up a figure and mentally separate it from the ground" (Bolles 1991, 25).

Frankl (1959) had described the making of meaning as essential to psychological life and developed a whole theory of therapy, logotherapy, around the making of new meanings. *Logos* is the Greek word for "meaning," although also for "spirit." Frank stated that "This striving to find meaning in one's life the primary motivating forces in man" (99). He coined the phrase "noogenic" (102) neuroses, in contrast to psychogenic neuroses from conflicts between drives and instincts to mean conflicts between various values, *noos* being the Greek word for "mind." Frankl reported that a survey of 7,948 college students revealed that 78 percent said their main goal was to find "'a purpose and meaning to my life" (99–100). He reported that 55 percent of the patients in the neuropsychology department of the Vienna Poliklinik Hospital had experienced "'a loss of the feeling that life is meaningful'" (108). For Frankl, there is a "will to meaning," not a drive (1988, 43–44), a "will to self-transcend" (138).

Existential philosophers and therapists see the creation of meaning as the task of people in a world that has no inherent meaning, where cultural worldviews (meaning systems) are believed to be socially constructed by people, as opposed to being given to people by a higher being. Tillich (1952), building upon the work of Heidegger and others, in analyzing the nature of anxiety, described three types of anxiety: the first being the anxiety of death, characteristic of the classical era of absolutism and tyranny; the second, the anxiety of guilt and condemnation, characteristic of the Middle Ages, but also apparent today when produced by the failure to realize one's potentiality; and the third, the anxiety of emptiness and meaninglessness, characteristic of our own time. Despair is the product of the three anxieties—a failure to find the proper identity. If one regards the meaning system as comprising the beliefs about self and the world, anxiety about survival of the meaning system encompasses both Tillich's second and third types of anxiety.

In psychoanalysis, it was Fromm (1992) who stated in a work published posthumously that making meaning was the major activity of people. Fromm is thought of as seeing the major forces affecting people as "biophilia (the love of life) and necrophilia (the love of death, decay, and so on)" (29). Although this is true, he saw Freud as trying to "understand all human passions as being rooted in physiological or biological needs," and making "ingenuous theoretical constructions in order to uphold this position" (28). In Fromm's own framework, however, "the most powerful human drives are not those aimed at physical survival (in the normal situation, where that survival is not threatened) but those through which man seeks a solution of his existential dichotomy—namely a goal for his life that will channel his energies in one direction, transcend himself as a survival-seeking organism, and give meaning to his life" (28). Meaning, then, was required for the love of life.

Recently, Brewin and Power (1997) have argued that all therapies are committed to transforming the meanings patients make of their symptoms, relationships and lives. They see the processes of meaning transformation as a way of integrating different psychotherapies at a theoretical level. Greenberg and Pascual-Leone (1997) apply this thinking to experiential, emotion-focused therapies, seeing emotion as a "primary meaning system" (159). Emotions are evoked so that they can be represented symbolically. Emotional experience is restructured and new meaning is created.

How meaning became a problem

It is difficult for an outsider to determine how meaning is provided or attained in other cultures. In non-Western cultures a sense of being part of the continuity of life by paying homage to one's ancestors seems to be a major way of feeling that life is meaningful. My host, Darta, in my home-share in Bali, explained to me that feeling a sense of harmony with nature and with others was the way the Balinese made meaning in their lives. Clearly though, the shrines to ancestors in all of the courtyards I saw and the Hindu ceremony where they were acknowledged each day also played a role in the sense of being part of a larger whole. Harmony with others included one's ancestors.

In Western society in the Middle Ages, Christians were oriented toward living a good life so that they might spend eternity in heaven. The crisis in meaning came when the belief in God was no longer accepted by everyone. The modern period and the secularization of society instigated a quest for fulfillment that could be achieved during life on earth. During the Romantic era, meaning was sought in passionate experiences, including love, artistic creativity, and development of the inner self. The Victorians sought fulfillment in domestic bliss and morality. Today people seek meaning through relationships, work, and play (cf. Baumeister 1991).

Becker (1973) suggests that people became "psychological" when they "became isolated from the protective collective ideologies" (191). Rank (1968a) also commented on Freud's lack of sufficient consideration of culture: "In the neurotic in whom one sees the collapse of the whole human ideology of God it has also become obvious what this signifies psychologically. This was not explained by Freud's psychoanalysis which only comprehended the destructive process in the patient from his personal history without considering the cultural development which bred this type" (143). He had earlier stated, "On the whole, psychoanalysis failed therapeutically because it aggravated man's psychologizing rather than healed him of his introspection" (1931, 10). Freud, had, of course, considered the role of culture in *Civilization and Its Discontents*, noting that it was the religious system that gave the common person a purpose and meaning: "One can hardly be wrong in concluding that the idea of life having a purpose stands and falls with the religious system" (23), he stated. He pointed out that without a religious system, one had to find meaning in creative activity, as Goethe had suggested: "'He who possesses science and art also has religion; but he who possesses neither of those two, let him have religion!'" (cited in Freud 1961, 21).

Religion is a major type of worldview. In fact, some anthropologists use the words almost synonymously—a religion being a kind of worldview that provides a way of living, differentiates what is right from what is wrong, and provides a way to avoid or escape from suffering. Religions respond to suffering and make it bearable, as do other systems of meaning. Systems of meaning, then, help to regulate emotions.

Religions help people explain events and experiences in the context of ultimate meanings. When people agree on these beliefs, the religion helps people to live and work together, the main task of culture (Baumeister 1991). According to Eliade (1978), early religions, prior to 10,000 BC (admittedly based on little evidence) explained how the earth and human beings came into existence and some idea about how to deal with death (e.g., ancestor worship), but did not offer doctrines about the goal of human life. The earliest notions of salvation began to appear in India around 600 BC in Brahmanism and Hinduism. These doctrines held that all life is suffering but that religion offers an escape from suffering. Why religions began to offer some sort of route to salvation is a puzzle. One hypothesis is that life became more stressful, that when life is pleasant, people are not in need of a way out of suffering (Stark and Bainbridge 1985). Religious faith is known to increase in times of war and other suffering, such as after September 11. Religions have offered the most persuasive promise of fulfillment of any belief system.

Freud noted that many people attempt to find happiness in loving and being loved, but that "every man must find out for himself in what particular fashion he can be saved" (1961, 39), referring to the way in which a person will find happiness. Freud himself lived in a culture where people were not likely to live alone and to lack a sense of belonging. Around the same time, it was Kierkegaard and Dostoevsky who were more aware of the sense of meaninglessness that can arise when people are isolated.

In the postmodern era, love and marriage have proved disappointing to many as a value. Bellah's (1985) research demonstrated that Americans expected marriage to provide a relationship in which their selves would grow, in which there would not be sacrifices to oneself because one would truly love the other. The idea became popular that if the relationship were detrimental to the self, it should be terminated. The divorce rate rose and many of those who stayed married had affairs. Conflicts develop when there are children. Love for a partner and love for children are often in conflict just as love for another and love for the self may be in conflict. Thus, finding fulfillment in love has been disappointing for many people.

Suffering and meaning

Suffering is relieved by making sense of it in terms of a larger meaning. The decline of religious faith has made it harder for people to recover from misfortune and tragedy. If someone is victimized and cannot make meaning of what has happened, meaningful thought stops (Janoff-Bulman 1985). A study of accident victims who ended up maimed or paralyzed found that all of them had asked "Why me?" and most had come up with an answer (Bulman and Wortman 1977). Incest victims continue to ask themselves this question for years (Silver, Boon, and Stones 1983). After twenty years, half had failed to make any sense out of it and 80 percent were still searching for some meaning. Those who were able to make meaning out of the event still thought about it, but were less troubled by the intrusive thoughts. Betrayal by someone who was supposed to take care of you wreaks severe havoc on one's meaning system, including views of self and others (Freyd 1996). Similarly, when couples can find no medical reason for infertility, coping is most problematic (Matthews and Matthews 1986).

Having an explanation, even if there is not convincing evidence that it is true, appears to be what is helpful. An explanation of almost any kind, not the particular attribution for the event, is what makes a difference (Taylor 1983; Bulman and Wortman 1977; Silver, Boon, and Stones 1983). As Baumeister (1991) has noted, it is not that any explanation will do, because the research examines only explanations that were "actually used" (268).

Making some sort of sense out of what has happened is one of the most common ways of coping. People often try to construct some type of meaningful narrative. As already noted, some people have the construction of new narratives as the major aspect of psychoanalysis (Schafer 1992). This new narrative may include finding some purpose or learning to the misfortune. For example, in a study of women with breast cancer, most of whom had breast removal, only 17 percent reported a negative change in their lives (Taylor, Lichtman, and Wood 1984). As many have found with AIDS patients, these women reordered their priorities in life so that they became more concerned with what was truly important in their lives. Another way of coping may be by putting the incident out of mind or by cutting it off from present experience. The idea of being born again as a religious experience allows for past mistakes to be cut off and seen as part of a former life (Baumeister 1991).

Justice as part of a meaningful worldview

In relationships, desires of individuals quickly run into conflict. Societies develop views about the ways to satisfy desires that lead to the fewest problems and ways of settling disputes when conflicts arise. Although societies exist for mutual advantage, the desired outcomes may not be available to everyone. For most people a meaningful worldview includes beliefs about how outcomes should be distributed—about justice—and that justice will prevail either in this world, in the next, or in both. "It is better to be a sinner in a world ruled by God than to live in a world ruled by the Devil," Fairbairn stated (1954, 66). The desire for fairness supercedes for many people the desire for self-esteem. The meaning system usually includes a way to maintain self-esteem by being of value in the larger community. When people are not valued, they may believe that the world is unfair, but that they will be compensated in the afterlife, as in the Christian and Muslim religions. This need can be seen by the belief in heaven and hell to provide ultimate justice if it does not occur in this world. If people believe that the world is fair, they have difficulty maintaining good feelings about themselves when not valued by others. Especially perhaps when there is no belief in an afterlife, people wish to believe that the world is just. A large body of research now demonstrates that people are motivated to believe in a just world (Lerner 1980).

If we consider two basic motivations—physical survival and the psychological survival of our meaning systems (our worldviews) or the meaning-making capacity itself (sanity), the belief that justice is a virtue and that justice will prevail is likely a part of the worldview. Although Fairbairn's statement is actually related to maintaining a view of the parent as benevolent or just and seeing oneself as bad, the concept makes sense when applied to the broader power structure in the world. The concept is similar to that expressed above in that people will decide that they are bad rather than see the world as ruled by the Devil, a force that will reward evil, or, in other words, unjust.

According to Freud (1961), a sense of justice was the first requirement of civilization. Becker (1973) believed that children were born with a sense of "rightness" (150). When people expect to suffer, they justify their suffering in some way (see Curtis 1989a, for a review). They have been found to make meaning out of their anticipated suffering by deciding that they deserve to suffer or that they are brave (Comer and Laird 1975). Others decide that suffering will improve their future performance at events both over which they have some control and over those due purely to chance (Curtis, Rietdorf, and Ronell 1980; Curtis, Smith, and Moore 1984). People create elaborate justifications for hurting others so that they may maintain an illusion of fairness. These justifications move the action to a higher level of meaning. Ends are seen as justifying the means. Invaders justify their murder in the name of various causes, the Romans by the bringing of civilization and a society of laws, the Jews through God's promise, the Christians in the Crusades and the conquest of lands in the Americas by the bringing of Christianity to those who converted, and the Nazis and Serbs by "ethnic cleansing."

For Erikson (1963), basic trust was necessary for a sense of fairness and the child's reliance on the justness of the world about her/him. The nature of the social environment provided the groundwork for the sense of justice well before prohibitions (related to the development of the superego) were internalized. Psychologists such as Lerner have argued that this need comes from self-interest—that people realize that just principles will most likely lead to the best outcomes for themselves, along with everyone else. Another tradition, however, suggests that empathy for others leads to distress when others are not treated as one would wish to be treated oneself (Hoffman, 1987). The desire to avoid pain leads to a motive for justice for oneself and others. Philosophers have described the rise of systems of justice as follows: "in the common interest, a compact is made not to injure, in return for not being injured. This compact is the basis of what we call natural right, and of what we call justice, and of law. . . .the compact is a natural product, growing out of the natural desire for self-preservation and self-assertion inherent in the individual, and for protection in the pursuit of his own ends" (Fuller and McMurrin 1955, 245).

Preservation of life and the meaning of life as related to other motives

In relational psychoanalysis, relatedness, or some sort of social or affilia-tive motive is considered to be primary. The interpersonal/relational point of view, dating back to Fairbairn and Sullivan assumes relationships as pri-mary. For Sullivan (1948), all manifestations of anxiety are of interpersonal origin: "In the study of any anxiety-fraught experience one discovers that the particular pattern of the situation which provokes anxiety can be traced to a past relationship with particular significant people in the course of which are experienced anxiety that was more or less clearly observed to be related to particular interaction with them" (10). Although it is unusual, there are peo-ple who live satisfying, even fulfilled lives, who momentarily do not have relationships, such as Thoreau on Walden Pond (cf. Storrs 1988), people preoccupied with an artistic pursuit, and spiritual hermits. For people who are born in a milieu embedded in relationships, or provided with a cultur-ally accepted worldview, the need for relatedness is probably not conscious. I suggest that finding meaning in relationships is only one way that people satisfy the desire to make meaning. It also seems likely that anxiety is trig-gered by threats to one's meaning system without being related necessarily to a pattern in a past relationship.

In Kohut's (1971) self psychology the need for a sense of self-cohesion is considered to be the primary motivation. This is achieved when there is a match between the ambitions and ideals and talents, capabilities, and skills. The ideals are part of the meaning system. For Lichtenberg (1989), the need for a sense of self-cohesion comes after the satisfaction of certain needs that are biological givens of the human infant. An advantage of the current model is that the desire for a meaningful worldview encompasses the need for a view of self, others, and the world that makes life feel worth living. The biologically "driven" motives described by Lichtenberg — attachment, aggression, sex — are all aspects of behavior related to survival. Attachment is required for human survival (Spitz 1945). Exploration helps in both the finding of food and shelter and in finding meaning in life; withdrawal and ag-gression are obviously essential to both survival and survival of the meaning system. Sexuality is also related to pleasure and to finding meaning. It can be argued that sensory pleasure is a motive in itself, separate from the major mo-tives described, although the origins of these pleasures may have been related to characteristics needed for survival. In Maslow's (1962) similar hierarchy of needs, the biological and safety needs are primary, again needs that must be met for survival, with belonging, self-esteem, and self-actualization the higher needs in his system. These last three needs are part of what I am calling the meaning system. Historically, the desire for self-actualization appears to have become a desire after the loss of other meaning systems.

Jay Greenberg (1991) suggested safety and effectance as the major motivations. Effectance is necessary for survival when needs are not satisfied without it. Control as a necessity is a Western idea. The greater need is for some optimum level of predictability, stability, and consistency. "Completeness and consistency are important aspects of the myth of higher meaning. . . . The faith in consistency is the belief that the world does not contradict itself, which again implies that things and people can be understood in a stable, predictable fashion" (Baumeister 1991, 73). Considerable research has shown that people often prefer to maintain consistency in their beliefs about themselves as opposed to the possible costs involved of experiencing something more positive. For example, people avoid someone who has a more favorable opinion of them than they have of themselves (Swann 1987). Anxious people may avoid success to keep people from expecting too much of them (Baumgardner and Brownlee 1987). Swann and his colleagues have conducted considerable research examining the effects of the conflicting motives for positive feelings and consistency. Consistency wins unless a person is uncertain about a belief in the first place. What many people often want is to maintain their beliefs about themselves, others, and the world, often even when one or more of these is negative. Some people, of course, are not motivated to maintain certainty in their beliefs but rather are "uncertainty-oriented" (Sorrentino and Roney 2000), but these people are likely confident that they will be able to make meaning in the world. Effectance, then, is in the service of survival, making and maintaining a sense of meaning, and pleasure.

Pleasure and the avoidance of pain have been suggested as the primary motives. This seems to be the case often in the short run. But people endure great amounts of pain in order to stay alive, so pain appears to serve as a signal of threatening experiences. Hedonism may be selected as a way of making meaning, but most people choose hedonism as a way of making meaning only if the pleasure will last for a while. This is why people avoid pleasurable, but dangerous activities. "People do experience temporary satisfactions, but they imagine and desire permanent satisfactions" (Baumeister 1991, 74). For most people the hedonic solution leads to an unfulfilling self-indulgence that is only temporarily satisfying. The loss of meaning is more devastating than the loss of happiness. This was demonstrated in a study of widows after the loss of their husbands (Parkes and Weiss 1995).

The search for meaning is also noted in theories of consciousness, such as that of Zeman (2003). Ramachandran (1996) has argued that belief systems

evolved to reduce the number of choices people have to make. Based upon research with patients suffering from anosognosia (denial of illness), Ramachandran argues that the left hemisphere always looks for meaning even when
there is none, including false information if it fits with a belief, whereas the
right hemisphere notices inconsistency and signals when it is time to revise
a belief system.

THE UNIVERSAL WOLVES

"And appetite an universal wolf / So doubly seconded with will and power,
/ Must make perforce a universal prey, / And last eat up himself," wrote
Shakespeare. For both Shakespeare and Buddha, desire eats us up inside. It
is the cause of suffering. But it is also the source of pleasure. People who are
depressed often seem to have no desire. Sex and power were the universal
wolves for Freud. I have suggested two other wolves—survival of the body
and the soul (or psyche). The paradox is that it seems if we desire this survival too much—or more correctly, if we fear death too much—we no longer
exist, as Tillich noted. We become eaten up with anxiety, afraid of life, and
psychologically dead.

SUMMARY AND CONCLUSION

I have argued that a dualistic theory of human motivation with the desire for
physical survival and desire for psychological survival—preservation of the
meaning system or the meaning-making system itself—as the two most basic motives. Although other motives, such as that for pleasure, may at times
supercede these motives, most biological and psychological desires can be
subsumed under these two categories. These two desires suggest two fears:
death and the loss of the meaning system, both ways of not being. Loss of the
meaning system involves a loss of any satisfying identity, leading to various
types of suffering and psychological problems for many people. The nature of
identity is the topic to be addressed next. The meaning-making system, that
is, the capacity for sound processing, will then be discussed in subsequent
chapters on conscious and unconscious processes.

Chapter 3

The Charioteer and the Two Horses: The Self and Its Representations

According to many historians, concern about the self is the central theme
of the last several centuries of Western cultures.

—Louis Sass, 1988

Psychoanalysis and psychology are both currently without widely accepted,
clearly spelled out, models of the self. Freud's model of the id, ego, and superego is as firmly embedded in psychoanalysts' psyches as Plato's model of the
charioteer with his two unruly horses. Yet in psychoanalysis Fairbairn (1952)
had rejected the ego–id model because sexual and aggressive urges were
partly conscious and it made no sense to relegate them to an unconscious id.
Brenner, a Freudian, concluded that the idea of "three agencies referred to as
id, ego, and superego is not supported by currently available data concerning mental development and functioning" (1998, 179). Some psychoanalysts
abandoned Freud's tripartite model and substituted either Kohut's (1977)
bipolar self (parental/societal ideals vs. personal ambitions) or a model of
multiple self-representations in interpersonal/relational psychoanalysis that is
not yet fully spelled out, but no model has taken hold in the field.

The Freudian model of id, ego, and superego had been excluded as a theory
in psychology from its conception because James, in its founding, had banned
the study of unconscious processes, calling them "the tumbling ground of
whimsies" (1890, 163), offering ten arguments against their existence, thus
rendering the whole concept of the id objectionable. Psychologists since
James have often refrained from offering any overarching theory of the self,
preferring to develop middle range theories of self-esteem, identity maintenance, and self-appraisal. In reviewing all the theories of the self in psychoanalysis and psychology, three major issues emerge: (1) a confounding of the
experiencing self with the representation of the self and lack of attention to

35

the experiencing self; (2) the importance of the distinction between actual and ideal self-states; and (3) the concept of self-regulation. I shall discuss these three issues and provide a new image of the self that makes these issues central. Then I shall elaborate upon social and visible forces, often unconscious, affecting images of the ideal self.

THE SELF AND ITS REPRESENTATIONS

In both psychoanalysis and psychology a major problem has been the conflation of the experiencing self with the representation of the self. This confounding of the self and the representation of the self has occurred with such theorists as Hartmann (1950), Melanie Klein (1964), and Kernberg (1976). The distinction between the self as an experiencing subject and the self as an object of thought is central in philosophy and must be given attention in any psychoanalytic/psychological model. In reviewing the psychoanalytic literature on the self, Cooper (1993, 41) commented, "Most contemporary psychoanalytic theorists fail to take a systematic stand concerning the self as distinguished from the self-representation." Recently, Meissner (2000) and Fonagy, Gergely, Jurist, and Target (2002) have made similar points.

In their summary for the *Annual Review of Psychology* Markus and Wurf (1987, 301) commented: "Self theorists have abandoned as somewhat premature efforts to describe the active 'I' aspects of the self, and have been temporarily content to elaborate the structural features of the self-concept." Harter (1983, 277) noted, in a review of developmental perspectives on the self, "The self as subject, process—active agent—has received far less attention." Likewise, Wolfe (1995, 362) stated, "Lurking in the background, virtually ignored by research, is the self as subject, the experiencing self." Obviously, a chair is different from an image of a chair. People have an image of themselves, just as they have an image of other people and objects, but the perceiver is not identical with what is perceived. Furthermore, a self-representation cannot act. Until recently, this confounding has led to a lack of attention to the experiencing self involved with sensory-motor responses and physical survival in contrast to the representations of self and the world—the more purely psychological self, oriented toward making meaning. Although attention to the experiencing self has been noteworthy in the psychoanalytic literature of self psychologists such as Kohut (1977), Stolorow and Atwood (1992), Lichtenberg, Lachmann, and Fosshage (1992), and D. N. Stern (1985) and also in the writings of Schafer (1976), G. Klein (1967, 1976), and Fast (1998), Stolorow and Atwood suggested that the idea of the person as an experiencing subject and agent lies outside the bounds of psychoanalytic inquiry: "Whereas the self-as-structure falls squarely within the domain of psychoanalytic investigation, the ontology of the person-as-agent, in our view, lies beyond the scope of psychoanalytic inquiry" (1992, 34). Lichtenberg, Lachmann, and Fosshage (1992) and Stern (1985), however, have included the person-as-agent aspects of self as essential to their models. Lichtenberg, Lachmann, and Fosshage (1992) amend Kohut's (1977) definition of self as an independent center of initiative and perception to include the self as an independent center for organizing and integrating experience and motivation as well.

In the psychological literature, Perls (1976), Guidano (1991), and experiential therapists (Gendlin 1962; Bohart 1993; Greenberg, Rice, and Eilliot 1993), have all emphasized the experiencing self. Leslie Greenberg (1995), it should be noted, however, criticized client-centered therapies for moving so much to the focus upon experiencing that they lost the emphasis upon the discrepancies between the actual and the ideal self important to Carl Rogers (1961). The discrepancies between the actual and ideal self were important not only to Rogers, of course. I shall return to the subject of actual and ideal selves shortly. Distinguishing the experiencing self from the representation of the self allows us to conceptualize therapeutic interventions affecting nonverbal and sensory motor aspects of self from those affecting the meaningful representations of self, others, and the world. Such a distinction does not imply that the bodily emotions are separate from cognitions, as will be addressed in the final chapter.

The use of the word "self" is a problem. The word comes from the Latin word "se" meaning sameness. It would be more appropriate to refer to an "experiencer" than an "experiencing self," but I shall consider this "experiencer" as part of the self, as it does experience sameness and continuity.

SELF-REGULATION AND THE CLASSIC CONTROL PARADIGM

Based upon the basic ideas of the general systems theory (Bertalanffy 1938), Miller, Galanter, and Pribram (1960) described a construct of a self-regulating system in which there is a comparison between an existing state and a predetermined standard. A thermostat is such a model (cf. Wiener 1948). Carver and Scheier (1981) applied the self-regulatory concept to social behavior, with a large number of articles on self-regulation then appearing in psychology journals and subsequently in educational and organizational journals. The concept of goals is used in psychology in place of the psychoanalytic concepts of wishes and desires. Goals are thought of as hierarchical and depend on unconscious (automatic) activation patterns (Bargh 1990). Systems that are based on hierarchies are much more stable, because failures don't destroy the whole system but only result in movement to the next stable subsystem level.

Prigogone and the Nobel Prize

Ilya Prigogine, a biologist, won the Nobel Prize for research showing that living systems change to fit in with the environment and maintain a self-organizing dynamic by a continuous exchange of energy with the surroundings (thus showing where Newton's second law regarding the dissipation of energy does not hold). The set-points change (the self as a dynamic system has been discussed more extensively by Piers 2000). Psychological change involves fluctuations in response to differing external realities to the extent that a "tipping point" (cf. Gladwell 2004) is reached, resulting in a new psychological organization.

Regulation of the psychological as well as the biological

Self-regulation models have been developed in social and cognitive psychology, experiential therapy, emotion theory, and in psychoanalysis. These models all overlap. For example, the development of a self-regulatory model and its failures in social psychology by Baumeister, Heatherton, and Tice (1994) seems almost to be a psychodynamic model—Freudian theory with new labels: "Impulses emerge from within (or minimally cued by stimuli in the environment) and these impulses must be controlled if the broad goal of adaptation to the social world is to be met" (1996, 37). Self-regulation processes entail the gatekeeping of what enters consciousness and what does not. I am suggesting that self-regulation and this gatekeeping will reflect the major motivations—survival and survival of a meaning or meaning-making system. Although the affect-regulation aspect of these models will be discussed in the final chapter, the point I wish to make now is that any model of the self must acknowledge in some way the issue of regulation. The experiencing self regulates discrepancies between the actual and the desired.

THE CHARIOTEER AND THE TWO HORSES: THE ACTUAL AND THE IDEAL

It has been hard for theorists to generate an image of the self that captures the imagination as much as Plato's and Freud's models did. Charioteers and steersmen make more attractive images of a regulator than a thermostat. I suggest we keep Plato's image and view the charioteer as *homo sapiens*, a smart, physical, experiencing creature with sensations, perceptions, and evaluations with an image of reality and its possibilities, mental images of what is and what might be, the actual and the ideal, as two horses before the charioteer. The horses in this model include social constructions of what one is and what is desired (as well as what is desired not to be, or feared). The desires include those that are socially constructed and their sources are often not conscious. Among the regulating tasks of the charioteer is keeping these aspects of self in balance.

When all of the models of the self are reviewed, discrepancies between the actual and ideal likely have been the most frequently discussed aspects in models of the self in both psychology and psychoanalysis. The ideal self is crucial to the psychoanalytic theories of Freud (1914, 1921, 1923, 1933), Horney (1950), Fairbairn (1952), Joffe and Sandler (1968), Schafer (1967), Kernberg (1976), and Kohut (1971, 1977). In psychology, the discrepancy between the actual and desired or ideal self is a predominant theme in James (1968), in cognitive psychology (Beck et al. 1979; Burns 1989), social psychology (Higgins 1987), and as mentioned previously, in experiential theories. A focus on the actual and ideal self does not in any way diminish the importance of unconscious experiences—they permeate all psychological functioning and shall be addressed later.

UNLIMITED DESIRES, THE EFFECTS OF THE MEDIA AND IDEAL SELVES

The true mystery of the world is the visible, not the invisible.

—Oscar Wilde

Attention to the discrepancies between realities and desires allow us to understand the self-regulation process in a way compatible with both psychoanalytic and psychological thinking. I shall now argue that images, largely those in the media, are increasingly affecting people's desires and their views of the ideal self, leaving many people with a chronic sense of dissatisfaction. These desires are created by external, social forces and differ from the intrapsychic urges so prominent in Freud's theory.

Gaps between these ideals and reality are the major determinant of dissatisfaction among people who have no physical threats to survival. "I should live in a better apartment," "I should be further along in my career by now." Where do these "shoulds," these ideals expressed by my patients come from?

Many terms have been used to get at similar, if not identical concepts. We speak of levels of aspiration, levels of expectations, standards, desires, values, goals, and so on. But where do they come from? When I asked a male patient where his "should" came from recently, he responded without hesitation, "television."

Images, especially visual ones, portrayed in the media in contemporary culture are having a profound effect upon standards and people's sense of relative deprivation. Although people may feel relatively advantaged when they compare themselves to the situations of their families in the past or others in the world less fortunate, when most people compare themselves to what is portrayed in the media, they feel they fall short. Although current theory in psychoanalysis suggests that if parents are sufficiently attuned to their child's needs, talents, and aspirations, this feeling of self-deficiency will be prevented, these beliefs ignore the strong influence of the consumer culture in which we live. We are largely unconscious of the effects of the cultural water of the twenty-first century in which we swim in and it is not our intrapsychic unconscious—our instincts—that are causing our suffering, but the ways in which our culture is affecting us that remain out of awareness.

The Hope of Parental Attunement

If one examines the recent theories of the self in American psychology and psychoanalysis, one notices a conspicuous lack of attention to the role of the culture in forming the ideal self. In the current literature in American relational psychoanalysis, one will see that ways of being in the world are viewed as derived from the internalization of identifications with significant caretakers, much of this process being unconscious. People are believed to repeat patterns learned in the past in an attempt to master situations that have been problematic, constructing unconsciously their contemporary world in ways consistent with what they experienced in the past.

In current relational thinking in psychoanalysis, children learn interactional patterns with their parents that are later generalized to interactions with others. These patterns have been variously referred to as "repetitions of interactions that are generalized" (Stern 1983) or "internal working models" (Bowlby 1973). When one looks at the model of the self that has emerged in psychoanalysis and psychology in its cultural context, one sees a self where defects are described as the result of inadequate parenting and the internalized representations from interactions with the family. When significant others behave properly toward the child (attuned, empathic, creating a sense of security, with the proper amount of freedom and discipline), the self supposedly grows in a healthy manner. According to this model, when significant others repair their relationships and allow the child to see their limitations, the child gradually becomes realistic and adapts to the culture. Patients are believed to have acquired maladaptive attachment patterns or internal working models that can be corrected by a new relationship with a psychotherapist. According to this perspective, good, attuned parenting leads to the development of a positive, cohesive sense of self leads to positive expectations, largely positive outcomes from a self-fulfilling prophecy, and a buffer against inferiority feelings based upon one's status in society. In relational psychoanalysis, one's social relations are viewed as largely the consequence of one's own internalized objects and subsequent social constructions. Pressure is removed from changing the socioeconomic conditions in the culture and the focus can be on individual change in psychotherapy rather than on sociopolitical interventions (cf. Cushman 1996).

Rowe (1994) began the critique of the "nurture assumption" by presenting the extent of genetic influences upon development. Harris (1995, 1998, 2000) criticized altogether the extent of parental influence upon children by arguing that parents have no important long-term effects on the development of the child's personality. She argued that group processes and the transmission of culture through groups, not the dyadic relationships with parents, are responsible for children's personality characteristics. In spite of criticisms (Vandell 2000), Harris (2000) has insisted that the impossibility of controlling for context and genetic effects precludes the rejection of the null hypothesis of zero long-term developmental effects of parenting on child outcomes. The ability of children to catch up who have been deprived of stimulation has been documented by Kagan and Klein (1973), with Kagan (1979) repeatedly criticizing the overemphasis upon early childhood determinants of problems in living.

Research on attachment styles is vulnerable to a similar critique. Although attachment style appears to be related to a number of problems in later development, the correlates of a secure attachment style may be contributing to, if not accounting for, the effects. Vaillant (2004), a psychoanalyst, has also found in his extensive studies of people across the life span that a childhood with "good" parents does not predict mental health in adulthood. Too many other variables have major effects.

Grandiosity is encouraged among children in the United States. They are led to believe that they can meet the cultural ideals by being told "you can be anything you want" and by being told that there is equal opportunity when neither is the case. Unlike previous eras where many people believed they were born into and would die in an inferior social status, people are told that they are all created equal. Some time by adolescence, reality sets in and young people often find they cannot be anything they want. Jobs depend upon relative abilities, connections, and educational opportunities. Romantic relationships are valued, yet marriages are not arranged by parents and the ideal of mutual romantic love often not experienced, leaving the percentage of single young people at a marriageable age larger and larger, many of them longing for and not having a committed relationship. The conscious actual self is one that feels deprived.

Mass Marketing and the Creation of Unlimited Desires

As I do my exercises, I have on one of the three television stations which I receive on my vacation. I am tempted to call to order all sorts of products I did not even know existed before—a hand sewing machine, a microwave egg poacher, calcium that will be absorbed quickly into my body, a steam clothes presser—the list goes on. I wonder why these wonderful products are not sold in the store and why I will receive a better price if I call within the next thirty minutes. Perhaps the reason is that after this morning, I won't remember that I wanted these items.

Material possessions have become very important to many people in defining the self (Belk 1988; Dittmar 1992; Kanner and Kasser 2004; McCracken 1986). Consumption is a way many members of consumer societies judge themselves and others (Rassuli and Hollander 1986). The way in which advertising has led to the creation of new desires has been documented by many scholars (Cohen 2003; Richins 1996). Galbraith (1969) had described how the main function of advertising is to create desires that did not previously exist. Before mass marketing, the desire for the new—the desire to be fashionable and stylish— had not come into being. Then there was the creation of a new desire—the desire to be "cool." At first our media was just selling products. But later our media began selling entertainment (Postman 1985). The United States began to sell its pop culture all over the world—our music, our television programs, our films. Culture became one of the largest U.S. exports. Whereas religion provided people with what they needed; television offers people what they want, Postman states. He questions the significance of the second commandment—that of not making graven images. Why would this be a commandment? What is there about visual images that would make them so important?

The Power of the Image

Art historian David Freedberg (1989) stated the following: "People are sexually aroused by pictures and sculptures; they break pictures and sculptures, they mutilate them, kiss them, cry before them and go on journeys to them; they are calmed by them, stirred by them, and incited to revolt. They give thanks by means of them, expect to be elevated by them, and are moved to the highest levels of empathy and fear" (1).

Art critic Dave Hickey (1997) went even further: "No image is presumed inviolable with our dance hall of visual politics, and all images are potentially powerful. Bad graphics topple governments and occluded good ideas; good graphics sustain bad ones" (17). It should be pointed out that Hickey does not provide any examples of images toppling governments, however, Volkan (2001) has described how cultures seize upon an image of a trauma in their past to rally aggression—their "chosen" trauma.

Images are processed by the sensory/affective processes in the brain as opposed to the semantic system, leaving many people often unable to verbalize what they feel. The sight of mutilated faces or bodies is especially frightening to both people and other primates (Hebb 1946). Such images related to survival are prewired to affect us very quickly. After Ambady and Rosenthal (1993) referred to such judgments of "thin slices of nonverbal behavior," Gladwell (2005) coined the term "thin-slicing" for these sorts of snap reactions. Gladwell defines "thin-slicing" as "the ability of our unconscious to find patterns in situations and behavior based on very narrow slices of experience" (23). Judgments gleaned from visual or other nonverbal stimuli are often made from longer exposures as well, of course. Gosling, Ko, Mannarelli, and Morris (2002) found, for example, that students who looked at another student's room for fifteen minutes predicted the resident's personality on three out of five dimensions—openness to experience, conscientiousness, and emotional stability (as measured by the most widely used personality test)—better than their friends did. Not surprisingly, the friends were better at predicting extraversion and agreeableness.

Visual imagery conveys a great deal of information, but not all of it is consciously processed. For example, my patients frequently report in their dreams the title, author, or other association from the books on my office shelves. Many years after first traveling to Vienna, I had a dream about a Ferris wheel in Vienna (cf. Curtis 1996b). When I went to Vienna again, I looked at my travel guide to see if there was any mention of a Ferris wheel. There was not. When I got home, I looked at my Frommer's *Europe on Five Dollars a Day* that I had used in 1968 to see if a Ferris wheel was listed as a site. It was not. Knowing that I had not looked at another travel guide in those days, I wondered where I had gotten the idea of a Ferris wheel in Vienna in the first place. Was it simply my imagination? Then I saw, next to the word "Vienna," a picture of a Ferris wheel. In my old Frommer's guide. (Fortunately, my hotel on that last visit was selling a postcard of the Ferris wheel at the check-in desk, so I did get there for a ride.) Considerable information is picked up by our brains but may not enter conscious awareness (the subject of chapter 5).

Many visual images are processed quickly without reaching conscious awareness. Words take more milliseconds to be spoken and so are more likely to be processed consciously unless masked in background noise or heard so softly that they are not necessarily heard.

Because we cannot give conscious attention to all the stimuli in our environment, we sense and store much information without "knowing" it. This is why when people are relaxed, such as when they are hypnotized, they can sometimes recall information that they cannot recall in normal waking consciousness (they can recall incorrectly, of course, as well). We subsequently act on the basis of this stored information, what Gladwell refers to as a "locked room," without knowing exactly why, by just having a "feeling" about something. "Thin-slicing" allows us to filter out the factors that matter most from the overwhelming number of stimuli reaching our senses. This is how "expert knowledge" develops in all fields, so that the "experts" can look at something quickly and make a decision based on the most essential features (Hoffman 1992).

Ekman (Ekman 1984; Ekman, Friesen, and Hager 2002) has now documented the varieties of facial expressions that convey emotions universally—three hundred combinations of two muscles. These expressions can be picked up by expert observers, such as his mentor Tomkins (1980) in a split second. Many people, however, miss them altogether. If all of these minute expressions are observed by someone who has gleaned knowledge of the emotions accompanying them, the observer can make very accurate predictions about the person's past and future behaviors. For example, when observing the discharge interview of a psychiatric patient, Ekman discerned a look of despair on her face momentarily when the psychiatrist asked about the future. She was allowed to leave the hospital, but subsequently attempted suicide. These nonverbal cues are often dismissed by what Schooler (2002) called verbal override. The semantic system pays more attention to words and the brains of many people give more weight to words than to visual and other sensory cues. (This happens with children developmentally. Young children remember eidetically (visually) until verbal memory takes over. A young child might visualize how many stripes were on a cat's tail and draw it correctly, while an older child must count them to get the number correct.) What determines the degree of "left brain" (verbal) or "right brain" dominance or the lack of dominance altogether is unclear.

Paetzold (1996) noted that Plato was so afraid of images that he excluded the arts from the ideal state. Status is often conveyed visually. Veblen (1931) noted that commodities also allocate social status or rank. Max Weber (1930) described how the industrial order led the making of money to become an end in itself. In industrial societies, people detach value from forms of the good life and reattach it to goods or exchange value. Paetzold (1996) reviewed the ideas of Cassirer, Benjamin, and Vitimo. Cassirer (1946) had argued that totalitarian states use images to convey their value systems. Benjamin had theorized that capitalist cultures are unable to control the economic process and that social relationships are mirrored through things. According to Benjamin, cultural processes provide society with images through which desires are structured. For Benjamin, freedom is only realized through the process of consumption and identity is constituted through acts of consumption: "I consume and therefore I am, and I am free." Benjamin (1931) coined the phrase "optical unconscious" in his article "A Small History of Photography." He argued that we discover this optical unconscious in photography, just as the instinctual unconscious is discovered in psychoanalysis. In discussing the work of the photographer Atget, he (1969) notes that the choice of lonely, deserted streets, for example, conveys something to us unconsciously and later comments that "mass movements are usually discerned more clearly by a camera than by the naked eye" (251).

Vitimo's 1992 (cited in Paetzold 1996) thesis is that the mass media undermine our sense of a stable and eternal world by the proliferation of images: "the flow of images driven by interests of capital leads to a 'weakening' of society's hold on reality" (104). Both Benjamin and Vitimo draw upon Marx's theory of the "phantasmagoria," or succession of images or illusions. For McLuhan and Fiore (1967), the "medium is the message." Derrida (1967) has taken this idea one step further. He states that the "medium is the meaning." In industrial society, capital and production become the meaning.

Benjamin (1931) also used the phrase "social unconscious"—a term Erich Fromm (1990) took up. For Fromm this social unconscious was the way we often think that our way of doing things is the natural way, and that our society represents just one of an infinite number of ways of dealing with how to live. The media and peers create an unconscious expectation of what ought to be with regard to one's possessions, lifestyle, and so on. The processing of this visually perceived information is automatic and sometimes not conscious (Lewicki 1986; Lewicki, Czyzewska, and Hoffman 1987), but has an impact on feelings and behavior, with their effects often unnoticed.

The Visual Image and Cultural Ideals

It is estimated that children in the United States spend approximately twenty-five hours each week watching television (Gentile and Walsh 2002). In addition to this time, children are exposed to visual images on the computer, video games, and at the movies on top of the multiple visual images of daily life that previous generations were exposed to.

The powerful influence of the media has been noted at least since Packard's (1957) book *The Hidden Persuaders*. Boorstin (1961) described what he called the "graphic revolution," beginning with the printing press and moving on through the development of the photograph and television. Explaining that ideals were related to ideas, but that the word "image" is related to imitating, he concludes his book entitled *The Image* by saying, "All around the world we have revealed a shift in our thinking from ideals to image" (241). He believes that Americans are now the "most illusioned" people on earth (240). Postman (1992) has chronicled the transformation of our society from one that uses technology to one that is shaped by it. The images in the media are processed by the sensory/affective system in the brain as opposed to the semantic system, leaving many people unable to verbalize what they feel is wrong. We see images of a tsunami wave and we feel what is about to happen and then what has happened to the people and animals engulfed. Ages ago it was declared, "A picture is worth a thousand words." Recently we have heard the more extreme idea that "image is everything." Marvin Hill, an artist, stated "The eye forms the world/ the world forms the eye" (cited in Koltko-Rivera 2004, 3). Hoffman (1998), the author of *Visual Intelligence*, explains that "We click icons because this is quicker and less prone to error than editing megabytes of software or toggling voltages in circuits" ("God or Not," *New York Times*, Jan. 4, 2005). According to Hoffman, visual intelligence interacts with, and in many cases, precedes and drives our rational and emotional intelligence. Visual effects lure us to films, entertain us for hours, and manipulate our spending.

Primates imitate what they see. The work of Bandura (Bandura, Ross, and Ross 1961) demonstrated that the people who are imitated most are those who are seen as warm and nurturing, powerful, and/or attractive. Media personalities often meet one or more of these criteria. We are driven to imitate them, not necessarily consciously. For example, I feel I know the television personality Katie Couric, whom I have never actually seen, better than many of the neighbors in my building whom I have actually seen many times in the elevator or the lobby and spoken with briefly. The images of people and scenes we see in the media are part of the culture to which we feel we belong. One patient told me that we know the problems celebrities have in their romantic lives the way the Greeks knew about those of their gods. The celebrities have become many people's gods.

Rubinstein (1983, 1995), an anthropologist, has documented how suicide became an epidemic among teenage boys in Micronesia. In the 1960s suicide on the islands of Micronesia was almost unknown. By the end of the 1980s there were more suicides per capita in Micronesia than anywhere else in the world. Males between fifteen and twenty-four make up the majority of such cases, with suicides occurring after not particularly important incidents—being rebuked for making too much noise, parents refusing to give the boy a few dollars or a graduation gown. Rubinstein reported that a number of suicide attempts seemed to be imitative play.

Phillips (1974) examined the relationship between suicides reported on the front pages of newspapers for twenty years and suicide statistics during the same period. Immediately after the stories about suicides appeared, suicides in the area of the newspapers increased. Marilyn Monroe's death was followed by a 12 percent jump in the suicide rate (Phillips 1979). Traffic fatalities also increased in the following four days, presumably because people commit suicide by crashing their cars. Phillips does not think this kind of contagion is rational or necessarily conscious. He thinks deaths give others a "permission" to die.

The idea that people conform to what other people are doing is an old one. Latane and Darley (1968) found that unfortunate effects of people observing the behavior of others in research when Kitty Genovese was murdered after being attacked three times on the street in Queens while thirty-eight of her neighbors watched from their windows without doing anything. Latane and Darley reasoned that people look around and see what others are doing and if others are not acting, they think they shouldn't either. Imitation effects are largest when the models are likeable and powerful (Bandura 1973).

To a large extent, the characters portrayed in the media and the celebrities who often portray them become unconscious ideals not focused upon by therapists unless patients discuss them. They are often not consciously thought about, but present only in dreams or if clinicians engage in techniques specifically asking patients what they are visualizing. For example, when one man was discussing his ideal male body, I asked if he had known someone with such a body. He referred to the Charles Atlas chest expander advertisement on the back of comic books he read as a boy.

Visualization and the "unsymbolized" nature of sensory information

Seeing is believing. "You know that's the truth because you see it right in front of you," state Ewen and Ewen (1992, 206). Social psychologists found that the vivid imagery of one case study had more influence than statistics involving very large samples (Nisbett and Ross 1980). Psychoanalysis has been heavily reliant upon the "talking cure," with psychoanalysis in much of Freudian and in Lacanian theory very dependent upon language. Obviously, this is not the case in the therapy in moments of insight, especially in the hot moments of analyzing transferential processes. Furthermore, Bucci (1997) has written extensively about the process of psychoanalysis as involving an increase in connections between the sensory, "sub-symbolic" systems and the symbolic (often verbal) system. But behavioral, experiential, EMDR, and, to some extent, cognitive therapy rely heavily upon the accessing of sensory-motor, imaginal, and emotional experiences. Horowitz (1983) asserted that "emotional responses to images of objects may be greater than those to purely lexical representations of object names" (81). There is no way to test this hypothesis experimentally, of course, since it is not possible to ever equate an image with a word. Whether a word or image will result in greater emotional reactivity would depend upon an individual's experience with both. For a person who had been threatened with a knife, the image of a knife might be more frightening than the word, but not for a person without such experience. On the other hand, a woman called "slut" by her mother might react more strongly to the word than to the image.

Sensory-affective events are not processed the same way in the brain as language, although language may quickly accompany sensory-affective experiences. Sensory-affective experiences, for example, are processed primarily by the limbic system, with information going through the amygdala as opposed to the hippocampus that mediates verbal information. For this reason, talking alone may do little to alleviate the physiological symptoms resulting from trauma and the reactivation of networks associated with trauma. Gazzaniga's (1967, 1998) research showed that visual information that was presented only to the right hemisphere in split-brain patients (patients for whom the corpus callosum connecting the left and right hemispheres had been lesioned) resulted in an emotional reaction as exemplified by facial expressions, although these patients were unable to verbalize what they had experienced. This research indicates the registering of visual information with the emotional system. Johann Huizinga, a scholar very knowledgeable about the art, literature, music, and manners of medieval Europe and a keen historian, stated, "Thought takes the form of visual images. Really to impress the mind a concept has first to take visible shape" (1954, 284).

Goldfried, Raue, and Castonguay (1998) found that master therapists rely upon visual imagery for understanding their patients. Levenson (2003) argued that the therapy process is more a right brain one, especially related to visual images, and questioned whether the verbal activity has any effect at all. There is some evidence for Levenson's radical idea that you do not even have to tap into the symbolic system in the work of Huber (1965). He told a woman with frightening hallucinations of snakes to tell him all the details about the snakes the next time he visited her. The hallucinations went away quickly. Here, becoming very aware of the visual image resulted in change without language, interpretation, or anything symbolic taking place. The woman simply became more aware of what was before her eyes.

Many cultures have displayed visual images of creatures to be idealized or feared—gods, devils, statesmen, athletes, and beauties. Recent art has questioned the experience of the thing itself in contrast to the image (Magritte's *"Ceci n'est pas une pipe"*) and images have no obvious cohesion (Rauschenberg's "Factum II"). In the United States we are finally reduced to numerous "reality shows" with no ideals to aspire to or terrors to be frightened of at all. Whereas the definition of art in an earlier era was "a work of beauty," today it is "a work that provokes us"—that makes us think or react. Most of our entertainment at best amuses us. At worst it occupies our time, distracts us from worries and our own meaninglessness, and creates new desires through advertising. "Postmodernists do not believe in what has traditionally been one of the main functions of narrative: to lend meaning to life, to our place in the world "(Van Alphen 1992, 21).

Effects of watching television

There are many studies demonstrating the deleterious effects on women of seeing culturally ideal women in the media. Watching even thirty minutes of television can alter women's perceptions of their bodies (Myers and Biocca 1992). Watching television commercials lowers self-confidence in women (Hargreaves and Tiggermann 2002). Looking at photographs of slender models also lowers the self-esteem and satisfaction of women with their bodies (Wilcox and Laird 2000). After viewing media images, women feel more angry, anxious, and depressed (Cattarin, Thompson, Thomas, and Williams 2000; Hargreaves and Tiggermann 2002). The work of Tversky and Kahneman (1973b) showed that events or images that are more readily accessible to memory have a greater impact on beliefs about what ought to be than less available images.

If the media affect women's standards of beauty and lead them to feel worse about themselves, it seems likely that images in the media affect other standards as well. Van Alphen (1992), in describing the bodybuilders in the contemporary art of Francis Bacon, states that the representation of the stability and control is idealized in images of the male body: "[I]t is easier to look like an erect penis than to have one" (182). In a consumer culture appearances and images of the body become a major interest (Featherstone 1991).

Great writers usually capture images and emotions better than psychologists do. Willy Loman, a character with whom many in the American public have resonated, sought popularity and financial success. Successful for a while, in the end he was not able to make it anymore. Miller's central conviction was that "as man is seldom defined by his social or political milieu, neither can he escape the impersonal forces which affect his image of himself" (Spiller et al. 1963, 1,437). Willy had to sell himself each day—his image was all he had. For many people in such a culture, identity becomes defined by outside forces. As Billy Bathgate mused upon his change in identity in the novel by Doctorow when he moved from a childhood as a street kid in the Bronx to gentility in upper New York State, "None of these things made sense except as I was contingent to a situation." He formulated what he called a "license-plate theory of identification," as discussed by Deaux (1991).

Studies by consumer researchers show that the more people watch television, the more they think American households have swimming pools, convertibles, tennis courts, maids, and private planes. Almost everyone in the United States overestimates standards of living. Television inflates ideas about standards of living for everyone except the very wealthy. Although there are some mixed findings, heavy television viewers in most demographic subgroups view Americans as richer than they actually are (Carlson 1993, Fox and Philliber 1978; Shrum, O'Guinn, Semenik, and Faber 1991). The more people watch television, the more in debt they are (Schor 1998, 81).

As more and more people around the globe see television or films, this phenomenon is becoming more widespread. A recent documentary one year after the arrival of television in the country of Bhutan included an interview of Bhutan's "cable guy" that documented the proliferation of desires. He stated, "I think so many people are aware of things they desire they didn't even know existed before. . . . Sometimes I forget my prayers" (*Frontline*, PBS, June 5, 2003). Belk and Pollay (1985) found that the level of affluence displayed in many advertisements is affordable only to the upper middle class. On the television show *Seinfeld*, the Seinfeld character and his sidekick Kramer rarely work but live in apartments many of my working patients can't afford. In an analysis of couples in five hundred magazine advertisements, Jordan and Bryant (paper cited in Richins 1996) found no old, poor, sick, or unattractive couples. Richins (1991) has argued that Americans most frequently compare themselves with media images. Campbell (1987) believes that the comparisons are made not with media images per se, but with daydreams stimulated by the media, including advertising. These fantasy images are even more idealized than the images provided by advertising.

Exposure to images also affects values. Massive exposure to sexually explicit materials results in greater tolerance for pre- and extramarital sexual activity, less endorsement of marriage as an institution, wanting fewer children, and beliefs that there are health risks to sexual repression. The media and the virtual others with whom we compare ourselves are affecting our standards and leaving us feeling that we fall short of these standards.

Visual images can be employed to have positive effects, too, of course. For example, Bandura's social modeling concept has been used in videos, street theater, and comic books to improve literacy in Mexico and improve education and reduce child marriages and HIV infection in India. Researchers found that the enrollment of girls in school had risen from 10 to 38 percent in one village after residents viewed a video portraying the benefits of education to a woman with an unfaithful husband (Smith 2002).

Subjective well-being

How can there be such widespread feelings of malaise when people's objective standards of living have been increasing? If we look at how people assess their subjective current state of well-being, we can look at objective aspects, their past outcomes, their expectations of future outcomes, and their goals. Relations between objective indicators and overall life satisfaction tend not to be very high. Ratings of past situations and future expectations are also poor predictors of current satisfaction, although ratings of only the past and future five years have been taken. Goals tend to be a much better predictor of subjective well-being. The gap between one's goals and one's present condition accounts for 35 to 41 percent of the variance. The size of the gap between goals and actual achievements has now been found to be the major determinant of satisfaction or happiness in a number of studies. Easterlin (1973) stated, "[R]aising the incomes of all does not increase the happiness of all. . . . The resolution of this paradox lies in the relative nature of welfare judgments. Individuals assess their material well-being not in terms of the absolute amount of goods they have, but relative to a social norm of what goods they ought to have" (4). Numerous subsequent studies from the United States, Europe, and Japan confirmed the 1973 findings (Easterlin 1995). Recent research (e.g., Fischer 2007 has indicated that this happiness paradox exists in some countries but not others and that surveys in developing countries are not well done, however (Hagerty and Veenhoven 2003).

The conscious actual self is one that feels deprived. In spite of the absolute level of affluence in the United States, there is a widespread sense of relative deprivation regarding the attainment of the cultural ideals presented in the images in the media. This is the "empty" self described by Cushman (1990). It tries to fill itself up with material goods, substances, and distractions such as film, TV, and video games, leading to increases in the sense of deprivation.

Theory of Relative Deprivation

In spite of the absolute level of affluence in the United States, there is a widespread sense of relative deprivation regarding the attainment of the cultural ideals presented in the images in the media. The sense of deprivation is encouraged by advertising urging consumers to buy products they do not need, keeping the marketing economy prosperous. In spite of absolute increases in the average square feet per house, the average number of automobiles and personal appliances of Americans from the 1950s to the 1990s, the happiness of Americans declined (Wachtel 1983).

The concept of relative deprivation was first put forth by Stouffer et al. (1949) in their study of American soldiers. The first formal theory was proposed by Davis (1959) who suggested that comparison with members of one's own group can produce feelings of relative deprivation if one's outcomes are poorer than another's. Comparison will produce feelings of relative superiority if one's outcomes are better. Runciman (1966), in his study of attitudes about social inequality in twentieth-century England, pointed out that comparisons with one's own outcomes in the past can produce feelings of relative deprivation or relative advantage. Comparisons of one's outcomes with those of another are obviously affected by one's sense of entitlement. Gurr (1970) proposed that a sense of deprivation is more likely to occur when people believe that it is not feasible for them to obtain the desired outcomes. The most elaborate theory of relative deprivation was developed by Crosby (1976). She proposed six necessary and sufficient "preconditions" for feelings of relative deprivation. In order for people to feel resentful about not possessing some desired object or state, she proposed people must perceive (1) a discrepancy between what they want and what they have, (2) that others are doing better, (3) a discrepancy between what they have and what they believe they deserve, (4) a discrepancy between what they have and their past expectations, (5) pessimism about the future, and (6) no feelings of self-blame. Hope for improvement has a somewhat surprising effect. Rising expectations can lead to the most discontent. Indeed, experimental research found some of the angriest complaints from participants come when their conditions were improving.

The theory of relative deprivation suggests that it is not people's material deprivation in an absolute sense that causes dissatisfaction, but rather the disparity between what they see as their own ratio of outcomes to inputs as compared to that which others are obtaining. This idea is consistent with the major theory of justice within social psychology—equity theory (Walster, Walster, and Berscheid 1978). According to equity theory, people act so as to make their own ratio of outcomes to inputs equal to that which others are obtaining. In order to do so, if their own ratio of outcomes to inputs is low, they may put in less effort or attempt to lower the outcomes of others, for example. Richins (1995, 1996) has documented how the idealized images of wealth and the good life lead to social comparison processes resulting in discontent and increased desire for more. Chiagouris and Mitchell (1997) found that materialism is increasing globally and Kasser and Kanner (2003) have demonstrated that the consumer culture is negatively affecting people's sense of social well-being. Kasser and Kanner make the case that psychologists cannot continue their reticence to investigate these topics.

The problem of envy has always been central to psychoanalytic theory (Freud 1914, 1921; Klein, 1964; Lacan 1964/1978). In anthropology, it is known that cultures engaged in practices to avoid the effects of the "evil eye"—the eye of envy. Interestingly, Rawls (1971), in his theory of justice, focuses upon the social derivation of envy and on society to mitigate its effects. Society will "reduce the *visibility*, or at least the painful visibility, of variations in men's prospects (536, italics added). Although the tradition in American WASP (White Anglo-Saxon Protestant) culture was to hide wealth from the eyes of the outside world, this tradition seems to have all but disappeared in the contemporary scene.

Krugman (2002) and others have pointed out that the disparity between the rich and the poor in the United States has been increasing in the past decade. Rawls (1971) justified disparities between the rich and the poor as long as a disparate distribution led to a greater amount for every person in the distribution. G. A. Cohen (2000), on the other hand, has argued that a great disparity can feel unjust in and of itself, even if the rule of distribution is viewed as fair. De Graff, Wann, and Naylor (2001) have called the suffering Americans feel as they fall short of the material standards they desire "affluenza." Kasser and Kanner (2003) have found that feelings of satisfaction and happiness are lower among people who value highly financial success and luxury possessions.

Although self-reported self-esteem is not lower for lower socioeconomic groups (Crocker and Major 1989), these measures ask questions about how people rate themselves on various qualities. People may rate themselves high on attractiveness, intelligence, and personality, and still feel a disparity with an even higher ideal presented by images in the media. Sennett and Cobb (1972), in *The Hidden Injuries of Class*, have given us a very different view of manual laborers and their families from their series of interviews. They report that lower class people feel that educated, upper-middle-class people are "in a position to judge them, and that the judgment rendered would be that working-class people could not be respected as equals. . . . The emotional impact of the class difference here is a matter of impudent snobbery, of shaming, of put-down" (38). The relative deprivation here leads to a sense of inferiority and shame. People do not feel the sense of dignity that we are all supposed to feel simply by virtue of being human.

It is not material deprivation that is most pernicious, however, but psychological deprivation of respect that leads to feelings of humiliation and shame (Sennett 2003). Gilligan (1996), in his study of prisoners who had committed violent crimes, concluded that it was shame, humiliation, and a sense of being invisible that led these men to violence. He cites Franz Fanon who described his response to being black in a world dominated by whites: "'Shame. Shame and self-contempt'" (203).

Consequences of the actual–ideal discrepancy

Comparisons to idealized images lead to negative feelings about oneself (Salovey and Rodin 1984; Smith, Diener, and Garonzik 1990). These negative feelings are sometimes motivating (Higgins, 1987; James, 1890). One response is to increase efforts to reduce the discrepancy between the comparison standard and oneself (Carver and Scheier 1981; Duval and Wicklund 1972). For those who perceive that increased effort will move them closer to the desired goal of more possession, media images will exacerbate the drive (Duval, Duval, and Mulilis 1992). Relative deprivation leads to different feelings depending upon whether people attribute responsibility for the deprivation to themselves or to others. Four major types of responses are possible. First, if the relative deprivation is attributed to failings of the self, depression often occurs. Second, if the relative deprivation is attributed to the other, anger occurs and/or one attempts to change the situation. Third, the relative deprivation may be blamed on the other initially, as in the case of felt discrimination, but rather than feel a sense of injustice threatening to the world view, one may act so as to deserve the poor outcome, behaving masochistically. Fourth, there may be a vacillation between a sense of deserving a great deal (entitlement), attributing the unfair deprivation to the other, and at another time, a sense of deserving very little (attributing the deprivation to one's own inadequacy), often unconscious. In other words, consciously, there is the sense of being unique, of being special, of deserving the best outcomes ascribed to the narcissistic character. This feeling alternates with a sense of being nothing, that satisfaction will never be attained, and that unlimited desires will never be fulfilled.

In contrast to the contemporary relational focus upon the internalization of representations occurring predominantly within the family, the Freudian superego and the Lacanian "symbolic" order were embedded with the ideals of the culture. In contrast, psychoanalysis in recent object relations theories and self psychology has focused upon the ideals of parents and significant others as leading to pathology, with the relationship between analyst and patient able to remedy the original lack of attunement to the child's own needs and desires. The gap between ideals and actualities in the social unconscious, however, is not one so easily rectified by a new relationship with a therapist. The gap created by visual images in our global village requires a larger social effort at transcendence of insatiable desires and empty selves.

Case Examples

Susan had worked successfully in the arts for many years outside New York City. She returned to New York where she had grown up when she married for a second time. She had divorced her first husband after he lost his business, became an alcoholic, and was hostile toward their sons. Her new husband was also in the arts and earned only a small income. Susan and her sons were unable to survive on two artists' incomes in New York City. She felt desperate about paying her rent and maintaining the lifestyle to which she was accustomed. Each session she cried and felt panicked. Susan refused to get a regular job, however, because she would be bored with anything that was not creative. The most difficult problem for me to sympathize with, however, was her refusal to think about selling her expensive second home outside the city, which she had been unable to rent. She rarely went to this home. She didn't have a group of friends who lived near it. Still, the idea of giving it up was not something she would think about. Nor was moving out of Manhattan a possibility she would consider. She would become angry if I said anything that might suggest lowering her standards. Susan saw herself as smart, talented, creative, attractive, and very energetic. This perception had been validated by her performance at school and comments from her teachers. I heard nothing about her experiences in her family that suggested she had narcissistic deficits. Her view of what she should be able to attain was derived from the culture, the media, and the comparison of herself to others. Her comparisons were not unrealistic. Yet the statistics regarding making a living in the arts were not in her favor. Although I saw her despair as coming from "tyranny of the should," she persisted until she fortunately, with lots of luck thrown in, figured out a way to make a living in the commercial arts.

My patients and students often have film and television stars in their dreams. At first, I thought this was because I have a number of patients who are actors. Now I realize that many nonactors have dreams permeated with actors as well. Meryl Streep comforts a young woman from Eastern Europe. Madonna is sitting on the grass in the middle of the Southern State Parkway. Patients also dream that I seem similar to one of these actors or that I am a psychotherapist on a television show, but quickly pick up that I seem unfamiliar with the television programs they mention. One such patient was Marie. Her case was a treatment failure. Not so smart, creative, or attractive as Susan, she refused to look for jobs paying less than $60,000—her former salary. She also refused to think about leaving Manhattan. Marie dreamed that robbers broke into her apartment and stole her purse. When the police came, she did not know her name or who she was without her wallet. She was taken to the police department and scientists walked around her, trying to figure out who she was. She had told me that she had always done whatever she thought her parents wanted, especially her very controlling mother. She did not even know the food she wanted to order in a restaurant. She just ordered whatever other people were ordering. Her parents had not pressured her to make so much money, however, and were quite proud of a sibling who had a much lower income.

Marie told me she was completely superficial. She didn't read or go to any cultural events—quite surprising given her educational background. She just watched TV and her dreams often contained television characters. She dreamed one time of me as a character from the show *Designing Women*. Marie fits the description of someone with an empty self. She stopped treatment, however, when I seemed unable to help her get the sort of job to which she felt entitled. Unfortunately, unlike my success with a number of other patients, I was not able to help Marie give up this desire, attain it, or find another solution.

Josephs (2004) has presented the case of James, a businessman who believes that given his background and breeding, he should have a trust fund and work as a museum curator. In addition to James, he notes a number of patients, born to upper-middle-class families and part of the bohemian, "Woodstock" generation who regretted not being more achievement-oriented as they aged and dealt with the expenses of New York City life. Josephs refers to what he calls "normative standards of affluence" that ensures that "one will always feel like a 'have-not' in a world of 'haves,' regardless of statistical evidence of one's relatively privileged position in the nation's (or the world's) economy" (407). He cites an article in *New York Magazine* by Kirkpatrick (August 7, 2000) in which college-educated New Yorkers making from $35,000 to $10,000,000 all feel poor. They believe they are failing to attain a middle-class lifestyle as they see it—a two or three bedroom apartment below 96th Street on Manhattan's east side, or below 125th Street on the west side; a nanny and private schools for the children; a country home; and the ability to dine out, go the theater, and travel. Josephs notes that failing to live up to this standard leaves many of his patients with feelings of longing, resentment, envy, and shame.

SUMMARY AND CONCLUSION

I have suggested a model of a biological self that attempts to keep actual and ideal respresentations of self in balance. Whereas in the previous century subjective desires unacceptable to the prevailing cultural worldview were kept out of conscious awareness, today unlimited desires created by visible images, yet invisible social and psychological forces, create a sense of lack often furthered by the absence of a socially created and agreed-upon self-transcendent sense of life's meaning. Whereas in the previous century unconscious forces that were intrapsychic led to considerable suffering, today unconscious forces that are social and visible are leading to suffering—depression, hurting others, and other responses. Psychoanalysis, with its recent focus upon internalized representations, the family, and the relationship between patient and analyst, has often neglected in its understanding of the self, its discontents, and in its theory about relieving suffering—the issues of the broader culture that Freud and the interpersonalists considered essential to the understanding of human beings. The question remains as to whether people who are not confident that justice will prevail in an afterlife will be able to create communal meanings that supercede individualistic desires now socially constructed so as to be competitive, unattainable by most people, unlimited in their nature and number, and forever frustrating in their quest. The visible images spreading throughout the world in the media, along with a culture that tells people that they can be anything they want, leaves people thinking that they, too, should have the lifestyle, if not of the stars, of the Manhattan singles and American families they see nightly on television. These visible images are often creating an unconscious, idealized vision of the self that wreaks havoc in self-regulatory capabilities. Many of the unconscious factors affecting our feelings and behaviors are right before our eyes.

Chapter 4

The Boogie-Woogie Rumble of Unconscious Processes

The Mind in Psychoanalysis and Psychology

Good morning, Daddy / 'Ain't you heard / The boogie-woogie rumble / Of a dream deferred?

—Langston Hughes

Andreas tells me that when he is not engaged in the energy of intense sexuality, he feels empty—dead. I ask more about the feeling. Cold. He indicates a feeling of blood being drawn out of his face. I ask about the first time he remembers such a feeling. He tells me that his mother didn't want him. She went to bed in her seventh month of pregnancy. When she was in labor, the doctor told whoever was present that only his mother or the baby could live and the doctor decided it would be the mother (who already had several children at home). Although both the mother and the baby lived, the mother was in bed for several months after he was born. I say, "You felt like you were almost a murderer before you were a day old." He said, "Yes," and then, "This is crazy, but could it be that I wished I were dead because she stayed in bed and held the picture of my dead sister in front of her every day? There were never any pictures of me. I wished I were dead so she would look at me like that."

How is it that feelings remain so unconnected in the mind? Andreas gets an insight in the above session, but it does not seem that an experience that was unconscious becomes conscious. Instead, it seems that he connects his dead feeling now with the dead feeling when he was young and did not have the gaze and the love of his mother. He had not been conscious of the connection. The "dead" feeling that is now sometimes a part of his identity, an aspect of his self-representation, is connected through sensory imagery with the wish to be dead or the dead feeling he experienced early in life. He is able to make sense of the feeling and it is not so terrifying anymore.

Was the lack of connection experienced by Andreas "repression" or "dissociation"? What are the current models of the mind in psychology and cognitive neuroscience and how do they affect our understanding of the controversy surrounding the existence of "repressed" memories or any kind of motivated forgetting or disconnecting? For almost a century, psychoanalysts and psychologists have worked from different models of the mind and different views of the role of consciousness in affecting human actions. Ideas about the processes of change have stemmed from very different models of the mind. Before thinking about change, it is important to recognize that there has been a convergence in models of the mind that allows us to integrate ideas about the psychoanalytic process with ideas about change in cognitive behavioral and other therapies.

Until recently, behaviorists viewed the mind and consciousness as irrelevant to change. Cognitive psychologists thought consciousness, but not unconscious influences, played an important role with the part of the mind that was unconscious being quite small. Psychoanalysts have always focused primarily on what is unconscious, although ideas about the likely contents of what is unconscious vary greatly among Freudian, Kleinian, and interpersonal and other analysts. Freud's iceberg image depicted the unconscious aspects as far larger than the conscious aspects. Now there is a convergence regarding the importance of unconscious processes, with social and cognitive psychologists agreeing that most processing is unconscious (Bargh and Chartran 1999; Velmanns 1991; Wegner 2002; Wilson 2002); although most of what is forgotten is not considered by social-cognitive psychologists to involve repression. After reviewing three models of the unconscious mind—the repressed, the dissociated, and the cognitive, I shall then show that the question of whether some sort of motivated not knowing and forgetting occurs is moot, as all perception, attention, and memory involve motivations related to people's primary desires. I shall then argue that current models of affect-regulation and controlled and automatic (unconscious) processes are similar enough to psychoanalytic ideas to allow for investigations leading to a unified model of the mind acceptable to psychoanalysts, psychologists, and other cognitive scientists.

THE MIND IN PSYCHOANALYSIS AND PSYCHOLOGY

As stated earlier, psychologists initially had described their infant science as the study of consciousness, with James (1892) offering ten arguments against the notion of an unconscious. Freud, believing that the role of conscious processes in human experience was much smaller than the role of unconscious processes, likened his discovery to those of Darwin and Copernicus in its assault on the superiority of the place of humans in the universe—they were not created first, their earth was not the center of the solar system, and they could now no longer believe that they had conscious control over their lives. Although Freud did not totally neglect the role of consciousness (cf. Natsoulas 2000), it was not his focus. (For an excellent review of the unconscious in philosophy, psychology, medicine, and literature 1750–1900, see Rand 2004).

The behaviorists, impressed by the extent to which reinforcements and punishments were able to predict behavior, saw consciousness as a sort of epiphenomenon, something that happened with people, but that was not relevant to how they acted. This position was supported by the philosopher Ryle (1949) who declared consciousness to be a "ghost in the machine," an observer of the machine's process, but not in control.

As discussed earlier, models of self-regulation such as Wiener's (1948) Cybernetics changed the thinking of many behaviorally oriented psychologists about the relation of consciousness to control. If a thermostat could be given a goal that determined behavior, then surely human beings could have conscious thoughts that affect behavior. With the cognitive revolution, more and more studies have accumulated demonstrating the effect of unconscious processes on behavior. Two sorts of unconscious processes resulted: the cognitive unconscious of psychology (sometimes referred to as the "psychological unconscious") and the dynamic unconscious of psychoanalysis.

Now some psychoanalysts are making an argument similar to some extent to that of the behaviorists, saying that change may sometimes come without conscious awareness from new procedural knowledge learned from a way of being with the therapist. (Beebe 1998; Fonagy 1998; Stern et al. 1998) or simply through unconscious processes that never become conscious (Levenson 2003). Morgan (1998) states, "In our model, then, the patient's gaining of insight is only part of the way change occurs, and the 'something more' is the acquisition of implicit relational knowledge" (330). According to these theorists, a space is created in the relationship between therapist and patient where something takes place that permits a new "'way-of-being-with-the-other'" in a "'moment of meeting'" (Stern et al. 1998, 300). Although these moments suggest a role for consciousness, other psychoanalysts think the relationship may be internalized without necessarily involving consciousness. So now we have psychoanalysts arguing that change can occur without unconscious processes becoming conscious and cognitive-behavioral psychotherapists recognizing that unconscious factors affect behavior.

Still, there is divergence regarding whether experiences are actively kept out of consciousness. And, although academic psychology has fully recognized the importance of unconscious processes in the mind, these processes still are not taken into account in any meaningful, extended way in nonana-lytic therapies. There has been a convergence in the thinking regarding the important role of unconscious processes in psychology and psychoanalysis, but the way these processes operate when the fulfillment of the desire for psychological, as opposed to physical survival, is threatened, has not been spelled out in scientific psychology.

The model of the mind in psychoanalysis and cognitive science has evolved considerably since Freud thought that making the unconscious con-scious would be helpful to people, or later that an integration of repressed contents of the id into the ego would lead to change. The limen of conscious-ness model of the mind endorsed by Freud, scientists and philosophers in the nineteenth century (see figure 4.1) now has been replaced by models of neural networks, connectionism, and multiple drafts. As Kihlstrom (1990) states, "A full century since the publication of Janet's (1889) *Psychological Automatisms* and James's (1890) *Principles of Psychology*, and five decades since the death of Freud, the study of unconscious life has been completely revolutionized" (460). Are there three different models of unconscious pro-cesses in the mind, or has one model emerged that accounts adequately for

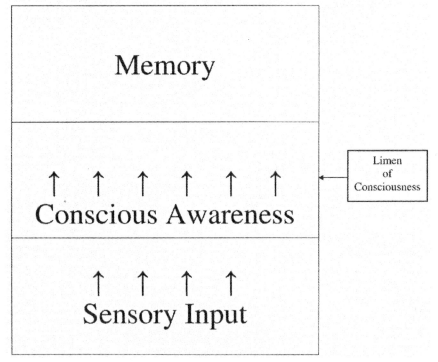

Figure 4.1.   Old Model in Psychology and Psychoanalysis

all of the observed phenomena? We know from Whyte's (1978) review in *The Unconscious Before Freud* that the idea of unconscious processes was prominent by 1800 and fashionable by 1870. In the limen of consciousness model of the nineteenth century (Herbart 1896), what was unconscious became conscious when it crossed over a line. Sensory processes crossed over the limen into conscious awareness and then might or might not be stored in memory. The current view is that sensory processes, perception, attention, memory, and conscious awareness are all operating in parallel, simultaneously. Instead of having to be conscious in order to be remembered, experiences show evidence of being remembered without having ever entered into conscious awareness. Some questions we still need to answer are how such processes are connected, how they remain connected or become disconnected, and whether such disconnections can be intentional or motivated as psychoanalysts have argued. Although the notion that unconscious processes can contribute to psychopathology was present in the writings of at least nineteen authors before Freud, this idea seems to have become associated only with psychoanalysis by the 1900s (Whyte 1978).

Although cognitive psychologists recently have embraced again and investigated unconscious processes, they have not studied the processes most important to people's views of themselves, others, and reality. As a leading cognitive scientist told me, researchers were not interested in anything "dirty." "Dirty" seemed to refer to sex and aggression—the traditional domain of psychoanalysis—or at least messy and hard to measure. Kilhstrom (1990) went on to say that research "has revealed a view of nonconscious mental life that is more extensive than the unconscious inference of Helmholtz, but also quite different—kinder, gentler, and more rational—from the seething unconscious of Freud" (460). Bargh (1989, 26) initially rejected the idea of unconscious motivation. He differentiated the cognitive unconscious from the "Freudian notion of unconscious goals and motivations in which the person is never aware of having such goals in the first place." The clean unconscious that cognitive psychologists discovered was quite dependent upon their method which never included, of course, free association with a trusted person. As Gladwell (2005) summarizes this point of view in his popular book, "The adaptive unconscious is not to be confused with the unconscious described by Sigmund Freud, which was a dark and murky place filled with desires and memories and fantasies that were too disturbing for us to think about consciously" (11). The "new" unconscious described by Hassin, Uleman, and Bargh (2005) and by Bargh (2006) also seems very "clean," although not without its biases.

We now need a model of conscious and unconscious processes that accounts for both nonmotivated ("cognitive") and motivated ("dynamic") at-

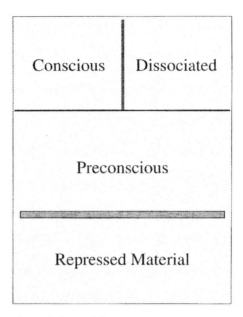

Figure 4.2.   Old Psychoanalytic Model

tention and forgetting and the differing sorts of connections and the lack of connections referred to as repressions, dissociations, and so on. We now have discussions of three types of unconscious processes: cognitive, repressed, and dissociated. Ideas about repression and dissociation and attempts to reconcile them have resulted in the rather unusual idea of the mind having "horizontal" and "vertical" splits (Hilgard 1977; Kohut 1977) and in some psychologists still remaining unconvinced that motivated forgetting of any sort exists. I shall argue that consciousness selects what it processes and that three different views of the unconscious mind are not necessary when all perception, attention, and memory are considered to be motivated by their very nature—that is, related primarily to the desires for self-preservation and preservation of a meaning-making system. If people are motivated primarily to survive and to preserve their meaning system—their representations of self, others, and the world—then all perception, attention, and memory will be affected by these major motivations.

Three Unconscious Minds

As stated earlier, three views of the unconscious minds have developed—a repressed unconscious from Freudian theory, a dissociated unconscious from Sullivanian and trauma theories, and a nondefensive, adaptive unconscious from cognitive theory. Recently, relational psychoanalysts have adopted a "dissociational" model of the mind for a variety of reasons, including the fact that repression is a term related to the squashing down of instinctive urges which they no longer see as the major motivational urges. Rejecting drive theory, the models of Sullivan (1953) and Fairbairn (1929) considered dissociation to be the primary mode of defense. Cognitive and other psychologists in the empirical tradition have also adopted the word dissociation, initially perhaps out of an attempt to distance themselves from the idea of the psychoanalytic unconscious, but also quite likely because of the lack of clarity surrounding the term "repression." Although both relational analysts and academic psychologists speak primarily of dissociations, there is greater overlap in the understanding of relational and other psychoanalysts about unconscious processes, however, than there is between psychoanalysts and empirical psychologists.

Returning to the example of Sirhan Sirhan described at the beginning of this book, we ask if psychoanalysts call Sirhan's memory repressed or dissociated? It fits Freud's definition for "repression" as "rejecting and keeping something out of consciousness" (1915b, 105). The memory involves what many may think of as a forbidden instinctual urge—murder. But the memory seems to be available in a dissociated state, so that many analysts would call it "dissociated." Although many psychoanalysts might agree that some examples of forgetting seem to be more clearly "dissociation" and others that are more clearly "repression," there is a great deal of overlap in these ideas. Let us look further at these two unconscious minds in psychoanalysis.

The Two Dynamic Unconscious Minds: The Controversy over Repression and Dissociation

Characteristics of the dynamic unconscious

As stated above, two views of the dynamic unconscious emerged in psychoanalysis—one, the Freudian model of the repressed unconscious and a more recent interpersonal/relational model of a dissociated unconscious. Regardless whether we look at the Freudian repressed unconscious or the interpersonal/relational dissociated unconscious, however, dynamic unconscious processes have in common a number of characteristics. They are related to desires, fears, fantasies, defenses, feelings, and behaviors. They are alogical, tolerant of mutual contradiction, timeless, impervious to contradiction and to external reality, and characterized by thinking that is called either "primary process" or "subsymbolic" (Bucci 1997), characterized by displacements and condensations.

There is a great deal of overlap between the ways the words "dissociation" (in the broad sense of "disconnection") and "repression" have been used. The phenomena of dissociation and multiple personality were known long before Freud (Carlson 1986; Ellenberger 1970). When Freud began to think about hysteria, he thought in terms of dissociation (1892–1893, 1956) and frequently used the terms synonymously. Early on he did not differentiate repression from dissociation. Soon, of course, he attempted to distinguish his "psycho-analysis" from Janet's (cf. Ellenberger) "psychological analysis" in a number of ways, including most prominently his idea of repression as distinct from Janet's concept of dissociation. There was a large difference. Of great importance was Freud's idea of unconscious motivation, of avoiding consciousness. For Janet, dissociation was the consequence of innate psychical weakness of the ability for psychological synthesis (1907). The idea of dissociation was also present in the mainstream psychological literature in the United States in the early 1900s, but did not reappear again until the latter half of the century.

The repressed unconscious

The Freudian dynamic unconscious consisted mainly of id impulses, in Freud's words "a cauldron full of seething excitations" (1933, 73). The nature of these impulses, primarily sexual and aggressive, was to seek immediate gratification without concerns about reality or other constraints. When one looks at the nature of the inhibiting process itself, it is not always so different from that described by later theorists who held a dissociational model of unconscious processes. What remains different is Freud's concept of the id and its contents.

Freud's early ideas about repression were formed from his experience observing Bernheim's work with hypnosis. Patients were instructed that they would forget that they were told how they would remember information and would only remember it given certain cues. Presented with these cues, they would recall the information or be influenced by it as they had been instructed, but upon return to waking consciousness would not remember the information. In his (1892–1893) report, "A Case of Successful Treatment by Hypnotism," Freud presented a "conflict theory of hysteria in which one element of the conflict is intentionally barred-'suppressed,' 'excluded,' 'dissociated' —from consciousness" (Erdelyi and Goldberg 1979, 361). Freud stated that "the distressing antithetic idea . . . continues to exist as a disconnected idea" (Freud 1892–1893, 1961, 122). Breuer and Freud (1893–1895) stated: "[T]he splitting of consciousness which is so striking in the well-known classical cases under the form of 'double consciousness' (1) is present to a rudimentary degree in every hysteria, and that a tendency to such a dissociation . . . is the basic phenomena of this neurosis. In these views, we concur with Binet and the two Janets" (12).

Repression was not always considered to be unconscious

Erdelyi and Goldberg (1979) have provided extensive evidence that this is the case. Among other quotations, they point to a lengthy footnote in the Studies on Hysteria "in which the reader is warned against falsely construing terms such as deliberate or intentional as implying conscious (1979, 365). In the case of Miss Lucy R., Freud states that for a hysterical symptom to develop, "an idea must be intentionally repressed from consciousness" (Breuer and Freud, 1893–1895, 1955, 116). Freud and Breuer (1893) stated also that "The splitting of consciousness in these cases of acquired hysteria is accordingly a deliberate and intentional one" (123–24). Although Freud used the concept of repression in a broad sense early on, later he used it in a narrower sense. In the broad sense he used the term as the process by which defenses keep a threat of conflictual ideation or affect out of conscious awareness. He (1915, 1956) had stated, "the essence of repression lies simply in the function of rejecting and keeping something out of consciousness" (105). This statement was made, however, before the development of the structural theory of the id, ego, and superego. In 1926 he sought to distinguish repression from other defenses such as isolation, denial, and undoing and used it to mean forgetting. After Freud developed his structural theory of the mind, he became more preoccupied with the agency of repression than with the nature of the repressed (Fairbairn 1944).

Sterba (1934) described the analytic process as one requiring a "dissociation of the ego." The analyst, he believed, must win over to his side part of the patient's ego. For Sterba the analyst's side was one of intellectual contemplation, but the winning over was to be reached through the positive transference. This "therapeutic ego-dissociation" (121) occurs by identification with the superego of the analyst. (This is akin to the process of connecting to the therapist's hope in the model described in the chapter in this book on therapeutic change.) Strachey (1934) in the same year also discussed the analyst's providing the patient with an auxiliary superego, but did not elaborate upon the patient's ego dissociation process.

Although I shall not discuss the split egos described by Klein, Kernberg, and Kohut, they deserve to be mentioned here. These sorts of splits are seen by these authors as a failure in development, but these splits are similar to the differing self-experiences of people who have suffered traumas. Failure to develop an integrated self-theory can be seen as arising either from the lack of a soothing, calm presence to offset intense feelings of excitement, rejection, deprivation, intrusion, fear of engulfment, annihilation, and so on, or from a requirement not to feel one's feelings in order to protect the caretaker's self-theory (Fairbairn 1954). A soothing, calm presence is similar to Sterba's

(1934) and Strachey's (1934) internalization of an auxiliary intellectually contemplative superego, Bion's idea of a container, Winnicott's (1958) holding environment, and Fonagy and Target's (1997) reflective functioning. This calm presence recognizes sensory-affective states of any sort and, in a sense, provides desensitization to anxiety in a state of relative tranquility.

The Dissociated Unconscious

A model of dissociated unconscious processes was developed by Fairbairn and Sullivan and more recently elaborated upon by Bromberg, Donnell Stern, Davies and Frawley, and Bucci. For both Fairbairn and Sullivan the lack of a concept of an id and their failure to continue adherence to Freud's hydraulic model likely led them to be more open to other ways of formulating unconscious processes.

Fairbairn (1929), in his only recently published medical thesis, entitled "Dissociation and Repression," described dissociation as a broader phenomenon than repression, but limited it to disconnections from a personal sense of consciousness: "Dissociation was defined as: An active mental process whereby unacceptable mental content or an unacceptable mental function becomes cut off from personal consciousness, without thereby ceasing to be mental—such mental content or mental function being 'unacceptable' with the meaning of this definition if it is either irrelevant to, incompatible with, or unpleasant in relation to an active interest. . . . Repression is in its essence just dissociation of the unpleasant" (69). This view of dissociation encompasses a much wider group of disconnections, not only those more extreme forms such as in dissociative identity disorder or in sleep. Fairbairn presents a model of the mind where unconscious self-other representations compete with conscious ones.

In Fairbairn's later writing he speaks of repression as leading to the formation of the different ego states. His idea of repression is not that of Freud's, however, because he is not speaking of repression of impulses. He is using the term for the disconnection of the unpleasant. It should be noted that Fairbairn, by acknowledging that experiences may be irrelevant to a personal sense of consciousness, allows for the cognitive unconscious and holds the same model that will be presented here in this regard. He does not discuss, however, two conscious states that are not connected—in other words, two experiences that may both be connected to a personal sense of consciousness (the "I-self") when they are activated, just never at the same time, as Bromberg (1996a) has recently suggested we must consider.

Fairbairn failed to develop a model that adequately describes motivation. To say that people are object-seeking may be true, but this motivation alone is far from complete in helping us understand how experiences enter consciousness or fail to do so. The lack of attention to motivation and affect in Fairbairn's model was addressed by Kernberg (1976) who suggested that affects organize internalized objects. Dissociation is the major defense, of course, for Sullivan (1956), interpersonalists, and contemporary relational psychoanalysts. Sullivan does not discuss the difference between dissociation and repression, however (although he uses the word "repression" at times), because he does not begin with a theory of instinctual impulses that are kept out of awareness. Experiences are kept out of awareness by selective inattention in order to avoid anxiety. Anxiety comes from threats to the self-system as will be discussed in the model presented in the next chapter.

Donnell Stern's (1997) ideas about dissociation are similar to those of Sullivan. He devoted three chapters of his book to dissociation, the strong form of which he considers to be an active defensive process—what most analysts have called repression—and the weaker, more pervasive form of dissociation being similar to Sullivan's (1956) selective inattention. For Stern, experiences are avoided by not interpreting, by not being spelled out, by remaining "unformulated," similar to the "unthought known" of Bollas. It is a restriction of the experiences we allow ourselves to have, a narrative rigidity. Harris and Gold (2001) have described this state aptly by referring to it as "when the fog rolled in." Reflective experience is created by what Finagarette (1969) called "spelling out" or interpreting. Dissociation, then, in Stern's way of understanding, is any type of function that keeps an experience from emerging into awareness. Stern pays short shrift to dissociations of ego states such as those described by Fairbairn, "splitting of the ego," dissociations from traumas, or the type of dissociation of incompatible conscious states Bromberg has described so well, although his concept of not spelling out certainly applies to these types of dissociations. Bromberg (1996) has described dissociations between what I would call different self-with-other states or cognitive-affective behavioral schemas that are conscious, but not in awareness simultaneously. These states are not felt as being in conflict because the person keeps them separated in the stream of consciousness that I would call the self-theory and others speak of as the personal narrative. Bromberg is speaking of the sorts of ego states described by Fairbairn and those that may be ways of coping with trauma. The task of the analyst is to help the patient become aware of these different states and to bring them into conflict—the area of classical psychoanalysis.

Davies and Frawley (1992, 1994) have provided examples of the sorts of dissociated self-states found in patients who were sexually abused as children and ways of accessing these different self-states. They have linked the differing states with the overstimulating and punitive states described by Fairbairn, but linking these dissociated self-states to Fairbairn's model is not necessary.

Davies (1996) noted three categories of unconscious experience: (1) those related to unacceptable wishes and fantasies about others within the context of a self-object dyad (close to the classical unconscious except that what is conscious and unconscious at any given moment varies; (2) mutually incompatible self-experiences that can't be maintained simultaneously in awareness of the sort that occurs after traumatic abuse; and (3) those dropped from the linguistic categorization of generalized experience due to their extreme or idiosyncratic nature (the unformulated aspects of experience described by Stern). Again, we have something that seems akin to what Freud called repression and two different types of experiences that have been called dissociation.

Bucci (1997) also considers dissociation as primary in her model of the multiple code system. She sees the lack of integration of the subsymbolic (the nonverbal in her 1985 article) and the symbolic (formerly verbal) systems as the source of psychopathology. Bucci discusses the problems inherent in Freud's ideas of primary and secondary processes from the point of view of connectionist views in contemporary cognitive science and suggests the subsymbolic and symbolic concepts as replacements. Her model differs from that to be described later in this chapter in that it does not specifically differentiate the experiences threatening to the self-theory (repression) from other disconnections. In her system, repression refers to dissociations among subsymbolic processes, between subsymbolic process and images, and between images and words. Although there are many similarities between her model and that presented here, her view of unconscious processes seems to be that they are nonverbal. Furthermore, she does not discuss the particular motivations to which emotions are related or the "control/automaticity" processes of cognitive psychology (to be discussed later in this chapter). In her system, therapeutic action comes from the integration of states—subsymbolic with symbolic, and the two symbolic states with each other—nonverbal and verbal. I shall discuss in the subsequent chapter a much broader model of therapeutic change.

Repressed and Dissociated Processes in Empirical Psychology

Dissociative processes are discussed at length in psychology in regard to altered states of consciousness, such as those involved in sleeping, dreaming, hypnosis, anesthesia, and meditation, as well as in instances of chemical or physical alteration of the brain (de Gelder, de Haan, and Heywook 2002). Dissociations are also investigated between implicit and explicit memory (Bargh 1997; Jacoby and Kelley 1992) and a variety of different perceptual processes—visual and semantic, for example. Repression, however, has been another matter. For a more extensive review of research regarding repression and dissociation, see Singer (1990).

Although there is considerable research supportive of a repressive personality style (Weinberger 1990), questions have always been raised about the evidence for repression in the laboratory in the sense of active exclusion from memory of threatening experiences and their later retrieval. Holmes (1990) declared "there is no controlled laboratory evidence supporting the concept of repression" (96), but also stated that "it should not be concluded that there is not selectivity in perception and recall"(97). His definition of repression included "the selective forgetting of materials that cause the individual pain" (86). Holmes reviewed studies that examined differential recall of unpleasant experiences, incomplete tasks and materials followed by a stressful experience. When one looks at the studies he reviews, there are no examples of threats to a person's meaning system. He cites Conant's (1948) idea that a theory is not usually overthrown by the data, but by a better theory. If we look at data for selective forgetting of experiences threatening to the self-view, we find plenty (Greenwald 1980; Taylor 1989). If the term "selective" or "motivated" forgetting is used instead of the term "repression," there is no controversy. I shall review what is known about selective memory in the next chapter.

The controversial idea remaining regarding "repression" is whether there is an active putting out of awareness that is unconscious. Wegner (1992) has demonstrated active "suppression" of ideas. The concept of repression is one involving networks that have been activated less frequently. Given the frequent occurrence of not being able to retrieve words or other experiences, and then eventually retrieving them, it seems reasonable to think that there may be some experiences much harder to retrieve (more upsetting or even traumatic) than the forgotten ideas in Wegner's experiments, such as white bears or sex. If we think of the active exclusion from consciousness of experiences threatening to survival or survival of the meaning system, most of us can probably think of times we have excluded upsetting thoughts. For example, in New York after September 11, some people eventually decided to stop watching the news and stop thinking about the possibility of a terrorist attack. People decide to stop thinking about the possibility of a loved one dying and to attend to other matters. In regard to experiences that threaten the meaning of life, the coping styles of people who have been threatened with or who have experienced significant losses seem more relevant to Freud's idea of repression than simply unpleasant words. This sort of conscious decision not to think about matters has not qualified as repression for cognitive psychologists, however, because it is not an unconscious decision.

Kihlstrom and Hoyt (1990) point out that Wegner's studies of suppression also do not involve unconscious thought suppression. Citing Hoyt (1987), they (202) suggest, however, that "recent information-processing analyses of attention (Egeth 1977; Kahneman 1973; Kahneman and Treisman 1984) and the acquisition of cognitive skills" (e.g., Anderson 1982; Schneider and Shiffrin 1977) afford us a mechanism for transforming consciously controlled thought suppression into unconscious repression—dividing attention. They conclude that "the information-processing approach to attention and cognitive skill suggests a mechanism by which the act of repression itself could be rendered unconscious" (202). Thus cognitive psychologists are open to the possibility of repression being demonstrated to their satisfaction, although they already accept evidence of dissociation. Erdelyi (1990) has pointed out that Freud thought of repression as conscious, anyway: "I repeatedly succeeded in demonstrating that the splitting of the contents of consciousness is the consequence of a voluntary act on the part of the patient; that is to say, it is instituted by an effort of will, the motive of which is discernible" (Freud 1894, 1963, 69). He argues that the idea of the process being unconscious came largely from Anna Freud, that later Freud allowed for the possibility of it being unconscious, but did not require it, and that this is a separate question in any event. Perhaps the word "repression" should be retired and "schema-threatening selective inhibition and forgetting" investigated instead.

Let us now examine briefly Kihlstrom and Hoyt's (1990) theory of dissociation. Following Anderson (1983), Kihlstrom and Hoyt identify "the conscious system with working memory, that portion of declarative memory that contains activated representation of the organism in its immediate environment as well as of the organism's current processing goals and goal-relevant memory structures activated by perceptual processing or memory retrieval" (201). Kihlstrom and Hoyt take off from Hilgard's (1977) view of divided consciousness. Hilgard (1977), choosing not to revive the Janet–Freud debate, described the repressive barrier as horizontal and the dissociative barrier as vertical. He saw the contents of the repressed unconscious as not amenable to conscious, voluntary control whereas the contents of material on either side of a dissociative barrier were available to introspective awareness and voluntary control, but segregated in some way from each other and executive control.

Cognitive psychologists separate memory into two major forms—declarative and procedural, with declarative knowledge being further broken down into semantic knowledge (facts) and episodic knowledge (events). There are many dissociations between these different forms of memory. Findings regarding amnesiacs suggest a dissociation between the events and facts. Schacter (1987) has further discussed dissociations between the explicit (conscious) and implicit (unconscious) forms of episodic memory, with explicit memory for events impaired in posthypnotic amnesia, but not implicit memory. Kihlstrom and Hoyt (202) state that "The ability to divide attention among two or more simultaneous tasks, as required by dissociative processes," may be one skill and "deploying attention away from unpleasant cognitive contents . . . as required by repression, may be another" (Wegner et al. 1987). In neuroscience Edelman (1992) has referred to repression as "the selective inability to recall" (145). Psychologists and psychoanalysts, however, have used the word dissociation to refer to selective inattention to external perceptual events in addition to selective recall.

"Dissociation" in the theory of early Freud, in the theories of Fairbairn and Sullivan, and in psychology seems to be a term often used for a broad category of disconnections and "repression" a specific disconnection with the dominant self-theory. Reyher (1978) limited the use of repression to the exclusion from consciousness of sexual and aggressive drives. Klein (1976, 24), for example stated that repression is "a meaning scheme that is dissociated from the person's self-conception." If use of the word "repression" continues, it makes sense to limit its use to the inhibition of behaviors that are inconsistent with the dominant self-theory. Dissociation remains a term used most frequently for the sequelae of traumatic experiences that lead to such a discontinuity in experience that another organizational system entirely emerges. In line with theories of complexity and chaos, the overload of inconsistent experiences is so great that the self-system bifurcates and an alternative self-system develops altogether. One can see in the case of Sirhan Sirhan that if he thought of himself as a good moral person who would never kill someone, murder would be kept out of awareness in the manner Freud suggested. Because it is still so difficult to distinguish these concepts clearly, it likely makes sense to abandon the words repression and dissociation altogether and think in terms of "motivated forgetting" and "motivated not-knowing." Singer (1990) reached this conclusion in his book on the subject:

"It is probably best that we consider using other terminology than 'repression' to describe persons who show systematic styles of avoiding thought or self-awareness of potentially troublesome life issues or who actively avoid situations that might remind them of such issues. . . Selective inattention, avoidance of labeling, avoidance of reminiscing and rehearsal, distraction through physical or social activity, and ruminative thoughts about trivialities all may interfere with the subsequent retrievability of troublesome experiences. Rather than invoke the concepts of defense and repression to close this book, we propose that individual differences in reliance on various types of selective, cognitive-affective strategies under certain circumstances and in particular domains of human concern may become the basis for differences in self-presentation, psychopathology, and physical health" (494).

The idea of a repressed unconscious was used largely to refer to sexual and aggressive wishes kept out of consciousness because they are inconsistent with a person's self-theory. The dissociated unconscious has included a much broader range of phenomena, except when it has been used to refer to the specific type of defense that develops in response to trauma and found in the extreme in dissociative identity disorder. In addition, research scientists refer to dissociations that are not related to motivated forgetting or defenses at all. Recently, there have been a large number of experiments also using the term "repression" and a body of research dealing with a "repressive" personality style. Among the results for individuals categorized as repressors is the finding that this group used more of a defense called "emotional dissociation" (cf. Bonanno 2001). (The research regarding the repressive personality style will be discussed more in the following section on selection in attention and memory.) It might be best if these terms were dropped altogether, however, as their usage has been so confusing. More specific words could be used instead, such as "motivated forgetting" or "schema-threatening selective forgetting" instead of "repression," and the types of disconnections specified when "dissociation" is used, such as "disconnected self-states" in multiple personality.

In addition to the process of rendering mental contents unconscious, there have been disagreements about the nature of what ends up out of awareness. For Freud, the major contents were clear. For many theorists since Freud who have focused their theories on interpersonal relations, the nature of what is kept out of conscious awareness has been broader, and might be summarized as anything that might lead to anxiety, particularly in relationships.

The Cognitive, "Psychological", or "New" Unconscious

In the past two decades, cognitive psychologists rediscovered unconscious processes (Greenwald 1992; Kihlstrom 1987; Kihlstrom, Barnhardt, and Tataryn 1992; Wilson 2002; Hassin, Uleman, and Bargh 2005). The burgeoning research on implicit memory among normal experimental participants, amnesiacs, hypnotized persons, on vision without awareness ("blindsight") among cortically injured patients, and research on patients while under anesthesia, along with a continuation of research on subliminal perception (Pierce and Jastrow 1884; Silverman 1983; Weinberger and Hardaway 1990) led to a new conception of mental functioning. From these studies, a model of the psychological unconscious emerged to explain many examples of apparently non-motivated forgetting, or perceptions and memory without awareness (Bornstein and Pittman 1992; Weiskrantz 1986). The word "unconscious" only appeared in a title in the experimental psychology literature, however twice (Jones 1935; Kennedy 1938) before Nisbett and Wilson used it in 1977. It was used by Stephen Jay Gould in biology in 1977, Shevrin and Dickman in 1980, Merikle in 1982, Marcel in 1983, with unconscious processing previously referred to as "implicit." Thereafter the word was used again quite frequently by cognitive researchers interested in differentiated conscious and unconscious processes in perception and memory. The word is still avoided in mainstream psychology texts on cognition, such as *Learning and Cognition* (Leahey and Harris 2001), where it is not found in the index and only once in the text—in regard to repression, the controversy over "repressed" memories, and noting that "there is little, if any, scientific evidence for the construct of repression in a century of research" (191).

In describing the sort of information dealt with by research on the cognitive unconscious, Greenwald (1992), a social-cognitive psychologist used the metaphor of "junk mail" sorting to explain how some material is attended to and kept in awareness and other material is quickly discarded as irrelevant. Kihlstrom, Barnhardt, and Tataryn (1992) were very careful, however, to distinguish the psychological unconscious from that of Freud and his colleagues: "Their unconscious was hot and wet; it seethed with lust and anger; it was hallucinatory, primitive, and irrational. The unconscious of contemporary psychology is kinder and gentler than that and more reality bound and rational, even if it is not entirely cold and dry" (789).

Until recently the cognitive unconscious was modeled after the computer. Psychologists tended to accept the "weak" version of artificial intelligence as formulated by Rumelhart in which the computer is considered a model of the mind, not a form, or an example. Reviews of the cognitive unconscious can be found in Greenwald (1992), Kihlstrom (1987), Shevrin (1992), Westen (1998), and Wilson (2002). Shevrin (1996) criticized Bargh's (1989) model of the cognitive unconscious for his failure to make allowances for unconscious intention.

The computer, or computation, model of the mind has serious limitations from a motivational point of view. Not only do computers lack "unconscious" motivation—they lack conscious motivation as well—they do not try to stay alive, preserve a meaning system, or experience pleasure. Furthermore, although there have been attempts to program computers to be similar to humans, no one has been able to program the successful handling of social situations because the number of unanticipated variables is unlimited. Recognizing some of the limitations of the cognitive unconscious, Kihlstrom, Mulvaney, Tobias, and Tobis (2000) have recently described an "emotional unconscious," although they still distance this unconscious from anything psychoanalytic.

Although mental states can be activated by priming (activating particular networks prior to a test phase of an experiment), the effect of the motivation to survive or other motivations have not been investigated by cognitive researchers. Differentiating conscious from unconscious motivation was not possible. Both normal and abnormal processes can now be understood, however, by consideration of schema or representation-irrelevant and representation-threatening experiences. Cognitive researchers and neuropsychologists usually examined the fate or representation-irrelevant information. Psychoanalysts, on the other hand, are interested in representation-threatening information.

Recently Wilson (2002) has written about the "adaptive unconscious." Among the four aspects of the "adaptive unconscious" are attention and selection as an unconscious filter and unconscious goal setting. For Wilson, the adaptive unconscious "is a set of pervasive, sophisticated mental processes" (5) with which we evaluate our surroundings, set goals, and initiate action, all without our awareness while we are consciously thinking about something else. Many bodily processes, movements, and emotional judgments are taking place simultaneously outside focal awareness. One of the rules it follows is "Select, interpret, and evaluate information in ways that make me feel good" (39).

According to Wilson, the adaptive unconscious has the following characteristics: multiple systems, an online pattern detector, concerned with the here-and-now, automatic (fast, unintentional, uncontrollable, effortless), rigid, precocious, and sensitive to negative information; whereas consciousness is characterized by a single system, after-the-fact checker and balancer, taking the long view, controlled (slow, intentional, controllable, effortful), flexible, slower to develop, and sensitive to positive information. Wilson reports a number of experiments have established that the adaptive unconscious is slow to respond to new, contradictory evidence.

Several authors previously described a dual coding system of images and words (Brewin, Dalgleish, and Joseph 1996; Bucci 1985; Paivio 1971, 1986; Singer 1978), or nonverbal (sensory in general) and verbal systems or experiential/rational systems (Epstein 1991). There are some parallels in these two sets of processes to the functioning of the right and left hemispheres of the brain, also referred to as "two minds", but the adaptive cognitive unconscious is not the equivalent of the experiential or right-brain mode of functioning. Nonverbal, experiential processing can be conscious and semantic processing is not always conscious.

Although social and cognitive psychologists now often refer to automatic processes as "unconscious" processes, behavioral psychologists and biologists still only use the term "automatic" processes. Whereas cognitive psychologists have looked at "cold," gentle information processing, biologists and behavioral psychologists have examined automatic processes that are linked to behaviors, often those crucial to survival, without the intervention of thinking—"quick and dirty" processes. In the behavioral view, however, the automatic processes were seen until recently largely as responses to environmental stimuli, not as conflicting with representations of self, others, principles, or plans of an organism motivated to preserve a meaning system.

Since 1977 many psychologists have worked from the model of controlled (conscious, systematic, strategic, reflective) and automatic (unconscious, heuristic) processes in information processing originally described by Schneider and Shiffrin (1977). This model has been elaborated in social psychology by a number of researchers and recently by Wegner and Bargh (1998). Although in these models, automatic processes were originally conceived of as emanating from external stimuli, the most recent conception of these processes as described by Wegner and Bargh (1998) and Glaser and Kihlstrom (2005) have noted the influence of unconscious desires affecting behavior. These recent models potentially provide a way of integrating the psychoanalytic understanding with psychological research, including research on therapeutic processes in the empirical clinical tradition.

There is now beginning to be a clear recognition in psychology that dynamic unconscious processes affect, and even guide, thought, feelings, and behavior. Smith (1998, 425) states: "Social psychologists in recent years have also emphasized the importance of preconscious and implicit processes (see Banaji and Greenwald 1994; Bargh 1994; Higgins 1989), on the grounds that such processes determine our conscious experience and therefore direct our thought, feelings and behavior." In contrast to Bargh's (1989) earlier position, Wegner and Bargh (1998) have acknowledged not only the influence of James' (1890) notion of habit, but also Freud's concept of latent, unconscious motives. Their thinking also draws upon the test-operate-test-exit model of comparison to standards of Miller, Galanter, and Pribram (1960), including the role of self-awareness as elaborated upon by Carver and Scheier (1981, 1990) and the hierarchy of control systems described by Powers (1973). I will now describe this model more fully.

In the thinking of Wegner and Bargh (1998), consciousness serves two functions: monitoring and controlling. Monitoring can be considered as either deliberate or event-driven. Consciousness allows symbolic systems to set control criteria for parts of complex action sequences. It is attracted to action primarily when the action is faulty. We may not be conscious of driving until the car veers off near the edge of the highway. It must be the case, then, that there are unconscious error-monitoring systems. Wegner (1994) suggested that such "error monitors" function to alert consciousness to the failure of control and reinstate conscious planning. The unconscious error-monitoring process has its own influence on behavior and can produce the very errors that are being monitored, according to Wegner's theory of "ironic processes of mental control." Wegner and Wenzlaff (1996) found, for example, that trying to control the expression of sexist thoughts led to saying more of the sexist things people were trying to avoid. Overconsciousness produces anxiety and more errors. Mental work space is needed to slowly work through the avoidance of errors.

Glaser and Kilhstrom (2005) have also argued for unconscious volition based upon studies demonstrating contrast effects and "reverse priming" (Glaser and Banaji 1999). People seem to correct biases for which they are unconsciously primed (racial prejudice) at times, suggesting that people may unconsciously monitor and correct their judgments. Although cognitive researchers are often careful to distance themselves from the Freudian unconscious, it is unclear what objections they would hold to views of a "relational" psychoanalytic unconscious.

Within psychology, literatures on both the new look in perception (see chapter 5) and the literature regarding skills acquisition inform our knowledge of automatic (psychoanalysts should read "unconscious") processing. Skills are started in motion consciously and then run in parallel with conscious processing once instigated intentionally. Two theories have offered similar understandings as to how conscious and automatic processes interact when they contradict each other. Posner and Snyder (1975) argued that automatic processes occur quickly, within two hundred to three hundred milliseconds. Conscious processing takes longer—at least five hundred to six hundred milliseconds, but is more flexible and can be adjusted to goals at hand. Conscious processes override automatic ones when there is sufficient time, but do not when time is lacking. Automatic processes do not adapt to short-term fluctuations, but conscious ones do. Automatic processes are not controllable. Some are driven by the environment whereas others require "the initial start" (Jastrow 1906, 45).

Wegner and Bargh (1998) see the understanding of conscious control and automaticity as "the place where human goals and mental processes meet, and where the daily tasks of survival become infused with larger purposes and direction" (484). When people have problems translating their goals into actions, they fall back on automatic processes (Gollwitzer 1999). Unfortunately from a clinical point of view, research regarding controlled and automatic processes has rarely investigated the role of anxiety experimentally. This is difficult to do ethically. Clinical researchers have, however, examined the way anxious, depressed, and nonclinical samples respond to various sorts of information. Emotional evaluation gets placed upon experiences in a preattention phase (Williams, Watts, MacLeod, and Mathews 1997). Anxious people (with generalized anxiety disorder) then focus attention on negative information while nonanxious people engage in a cognitive avoidance strategy. This strategy then leads to greater recall of information overall to be remembered by the nonanxious group. Activation spreads for the anxious people, leading to thinking about possible implications of specific information. Anxious people are unable to inhibit the spread of activation. This depletes processing capabilities. Bonanno (1988–1989) had found that thoughts were more difficult to control when people felt threatened. "Hot" information leads to such implicational thinking and poorer explicit (conscious) memory. The cognitive avoidance strategy (repressive style) leads to better information recall, likely through better conceptual elaboration (activation of associated representations). Differences have been found, however, for patients who show greater or lesser left hemisphere advantage, depending when semantic stimuli are presented, and with patients suffering from panic disorder (Cloitre and Liebowitz 1991).

For researchers in the behavioral tradition, automatic responses were viewed as coming solely from external stimuli. With current research in social psychology showing the importance of unconscious goals, however, the framework of the control/automaticity model provided allows us to integrate the dynamic social-cognitive and clinical empirical unconscious—influenced by motivation and affect at every step—with the dynamic unconscious of psychoanalytic theory. And when nonanalytic clinicians urge patients to relinquish conscious control and free associate, or to "stream," as Mahoney (1991) calls it, they may find unconscious processes that resemble Freud's "seething" cauldron more than Hayek's (1952) tacit rules of order.

As a model of conscious and unconscious processes, the control/automaticity model has a number of limitations. It does not easily account for conscious processes that are not experienced as under control, such as intrusions of thoughts and flashbacks. It fails to characterize the different sorts of control processes—what psychoanalysts would call the variety of defensive processes. Furthermore, unlike the psychoanalytic literature, it does not offer any guidance as to what motivations may be outside awareness. Still, it provides another methodology for investigating processes outside conscious control and allows psychology and psychoanalysis to be "on the same page."

The Cognitive Unconscious of Neuroscientists

De Gelder, deHaan, and Heywook (2002) have asked if we can learn without consciousness. They present evidence for unconscious processing across a range of sensory modalities, including vision, audition, memory, emotion, and action. Squire and the Nobel Prize–winner Kandel (1999) have enumerated a number of types of nondeclarative (nonfactual) memory—emotional learning, classical conditioning, perceptual learning, skill learning, habit learning, and psychotherapy. They explain that some of these types of learning involve the motor systems of the brain, which can record unconscious memories. But others are based on complex perceptual and cognitive abilities yet "like all forms of nondeclarative memory, they can occur even when we have no awareness about what was learned" (173). Zajonc's (1980) work on liking and disliking is a form of emotional learning without awareness. People come to like pictures and shapes to which they have been exposed more frequently (for about one millisecond each) even though they scarcely remember seeing anything and can not recognize what they had seen or not seen. Nevertheless, when asked to indicate their preferences, people prefer the shapes they saw over shapes that were new. Le Doux's (1996) work shows that information regarding fear-provoking stimuli travel fast to the amygdala and emotional reactions communicate the fear state widely to many systems while the cortex is still evaluating them. Information about the fearful stimulus also travels a longer route through the cortex and then back through the amgydala. Parallel circuits are in operation that may explain our startle reaction when someone unexpectedly enters a room. Signals alert the fear system first and then we realize that the person is a friend after the cortex has made finer discriminations about the nature of the intruder. Although the hippocampus is required for declarative memories, habits can be learned when the hippocampus has been damaged. Squire and Kandel note that learning can take place without unconscious material becoming conscious. Citing the work of others (Stern et al. 1998) in psychotherapy, they even suggest that therapy can occur through a process other than making the unconscious conscious.

The theme of cognition without language has been important in neuroscience ever since the work on the split brain by Sperry (1964) and Gazzaniga (1967). These researchers found that patients in whom the corpus callosum had been lesioned to prevent epileptic seizures would be able to point later to objects presented experimentally only to the right hemisphere, but when asked what they had seen would say nothing. When instructions went to the right hemisphere to walk, a patient walked, but when asked why he walked out, he stated, "To get a Coke." The left hemisphere had no access to the command "walk," but came up with a plausible meaning. Solms (2000) has found similar confabulations in patients with frontal lobe damage. These disconnections as a consequence of physical damage are referred to as dissociations throughout the neuroscience literature. Obviously, these dissociations from physical processes are not related to motivation in any way. Attempts to integrate the neuroscience perspective with the psychological perspective have merged in a field called "social cognitive neuroscience (Ochsner and Lieberman 2001) and a new journal *Cognitive, Affective, and Behavioral Neuroscience.*

Summarizing the cognitive unconscious, we find conceptualizations of automatic or adaptive processes related to survival mechanisms that are not processed symbolically or consciously, other dissociations due to physical processes, and other "implicit" processes that occur outside awareness because networks are not activated or actively inhibited. It is this last group of processes to which I would now like to turn. If we consider all unconscious experiences (except those physically impossible) as resulting from a failure to be selected for consciously controlled processing, then we do not need to think of three different types of unconscious processes. What we know about the processes of selection in perception, attention, and memory will be discussed in the following chapter.

Three Unconscious Minds or One?

Some theorists, such as Shevrin (1992), have thought that integrating the Freudian unconscious and the cognitive unconscious was problematic. Shevrin, after reviewing the two, concluded that "the shift by some psychoanalysts to an 'information' metaphor" (324) did not represent any advance. The "cognitive unconscious" he discussed, however, was at that time still one devoid of motivation. He believed, however, that theories of attention would provide "the bridge across which psychoanalysts and cognitive scientists will cross over to each other's side of the river" (324).

Eagle (1987) also examined the psychoanalytic unconscious and the cognitive unconscious, but largely from the perspective of an unconscious composed of "pathogenic beliefs" derived from the therapy of Weiss, Sampson, and colleagues (Weiss, Sampson, and the Mount Zion Psychotherapy Research Group, 1986). The tacit rules he noted his patients following were not directly related to the Freudian unconscious, but might be of the nature, "If I separate I will not survive" (167). He found that these rules did not easily fit into the Freudian model of repression. Instead, they seemed to be rules that were never directly subjected to test. Although he acknowledges that these fears might be seen as symbolically equivalent to murder or incest, Eagle thinks, citing G. Klein (1976), that the relegation of mental contents to unawareness comes from a failure to integrate contents into one's overall sense of personal identity. Departing from the concept of the Freudian unconscious, he does not see the integration with cognitive psychology as difficult. He thinks that psychoanalysts must be able to formulate their ideas in terms of ordinary cognitive processes and the "more affective, motivational, and vital material which psychoanalysis deals" (186) will have to be taken into account by the cognitive unconscious. I think that integrating the cognitive and dynamic unconscious is now possible and have suggested that experiences are kept out of consciousness through selective inattention (or more precisely, a failure of selection) and forgetting.

Rather than three types of unconscious minds, it is possible to think of all processes of attention, memory, and forgetting as selective in nature. Some contents that are relevant to behavioral tendencies would be inconsistent with frequently activated self- (cognitive-affective-behavioral) schemas (those associated with "repression"), some schemas that cannot be activated simultaneously with others, (those associated with traumatic "dissociation"), and other experiences either not relevant to meaningful schemas, or never connected to relevant schemas due to inconsistencies ("dissociation" due to selective inattention). It is easier to integrate a model of dynamic unconscious processes that speaks of selection processes in attention and memory, such as those associated with Sullivan and Donnell Stern, than one that uses the unclear term "repression," although, as has been seen, the processes actually described as repression and dissociation often overlap when these words are used in a broad sense and considered to be the major form of disconnection. As was noted, the models of the adaptive unconscious and of automatic processes from social/cognitive psychology have had serious deficits until recently in their conception of unconscious processes as emanating only from stimuli in the environment and as not involving unconscious intentions. In the more recent formulations of controlled and automatic processes, however, unconscious desires have been recognized and research findings from these models can be integrated with findings from psychoanalytically-derived research to provide a broader knowledge base of conscious and unconscious processes. Psychoanalysts and psychologists are now ready theoretically to move along with neuroscientists towards integrated models of the mind. Cognitive researchers can now investigate psychoanalytic hypotheses. Such research requires presenting people with stimuli relevant to their own personal conflicts and examining the differential processes that are activated unconsciously and consciously.

Shevrin (Shevrin et al. 1996) has done this in his recent work with phobics. After determining through interviews what words might be related to hypothesized unconscious conflicts, when these words were presented subliminally, but not supraliminally, the phobics later put them in categories together. Other research showed that arachnophobics who scored high for repression on the Hysteroid-Obsessoid questionnaire were slow to detect spiders, but not rectangles. Men presented subliminally with stimuli saying "Beating Dad is OK" performed better at dart-throwing than men presented with control stimuli such as "Beating Dad is wrong" or "People are walking" (Palumbo and Gillman 1984). Similarly, when Weinberger, Kelner, and McClelland (1997) presented participants with messages subliminally that from a psychodynamic perspective should make them feel better, such as "Mommy and I are one," these messages but not others improved their moods. Men who consciously report homophobia have been found to be more aroused physiologically (as measured by penile circumference through genital plethysmography) when watching videos showing men engaged in homosexual sex, whereas men who were not homophobic did not show such arousal (Adams, Wright, and Lohr 1996). Similarly, women who self-report more sexual guilt and less sexual arousal were found to experience greater physiological arousal when watching an erotic video (Morokoff 1985). Such findings demonstrate defensive processes that are supportive of psychoanalytically derived hypotheses.

The way unconscious desires interact with conscious desires to affect behavior will be better understood as more research is conducted investigating psychoanalytic hypotheses. Possible links between unconscious motives and symptoms can be examined in a way so that any positive results will be convincing to the larger psychological community and negative results at least lead psychoanalysts to look again at their assumptions. When asked by a reporter from the *New York Times* recently, "What do you believe is true even though you cannot prove it?" Roger Schank, a computer scientist responded, "People believe they are behaving rationally . . . but when major decisions are made . . . people's minds simply cannot cope with the complexity. When they try to rationally analyze potential options, their unconscious, emotional thoughts take over and make the choice for them" (*New York Times*, January 4, 2005, F3). Thus, groups and individuals often fail to make the choices that would avoid disaster or harm or at least achieve a better reward–cost ratio. It would be of great use to societies as well as to individuals to have more knowledge of the conditions that allow negative and important information inconsistent with cherished beliefs to be processed in a nondefensive manner by people with different defensive styles and various personality characteristics.

SUMMARY AND CONCLUSION

Until the "cognitive revolution" in psychology, psychologists and psychoanalysts had different models of the mind. Not only were unconscious processes unimportant to behavioral psychologists, conscious processes were not important as well. Once the "cognitive revolution" took place in psychology, conscious processes, and eventually unconscious processes were believed to be crucial again in understanding human behavior. The experiences that are unconscious in cognitive psychology are not, however, experiences that people appear motivated to keep out of awareness. They are experiences that are simply not activated by current situations. The psychoanalytic unconscious has continued to represent experiences that either do not reach awareness or get pushed out of awareness—in other words threatening experiences of which there is motivation to remain unaware in order to maintain the functioning of the meaning-making system. Knowledge that neural networks are activated by incoming experiences, especially those related to physical and psychological survival, and that the organization of experiences takes place on an ongoing basis, can unify psychology and psychoanalysis in their understanding of conscious and unconscious processes and their interplay. Unconscious experiences are those that are not connected or "dissociated" from the conscious processes activated at any given moment. Psychoanalysts can join mainstream neuroscience and scientific psychology by laying the term "repression" to rest and thinking instead in terms of "motivated forgetting" and of threatening experiences as sometimes "dissociated." It is useful, however, to conceptualize unconscious processes not only as repressed, dissociated, or "adaptive" (or maladaptive), but as a cauldron of generative experiences—perhaps burning, perhaps murky, but always rumbling in the shadows of the mind. This last conceptualization of unconscious processes will receive more attention in the final chapter of the book.

Returning to Andreas, with whom the chapter started, it is noteworthy that his insight into the origin of his "dead" feeling did not eliminate the compulsive sexuality that bothered him so deeply. His behaviors developed to cope with the dead feeling required learning other ways of handling his feelings, not only an awareness of the origins of his feelings. Specific strategies about alternative ways of responding that some clinicians might consider "nonanalytic" were helpful to him until he became involved in a more meaningful relationship with another man. The many ways that change takes place will be addressed further in the following chapters.

Unconscious processes are a sort of "boogie-woogie," always rumbling in the background, with desires waiting to be satisfied and connections waiting to be forged. They rumble like a "boogie-woogie" out of awareness all of the time until they are activated by external or internal experiences. Now that the thinking in social/cognitive psychology has included the possibility of unconscious goals, or "dreams deferred" in Hughes' language, more research by psychologists can potentially include arousal of the conflicting unconscious desires most important to people. A broader conceptualization of unconscious processes as creative can unify both psychoanalytic and cognitive understandings of unconscious processes and will be discussed further in the final chapter. It encompasses all of those discussed in this chapter.

If we think of the mind as having various aspects of self-representations that are not fully activated aspects of self, these aspects might be influencing our feelings and behaviors without our full knowledge—like Baudelaire's (1857) "city full of swarming ants, city full of dreams where ghosts in plain daylight grab at passers-by" (author's translation).

Chapter 5

Big, Bad Blinks: What Happens to Threatening Information and What Is Selected for Conscious Processing?

> The last peculiarity of consciousness to which attention is to be drawn in this first rough description of its stream is that . . . it is always interested more in one part of its object (thought) than in another, and welcomes and rejects, or chooses, all the while it thinks.
>
> —James, 1890

Gladwell (2005) has recently documented a large number of effects of unconscious processing in his popular best seller *Blink*. But he does not address what happens to threatening experiences. Although experimental psychologists have argued that there is no scientific evidence for "repression," I have shown that this term is confusing and suggest that we think in terms of "motivated forgetting" instead. Attention and memory are always affected by the primary motivations. The difficulties incorporating threatening experiences into the meaning system that clinicians have called repression and dissociation can be understood as operating by the same selection processes that govern all attention and memory. Although researchers have investigated threats related to survival, only recently have they begun to investigate threats to individuals' personal meaning systems—threats to identity and to their major belief systems—the threats with which psychoanalysis has been concerned. I shall show that the sort of forgetting that psychoanalysts have seen as crucial is now supported by scientific psychology.

SELECTIVE ATTENTION

We cannot give everything in our environments conscious attention. The amount of information we can keep in mind at any one time is limited

(Lachman, Lachman, and Butterfield 1979). "Attention is selective, focusing on some stimuli while ignoring others," state Bernstein, Roy, Srull, and Wickens (1988, 191). Like a flashlight on a dark night, the beam of attention is narrow and must scan the environment sequentially (Wachtel 1967). "In the competitive world of species survival, attention is determined primarily by motivation" (97) state Lang, Bradley, and Cuthbert (1997). Sullivan's (1956) ideas about selective attention, inattention, and dissociation, of course, presented this line of thinking.

Sensory processes are also selective. For example, in the visual system, certain cells in the visual striate cortex select for orientation and others select for direction of movement. Most salient to our attention are stimuli that are novel, unexpected, aversive, and pleasurable (Kanwisher 2004). We are particularly attracted to people, places, bodies, and body parts (Kanwisher 2004) as part of our evolutionary heritage. Attention is "selective" (Freiwald and Kanwisher 2004, 575). Looking at all perception, attention, and memory as related to motivation renders the distinction between different kinds of unconscious processes—one for the cognitive and the other dynamic—unnecessary. For human beings, all perception, attention, and memory developed in an organism motivated to survive and thus subject to the biological selection principles that favor adaptive functions. All perception, attention, and memory are selective and therefore, in a sense, motivated by their very nature (Curtis 1992b). Neural pathways leading to behaviors that enhance survival are selected in what is referred to by neuroscientists as the value system. There is a general consensus that the major value is usually survival. Although both Freud and Wilson (2002), in his book on the adaptive unconscious, have argued that selection occurs in order to feel good, I have suggested in an earlier chapter that the motivations of physical and psychological survival are often more important and that these needs must be satisfied in order to feel good. How, then, are certain experiences selected for conscious processing and others neglected?

Consciousness is useful with problems of a nonroutine kind (Popper and Eccles 1977). Popper and Eccles saw consciousness, perception, and memory all as selective, with consciousness needed to "select, critically, new expectations or theories" (126). Edelman (1989, 1992) argued that the brain operates according to the same principles that Darwin proposed for species evolution—variation and selection. His theory suggests that the brain can develop all the neural pathways it needs for adaptive responses without specific genetic instructions. Developmental selection provides an almost infinite variation of ways for neurons and synapses to be organized. The connections that are selected through experience are then strengthened. An analogy is that the routes taken most frequently by water running down a mountain will become deeper. Bidirectional signaling allows for mutual influence through a process he calls reentry. For Edelman, selective attention and the ability to select quickly one action pattern over another confers considerable advantage for survival. Attempting to undertake two incompatible actions simultaneously would be deadly for a threatened animal. Value and belief systems also allow for quicker decision making. Posner (2004) also argues that people often ignore risks of low probability because human beings would not have survived in early environments if they let their attention wander from circumstances fraught with a high possibility of immediate danger—death. Still, the quick, evolutionarily "primitive" emotional responses that are not routed through the cortex often prevail when survival is at stake, especially when the risk is very high. Selective processes operate at early, intermediate, and late stages of attention, including those that operate prior to identification (Luck and Hillyard 2000). We shall now look at the selective nature of attention and memory in more detail.

Selective Attention and Memory for Goal-Relevant Experiences and Activated Networks

All perception, attention, and memory are motivated: "If motivation is a necessary element of all conscious experience, then distinguishing between conscious and unconscious forms of information processing would hinge on understanding the role of motivation and emotions in all modalities of conscious experience and thought," state Ellis and Newton (2000, x). Motives bias interpersonal perception (Maner et al. 2005). Activating a self-protective goal led participants to perceive greater anger in Black and Arab faces, and activating a mate-search goal led men to perceive more sexual arousal in attractive women. Motives influence perceptions of ambiguous stimuli. When a series of dots is presented very quickly tachistoscopically, they will not be perceived consciously if the duration of each stimulus presentation is too short. "If the duration is lengthened to a few milliseconds, under normal conditions the subjects still say, 'I see something but I don't know what'. However, if the subject is deprived of food, they (sic) will say 'I see pieces of meat'" (Pally and Olds 1998, 983). It seems reasonable to think that psychological values, such as a favorable self-view, might operate in a similar fashion.

Motives and emotions often remain or become activated out of awareness. Research on the transfer of excitation has demonstrated that although participants lose awareness of arousal after vigorous physical exercise, they subsequently respond with greater aggressive or sexual excitement (depending upon the cues) than participants not aroused (Cantor, Zillmann, and Bryant 1975; Zillmann and Bryant 1974). Early research by Schachter and Singer (1962) had demonstrated that emotions have two components—physiological arousal and a verbal (cognitive) label. Experimental participants given epinephrine and then placed in a room with a confederate who acted giddy or angry labeled their own emotion happiness or anger, depending upon the external cue. People experience feelings, but are not aware of either the arousal itself or may be aware of the arousal, but not its cause. This source of arousal due to unconscious factors has been known for a long time: Ovid advised suitors to take a woman to a gladiator fight. The woman would become aroused, but attribute her arousal to romantic attraction. These ideas have been tested experimentally.

That motivation affects memory is demonstrated by research on instructions to remember or forget. The research on directed forgetting and memory has shown that people will forget more of what they are instructed to forget than of what they are instructed to remember (Bjork 1989; Davidson and Bowers 1991; MacLeod 1975, 1989; Paller 1990; Wetzel 1975). These results provide support for the idea of motivated forgetting. Forgetting has been attributed to less rehearsal or elaboration during encoding (Woodward, Bjork, and Jongeward 1973), restricting attention during exposure (Koutstaal and Schacter 1997) or active inhibition (Anderson 2001). People who have been sexually abused have been found to have greater ability to forget words designated for forgetting (Cloitre, Brodsky, Dulit, and Perry 1996). Repressors are also especially good at forgetting if instructed to do so (Myers et al. 1998). A shift in perspective, however, will help people recover forgotten information (Anderson and Pichert 1978).

Goal-Relevant Experiences

The selective activity of consciousness most likely lies in the selective attention and recall of goal-relevant experiences (Carpenter 1988), which include self-relevant information (Rogers 1981). Normal participants have been found to recollect arousing slides (a boy hit by a car with his legs severed) better than neutral slides although patients with amygdala damage do not show this advantage (Cahill et al. 1995). Normal participants (without amygdala damage) have generally been found to forget fewer arousing words than neutral words (LaBar and Phelps 1998).

Schema Activation

Once schemas are activated by external or internal associations, they affect the perception of ambiguous stimuli. When people are made anxious experimentally, they are more likely to see others in stereotyped ways (Stephan and Stephan 1985). In terms of activating mental networks, the arousal would lead to greater activation of often-used pathways and fewer connections between seldom-used pathways. The often-used pathways would be ones that had alleviated anxiety in the past. The various forms of selective perception, including those labeled as perceptual defense, prevent consciousness from becoming flooded with threatening experiences. When consciousness becomes flooded, its control function, in the sense of selecting, fails. The failure of selection leads to anxiety of various types, such as uncontrollable, intrusive thoughts or paralysis in a more extreme form. For example, in contrast to patients suffering from panic attacks who scored high on a self-report of anxiety, patients who suffered from obsessive-compulsive disorder showed a deficit in the capacity to selectively ignore intrusive thoughts (Clayton, Richards, and Edwards 1999). The patients with panic attacks keep the threatening content out of awareness, but not the anxiety related to it. The patients with obsessive-compulsive disorder are bombarded, however, both by the content and the anxiety.

More Attention to Threatening Information

In spite of clinicians' interest in selective inattention, defense, and "repression," overall research has indicated that people pay more attention to negative and threatening information (Broadbent and Broadbent 1988; MacLeod and Mathews 1988; Mogg et al. 1992), although they do not always bring this information under conscious control. For example, when film clips were shown with two alternate scenes presented at one moment (a check versus a gun being held toward a cashier), attention as measured by eye fixations was greater for threatening information (Loftus, Loftus, and Messo 1987). Or, when one slide varied, such as a boy either still riding his bicycle, or lying on the ground bleeding, more eye fixations were obtained for the upsetting slide (Christianson, et al. 1991). Both state and trait anxiety have been found to increase attention to threatening stimuli (Rutherford, MacLeod, and Campbell 2004).

Fear-relevant pictures such as snakes or spiders have been found to capture more attention than fear-irrelevant pictures, such as flowers or mushrooms (Ohman, Flykt, and Esteves 2001). Anxious people have a disproportionate tendency to identify and detect emotionally negative stimulus words (Burgess et al. 1981; Foa and McNally 1986). People who suffer from panic attacks attend more to threatening stimuli than those without this disorder (McNally et al. 1990; Cloitre and Liebowitz 1991) and those who are high in trait anxiety attend more to threatening information when they are in an anxious state (MacLeod and Mathews 1988). Another recent study shows that everyone, not just anxious people, attend more to strongly threatening information and away from mildly threatening stimuli (Wilson and MacLeod 2003). Use of functional MRIs has indicated that there is reduced top-down control when people are anxious (Bishop, Duncan, Brett, and Lawrence 2004). Although Bradley and Schupp (Bradley et al. 2001; Schupp et al. 2004) have found support for a motivated attention model with heightened attention to both erotic scenes and scenes of mutilation—suggesting both defensive and appetitive motivations—other researchers have found stronger attentional biases for threatening than for positive stimuli (Ruiz-Caballero and Bermudez 1997).

Research indicates that depressed people (Ellenbogen et al. 2002), trait anxious people (Fox, Russo, and Dutton 2002), those diagnosed with social phobia (Amir et al. 2003), and physically abused children (Pollak and Tolley-Schell 2003) all take longer to disengage from threatening stimuli and threat-related ambiguous cues. Once people are threatened, they usually devote attentional resources to the threat, raising the accessibility of affectively similar information and biasing the perception of such information towards a negative evaluation. This process also explains the activation of threatening stereotypes. Participants were more likely to think a hand tool was a handgun after a Black face prime than after a White face prime (Payne 2001; Payne, Lambert, and Jacoby 2002). It is likely that the prime activates stereotypes about what is associated with being Black or White (Judd, Blair, and Chapeau 2004). A similar phenomenon occurred when the Black and White faces were replaced by snakes and spiders and bunnies and kittens (Larsen, Chan, and Lambert 2004). Furthermore, after a Black face rather than a White face, people were more likely to think a nonthreatening animal was a threatening one. Unpleasant stimuli evoke larger emotional responses, longer duration responses, and have a broader impact than pleasant ones (Baumeister, Bratslavsky, Finkenauer, and Vohs 2001; Larsen and Yarkoni 2004). An automatic vigilance system is likely an explanation for these findings.

A body of research showing poorer recall for words following threatening words (Kulas, Conger, and Smolin 2003; MacKay et al. 2004; Raymond, Fenske, and Tavassoli 2003), suggests that emotional stimuli may receive more elaborate assessment. Extra attention, though not clearly conscious, appears to account for the extra time taken for emotional words on the "emotional Stroop" (McKenna and Sharma 2004; Williams, Mathews, and MacLeod 1996). Like the original Stroop test, the experimental participant is asked to state the color of a word. The longer time is especially true if the word is related to personal concerns (Mathews and Klug 1993; Rieman and McNally 1995) and if the affect aroused is negative (Williams, Mathews, and MacLeod 1996) and holds when length and frequency of the words are controlled (Larsen et al. 2004). Effort can sometimes suppress the interference. For example, if phobic patients know they are in a highly anxious situation, they show less interference for socially threatening words than if they do not believe they were in an anxiety-producing situation (Amir et al. 1996). These results were interpreted as showing that interference effects occur when an individual can no longer expend the extra effort required to override the attention that an emotional stimulus elicits (Mathews and MacLeod 1994). These findings are all consistent with the concept of a preattentive system that screens for threatening information. It is believed that the interference represents a failure to inhibit intrusive thoughts among anxious people (Kindt and Brosschot 1998), with anxious people showing delays related to all stimuli presented after a threatening display, not simply a delay in naming the threatening information itself.

Blindness after Threatening and Sexual Information

People are also less likely to perceive other images after threatening and erotic pictures. When participants were shown slides rapidly, they usually had no difficulty picking out a picture turned ninety degrees from the rest. After seeing a bare breast or a severed limb, however, they had a greater chance of missing the perpendicular image (Chun and Marias 2002). Only students who were low in anxiety were still able to perform well after the threatening picture. Even they, however, had difficulty after the erotic ones.

Fewer "Blinks" in Attention with Threatening Material

Attention appears to "blink" under certain circumstances (Chun and Potter 1995; Raymond, Shapiro, and Arnell 1992). If two items in a list of fifteen presented very quickly (one every one hundred milliseconds) are to be identified, the second target is likely to be missed if it is presented soon after the first target. But if the second item is arousing as opposed to neutral, this "blink" effect is diminished (Anderson and Phelps 2001), again showing greater attention to arousing stimuli. The amygdala receives information about the emotional salience of a stimulus from the visual cortex early in perceptual processing and in turn modulates a later perceptual processing (Phelps 2005).

A Preattentive Evaluative System

Given the large amount of research demonstrating greater attention to threatening information, how are we to understand the psychoanalytic ideas of avoidance and forgetting of threatening experiences? It would seem that attention to such threats would be helpful to survival. The answer lies in a preattentive evaluation system. There may also be differences in the ways information threatening to physical survival is processed from the ways information threatening to the meaning system is processed.

The research on perceptual defense referred to as the "New Look" (Bruner and Postman 1949) and "New Look 2" (Allport 1955; Bruner 1957; Dixon 1981; Erdelyi 1974; Greenwald 1992) suggested a preattentive evaluative system that led people to take longer to perceive threatening information. This work was discredited when it could not be resolved if conscious perceptual experiences as opposed to preconscious effects accounted for the results (cf. Eriksen 1960) and signal detection and behavioral theories developed prominence. Now experimental psychologists have again endorsed the notion of "preattentional" processes (Bargh 1997; Ohman 1992; Williams et al. 1997) with entry into consciousness affected by the relevance of the activated meanings to the goals of a person.

Evidence for Perception without Awareness

Broadbent's (1958) work on selective attention demonstrated that some information did get through an attentional barrier and was processed despite the fact that it was not attended to consciously. The research on "selective attention" in cognitive psychology instructs people to focus attention on one channel of information in a dichotic listening or dichotic viewing procedure and then examines what additional information they have received that they were not attending to. Dichotic listening experiments were consistent with Broadbent's finding (Triesman 1960). The experiments regarding selective attention have been used to document the fact that information not attended to is perceived unconsciously. This body of research assumes that attention is selective but that information of "high relevance" will be perceived when it is not specifically attended to (Johnson and Dark 1986). When different stimuli were presented to each ear, galvanic skin response was greater for words related to shock than for other words when presented to the ear not attended to, although participants did not recall the words (Corteen and Wood 1972). This work on selective attention has led to a revival of interest in "perception without awareness" (Bornstein and Pittman 1992; Wegner and Bargh 1998).

Preconscious Analysis

In Neisser's (1967) view, experiences seem not to be as much "filtered out" as they are not activated. The extent of preconscious analysis depends upon the match between the external information and the accessibility of memory schemas relevant to that information. Kent (1981) has also described a model of the brain where there is an anticipatory system that makes assessments so that people can "look before they leap." People, in essence, get a "snapshot" of a situation and compare it to previous situations so that they can selectively inhibit behavior. This process is going on during a preattention phase of mental processing. An inhibitory effect suppresses what is irrelevant. Kent's model is useful in accounting for the ways threats are handled. Levin (1991) argues that the perceptual system is "directed to pay attention to selective features of the world as they relate to some specific goal" (88).

Early research had demonstrated that meaningful and important information is more likely to break through our limited attention resources and reach awareness (Moray 1959). Ohman (1993) and Williams, Watts, MacLeod, and Mathews (1997) have suggested a "preattentional" mechanism and Bargh (1997), similarly, a "preconscious" one. The amygdala has been found to respond to faces presented so quickly that participants were unaware of their presentation (Whalen et al. 1998). Its responses appear to be automatic, not requiring additional cognitive processing (Morris, Ohman, and Dolan 1998). Lang, Bradley, and Cuthbert (1997) commented that the "psychophysiological laboratory provides a virtual window into a Darwinian world of natural selective attention" (129) where reactions provide information about the cognitive processes of orienting, affective mobilization, and the early stages of defense related to our primitive survival system. "From the functional, evolutionary perspective, it follows that the burden for the discovery of threat should be placed on early, rapid, and parallel preattentive processing mechanisms, which define threat on the basis of relatively simple stimulus attributes" states Ohman (1997, 169). Ohman cites LeDoux's (1990) differentiation of the "quick and dirty" emotional route that bypasses the longer thalamic-cortical emotional route to the amygdala. This processing does not require a full meaning analysis and does not require much contact with memory.

Orienting reflexes under some circumstances are initiated by preattentive processing mechanisms of which the participants are not aware (Ohman 1997). Ohman's analysis is based on two types of research. One line of research has followed up on Hansen and Hansen's (1988) finding that people were faster locating a deviant angry face in a background crowd of happy faces then vice versa. Although the Hansen and Hansen study was criticized on a number of methodological grounds, follow-up studies eliminated the methodological confounds and supported Hansen and Hansen's finding (Ohman, Flykt, and Lundqvist 2000). Anxiety enhances the normal bias to be faster in detecting the threatening stimuli (Byrne and Eysenck 1995).

The other research by Ohman and his colleagues involves a procedure where the pictures are presented so quickly that participants can not consciously differentiate what they are seeing above a random rate of recognition. Ohman and Soares (1994) found that an elevated skin conductance (a sign of anxiety) occurs when certain stimuli (snakes and spiders) have previously been paired with shock, but not other stimuli (flowers and mushrooms) in these very quick presentations. Similarly, learning of associations of shock occurs to angry faces presented in this masking procedure, but not to happy faces (Esteves et al. 1994). Esteves, Dimberg, Parra, and Ohman attribute the unconscious learning that occurs to "preparedness," referring to the ease of learning a particular association as based on the functional, evolutionary relatedness. It would not be possible to have avoidance without some level of detection. Zajonc (1994) argued that the existing research provided evidence for nonconscious emotions. Recently, Etkin, Klemenhagen, Dudman, Rogan, Hen, Kandel, and Hirsch (2004) have in fact demonstrated a biological basis for unconscious emotional vigilance in the amygdala when people detect fearful faces in research using functional magnetic resonance imaging (fMRI).

At least in regard to the perception of movement by other mammals, the detection of such movement appears to occur by the "mirror neurons" newly discovered by Rizollatti (Stamenov and Gallese 2002). Ramachandran (as of January 30, 2005) has stated that the development of these neurons represents "the great leap forward" and the "big bang" of human evolution. Rizzolatti's discovery was that these mirror neurons fire in monkeys when another monkey performs an action or even starts to do something. Ramachandran thinks these neurons also occur in humans because patients who are paralyzed and deny their illness (a disorder called anosognosia) also deny the paralysis of another patient whose inability to move is clearly visible. This would happen if their mirror neurons were destroyed. Furthermore electroencephalography research showed that a brain wave called the MU disappears not only when people move their hands, but also when they watch someone else moving his hands but not when they watch a similar movement by an inanimate object. He conjectures that the extraordinary advances the quick transformations that occurred with the invention of fire, tools, and art may not have been possible if Homo erectus and Neanderthals did not have an advanced enough mirror neuron system. He points out that these advances would not have occurred without being immersed in a culture that can take advantage of such learnability. The human brain and human culture co-evolved like mutual parasites — without either human beings would not have evolved. Once they evolved, these neurons allowed mammals to detect movement when another mammal was intending to move, leading in many cases to split-second life-saving action.

Vigilance versus Avoidance

After this initial preattentive detection, there is enormous evidence for two different reactions—vigilance and avoidance (Krohne 1993). Although how preattentive biases toward either type of response is likely a function of genetic predispositions and environmental factors, few empirical results are available to offer convincing arguments for what these factors may be (Borkovec and Lyonfields 1993). Krohne 1993 has suggested two underlying variables—intolerance of uncertainty and intolerance of emotional arousal. Those low in tolerance of uncertainty are prone to vigilance (sensitizers) while those low in tolerance of emotional arousal may be prone to avoidance (repressors). This formulation suggests that those tolerant of both uncertainty and emotional arousal should be less biased to use either strategy (nondefensive) and should be more able to adapt their ways of coping to specific situations. Those who are intolerant of both uncertainty and arousal are anxious, according to this model. With a difficulty tolerating uncertainty, those prone to vigilance (sensitizers) perform worse on unstructured tasks, but no differently on structured tasks than those prone to avoidance (repressors), and worse in a number of critical situations in the course of athletic competitions, especially in tiebreakers (Krohne and Hindel 1988). Nondefensiveness would lead to vigilance—an intensification of the search for information when this can improve control over the situation, instrumental action when this is the best way to bring about a desired effect, and distraction from threat-related stimuli in an anxiety-provoking situation where the situation is beyond control. Overall, however, it is proposed that anxiety makes it less likely for multiple subsystems to be connected, so that a person either focuses more on the threatening information or on other information, but not both. Relaxation, on the other hand, leads to a decrease in noradrenagenic activity, making it more likely that multiple networks are connected.

Avoidance

Although clinicians are familiar with attempts to avoid threatening experiences in phobics, procrastinators, and the use of defenses in general, much of the experimental research regarding avoidance suggests conscious attempts to keep such experiences out of awareness. These studies include those demonstrating the avoidance of thoughts and memories (Bonanno 1990; Davis 1990; Erdelyi 1990; Kihlstrom and Hoyt 1990) and recall of an absence of negative experiences by those motivated to do so (Higgins and Tykocinski 1992). Wegner's (1992) work on thought suppression shows that the thought to be suppressed remains activated unconsciously. People instructed not to think about sex, for example, remained physiologically aroused. Newman, Duff, and Baumeister (1997) found that people who avoid thinking about threatening aspects of themselves become chronically vigilant toward those traits they wish to disavow. This effect occurs both when people suppress thoughts about their traits in response to instructions and when they do so as a consequence of their own dispositional repressive tendencies.

As mentioned earlier, New Look and New Look 2 researchers found that people took longer to perceive threatening information. An example of the findings from this body of research was that participants more readily perceived neutral than taboo words presented briefly on a screen and showed higher skin conductance for the taboo words prior to conscious recognition of them (McGinnies 1949). Overall, the perceptual defense experiments were criticized regarding the frequency of threatening versus nonthreatening words in past experience, differences in expectancies, and response suppression as opposed to perceptual avoidance (Brown 1961). The findings held in spite of many possible alternative explanations, however (Broadbent 1977; Dixon 1981; Erdelyi 1974, 1985). Although signal detection theorists argued that there is no limen or perceptual awareness threshold and that responses to conscious perceptual experiences accounted for the results, Erdelyi (1990, 2001) has frequently argued that Freud's concept of repression did not require unconscious processing. In any event, the results of these thousand or more studies do demonstrate some sort of avoidance. Determining if experiences are "conscious" is a thorny problem and researchers have now turned instead to looking at whether experiences are under conscious "control" (Jacoby, Lindsay, and Toth 1992). Furthermore, I have suggested that the idea of preattentive processing has now found support in other research.

Motivated forgetting is an avoidance of recall. Anderson and his colleagues (Anderson and Green 2001; Anderson and Levy 2002; Levy and Anderson 2002) have demonstrated poorer recall when participants are instructed not to think about words for a period of time. The frequency of occasions the undesired words need to be excluded from thought increases the inhibitory effect. There are also several studies now demonstrating forgetting that does not appear to be necessarily intentional. Participants who were made anxious tended to be less likely to remember information inconsistent with their prior beliefs about themselves (Curtis, Pacell, and Garzynski 1991) or others, whether or not this information was positive or negative. Green and Sedikides (2004) reported greater forgetting of negative feedback central to people's identity. In another study, the forgetting was found for negative information as opposed to information inconsistent with people's self-conceptions. Recently, Green, Pinter, and Sedikides (2005) found evidence for forgetting of feedback related to the self-conception that was not modifiable. It is noteworthy that in these studies showing poorer recall for threatening information, the information forgotten was feedback threatening to the person's view of self and others—threatening to the person's meaning system. These studies represent a new stage in research on motivated forgetting and demonstrate large "blinks" or blind spots of the sort with which psychoanalysts and other clinicians have been concerned. The threats are not simply spiders or snakes that might threaten survival or even sexual or aggressive stimuli, but experiences identified as threatening to psychological survival of the worldview.

There is also a large body of research on the "repressor" personality style demonstrating avoidance and forgetting of threatening information. As measured by Daniel Weinberger (cf. Weinberger 1990 for a review) a repressive coping style is shown by people who report little anxiety but score high in defensiveness. Inflexible adherence to a predetermined self-image was found to be a characteristic of repressors whereas adaptability was found to be a feature of a low anxious, well-adjusted group (Cook 1985). Repressors are much more likely than others, especially sensitizers, to engage in "selective exposure" to materials consistent with their beliefs (Olson and Zanna 1979) and to focus on positive rather than negative personality attributes (Mischel, Ebbesen, and Zeiss 1973). They are less likely to remember memories of fear and anger (Davis 1990). Repressors are more reactive, however, than their counterparts on physiological measures (Hare 1966; Lazarus and Alfert 1964; Parsons, Fulgenzi, and Edelberg 1969) suggesting that the repressive tendency may prevent overstimulation.

A number of studies have found that although anxious patients perceive threatening words earlier, they have poorer recall (Williams et al. 1997). This pattern only occurs in anxious people, not depressed patients. The interference of anxiety, then, is not one of attention or perception, but occurs in the distribution of processing afterwards. Anxious people have difficulty ignoring the emotionally negative content of material. Some research indicates that anxious people begin to elaborate upon the implications of stimuli, and that this elaboration interferes with recall of the event to be remembered. The forgetting that is seen as a consequence of anxiety, then, is a failure of consciousness to adequately select and distribute the number of experiences arriving in what Baars (1997) called the global workspace or theater of consciousness. The forgetting that is seen as a consequence of anxiety, then, is a failure of consciousness to adequately select and distribute the number of experiences arriving in this workspace. According to Lavie (1995), selective attention operates only under conditions of high perceptual load. Armony and LeDoux (2000) note that what is added to working memory, when the fear system is activated, is a greater number of inputs. If selection is an attempt to protect verbal or symbolic processing (Joseph 1996), the selective mechanism works so as not to overwhelm the capacity to evaluate and choose among alternative responses.

Selection for Conscious Processing

So what can we conclude is being selected by perception and attention for conscious processing? It appears that goal-relevant information is being processed both through an emotional response system and often through the cortex in a process that feeds back to the amygdala for further processing. There is a pre-attentive evaluation, a sort of way station judgment that leads to attention or inattention. The variables leading threats to get consciously processed resulting in an overload are not yet known, but are likely a consequence of biology and past experiences of success with such processing. Cognitive avoidance is likely learned in situations in which escape is not possible (Freyd 1996) and where the lack of integration maximizes survival by allowing the threatening experience to remain disconnected. It may be that a preattentive evaluation is made whether conscious processing might help with a better solution than automatic processing. If the information is threatening and there is a preattentive evaluation that the probability is low that conscious processing will result in a better solution than automatic responses, the information may not get consciously processed. Or, if such processing would result in overwhelming the processing capabilities and paralysis, it may not receive conscious attention. This may be what occurs with the "repressor" personality type. It may also be that information becomes conscious, but is kept disconnected so as not to overwhelm the processing of other information, as in dissociation. Or, a person may be able to integrate the threatening information and continue with other processing as well. In some cases, however, the individual may be unable to inhibit activation of implications of the threat and may become overwhelmed and unable to process other experiences.

For events to be consciously perceived, they must be significant to the self (Pally and Olds 1998). Consciousness involves shifts back and forth between self-system representations and representations of sensory images (Damasio and Damasio 1996; Edelman 1989). Libet, Gleason, Wright, and Pearl's (1983) work shows an electrical potential in premotor areas of the brain almost half a second before conscious awareness of a decision. Many decisions to act are initiated first. Then, some of them enter consciousness. Consciousness lets us know what we planned to do and fine-tunes behavioral responses. Consciousness allows us to choose between a number of responses and modify our plans.

Consciousness acts to hold in check the number of experiences that require thought. It monitors the changes, inconsistencies, and anomalies that are picked up (by the right hemisphere according to Ramachandran [1996]) for

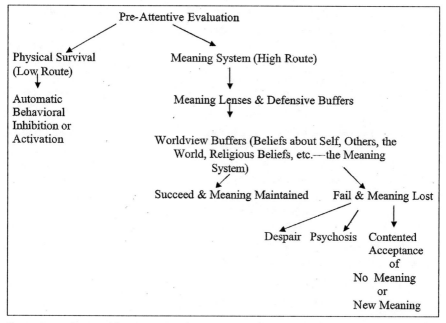

Figure 5.1. Routes After Pre-Attentive System Evaluates Experiences as Important

experiences that may require adjustments other than the automatic ones. Ramachandran's ideas are reminiscent of LeDoux's two emotional response systems, with type II responses involving cognitive processes and comparisons to previous situations. Sroufe (1996) has suggested that affects are regulated so that organization can be maintained in the face of tension. The cognition is not controlling the affects, but a process is occurring so that overwhelming affects optimally do not overwhelm cognitive processing.

If too many experiences enter consciousness, its resources become overloaded, leading to errors, like an air traffic controller with too many planes trying to land. At an extreme, the process may get so flooded that it becomes paralyzed. Belief systems may serve as a buffer so that information can be dealt with quickly and not thoroughly processed. As affect becomes more intense during threats, meaningful processing by the hippocampus decreases. The responses become more automatic, more routine, more rigid and the person may eventually freeze. Figure 5.1 depicts the two routes by which information may be evaluated after preattentive processing and the buffer role that belief systems may provide.

Information is prioritized according to the relative motivational importance and temporal urgency of potential threats (Allport 1989, 653). Motives other than the one momentarily prioritized most highly then can be processed simultaneously. Relating these ideas to psychoanalysis, Allport's ideas allow for unconscious motives to be processed simultaneously with conscious ones. People have two separate processors—a "top-level processor" and an "intuitive processor" (Smolensky 1988). A "top-level processor" uses verbally encoded and culturally transmitted knowledge as its "program" and is responsible when people engage in conscious, effortful reasoning. It works by manipulating linguistically encoded symbols. Because only one linguistically encoded pattern can be operated on at a time, this process must be sequential and relatively slow. An "intuitive processor" mediates most human behavior, including perception, skilled motor behavior, intuitive problem solving and pattern matching, via connections networks. This processing is associative. Others, such as Cohen, Servan-Schreiber, and McClelland (1992) and Sloman (1996) have suggested similar separations. This top-level processor seems related to LeDoux's type II emotional response involving symbolic processing, whereas the more intuitive processing seems related more to type I "quick and dirty" survival-related emotional responses.

From Selection to the Construction of Meaning

When people are aroused, they look around them to find the meaning of their arousal (James 1890; Damasio 2003). They are not clear about the actual source of arousal or influence (Schachter and Singer 1962). Arousal leads the conscious mind to seek out understanding, as Carver and Scheier have described in their control theory. For Gazzaniga (1998) the left hemisphere serves as an interpreter. Meanings consistent with a person's desires and values are then imposed upon the experience. The selection process moves into a process of constructing meanings. Belief systems reduce the degree of conscious processing needed for each individual decision. In Edelman's theory values are a component of the selection process. According to Armony and LeDoux (2000) the mechanism of consciousness is the same for emotional and nonemotional subjective states. When the fear system is activated, however, a greater number of inputs are added to working memory.

The Failure of Selection

What becomes more puzzling than the fact that consciousness is selective or defensive in nature is that the selection process fails. This is seen in panic states, trauma, and phobias. The person may become paralyzed and unable to think. A number of possibilities for the failure of successful selection exist: (1) cognitive processing may be overwhelmed by the type I survival-related physiological reactions described by LeDoux affecting the working of symbolic processing in the hippocampus and possibly in the neocortex; (2) conflicting higher-order goals may prevent one mode of action from being decided upon; (3) a sort of freezing response, like that which occurs physically when fight and flight responses are blocked, occurs cognitively; (4) conscious evaluation was rewarded in the past and/or automatic processing punished, so that conscious processing is attempted although a solution is not readily forthcoming in the current situation.

Differences Between the Current Model and the Freudian Model

There are four differences between the model of mental processes being presented and that which has prevailed in psychoanalysis: (1) there is not an unconscious (or three unconscious systems), but many cognitive subsystems which are not in conscious awareness at any given time; (2) it is not only lack of integration into conscious awareness that leads to lack of optimal functioning, but also lack of connections between subsystems whether or not they are conscious; (3) as differentiated from later Freudian theory, any experiences which are threatening to survival or to the mental representations of the meaning system can remain unconnected, which depending upon the culture, may or may not be primarily aggressive and sexual wishes; and (4) representations, including those of self and others, are differentiated from working memory and the executive control system (Curtis 1992b). It is important to understand that the processes that lead to dysfunction are the same ones that lead to functioning. Shortcuts are learned to avoid pain involving the repetition of certain neural pathways. Cues in conscious awareness signal automatic reactions to previously threatening stimuli including interpersonal interactions, just as sitting in front of the steering wheel of a car triggers certain networks.

It is obviously not possible to begin to present a complete diagram of the complex neural networks involved in the processes of the mind. Unlike the earlier models, any experiences can be unconscious and remain so when there is difficulty retrieving them. It is important, however, to attempt to present some sort of image that differs from those provided in the past. A simplified image of a neural networks model would look something like that in figure 5.2. Obviously, activation of networks is not likely to be as discrete as presented here. In figure 5.2 conscious monitoring and control are indicated in the center. This control center is connected to cognitive-sensory/affective-behavioral networks of the self, others, and so on. Although it is connected to both cognitive-sensory/affective self-network 1 and cognitive-sensory/affective self-network 2, these states are not directly activated by each other. Furthermore, network 3 is not connected directly to conscious control and inhibited by activation of network 1. Network 3 may

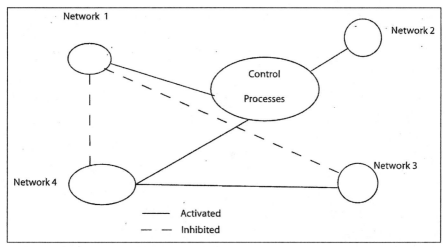

Figure 5.2. New Model: Association and Dissociation Among Neural Networks Including Conscious Control Networks

contain material that is traditionally thought of as repressed—that is, it is incompatible with a dominant (or frequently activated) self-state and actively disconnected from conscious control. Network 1 and 2 can be activated simultaneously, but networks 1 and 3 cannot be activated simultaneously. Network 4 can be activated by Network 3, but not simultaneously with network 1. Network 4 is connected directly to conscious awareness and can be activated simultaneously with network 2. States 1 and 4 are traditionally thought of as dissociated from one another. They each can be activated, but not simultaneously.

Usually, only when there are problems do we begin the self-aware metaprocessing that is part of regulation. This reflection on the automatic processing may lead someone to seek the help of a professional to determine what is going amiss. In terms of Wegner and Bargh's (1998) model, conscious control processes sometimes launch automatic processes, are sometimes transformed into automatic processes, and are sometimes overridden by automatic processes in ways that may no longer be desirable. One route to change is for the therapist to help automatic processes become transformed into consciously controlled processes and for consciously controlled processes to override automatic processes until new ones are learned. This is the process that traditionally occurs in most types of therapy.

What are the conditions that make it more or less likely for experiences in different subsystems to become connected, never to be connected, or to become disconnected? It is proposed that anxiety makes it less likely for multiple subsystems to be connected, and relaxation, that is, a lack of a sense of threat makes it more likely for multiple networks to be connected. If the patient feels safe in the psychoanalytic situation, the patient is able to relax on the couch and relinquish a large degree of conscious control, knowing that the trusted analyst is maintaining it. This experience is similar to that of hypnosis, but in hypnosis, the hypnotized person likely relinquished greater control. In the psychoanalytic situation, the connections or associations increase, the patient is highly suggestible, and the relinquishment of control resembles that of an altered state of consciousness.

Anxiety interferes with holding in awareness simultaneously multiple subsystems and the integration of subsystems. Arousal leads to performance of the dominant response. This can happen behaviorally or by activation of a belief system that defends against anxiety. When some people are threatened, they may be able to focus on the anxiety-provoking experience while simultaneously remaining aware of experiences located primarily in other networks. In this case, the possibility for creative problem solving is optimized. But if the person is threatened, fearing in the worst cases physical or psychological annihilation, and is unable to keep different networks in mind simultaneously, the person either attends almost exclusively to the anxiety-provoking experience or attends to the other experiences, making it more difficult to process the threat simultaneously with other information—vigilance or avoidance. If the basic beliefs about self and the world are threatened and many networks remain activated, conscious controlled processing may be flooded and unable to direct action, resulting in panic.

If the person keeps the threatening experience disconnected from other subsystems, the experience continues to affect certain mental processes and behavior, but not others. Such experiences affect behavior whether the "dissociations" occur from controls intended to maintain a satisfactory level of conscious processing or due to physical damage. From these studies, we know that the unconscious mind picks up information more quickly than the conscious mind does, and shows evidence of what was perceived without awareness under many special conditions. I am arguing that some information may not reach conscious awareness due to selective attention processes in favor of schema-relevant information and some information may not reach conscious awareness due to an attempt to prevent overload from experiences inconsistent with the current organizing processes.

A model of selective attention and inattention with dissociations between subsystems seems most easily to accommodate all of the data from both psychoanalysis and cognitive science. A selective attention model can most easily deal with selective perceptions of both inner and outer experiences. The language used for such processes, however, is not as important as understanding the mechanisms involved, as we are now beginning to do.

SUMMARY AND CONCLUSION

In the current model integrating psychoanalysis and psychology we have self-preservation and preservation of meaning as primary human motivations in place of ego instincts and id instincts of sex and aggression. In place of structures of ego, superego, and id we have the experiencing self, representations of actual and ideal self-states, and unconscious aspects of self. More precisely, we have many neural networks that can be activated by external situations or inner urges — conscious control/monitoring functions and mental representations, including those of various selves, some frequently activated, some usually unconscious. In place of three different "its", we have preattentive evaluations of relevancy to goals and consistency with already existing representations, responding automatically or with selection for conscious processing. Because people are motivated not only to sustain life, but also to preserve its meaning, mental organizing processes are motivated by their very nature, with people integrating, ignoring, or inhibiting new experiences both consciously and unconsciously.

These experiences are selected just as surely as are genetic variations. Darwin (1859) stated: "I have called this principle by which each slight variation, if useful, is preserved, by the term Natural Selection" (chapter 3). Each slight variation of neural connections, if useful, is also preserved (more likely to be activated again) by a similar process of natural selection.

Chapter 6

Abandonment of the Interpretation-Insight Model and the Tsunami of the New Experiences Model of Change

All those analysts want to talk about is themselves.

—Pedestrian commenting to another pedestrian
on a sidewalk in Manhattan

Right now in psychoanalysis we have more than a sea change. We have a tsunami. As described in previous chapters, our models of motivation, the self, and the mind have all been changing. As discussed earlier, the view of unconscious processes as an internalization of interactions with significant others (Newirth 2004) has contributed to an unfortunate focus upon interpreting transference and countertransference as the major route to change (cf. Curtis 2000). This affinity has come at the expense, in many cases, of the broader goal of expanding awareness of unconscious processes. I wish to address first this tendency. In so doing, I shall suggest that we no longer have an "interpretation-insight" model of change, that a "new relationship" model of therapeutic action is also grossly insufficient, and that we have moved to a "new experiences" model of change. This new model allows us to incorporate shamelessly interventions derived from other theoretical orientations to psychotherapy.

Recently there has been an increase in the tendency in American psychoanalysis to focus more and more attention upon interpreting transference and countertransference processes, probably stemming largely from the influence of Merton Gill (1982). Strachey (1934), Glover (1955), and early interpersonalists (cf. Cooper 1995; Sullivan 1953), however, valued analyzing the extratransferential feelings of the patient, considering it often too anxiety provoking or unimportant to the patient to focus on the patient's feelings toward the analyst. Strachey pointed out that analysis could not be limited to the analysis of the transference. "A cake cannot be made with nothing but currants," (290), he quipped. Gill's focus upon what was going on in "the here and now" of the transference was likely largely a reaction to the excessive emphasis upon the past in many of the analyses of the 1950s.

It is also possible that psychoanalysts are tending to focus more upon the transference out of the belief by many that this is the primary way that psychoanalysis differs from other forms of psychotherapy. An examination of the table of contents of Slipp's (1982) *Curative Factors in Dynamic Psychotherapy*, reveals that Gill's title "The Analysis of the Transference" is the only title out of seventeen that mentioned transference (another is on countertransference). He begins his paper by stating, "The analysis of the transference is generally acknowledged to be the central feature of analytic technique" (1979, 273). The change from 1979 to the present is evident in the excessive focus of analysts in recent years on transference as noted by Eagle (2000a) in a review of Mitchell and Aron's (1999) edited volume *Relational Psychoanalysis: The Emergence of a Tradition*. Eagle remarks as follows: "Many of the contributors to this volume (more than half, as I count them) focus on the clinical situation, in particular, on the patient-therapist interaction. This is but one expression of the strong tendency in the contemporary psychoanalytic literature to view near exclusive attention to the transference-counter-transference interaction as the 'common ground' of psychoanalysis. . . . Enormous attention is given to an examination of all the nuances and complexities of patient-analyst interactions without any focused consideration of the question of whether such an examination is related to therapeutic outcome, let alone providing evidence that it is." Examination of *Psychoanalytic Practice: Clinical Studies* (Thomä and Kächele, 1994) reveals that the second chapter is on transference, the third on countertransference, with the fourth and fifth on resistance and dreams, respectively,

Comments from analysts in training and patients reveal this contemporary American focus upon transferential issues. One of my colleagues in training was told by his supervisor that all the supervising analyst wanted to hear about was transference and countertransference. The overuse of the focus upon the transference was also evident in the remark I quoted at the beginning of this chapter that I heard walking along the street in New York City near a psychoanalytic institute. I overheard the person on the sidewalk near me say to her companion, "Oh, don't go to that institute. All those analysts want to talk about is themselves." I doubt that the analysts were actually talking about themselves. More likely, what the person meant was that her analyst had asked a lot about her feelings about him or her and their relationship.

In speaking with another analyst recently, I stated that the problems a patient is having in relationships may not be occurring in the relationship with the analyst. His immediate response was that the patient was not aware that these problems were happening with the analyst (as if the analyst knew what was really happening). This was not what I had meant. I had meant that the problematic pattern of interaction was a pattern not occurring with the analyst. When a senior analyst at the W. A. White Institute commented that nothing transferential happened for the first three years of an analysis, the audience was shocked. This did not seem to be a provocative comment to someone trained many years ago, but younger colleagues expect to "work in the transference (referring to the therapist-patient relationship)."

Although the analysis of transferential and countertransferential processes may be the most powerful tool at the disposal of analysts, the question I am raising is whether this focus is being overly used. I am arguing that there can be major problems when this focus is applied to once or twice per week therapies and when this focus is used to the detriment of other sorts of interventions that have been found helpful. It would, of course, make the job of analysts a lot easier if it could be assumed that any problem the patient was having in an interaction with another individual was also occurring with the analyst, but there is no evidence that this is true. In fact, as I will discuss shortly, most people have a variety of ways of relating and only perhaps very disturbed patients will get quickly into a similar interactional style with everyone, or almost everyone. For example, I have several patients who were ignored by their mothers. With my listening to their every word, they do not feel ignored by me. Some analysts then say one has to look at the patient's responses at the end of the session or when the analyst goes on vacation to find out about feelings of being ignored. But high-functioning patients are able to differentiate a vacation from being ignored. It can take quite a long time for the patient to become aware of any such feelings when they have a very different impression of someone. Even Hoffman (1996) made this criticism of Gill: "In my view, Gill in his enthusiasm for the analysis of the transference may have been excessively impatient regarding the time it might take for certain transference-counter-transference patterns to unfold and for the participants to work their way out of them" (48).

This question was addressed previously by Menaker (1991) in a chapter entitled "Questioning the Sacred Cow of the Transference." Although Freud's idea that what is not remembered is repeated is indeed a brilliant one, Menaker objects to consideration of the value of examining the projection of qualities onto the analyst while neglecting the value of the patient's introjection of qualities of the analyst. Although she sees that clearing up projections may help alleviate problems originating in the past, she sees the new positive introjects from the analyst as facilitating growth. Schacter (2002) has also questioned the use of transference, largely on theoretical grounds, and suggested focusing instead on habitual relational patterns and defenses related to them. Schacter has also asked if transference is a "shibboleth," referring to a password "that enables an unknown to identify himself or herself as a member of a particular group" (2). Although Freud had referred to dreams as "the shibboleth of psychoanalysis (1914, 57), Person (1993) wrote that "The development of transference and its analysis appear to have replaced dream analysis as the 'royal road' to the unconscious" (5). Schacter's excellent critique *Transference: Shibboleth or Albatross?* fails to report, however, the research on the effect of transference interpretations.

In Freud's conceptualization of the phenomenon of transference, he seemed to highlight the importance of a predominant pattern, although he left open the possibility that multiple patterns might be present. Sullivan (1953) noted the multiple types of transferences. Stone (1967) commented that the sheer variety of relationships to other people will never be reproduced in the relationship with the therapist. Yet many analysts believe that the relational pattern that occurs with the analyst is the predominant relational pattern in the patient's life or that large amounts of time dedicated to examining the patient-therapist relationship will be beneficial to the patient. Crits-Christoph and Luborsky (1990) using the core conflictual relational theme method found that the main wishes of thirty-three patients were present in 66 percent of the patients' narratives, indicating that most patients experience a single pervasive relationship theme. A subsequent study by Connolly, Crits-Christoph, and colleagues (1996), however, found that the predominant relational pattern of the patient is often (40 percent of the time) not occurring with the therapist. Or, in other words, in the narratives of 40 percent of the thirty-five patients, the pattern occurring with the therapist was not the patient's most common relational pattern. Although their work did not investigate long-term psychoanalysis, their findings make problematic the assumption of some analysts and psychodynamic therapists that analyzing the transferential pattern will help the patient with his or her predominant maladaptive pattern. For example, a patient may show a pattern with some people of a wish for the other to be loving and approaching. This may be the pattern with the analyst who seems to be a benevolent authority figure. The predominant pattern for the patient with most other people may be, however, one of wishing to be asserting and separating. Although a psychoanalyst will undoubtedly spend a good deal of time examining the analyst-patient relationship, when the model of analyzing transference-countertransference is applied as the primary theory of a once-a-week therapy, it is potentially more problematic.

Assuming that the analyst can simply examine his or her own countertransference as a clue to what is happening in other interactions is another pitfall of the perspective that the patient's problematic interactional style will undoubtedly occur with the analyst. The problem with this perspective has been criticized recently by Eagle (2000b). He states that "the analyst's counter-transference reactions tend to be seen as a virtually unerring guide to the patient's mental contents" (24). Eagle provides examples of situations in which the analyst is having a feeling that does not correspond to what the patient is feeling and criticizes the idea of the analyst as an empty container as similar to the earlier idea of a blank screen. He (27) criticizes Levine (1997) who wrote the following: "I hope to demonstrate that there is a pragmatic value in assuming that even those thoughts and emotional experiences that clearly arise within the analyst from the analyst's own personal life and have seemingly little to do with the specific patient at hand—for example, when the analyst's personal life events intrude upon the hour to such an extent so as to encroach upon or even override his/her capacities to analyze effectively— can be presumed to have a patient-related component that contributes to their appearance in a given hour in a particular way" (48). Well, yes, everything in the world may be related in some way. It is likely, however, that what intrudes on the analyst about his or her personal life says more about the analyst.

Supporting the view that these intrusions reveal more about the analyst than the patient are the findings in a recent study. Holmqvist (2001) asked nine therapists to provide reactions to a number of patients on a "feeling word" checklist after each therapy session. Reactions to twenty-eight therapies were analyzed in this way. One of the main results was that the therapists' own habitual styles were very important to the emotional reactions to different patients. A discriminant analysis showed that 93 percent of the checklists could be correctly classified according to the therapist using a cross-validation method. (The discriminant power within the therapist according to the patient was smaller.) The reactions of the therapists to particular patients were quite different, suggesting that the therapists' feelings said more about their own personalities and transferences than about the patients' and that it is hazardous to think that patients evoke consistent countertransference reactions. Although classical analysts certainly did not rely upon their countertransference to understand the patient, this tendency has grown so popular in recent years that Hoffman (1996) recently stated the following: "Systematic use of the patient's associations as a guide to understanding the patient's resisted ideas about the counter-transference is a critical element of the interpretive process in the social paradigm. Without it, there is a danger that the analyst will rely excessively on his or her own subjective experience in constructing interpretations. The analyst then risks making the error of automatically assuming that what he or she feels corresponds with what the patient imagines to be the case. In fact, Racker (1968), whom I have cited so liberally, seems to invite this criticism at times, although he also warns against regarding the experience of the counter-transference as oracular."

In a recent study of interventions that seventy-five analysts from the White Institute in New York and the Institut für Psykoterapi in Oslo found helpful and hurtful in their own psychoanalyses (when they had been patients themselves), the transference questions were significantly correlated with perceived change, although altogether forty-four of the sixty-eight analyst behaviors were correlated with change as perceived by these analyst-patients (Curtis et al. 2004). The analysts reported that their own psychoanalysts' behaviors related to genuineness, openness, and warmth were the most helpful and the item most correlated with change was "helped me become aware of experiences I was avoiding"—a question related to unconscious processes, but not necessarily transferential ones. The conclusion of the study was that active interventions in the context of a supportive relationship best predicted overall reported change, not simply "the relationship" nor analysis of it.

REASONS FOR THE FOCUS ON TRANSFERENCE

Two reasons have already been provided for this strong emphasis on analyzing transference. The first is the shibboleth idea already discussed. The focus on transference makes one a real psychoanalyst working with the "gold" described by Freud. The second, and probably the major reason, is that analyzing what is going on in the here-and-now is very powerful. Analyzing what is going on with the therapist seems more effective to analysts than other interventions, such as reconstructing the past or discussing relationships outside the consulting room. Psychoanalysts have found the analysis of the relationship with the patient in the moment can be very powerful and then have used what has worked for them in the past.

The psychoanalytic tradition of reconstructing the past to understand how reactions, beliefs, and behaviors came about provides an excellent means for understanding how people came to be the way they are. An intellectual understanding of the etiology of a problem does not lead to change, however, as psychoanalysts have long noted. So it is the theory of change that is at question here—and it is generally agreed that something in the present, like whatever is wished for from the analyst, is maintaining a feeling or behavior.

A third reason for reliance upon analyzing transference is the difficulty getting a sense of what is happening in other relationships. If psychoanalysts hear about other relationships, it is often not possible to ascertain if the patient's reaction to the other person is unusual, to know what is being omitted, or to know how the other person is reacting. In contrast, analysts do have some knowledge of how they themselves feel and how other people behave in response to them, and, hopefully, how people report feeling in response (group therapy experiences are indispensable in this regard, but not required, to my knowledge by any training programs). Sometimes it can be difficult to get a clear picture of what is going on in other relationships from the patient's reports. It is only when an interaction occurs with us that we get a sense of what the problem is.

A fourth reason may be an ignorance of—or deficit of—other skills by persons eventually trained in psychoanalysis. For example, psychiatrists today and social workers get a minimum of training in psychotherapy. Most psychologists get little exposure to psychoanalytic technique in their Ph.D. programs—usually predominantly cognitive-behavioral or person centered, or, if the program is psychoanalytically oriented, little exposure to other approaches. A fifth reason is that psychoanalysts often feel guilty if they are doing something of which their supervisors wouldn't approve or feel anxious when they try something that would receive a negative reaction from their peers. So psychoanalysts do what they know and what they think they should do: ignorance is bliss. A sixth reason is that the writers and teachers in the institutes are the people most likely to have patients for whom analyzing the transference works well. Their patients usually earn a decent income and are verbal and psychologically minded, with high motivation, good impulse control, and a history of positive interpersonal relations (very often they are mental health professionals in training). As will be discussed next, research has shown that these verbal, educated, well-functioning, psychologically minded patients are the ones for whom transference interpretations are effective.

Empirical Research on Transference Interpretations

Gill concluded that the relative prominence of transferential versus extra-transferential interpretations has faded in and out due to the almost total lack of research in the psychoanalytic tradition. In fact, there has never been clear empirical evidence that the analysis of transference is related to good outcomes. Many psychoanalysts believe that empirical research is not a litmus test for the validity of psychoanalytic hypotheses, but that the consulting room is. Empirical research can call into question psychoanalytic beliefs, however. If we are interested in all forms of knowing, it is curious that some psychoanalysts exclude empirical research from awareness altogether.

Several studies have found that interpretations inhibit therapeutic progress (Connolly et al. 1999; Fisher and Greenberg 1977; Henry et al. 1994; Hoglend 2004; Ogrodniczuk et al. 1999; Orlinsky and Howard 1986; Sloane et al. 1975; Spence 1993). In three studies (Malan 1976; Marziali 1984; Marziali and Sullivan 1980), only when the transference interpretations were linked to relations with parents were the interpretations related to a positive outcome. One study found an inverse relationship between simple transference interpretations and improvement in relations with friends and sexual adjustment (Piper et al. 1986). In a follow-up study, a high dosage of transference interpretations was predictive of poorer outcome (Piper et al. 1991). Although it was possible that therapies with a high dosage of transference interpretations meant fewer "correct" interpretations, another study showed that the high dosage or concentration was not confounded by correctness or lack of correspondence (Piper et al. 1993). In this study, a high dosage of transference interpretations was related to a positive outcome for patients with a high quality of object relations, but to a poor outcome for patients with a low quality of object relations. Ogrodniczuk and Piper (1999) drew three conclusions in a review of studies of transference interpretations in treatments of patients with personality disorders: (1) a strong therapeutic alliance is necessary for successful exploration of the transference; (2) transference-focused work should be balanced with supportive interventions, and (3) the patient must have a high quality of interpersonal relations.

McCullough and her colleagues (1991) compared the effects of transference interpretation, patient-and-significant-other interpretations, and clarifications on patients' affective and defensive behaviors. Transference interpretations followed by affect were related to favorable outcome, but defensiveness was associated with negative outcomes. These findings highlight the importance of the therapist being aware of the patient's responses to interpretations.

In a study of fifteen patients with personality disorders in dynamic psychotherapy of brief to moderate length (nine to fifty-three sessions), four patients were deemed suitable for transference interpretations by using Malan's (1976) criteria of circumscribed conflict and high motivation for self-understanding (Hoglend 1996). These four patients had less favorable change at two and four year follow-ups. They asked for more advice, missed more sessions, and increased their maladaptive patterns. Transference interpretations were found to have a greater impact—both positive and negative by Gabbard and colleagues (1994). They suggested using supportive interventions first. Kernberg et al. (1989) also argued for giving interpretations to an "emotionally prepared patient" (16) by paving the way first. Hoglend (2004) reports a negative association between frequent transference interpretations and immediate or long-term outcomes in eleven different studies. A high concentration of transference interpretations, then, may be harmful. Several authors have argued that a moderate use of transference interpretations is essential in psychoanalysis and long-term dynamic psychotherapy, but should be completely avoided in brief psychotherapy (Berliner 1941; Deutsch 1949; Pumpian-Mindlin 1953). The research findings suggest that there is a subgroup of patients who benefit from transference interpretations in short-term therapy, but that this group is limited. Sifneos's (1987) success with transference interpretations has been largely with Harvard students who are verbal, young, and well-functioning in their work.

Although positive outcomes have been found to be related to accurate interpretations based on Luborsky's core conflictual relationship themes (Crits-Christoph, Cooper, and Luborsky 1988) and interpretations compatible with the patient's plan using an adaptation of the plan formulation method of Weiss and Sampson (1986), interpretations related to patients' unconscious plans were found to be helpful whether or not they were transference interpretations. (Fretter et al. 1994). Although these studies present a limited view of the vast enterprise considered to be the analysis of transference, their findings are worth at least considering. There is still no research pointing to the superiority of therapies that address transference over those that do not. What we do have is a plethora of studies demonstrating the importance of a warm, genuine, open relationship (Norcross 2002) and a positive alliance (Horvath and Bedi 2002), but not necessarily the analysis of it, or the preoccupation with discussing it that the contemporary American psychoanalytic literature suggests. Hoglend (2004) concludes that a moderate use of transference interpretations may be productive with patients who have a history of good interpersonal relations, but that it may be more important to focus on relationships outside therapy.

Freud had suggested leaving alone a positive transference. He regarded transference analysis as a means of overcoming resistance. The feelings that occur with the analyst may not be those most warded off or dangerous. If patients can discuss the relationship with the analyst, they will likely then be able to have similar discussion elsewhere in life, or able to explore their own subjectivity in another relationship as well. Of course, this depends upon the capacity of the other person with whom they are interacting. Furthermore, some patients come into analysis already able to discuss relationships in the here-and-now, and some become able and even happy at times to explore such processes, without their major problems being addressed. As long as such processes are not being kept out of awareness, what is the point of so much emphasis? Here there is not a question of hurting the patient by analyzing the transference, but of negligence in addressing the most important problems with which the patient is concerned. Although analyzing the transference may shed light on how a problem came about, it will not necessarily lead to changing the problematic behavior in the present when the problem is an addiction or phobia, for example.

Discussing the transference or what nonanalysts call the patient-therapist relationship can be an extremely valuable route to change. When this focus is overly emphasized or the only one that therapists rely upon, however, opportunities for other routes to change are lost.

Interpreting Unconscious Influences on Experiences

Strachey (1934), in his theory of mutative interpretation, noted that only a "relatively small proportion of the psychoanalytic literature . . . has been concerned with the mechanisms" (127) by which the therapeutic action of interpretations is achieved. He went on to say that although little was known about interpretation, "it does not prevent an almost universal belief in its remarkable efficacy . . . [possessing] many of the qualities of a magic weapon" (141). Spence commented in 1992 that "more than half a century later, we still celebrate Strachey's model, despite the absence of compelling clinical confirmation" (558). He criticizes the belief in the mutative power of interpretations as coming from analysts who have been exposed to the theory and are biased in recalling their own experiences consistently with received wisdom. According to Spence, interpretations "unlikely achieve any mutative effect unless—and this is a critical condition—they happen to coincide with a state of positive transference or an enabling therapeutic alliance" (570). These are the conditions for interpretations with which most analysts are familiar.

Hobbs (1968), in his presidential address to the Division of Clinical Psychology of the American Psychological Association doubted the role of interpretation and insight in therapy (a doubt raised by some psychoanalysts as well). He argued that insight might have nothing to do with behavior change, or, that at best, it might follow such change. He presented five arguments against a special role for insight. First, interpretations may be acceptable to clients only after they have "achieved sufficient self-organization for the interpretation no longer to be relevant," so that they can accept, but no longer "need" the interpretation. Second, concrete experiences without interpretations lead to good results with children. Third, the occurrence of an insight merely means that the client is catching on to the therapist's personal system for interpreting the world of behavior: "The therapist does not have to be right; he mainly has to be convincing" (14). Fourth, it may be the intimate, nonhurtful relationship with another human being and the reduction of anxiety which are therapeutic, and fifth, the lack of needing previously useful tactics, the development of a sense of agency, and learning new ways of responding that are helpful in therapy, not interpretations.

Psychologists since Dollard and Miller (1950) have also raised the possibility that interpretations are desensitizing the patient to anxiety-provoking experiences. Another possibility is that they are helping the patient to be more open to all experiences, presenting not what is necessarily out of the patient's awareness—the "bad me" or "not me," for example, but another possible way of being for the patient to consider—what Blechner (1994) has called the "maybe me." With both of these possibilities regarding the effect of interpretations, it is not the specific content of the interpretation that is important, but the allowing of many possibilities into awareness that is therapeutic. This is not to argue that awareness is essential for change to occur, but that it is one way in which change takes place.

Hammer's (1968) response was that interpretations might be helpful, not in place of the above factors, but in addition to them. Some of his arguments were that the patients hear the more tolerant therapist and increase self-acceptance, that they bring dissociated material into awareness, and that they inaugurate experiments in less defensiveness. Hammer states that none of his arguments are "to imply that interpretation is the principal ingredient of therapy" (26).

The Waning of the Interpretation-Insight Model in Psychoanalysis

A number of alternative routes to change have been posited by psychoanalysts over the years. Reviewing a broad range of views of therapeutic action, in 1980 Eagle and Wolitsky suggested that these theories fall into three categories: (1) theories about insight into the relationship with the analyst; (2) theories about insight into other patterns of relating; and (3) theories about the relationship itself as mutative. Kavanaugh (1995), in a comprehensive overview of theories of therapeutic action in interpersonal psychoanalysis, divides them into hermeneutic-interpretive theories and relational-experiential theories. Stark (1999) categorized theories of therapeutic action in psychoanalysis as models of knowledge, relationship, and experience. I shall present a very broad overview of some of the theories that have been offered, usually not as replacements to the interpretation-insight model, but for the most part as additional avenues to change.

Ferenczi (1932), for example, thought that regression was central to therapeutic change. In this regression the patient would have benign, new experiences which would allow a new development of personality. Bion (1977), Winnicott (1958), Guntrip (1969), and Tuttman (1982) continued with this view of change. In this model, safety—a sense of being held (Slochower 1996)— leads to the relinquishment of control and defenses, leading in turn to new experiences. This model is akin to that of experiential psychotherapies, but informed by psychoanalytic theory.

Defense Analysis

Defense analysis was the major technique of Reich (1949). Although the interpretation of defense was advocated by analysts when the patient was not free associating in a way that allowed the analyst to interpret content, defense analysis recently has been advocated as a way to access affect in many of the short-term dynamic therapies (Davanloo 2000; Fosha 2000; McCullough-Vaillant 1996). Although Davanloo's particular type of defense analysis appears too aggressive and assaulting of the dignity of the patient to many psychoanalysts, experiential therapists, and other therapists as well, Fosha and McCullough have presented transcripts and videotapes of gentler forms of this type of treatment. One could argue that these therapies interpret defenses, but the major therapeutic action appears to occur with access to emotions and their diminishment or transformation (McCullough-Vaillant 1996).

New representations of self and others

Many psychoanalysts have viewed the development of new representations of self and others as a consequence of the relationship with the analyst as central to change. For Fairbairn (1952), it was the relinquishment of ties to old "objects" that was curative. Harris (1996) has emphasized the mourning of lost "objects." Loewald (1960) described the process of developing a new "object relationship" (17) as integral to change, although he thought that the therapeutic process is "not simply internalization of 'objects' but also integrating the preconscious and the unconscious" (30). Jay Greenberg (1986) has also described the process of developing new views of self and others. For Greenberg, the patient sees the analyst according to the old pattern, but realizes simultaneously there is something new. Fonagy (1999, 2000) has argued that the change in relationship representations is the curative aspect of the psychoanalytic process, not the recovery of memories. As will be discussed below, he sees change coming about through new representations as a consequence of the relationship with the therapist. Lichtenberg, Lachmann, and Fosshage (2002) also have viewed the reorganization of representational schemas as part of the therapeutic process, along with the expansion of awareness and the natural tendency toward self-righting and resilience that occurs when an inhibitory stress is removed.

Increasing awareness of interpersonal relations

Sullivan (1940) viewed an increase in awareness as the major route to change: "[O]ne achieves mental health to the extent that one becomes aware of one's interpersonal relations" (207). The idea of increased awareness is obviously not different from that of the interpretation-insight model, but the content of the awareness was different. Furthermore, Sullivan suggested inquiry as a major technique to achieve this awareness, but he did not exclude interpretations. He believed, however, that "the supply of interpretations, like that of advice, greatly exceeds the demand" (187). "[D]isabuse yourself of the idea that you can tell anybody what ails them in a fashion that will be simply helpful to them," he is reported to have said (Kvarnes and Parloff 1976, 21). Thompson (1953) summarized his position as follows: "[I]n Sullivanian terms, therapy consists of the gradual clarifying for the patient of the kind of things he is doing to and with other people" (29).

In recent years psychoanalysts have rejected the idea that they can "know" what is in the patient's mind and many present interpretations in the form of an inquiry or as hypotheses.

Empathy

Recently, especially with the influence of Kohut (1977), analysts have learned to value the empathic responses valued by Rogers (1961), whom Kohut failed to cite. Kohut's (1984) view of the change process comprises three steps, the first two being defense and transference analysis, and the third being empathy—in his words "the new channel of empathy . . . supplants the bondage that had formerly tied the archaic self to the archaic self-object" (66), similar to Fairbairn's idea of the tie to the "old object." Josephs (1995), who has written extensively about combining interpretation with empathy states "an interpretation is experienced as empathic to the extent that it stabilizes and bolsters the sense of self and will be experienced as unempathic to the extent that it stabilizes and undermines the sense of self (110). Mann (1992) has also emphasized the role of empathic responses in his time-limited psychodynamic psychotherapy. Process-experiential, emotion-focused (Greenberg 1993; Gendlin 1962: Bohart1993) therapists and intersubjective analysts (Lichtenberg, Lachman, and Fosshage 1992) have now elaborated extensive ways of intervening that extend the notions about empathy that Rogers and Kohut advocated.

The therapeutic relationship

Some analysts, such as Ferenczi (1926), Suttie (1935), Balint (1952, 1968), and Thompson (1950) believed that it was primarily the relationship that leads to change. Even Freud, on at least one occasion, commented that the relationship was the major factor in change: "What turns the scale is not intellectual insight, but the relationship to the doctor (1916, 445). Guntrip (1975) reported Fairbairn as saying, "'You can go on analyzing forever and get nowhere. It's the personal relation that is therapeutic'" (145). For Guntrip, psychoanalytic psychotherapy is "the provision of a reliable and understanding human relationship of a kind that makes contact with the deeply repressed traumatized child in a way that enables one to become steadily more able to live" (154).

In his book, *What Is Effective in Psychoanalytic Therapy: The Move from Interpretation to Relation*, (1991) Meissner also obviously focused on the value of the therapeutic relationship: "Rather than interpretive resolution of the oedipal transference as the major agent of therapeutic change, emphasis falls on the analytic setting and the relation to the analyst as bearing the major weight of change in successful psychoanalytic treatment" (183).

As noted by Wallerstien (1995), the relationship has been emphasized more recently by Pulver (1992), Blum (1992), Chasseguet-Smirgel (1992), and Jacobson (1994). Although Blum comments that insight is "the unique, critical agent of psychic change in clinical psychoanalysts" (257), he goes on to say that "with some very disturbed, regressed patients, interpretation really turns out to . . . have a secondary, synergistic role to that of the analytic relationship" (329). Jacobson, according to Wallerstein, "turned Eissler's conception of parameters around completely" (331), referring to this passage from Jacobson (1994): "In other words, we can [now] see such non-interpretive interventions as integral aspects of the analytic work, rather than being restricted to viewing them as gratification, as suggestions, as distractions from the optimal emergence of the instinctual drive derivatives, or as merely incidental or supportive" (31).

Recently, infant researchers have suggested the relationship as the major route to change. It does not make sense that problems emanating from non-verbal experiences with caregivers, likely not remembered in declarative memory, would be helped by verbal interactions. Fonagy (1998), in citing the four hundred different types of psychotherapy, all often effective, commented: "[T]he relationship component of therapy must contain an effective ingredient because this is the only feature that the curative technique of talking can share" (350). He had stated, "The relegation of the transference phenomenon and its interpretation from a 'star' to a mere 'supporting role' in the therapeutic play, may seem like an extravagant and even an impious claim" (349). Infant researchers (Beebe 1998; Lyons-Ruth 1998; Morgan et al. 1998; Sander 1998) have noted the importance of procedural memory in the way people interact in relationships. They have suggested that there are "now moments" (Freeman 1994) when the patient is alone in the presence of the therapist where a shift occurs in the patient's way of relating, such as taking on more of a sense of agency. Tronick (1998) has even gone so far as to suggest, "I interact, therefore I am." He suggests that dyads create their own states of consciousness and that states of consciousness "can be expanded into more coherent and complex states in collaboration with another self-organizing system" (290).

The "nonspecific" or "common factors" in the therapist have been found consistently in research to be the most important variables of the therapist accounting for change. Lambert, Shapiro, and Bergin (1986) in a thorough review of all of the available research on therapy outcome concluded that approximately 40 percent of change occurred from extratherapeutic factors, 30 percent from common factors, 15 percent from interventions, and 15 percent from expectancy (placebo) effects. If psychoanalysts believe that these variables are a primary component in the change process and that new representations of self and others can arise in any type of therapy, psychoanalysts must make clear what they are offering that leads to anything different from what other therapies are providing. Most psychoanalysts see a positive relationship as necessary, but not usually sufficient, for the greatest therapeutic traction, however. In research by Curtis, Field, Knaan-Kostman, and Mannix (2004), relationship factors and specific interventions together predicted 42 percent of the variance in reported change by psychoanalysts in their own analyses. Passing relational tests, that is, disconfirming pathogenic beliefs about others, is emphasized as the curative factor in the control-master theory of Weiss et al. (1986). New relational experiences have been stressed as mutative in a number of short-term dynamic psychotherapies (Balint et al. 1972; Luborsky 1984; Strupp and Binder 1984). Although insight is still considered important in these therapies, interpretation "is thought to facilitate patients' new kinds of experience of self with others" (Frank 1999, 256). Identification with the therapist, in the tradition of the introjection of a kinder superego, has been emphasized by Volkan (1982) and Menaker (1991). "Mutual recognition" has been seen as central by Benjamin (1990).

The integration of disconnected self-states

Bromberg (1996) has argued convincingly that conflicts can be analyzed when there is some awareness that there are experiences in conflict, conflicting wishes, conflicting fears, or a wish and fear in conflict, for example. This requires being able to hold in awareness simultaneously different experiences. When experiences and their related self-states are dissociated, the task of the therapist is to bring these disconnected states into awareness simultaneously. These self-states, however, are not necessarily unconscious. What remains out of awareness is their conflictual nature.

THE NEW EXPERIENCES MODEL IN PSYCHOANALYSIS AND PSYCHOTHERAPY

"The patient needs an experience, not an explanation." This remark, usually attributed to Freida Fromm-Reichmann (cf. Kavanaugh 1995), is often quoted among interpersonal analysts. Eissler (1953) and Stone (1954) believed new experiences to be the major route to change in psychoanalytic psychotherapy, but interpretation to be central to therapeutic action in psychoanalysis proper. Recently, relational analysts, as summarized by Curtis and Hirsch (2004), have adopted a model of therapeutic action within psychoanalysis proper more akin to the interpersonal tradition. Aron (1996) states "While insight and interpretation (verbal symbolization) continue to be valuable for relational analysts, they do not retain the centrality that they have for classical Freudian and Kleinian authors. . . . Relational analysts generally believe that what is most important is that the patients have a new experience rooted in a new relationship" (214). He continues, "Old patterns are inevitably repeated, but, it is hoped, the patient and analyst find ways to move beyond these repetitions, to free up their relationships and construct new ways of being with each other. This is what is critical and ultimately what leads to change" (214). Aron sees insight and new forms of interpersonal engagement as working synergistically as Gill (1993) had noted: "We are, of course, on the familiar ground of whether it is insight or experience that is mutative. Clearly, not only may both be, though I grant that experience alone is more likely to be successful than insight alone, but the interactive perspective makes clear that insight is simultaneously an experience, while experience, as I suggested, is simultaneously an 'insight'" (116). And, in concluding his 1994 book, Gill stated, "What is mutative is not solely insight but insight in the context of new experience" (156). Gill cites Jacobs (1990) who wrote that "insight and 'corrective' experiences have in fact turned out to be rather intimate partners. They are not, as we were once taught, mutually exclusive processes technically and theoretically words apart" (454). Jacobs continues, "They are rather, synergetic forces in treatment, on paving the way for the other, each important, each contributing in essential ways to the therapeutic action of psychoanalysis" (454). Gill (1984) had stated previously that "in prevailing theory the role of new experience in bringing about change is understated" (172). By 1994 Gill wrote that "[S]uggestions are appearing about how action and interpretation can be employed in combination for more effective therapy . . . sometimes a directive, a piece of advice, a suggestion about how to behave in a difficult situation may seem desirable to break an impasse or an obsessional vicious circle. The possible utility of such analyst actions seem much more acceptable with the recognition that interaction is constant anyhow and with attention to the analysis of such interaction" (57). His interest in such combinations of action and interpretation was evident in his attending the meeting of the Society for the Exploration of Psychotherapy Integration in Chicago in 1988.

Levenson (1972), in elucidating what he saw as the three psychoanalytic models of the mind and change, had described the "machine" model where interpretation leading to insight is curative; the "communications" model of the early interpersonalists where clarifying and demystifying communication is curative; and the "organic systems model" where the analyst and patient become aware of the interpersonal binds in which the patient places others and where they find themselves trapped. According to Levenson, in classical theories, change was believed to occur through the lifting of repression and insight through interpretation, but in contemporary theories change occurs from new experience and the awareness of interpersonal entanglements. Attention is directed to what was avoided. Change comes about from elaborating patterns of experience. For Levenson (1972) and Witenberg (1987) insight follows change.

Mitchell (1997), building on Levenson's interpersonal model, contrasted the interpretation—insight model with the model of relational psychoanalysis by describing the process of "bootstrapping" where analyst and patient must somehow pull themselves "up by their bootstraps" out of the interpersonal entanglement in which they find themselves inevitably as the patient plays out repetitive interactive patterns. He contrasted his model of change with the interpretation-insight model. Mitchell and Aron clearly move to a new model, not excluding insight, of course, but not seeing it as the primary mode of therapeutic action the way some of their predecessors had.

Wallerstein (1995b) dedicates two chapters to the issue of new experiences, focused upon the concept of new experiences in relationships as conceived by Stone, Loewald, and later theorists. Loewald (1960) stated, "While the fact of an object-relationship between patient and analyst is taken for granted, classical formulations concerning therapeutic action and concerning the role of the analyst in the analytic relationship do not reflect our present understanding of the dynamic organization of the psychic apparatus (16). Later he says that "The analytic process . . . consists in certain integrative experiences between patient and analyst as the foundation for the internalized version of such experiences: reorganization of ego, 'structural change'" (25). Later Loewald (1988) commented that his view of the analyst's role as educator and parent was not limited to the opening phase of analysis as Gitelson (1962) had suggested. Cooper (1988) acclaimed Loewald a revolutionary who used "new ideas of interpersonal interaction and communication as his inspiration for a new description of the method of analytic therapy" (19).

Valenstein (1983) had commented: "If insight is not enough, if insight in itself does not quite do it, does not lead to definitive change, then we must consider other factors" (354). Although Valenstein believed in the interpretation-insight model for neurotic patients, he suggested "more interactive and experiential therapeutic features" (362) for sicker patients. De Jonghe, Rijnierse, and Janssen (1992) concurred that interpretation leading to insight was the most important factor in the analytic process, but argued that another factor, "the analyst's support leading to a specific experience by the patient . . . has long been a controversial issue" (475–76). Later they state, "It is clearly not the support in itself that is mutative, but the experience it provokes" (484). Summers (2003), more recently, has also elaborated upon the creation of "new ways of being and relating" (394) in psychoanalysis in his response to Stolorow's (1994) views about the therapeutic action of interpretations.

The "new experiences" model of therapeutic action is more comprehensive than the interpretation-insight model. "New experiences" includes, of course, new awareness or new insight and new meanings of experiences that might come through interpretations or otherwise. These new experiences may be arrived at through analysis of transferential processes or through a number of other avenues. The extent to which transference is analyzed will still differentiate psychoanalysis from other approaches. In the new experiences model in psychoanalysis it is still assumed that almost always, if not always, something unconscious underlies the patient's problem whether it is declarative or procedural in nature. The new experiences model, however, allows for the possibility of other therapeutic interventions, especially those intended to help the patient explore unconscious conflicts and disavowed aspects of self. It also allows, as described by Bromberg and others, for the exploration of conscious, yet conflicting self-states that are not experienced simultaneously. The psychoanalytic approach is an excellent one for investigating the role of unconscious factors on experience. Gestalt psychotherapists have developed excellent techniques for helping patients become aware of disavowed aspects of experience. Cognitive psychotherapists, on the other hand, have spelled out techniques that are effective in helping patients deal with conscious aspects of their experiences that are creating problems in their lives. A new experiences model in psychoanalytic theory allows psychoanalysts to include these approaches to addressing conscious thoughts while still engaging in psychoanalysis. More will be said about these approaches later.

IMPLICATIONS OF THE CURRENT MODELS OF THE SELF AND THE MIND FOR THE CHANGE PROCESS: NEW EXPERIENCES AND NEW MEANINGS OF EXPERIENCE

When the self is thought of as composed of an experiencing, phenomenal self with nonverbal sensory aspects and tendencies toward behavioral activation and inhibition, as well as a symbolizing self with nonverbal symbolic aspects in addition to verbal symbolic ones, new possibilities present themselves as entry routes to change. Freud's model of change was a disease model in which an unconscious pathogen was removed from the unconscious by the process of interpretation. Psychoanalysts have developed the most comprehensive method to date for understanding the meanings people make of their existence and for the integration of various self-representations, especially unconscious ones. But as we have seen, contemporary models of the therapeutic action, especially in relational, interpersonal, self psychology, and intersubjective approaches to psychoanalysis, have focused upon new experiences themselves and not simply the meanings of experiences as a route to change. Our current models of the self and the mind suggest that it is not only by making the unconscious conscious or integrating unconscious processes into the self-theory through free association, as important to change as these processes may be, but also by integrating various aspects of already conscious experiences, changing one's conscious thinking, behaving in new ways, and so on, that change occurs. New thoughts, new sensations and feelings, new images, new behaviors—all become potential avenues to change. Conceptualizing therapeutic action from the standpoint of new experiences provides psychoanalysis a framework compatible with learning theory and emotion theory in psychology. Gabbard and Westen (2003) have also argued that the interpretation model of therapeutic action is no longer sufficient for describing how analysts conceive of change within psychoanalysis and that "secondary strategies" (834) can contribute meaningfully to change. They ask that psychoanalysts consider not what is and what is not "psychoanalytic," but instead what is "therapeutic" (826).

Limitations of the Interpretation-Insight Theory of Change

The strength of psychoanalytic theory came from Freud's abandonment of trauma theory and the investigation into the meanings and fantasies people make of their experiences—the secrets of vast inner worlds. This has also become its weakness. Although psychoanalytic theory(ies) can account for the etiology of difficulties in living and provides a theory for changing the meanings of experience and our representations of self, others, and the world, interpretation-insight theory of change does not adequately address problems stemming from our animal consciousness, the aspects of our functioning that are linked to desires for survival, and extrinsic factors that affect the more primitive areas of the brain—the type I emotional responses described by LeDoux (1996). Learning and trauma theories have more adequately addressed how to understand and approach such problems. Only a new experiences model can account for such changes. In addition, changes outside awareness, such as those described by Squire and Kandel (1999) cannot be accounted for by the interpretation-insight model. I shall elaborate more on these processes of change shortly.

Indulge me to report the experiences of my dog Sgt. Pepper for a minute. Sgt. Pepper hit one of the tripod legs of a black, metal outdoor barbeque grill one day, resulting in its falling over, making a loud bang (fortunately, it was not hot). Subsequently he would bark ferociously at any large, black object, like the black lobster pot. Many fears of people are learned, such like Sgt. Pepper learned to fear large, black pots, and we do not need to look for unconscious meanings to understand the fear whereas other fears may have unconscious and/or more generalized meanings. Talking about the fears with people may help—explaining what happened and why it is unlikely to happen in different situations where the fear is irrational. With fears that are physiologically conditioned, however, talking alone does not seem to help much. We see this especially with women who have been sexually abused as children, although other types of abuse may result in a similar sort of paralysis. When danger signs occur with men, these women simply freeze.

Wachtel (1992) is the psychoanalyst who has enumerated five limitations of the psychoanalytic perspective more articulately: (1) an overemphasis upon early childhood determinants of problems in living; (2) an overemphasis on insight as leading to change; (3) a lack of clarity about the process of change and under-utilization of Freud's revised anxiety theory; (4) insufficient attention to the role of social skills; and (5) the importance of active interventions. Regarding the reliance on insight, Wachtel has argued that psychoanalysts claim post hoc that insights are only intellectual when they do not seem to work. Wachtel argues that new experiences generally, not just in the relationship with the therapist, disconfirm neurotic expectations. Others, such as Goldfried (1980) and Curtis (1991a), have argued that these risk-taking behaviors are essential to change.

Wachtel finds the process of "working through" in psychoanalysis rather vague and that Dollard and Miller's (1950) description of the extinction of anxiety captures better the implications of Freud's (1926) insights. Similarly, learning social skills requires considerable observation and practice. Although Wachtel discusses these deficits in terms of experiences avoided due to anxiety, his inclusion of the necessity of observation points out that for some people bad habits are simply learned by imitation or more constructive ways of behaving not known. In regard to active interventions, Wachtel thinks that the possibilities are too potentially useful and Freud's work too valuable "to be embalmed in a method that was essentially a preliminary, early-20th-century stab at how to apply the new insights" (343).

The Movement from Experiences to Meanings
of Experiences in Freudian Psychoanalysis

Freud's psychoanalysis underwent a major change when he abandoned the seduction theory, a theory of actual experiences, in favor of his theory of Oedipal wishes. At that time psychoanalysis became focused upon fantasies and the meanings of experiences in a way that has brought about an elaborate understanding of the mind. Since that development, however, other clinicians have attempted to deal with realities themselves while classical psychoanalysis in the Freudian tradition has remained interested in meanings, especially unconscious ones. Ferenczi treated patients who had experienced the reality of sexual abuse (e.g., Clara Thompson) and found that he needed techniques other than the ones Freud was advocating. From the beginning, the reality of trauma and the failure to find early childhood precursors to the inability to master traumatic symptoms has been a problem for the interpretation-insight model of therapy.

In a 1920 paper by Freud (not published until 1956) Freud reasserted his view that the neurotic symptoms from war stemmed from psychological conflict and the repression of the desire to flee the terrors of war to avoid the experience of shame. Relying upon Freud's theories which were prevalent after World War II in Germany, the German government claimed that the posttraumatic neuroses of concentration camp survivors were reactions related to childhood abuse and refused to pay reparations (Horowitz 1999). Research by Eitinger (1971) resolved this issue by finding that 99 percent of Norwegian concentration camp victims suffered symptoms after the war and that adult traumatization had caused their reactions. The failure to use methods to address conscious experiences and conditioned emotional reactions that have not been symbolized still plagues some psychoanalytic treatments intent on finding unconscious meanings, although there are notable exceptions (e.g., Saporta, as reported in Ostow and Bates, 2000). As discussed earlier, traumatic experiences are not encoded symbolically (van der Kolk, 1994, 1999).

Freud attempted to connect bottom-up processes with top-down ones—the biological drives with the meaning-making system of the ego. Although change may occur through greater conscious acceptance of previously unconscious biological impulses, current research and clinical experience indicate that there are many other routes to change. As discussed earlier, within psychoanalysis itself there has been increasing attention to change through greater awareness of relational patterns without specific reference to biological drives or processes in the interpersonal and relational schools and somewhat, perhaps, to various sorts of wishes, especially interpersonal ones, in the Freudian tradition (Luborsky and Crits-Christoph 1990; Luborsky

1998). At the same time there has been an awareness of changes in ways of relating through experiences that are not interpreted and not ever necessarily made conscious (Lyons-Ruth 1998; Tronick 1998). This tendency has led some psychoanalysts to reconsider the role of the body (Aron and Anderson 1998; McDougall 1989), somato-sensory processes (Leuzinger-Bohleber and Pfeifer 2002), and emotion (Spezzano 1993) in psychoanalysis and leads us to rethink the nature of therapeutic action and routes to change. When we think of our model of therapeutic action as one of new experiences, we can expand our repertoire of approaches beyond the interpretation of unconscious processes.

SUMMARY AND CONCLUSION

The interpretation-insight model of change in psychoanalysis has been replaced. Psychoanalysis has moved to a new experiences model, with insight only one type of new experience among many. As important as transferential processes are, an overemphasis on the interpretation of transference (referring specifically to interventions related to the relationship with the therapist) as the major source of therapeutic action still occurs in the psychoanalytic literature. The new experiences model of change brings to the fore other possibilities, namely a change in already conscious experiences, belief systems, and the controversial issue of suggesting fantasies and behaviors. When symptoms themselves are a problem apart from any other meanings they may have, a new experiences model of change allows for addressing those symptoms while maintaining a psychoanalytically informed treatment addressing broader meanings, both conscious and unconscious, that these symptoms may serve. This model also allows a flexibility to use many other routes to change developed by psychoanalysts, other therapists, and facilitators of change in other cultures not constrained by the interpretation-insight model.

Chapter 7

Top-Down and Bottom-Up Processes: Focusing on the Experiencing Self

Frances tells me that she had a very moving experience in her yoga class. A memory came to her—she must have been under two years of age—when she attended a yoga class with her mother. She recalled the presence of the individuals doing yoga and a feeling of "peace, love and awareness." There was one person who seemed to love her especially. She had begun to cry in her yoga class and cried a long time afterwards about the loss of that person and that time. Her parents had separated shortly thereafter and she had lived only with her mother.

"I'm scared of connection," she states, and cries.

"What makes you scared?" I ask.

"It has to end—they have to stop it or I do." She then tells me that a friend had talked about her own therapist's similarity to her guru. "Your eyes remind me of my father's—wise and kind," Frances then says.

"You've been afraid to connect with me, but you are letting yourself," I say. She nods and smiles. It was a moment for which I had long hoped. Frances seemed to be recalling a nonverbal experience that was symbolized or abstracted nevertheless. She was able to connect her experience with me, her father, and with other people who emanated love and peace.

Thinking of change as involving both top-down and bottom-up processes allows us to think about the potential effectiveness of types of interventions derived from various theoretical approaches to psychotherapy. The symbolic system has been the forte of psychoanalysis, especially in regard to unconscious meanings. As has been noted, however, the emphasis within this tradition has been largely upon interpretations and the verbal system.

Historically, psychoanalysis has relied primarily upon interventions directed at verbal associations and the meaning system. Interventions directed at sensory imagery and behavior, however, may impact more directly the emotional limbic system or trigger networks not activated verbally. Such interventions are consistent with the new experiences model of change and what we know about the brain. I shall now discuss what we know about the brain, attention to sensory processes, and then how behavioral interventions might be integrated into psychoanalytically oriented treatments.

THE TRIUNE BRAIN AND TWO ROUTES TO BEHAVIOR

MacLean (1973) described three separate and relatively independent subsets of the human brain—the reptilian complex, the limbic system, and the neocortex, although his view may be too simplified (Reiner 1990). The reptilian and limbic systems are more related to behavior and emotional processing whereas the neocortex deals more with meaningful processing. Cognitive scientists have referred to "top-down" processes, starting with the symbolic system of the neocortex, and "bottom-up" processes, starting with physiological or sensory-motor systems. Indeed, Goldapple, Segal, Garson, Lau, Bieling, Kennedy, and Mayberg (2004) demonstrated that talk therapy and psychoactive drugs acted on different parts of the brain, so that these two routes to change can be seen as complementary. As suggested, interventions directed to sensory processes may also activate networks in the limbic system responsible for emotional processing more directly than verbal associations.

According to LeDoux's (1996) neural model of anxiety, the amygdala within the limbic system plays a crucial role in the appraisal of danger because it receives not only "quick and dirty" sensory inputs via the thalamus, allowing for rapid responses on the basis of limited information, but also more detailed information via longer and slower neural pathways from the hippocampal and cortical regions. Once the amygdala has been activated, it may influence a range of cognitive processes. Bucci (1997) has suggested that the nature of change in psychoanalysis consists of links foraged between three systems—two symbolic systems, one of language and the other of images and a subsymbolic (nonverbal, sensory) system. The symbolic system is equivalent to what I have called the meaning system, whereas the subsymbolic system is related to the sensory-motor aspects of survival and threats to physical well-being shared by animals. The interpretation-insight model of change assumed this sort of linking between a meaningful (verbal and symbolic) context and emotions, especially during the analysis of transference. In spite of this assumption, Freud's belief in the supremacy of rational, verbal process had a profound effect upon the development of psychoanalysis.

It is widely believed that conscious thought involves processing by the hippocampus (Squire 1987), although such processing does not appear to be sufficient for consciousness. The research has now differentiated some types of fear responses learned by Pavlovian conditioning that are processed through the amygdala without involvement of the hippocampus (LeDoux 1996) which is required for any sort of learning related to context (Fanselow 2000). The absence of direct connections from the lateral prefrontal cortex to the amygdala "may be related to why talk therapy for psychiatric conditions that involve amygdala-related conditions is relatively inefficient" (LeDoux 2002, 292).

Behavioral therapy is more dependent on extinction processes involving the medial prefrontal cortex. LeDoux continues, "The direct connection of the PFC-M [medial prefrontal cortex] with the amygdala may explain why cognitive behavioral therapy is more efficient for certain fear/anxiety related problems" (292).

The research on fear responses not mediated by the hippocampus and cortex helps us understand traumatic experiences. Whereas arousal of the amygdala enhances recall when the arousal is at a moderate level (Phelps, 2005) the work of Squire and Zola-Morgan (1991) indicates that high-level stimulation of the amygdala interferes with hippocampal functioning, inhibiting semantic representation and cognitive evaluation and semantic representation: "Memories are then stored in sensorimotor modalities: somatic sensations and visual images" (van der Kolk 1999, 314). The substantial literature on the psychobiology of posttraumatic stress disorders (van der Kolk 1987, 1994; Friedman, Charney, and Deutch 1995; van der Kolk, McFarlane, and Weisaeth 1995) indicates that flashbacks and nightmares can be understood as eidetic (photographic) memory disconnected from context. Extreme stress produces cognitive and behavioral "shutting down" and freezing (Leaton and Borszcz 1985).

The associative learning process follows the principles of classical conditioning to environmental stimuli. An example of this would be a panic attack precipitated by helicopter noise. Gunfire, for example, may produce nonassociative neuronal responses. Van der Kolk (1994) stated that this sort of arousal is activated when conscious control over limbic system activity declines, as under stress and during sleep. Intense stimulation of the amygdala may interfere with hippocampus functioning and the linguistic and symbolic categorization and organization essential to meaning and narration, leading to sensorimotor, affective, and somatic memories without symbolic or semantic coding. One study (Rauch et al., 1996) looked at flashbacks occurring during script-driven imagery. Although activity increased in some areas, activity was decreased in Broca's area, which would be required to find words related to these experiences. It seems reasonable to think these sorts of reactions that do not involve symbolic processes require some sort of therapeutic technique other than free verbal association and interpretation. When fear responses are conditioned by pairing words with shock and then people are assured that the shock will not happen again ("instructed extinction"), for example, electrodermal responses take a while to diminish and require exposure to the previously threatening stimulus in order to be eliminated completely (Lipp and Edwards 2002).

These studies all demonstrate reactions that are not related to the verbal symbolic system and that require traditional behavioral interventions to change. Although psychoanalysts and other therapists may not wish to be involved in helping people with such problems and may prefer to refer patients elsewhere for suitable treatment, a comprehensive theory of psychological change must account for these processes. I shall address ways to integrate behavioral treatments into psychoanalytically oriented treatments later in this chapter. For now, first I would like to discuss further the importance of attention to top-down conscious experiences and then discuss more "bottom-up" processes such as sensory experiences— the body and the use of visual imagery—all aspects of the experiencing self. These interventions do not involve any philosophical incompatibility with traditional psychoanalytic approaches and have been used widely in many behavioral treatments, as well as psychoanalytic ones.

"TOP-DOWN" PROCESSES:
REGULATING MEANING SYSTEM ROUTES

Both top-down and bottom-up processes are essential for effective functioning and creative living. The poet, playwright, and filmmaker Jean Cocteau (1947, 56) expressed the interplay of these processes well: "These unknown forces work deep within us . . . and when they burden us and oblige us to conquer the kind of somnolence in which we indulge ourselves like invalids who try to prolong dream and dread resuming contact with reality . . . we can believe that this work comes to us from beyond. . . . For it is at this moment that consciousness must take precedence over the unconscious and that it becomes necessary to find the means that permit the unformed work to take form." Just how is it that conscious processes can be aided in taking over?

More Attention to Conscious Thoughts

From the dearth of writing in psychoanalysis on how conscious factors affect experience and the abundance of writings on how unconscious factors affect experience, one might get the impression that psychoanalysts think that conscious thoughts never lead to problems in living. Sometimes, however, it is conscious thoughts themselves that are troubling. Often, conscious constructs, attributions, and interpretations affect reactions to other events. Recently, several articles in psychoanalytic journals have addressed consciousness (Busch 2004; Gabbard and Westen 2003; Solms 1997), with Gabbard and Westen suggesting the use of techniques from cognitive psychotherapy in psychoanalysis. The psychoanalytic literature itself provides guidance for dealing with conscious problems related to transference and conflict, but not necessarily other troubling conscious thoughts. (A major exception is Wachtel's 1996 book, *Therapeutic Communication*.) Beck and Ellis, both trained as analysts (Gurman and Messer 1997) although cognitive therapists, noted common sorts of conscious dysfunctional thinking, such as catastrophizing and categorical thinking. There is nothing inherent in psychoanalysis that prevents pointing out the sorts of dysfunctional thinking, such as catastrophizing and categorical thinking, noted by Beck (1979) and other cognitive therapists. As we have seen in the research demonstrating spreading activation among anxious patients, this group of people can benefit from help with inhibiting such processes and substituting more beneficial ways of thinking. Psychoanalysts likely question dysfunctional beliefs frequently, although such questioning is not related to the traditional interpretation-insight model of change. A clinical example will illustrate the sort of intervention I mean.

A patient seemed happy but reluctant to let me know—to act in a way that would indicate she felt so. When I inquired about what was going on, she explained, "I don't want to be too happy—you know—all laughter ends in tears." I said I didn't know what she was talking about. She said, "You know, the old phrase—'All laughter ends in tears.'" I said I had never heard of this phrase. She seemed very surprised. I asked where she had heard it. "My mother said it all the time," she responded. Her mother was a Jewish woman from Austria who escaped with her family to the forests during the war and hid in cramped quarters often during much of it. It was understandable that her mother had learned and repeated this phrase. In this case, pointing out the dysfunctional implications of this accepted belief was useful.

As discussed earlier, beliefs are not only developed through the association of experiences, but are also transmitted through the family and culture. Beliefs and belief systems, such as religion and other cultural word views, have major impacts upon people's lives. These aspects of existence need to be addressed specifically when they lead to dysfunctional feelings and behaviors. Reinecke and Freeman (2003) state that clinicians who conceptualize patients dynamically often report using cognitive techniques. Addressing dysfunctional beliefs is not consistent, however, with either the interpretation-insight or the new relationship models of change. I shall mention a few examples here to clarify what I mean.

A conflict frequently comes up between religious values and feelings of aggressiveness. The issue is not one of being unconscious of aggressive feelings, but of trying to suppress them because they are believed to be wrong. An example is that of a patient brought up in a Catholic family. His wife had been raped before they were married. He felt very angry at the man who had raped her, but his religion had taught him that he should not even feel as if he wanted to kill the rapist. I explained that this was a fundamental difference between psychoanalysis and his religion. I said something like the following: "Your religion teaches that it was wrong to feel like wanting to kill someone. Psychoanalysts think, on the other hand, that all people do have such feelings. What is important is not to act on these feelings. People like you who have never physically hurt someone are less likely to act on such feelings when they are fully aware of them. There is a large difference between fantasy and reality. Psychoanalysts think that it is helpful to allow all feelings and thoughts into awareness, but not necessarily to act upon them." When no one was home the young man then went through a number of episodes of screaming and attacking the rapist in fantasy. After doing this he was much less anxious and able to act more assertively in his work.

A woman in a group said that if she told her father she was moving out, he would have another heart attack and die. She felt it was wrong to act in a way that would kill her father. The group members told her that she should tell her father that it was not right morally for him to tell her this—that a father should want his daughter to grow up and function on her own. She became convinced that the group members were right and began to speak with her father about moving out on her own.

These examples, I think, are quite typical of work that goes on frequently in psychoanalysis and psychoanalytic therapy. Although there is nothing "psychoanalytic" about these interventions, I am arguing that these conscious beliefs have major effects upon patients and should be addressed not only in any therapy, but also in the theory of change.

Although there may be unconscious determinants of dysfunctional thinking and behavior, and although becoming aware of such determinants may be helpful, such awareness does not necessarily lead to change when they stem from deficits in learning. For example, there is no reason that knowing one has few friends as a consequence of not being interesting will lead to a change in behavior. Not being "interesting" can come from a deficit in learning, not just from conflict. With a patient from a rather deprived background, who had nothing to say at dinner parties with her journalist husband's friends, I inquired if she read the newspaper or watched television news before going to the dinner parties. She did not, but when tried this, she found it worked quite well. Such a deficit is not related to the sorts of arrests at developmental stages described by psychoanalysts, but is a simpler type of deficit in learning associated more frequently with lack of education or other sociocultural factors.

Milton (2001) has recently argued that although psychoanalysts routinely use cognitive interventions, there is a loss if the psychoanalytic stance collapses. On the other hand, she argues that there are certain patients who cannot tolerate the psychoanalytic situation. The psychoanalytic stance is providing deeper emotional work and allowing for more irrational experiences. In preventing the overuse of cognitive solution-oriented techniques at the expense of full awareness of troubling emotions, Stiles et al. (1990) have suggested that patients must start from the "left" hand of experiencing troubling feelings and move to the cognitive focus on the "right" hand that helps in coping with, or mastery of, the emotions and thoughts. Whereas cognitive techniques are lacking in the first sort of experience (Holmes 1998), psychoanalysts do not emphasize coping skills to the extent cognitive-behavioral therapists do.

THE "PRIMITIVE" BOTTOM-UP SURVIVAL SYSTEM: SENSORY-MOTOR ROUTES

Focus on Sensory Experiences

We know that memories are very influenced by context (Bower 1981). When people are depressed, they are more likely to recall sad memories. But the memories people report are even influenced by reading a sad or a happy list of words. Although psychotherapists are often limited to inquiring verbally about what has happened and how someone is feeling, taking someone to the actual situation in which an emotional reaction occurs or in which a traumatic event actually happened will elicit a much stronger feeling. Readers are likely familiar with the Hitchcock film *Vertigo*. Not until the Jimmy Stewart character returns to the tower of the church does he remember exactly what happened. Sights, sounds, and smells eliciting memories are an everyday occurrence, with Proust's taste of the madeleine bringing forth memories of his childhood likely being the most famous example. When therapists inquire about the sensory aspects of a situation—what is visualized, heard, smelled, tasted, and felt tacitly—patients often recall memories that have eluded them with fewer specific cues. The procedure of using sensory imagination to stimulate emotional responses is the technique employed in "method" acting developed by Stanislavski and Strasberg so that an actor can not only experience an emotion, but lead people in the audience to experience it as well. Classes in method acting use a procedure of relaxation and sensory exercises in each session prior to engaging in scene work. The relaxation exercises include both muscle relaxation and a process of "talking out." In this talking out process, students say whatever comes to mind, just as in psychoanalysis. Other acting students are doing the same thing, so there is some possibility that other students or the teachers will hear what they are saying. To the extent that they can feel free to talk in this situation, they are doing something similar to free association. The difference, however, is that the others present are not supposed to be listening and will not respond. This relaxation seems to be a way of helping the actors feel private in public and tap into the ways of being, including the emotions they feel in a particular role.

In order to have an affective experience on the stage, Strasberg (1991) tells us, actors must draw from both sense memory and emotional memory. Method actors engage in sense memory exercises in which they must recall particular sounds, smells, and tastes and feel them on stage. For example, they must feel grass under their feet or sunshine. They go through moments of feeling they "have it' or they "don't have it." This sort of sensory experience seems closer to the emotions than simply talking about experiences. The teacher is constantly reminding them to "get out of their heads." Bucci (1997), as mentioned previously, has argued that the use of vivid language in psychoanalysis allows connections between what she calls the symbolic, generally the language, system, and the nonsymbolic, or sensory-emotional system and that these connections are the essence of change in psychoanalysis.

I have had at least twelve actors trained in the "method" in treatment. The images evoked in the acting studio have often brought about forgotten experiences. Jack, for example, was trying to imagine being in a sanctuary in one of his exercises. In class he had recalled the appearance, sounds, smells, and so on, of the church he attended before he was five years old. When he came to therapy the next day he was still remembering being there with his grandmother. He disliked the church—it was in a poor neighborhood, dark inside, and rather depressing to see. When he began to talk about the experience in therapy, he recalled missing his grandmother's funeral because he was scheduled to be in a college friend's wedding in California that weekend. He went to a wake and then left town the next day, his mother having told him that she didn't think his grandmother would have wanted him to miss his best friend's wedding. He had never mourned his grandmother's death and cried and cried during our session. I was aware that he felt his grandmother was much more loving and warm than his mother, but I was not aware that he had not mourned her death. Although he might have somehow gotten around to this eventually, I am not certain that he would have had it not been for the sanctuary exercise.

Therapists who work with patients who have been traumatized frequently have found that descriptions by patients of the sensory impressions elicit recollections that patients often have not remembered for a long time (Davies and Frawley 1994). Therapies oriented specifically towards getting at affect often inquire "Where in your body do you feel that?" The focus on the body work has also been emphasized by Gestalt psychotherapists who ask patients to exaggerate a movement in order to become more fully aware of it. Often the patient then spontaneously explains the meaning of the movement.

In addition to a focus upon sensory experiences to elicit affect, such a focus can be therapeutic in itself. When people have experienced traumas, their flashbacks and other symptoms—not simply the meanings of these traumatic experiences—are disturbing. Both meditation and twelve-step programs encourage people to focus upon the sensory experiences of the moment and to create positive moments when thoughts about the meanings of experiences are all upsetting. The relaxation that comes from this sort of sensory focus is apparent in the increasing popularity of spas and massage. At spas people receive facials and various body treatments, such as mud baths, often accompanied by sounds. Many writings have now suggested a link between psychotherapy and mindfulness (Linehan 1993; Martin 1997) and Buddhist meditation techniques (Epstein 1996; Safran 2003).

Flashbacks and physiological symptoms in the presence, actual or imagined, of certain images, often occur in patients who have been traumatized. There appears to be a general recognition that traumatic experiences themselves have negative repercussions, not only the meanings of these experiences. Although Freud had abandoned trauma theory in his focus upon the latent meanings of experiences, Ferenczi (1955, 1985), in his treatment of difficult patients, took very seriously the actual experiences that had taken place. Recently, in treating so many patients who have experienced sexual abuse, war, torture, natural disasters, terrorism, and so on, many analysts have incorporated the work of van der Kolk (1987), Herman (1992), Putnam (1996), Davies and Frawley (1994), and others regarding trauma and developed more fully their own forms of treatment. Here there is recognition that conscious experiences, and a lack of defenses, not unconscious factors, are a major source of the patient's problems. Because traumatic experiences often have sequelae that occur as dissociated self-states, therapy with patients suffering from such experiences has been the source of considerable recent literature. Although talking about traumatic experiences may desensitize patients over a period of time, as discussed previously, behavioral psychologists have found that a gradual exposure to frightening images, when a person is relaxed and when the images are presented in a fashion so that images that are not distressing are presented first, results more quickly in a decrease in symptoms.

Advocates of eye movement desensitization and reprocessing use another technique that will be discussed briefly later. Van der Kolk (1996) has cited research by Rauch and his colleagues indicating that when people with post-traumatic stress disorder are exposed to stimuli reminiscent of the trauma, they show an increase in perfusion of the areas in the right hemisphere associated with emotional states and autonomic arousal and a decrease in oxygen in Broca's area, a region of the left frontal cortex responsible for attaching words to internal experiences. Experiencing these images while relaxed and attaching words to the experiences, appears to be helpful.

The woman all covered with snakes

As mentioned in chapter 3, Huber (1965) gave an example of a Zen Buddhist nun who began to behave strangely after going to a large city for the first time. She was put to bed by the other nuns because she was terrified at the snakes she saw crawling over her body. Psychologists, psychiatrists, and physicians could do nothing. Finally, a famous Zen psychiatrist was brought in. The psychiatrist was there for only five minutes and then said, "I must leave now, but I shall come back to see you in a week. While I'm gone, I want you to do two things. First complain to no one. Say nothing of this matter to anyone. And second, observe the snakes very carefully so that when I return you will be able to describe their movements accurately to me" (3). In a week when the psychiatrist returned, the nun reported that when she observed the snakes carefully, they were gone.

This description exemplifies a change without any "psychoanalytic insight." The woman did, however, become more aware. Her view of her therapist, the monk, could not have been more positive. Her improvement shows the sort of change that can come about from getting someone to become aware of all the sensory details and plan to put them into words. The sort of awareness suggested by the monk represents a place where the work of psychoanalysts, therapists, and meditators, overlaps.

Thinking of the self as behaviorally activating — as having a motoric, enactive aspect — leads us to consider focusing on this aspect of experience as potentially therapeutic. If we think of the self as experiencer — the observing, perceiving I-self, the self as subject and agent, and not simply as the self-representation, we may think about altering conscious experiences themselves, not only the meanings of experience. When people have experienced traumas, when they have been betrayed by friends, colleagues, and family, when parents have driven their children crazy, and so on, attempts to alter the meanings of experience may be futile. When people have lost all that they have attempted to create in their lives, mourning and starting all over are extremely difficult and attempts to do so may be discouraging. Focus upon sensory experiences in the moment; physical movement can provide a relief from the problems of meaning. Meditators have long suggested a focus upon breathing. Increasingly, therapists are recommending breathing retraining and exercises (Fensterheim 1994), and some psychoanalysts have even suggested a focus upon breathing (Eigen 1977). Barlow (2002), a behavioral psychologist, has developed an effective short-term procedure for inducing panic attacks in the laboratory and getting patients to learn how to stop them. Attention directed to any sort of individual physical exercise can provide a sense of control. Often patients seek out exercise on their own and mention it. If not, the degree of physical exercise makes sense as a typical area of inquiry.

THE BODY

Psychoanalysts have for a long time tried to get at phenomena that were not expressed verbally. Freud had, of course, discovered that what was not remembered was repeated. He had also stated in 1923 that the ego is "first and foremost a body–ego" (17). He wrote: "The ego is ultimately derived from bodily sensations, chiefly from those springing from the surface of the body. It may thus be regarded as a mental projection of the surface of the body" (16). In 1915, he had written that "affectivity manifests itself essentially in motor (i.e., secretory and circulatory discharge resulting in an (internal) alteration of the subject's own body" (1915a, 179n). Freud's interest in somatic experience declined, however, as he turned away from neurology towards psychoanalysis (Mikail, Henderson, and Tasca 1994). Ferenczi, in 1919, also tried to get at the bodily and muscular expressions of his patients, calling his technique "analysis from below" (cited in Lowen 1971, 12). In addition to enactments, Melanie Klein (1964, 1975), Winnicott (1954), Bion (1967), and Alexander and French (1946) noted somatizations and feelings within themselves that Bion and Klein labeled "projective identification." Reich (1949) and Lowen (1971) broke with psychoanalytic tradition by using techniques of intensive body contact with the patient, a practice most clinicians in a litigious society will eschew, even if it is effective.

Many therapists recently have been attempting to get at the communications of the body more directly (Aron and Anderson 1998; McDougall 1989; van der Kolk 1994). Getting at bodily sensations was, of course, something a large number of therapists outside psychoanalysis have advocated (Gendlin 1981; Greenberg and Safran 1987; Lowen 1971; Smith 1985, to name only a few).

Although the centrality of the body has remained important in psychoanalytic theory (Loewald 1980; Winnicott 1954), the movement away from

Freud's dual instinct theory left bodily concerns neglected in the focus upon interpersonal relationships. In a volume attempting to rectify this neglect, Aron commented: "By attempting to differentiate themselves from the Freudians, the interpersonalists may have created an atmosphere in which for analysts to acknowledge sexuality and the body as an area of focus in their clinical work was to risk being viewed as 'too Freudian'" (Aron and Anderson 1998, xxv–xxvi). Gill (1994) had distinguished between the "body as such" and the "body in terms of its meanings (139) and emphasized the metaphorical aspects of bodily processes. The chapters in *Relational Perspectives on the Body* (Aron and Anderson 1998) focus on these experiences, but most authors do not explicitly address the model of change inherent in directing attention to the body, perhaps implicitly assuming that an openness to bodily experience occurs in the relational encounter and that becoming aware of this experience, its verbalization, symbolization, and self-refection is transformative. An exception is Hopenwasser who discusses the different neural pathways related to somatic memories.

Grounding her discussion of work with a traumatized patient on the work of Fair (1992) and others, Hopenwasser (1998, 227) notes Fair's differentiation of cortical routes and subcortical (limbic system–brain stem) routes and that memories may be resistant to "reactivation via the usual cortical routes" (Fair, 56). Hopenwasser describes her work with a twenty-eight-year-old woman who had attempted suicide after the termination of a previous treatment. She began to recall experiences with her grandfather and somatic memories of pain and excitement during the night, reporting such experiences as the following one: "I'm laying on my stomach. He's over me. I have a feeling it's my grandfather; it's just a feeling. He's touching me all over—it's not sexual—it's cruel" (Hopenwasser 1988, 222–23). The patient's panic attacks and anxiety had decreased and she was moving to better jobs and higher salaries, but her fearfulness of men persisted. At this point Hopenwasser introduced eye movement desensitization and reprocesssing (Shapiro 2001). The patient then began to have sexual experiences in a nondissociated state and had maintained an intimate relationship for more than a year. Hopenwasser saw this procedure as getting more directly at the retrieval of mediated memories. Hopenwasser has also suggested that patients become certain parts of themselves. With a patient previously diagnosed as having dissociative identity disorder, Hopenwasser suggested that the crack-using part of the patient needed to participate in the treatment. At this point the patient "went into a trance and swiftly developed rhinorrhea, lacrimation, pilomotor activity on her arms (gooseflesh) and diaphoresis" (224). Within moments of switching back into other parts of herself, the physical symptoms stopped. Another patient was distrustful of taking medication. At Hopenwasser's request to work on those parts, the articulate, healthy woman "manifested a left facial droop, with subsequent uncontrolled salivary drooling and slurred speech" (224) and spoke about childhood years in a convent where she alleged she was given drugs, restrained, and sexually abused.

Smith (1985) instructs patients to close their eyes, relax, breathe comfortably, and check out their bodies to see what they find, noting anything that calls attention to itself. He goes on to say: "Just monitor your body, inch by inch, from the tips of your toes to the top of your head and down to the tips of your fingers. In particular, note any hot spots, cold spots, tight or tense muscles, pains, tingling, or anything happening in your body" (107). Fosha (2000) also gives an example of where this sort of inquiry can lead. When a patient reports a tingling in her face, the therapist asks the patient to focus on it and describe it. After a few minutes of floundering the patient recalls a consultation with a previous therapist who noted she had a hard time with feelings of anger. When the therapist asks for a specific example, the patient recalls her father getting angry outside a McDonald's and slapping her across the face (199). Fosha considers the visceral experience as the center point of the cycle of core affect and the hallmark of the affective model of change and "where it becomes differentiated from both academic (i.e., nonclinical) emotion theory and other psychodynamic (i.e., nonexperiential) treatments" (24–45).

Hopenwasser describes how the body seems to "'hold' information, as in a potential state, even if the associational pathways to mental representation are somehow blocked" (1998, 233). Sometimes sensations are felt in the analyst's body that may provide information about something the patient has experienced. Leuzinger-Bohleber and Pfeifer (2002), for example, described an analysis in which the analyst felt horrible pains and eventually found out that the mother of the patient had wanted to abort her. Leuzinger-Bohleber and Pfeifer present their understanding in the context of Edelman's (1989, 1992) ideas about embodied memory. My patient Andreas, whom I described in a previous chapter, experienced an embodied memory of deadness. A PhD candidate recently described a patient's spontaneously "embodying" an experience. She had discussed being punished by having to kneel on a cheese grater with her back straight and balancing a book on her head. She reported this with no emotion. When the therapist commented on the discrepancy between the content of the memory and the emotionless presentation, the patient asked if the therapist wanted to see how she used to kneel. The patient and therapist sat in silence for a few minutes and then the patient seemed to crawl back to her seat. For the first time she exhibited some show of emotion over the abuse, exclaiming, "I can't believe I did that, but I had no choice—my body just took me there."

GREATER USE OF VISUAL IMAGERY

Imagery also involves accessing memory structures that tie into physiological responses (Lang 1985; Foa and Kozak 1986). Lang has demonstrated that articulating verbally produces little physiological response whereas imagining the same material produces a strong response. The symbolic verbal system does not tie into the sensory/affective system as strongly as the imaginal system. Freud (1923) had stated, "Thinking in pictures . . . stands nearer to unconscious processes than does thinking in words, and it is unquestionably older than the latter, both ontogenetically and phylogenetically" (21).

The woman all covered with snakes described above provides an example of a change through increased visual imagery. The importance of the nonverbal system in change has been highlighted recently by a number of psychoanalysts. Beebe, Knoblauch, Rustin, and Sorter (2003) have argued that infants detect action and interaction sequences before symbolic forms of cognition begin toward the end of the first year and that many other transformations occur prior to adult forms of symbolic intelligence. They point out that psychoanalysis has addressed the concept of intersubjectivity primarily in the verbal/explicit mode whereas infant research has addressed this concept in the nonverbal/implicit mode of action sequences. They utilize the distinction between explicit (conscious) knowledge and implicit (unconscious) procedural and emotional knowledge.

Rosenblatt (2004) similarly has emphasized the role of procedural knowledge and the relevance to therapeutic interventions beyond interpretation. The importance of nonverbal exchanges within the treatment situation have also been noted by Pally (1998), Knoblauch (2000), and Levenson (2003). Pally (1998) stated, "Emotional and nonverbal exchange may play at least as much importance in analytic treatment as does verbal exchange (360). Galatzer-Levy (2004) described changes in a patient which he thought resulted from the analyst's calmness and "sighs and giggles" when confronted with what the patient believed to be very urgent pressing issues until, in the patient's words, his "fears slowly melted away."

Early on, before *The Interpretation of Dreams* (1900), Freud had used an imagery association method when he employed hypnosis. In this procedure he held the patient's head and encouraged a stream of visual pictures. He reported that patients began to see a succession of scenes related to central conflicts. It is likely that Freud viewed visual and auditory imagery as regressive or as primary process phenomena that needed to be verbalized. He decided against using imagery and remarked, "My therapy consists in wiping away these pictures" (Kosbab 1974, 284).

As images are an important part of mental representations, a focus upon them can be employed without contemplating a different theory of change from that of traditional psychoanalysis. Bucci (1997) has listed a number of the characteristics of speech which are high in connections between the sub-symbolic (sensory, nonverbal) and symbolic systems: concreteness, imagery, specificity, and clarity. As discussed previously, Bucci sees making links among the subsymbolic system, imagery, and words as key to the psycho-analytic process of change. Ahsen (1973) had a similar view. In developing his eidetic psychotherapy, he developed the concept of "Image, Somatic Correlates, and Meaning," always trying to link the three.

Ferenczi (1985) also inquired of patients what sort of image was occurring when various sorts of motor activity were taking place. For example, if a patient's foot were swinging, he might inquire what the patient was seeing. Jung (1916) advocated a procedure called active imagination. He believed that people became conscious of the images within only if they focused upon this world instead of the external one: "[W]hen we concentrate on inner pictures, and when we are careful not to interrupt the natural flow of events, our unconscious will produce a series of images which makes a complete story (1916, 172). According to Watkins (1976), Jung recommended the use of imagery in the following circumstances: (1) when the unconscious is obviously overflowing with fantasies; (2) to reduce the number of dreams, when there are too many; (3) when not enough dreams are being reported; (4) when someone seems to be under a sort of spell of indefinable influences; (5) when adaptation to life has been injured; and (6) when someone falls into the same hole again and again. He believed that these images and fantasies were superior to dreams in defeating resistance and shortening the analytic process. Jungians have continued to employ considerable work with imagery. Due largely to Jung's ostracism by Freud, and perhaps also because of the linkage with archetypes, this sort of imagery work does not seem to have had much impact upon mainstream psychoanalysts.

A number of therapies in Europe and Africa, however, used the directed daydream (Desoille 1945), guided affective imagery (Leuner 1975), and guided imagery (Edwards 2001), the latter being drawn from Teasdale's (1997) interacting cognitive subsystems model. The European therapies were variously known as "waking dream therapy," "dream therapy," and "oneiro-therapy" (from the Greek "oneiros" meaning "dream") (Fretigny and Virel 1968). Relaxation is often encouraged first, including muscle relaxation. The imagery is discussed along with associations and memories in order to obtain information about the desires, conflicts, and perceptions of the patient. Surprising images are especially explored. Leuner (1975) also investigated the use of imagery in Japanese Morita therapy. Fretigny and Virel claim four advantages for the use of imagery: (1) it can be used with people incapable of reflection because of their low level of sophistication; (2) the snares of rational thinking are avoided; (3) sterile rumination is avoided; (4) imagery is more directly linked to affective experience. Fromm (1955) also stated that more active methods than conventional free association are needed to access the patient's affect: "There are other active methods to stimulate free association. Let us assume you have analyzed the patient's relationship to his father, but want more unconscious material than he has offered in his association; you tell the patient: 'Now, concentrate on the picture of your father, and tell me what is the first thing that comes to your mind' . . . or, 'Visualize your father now, and tell me what is on your mind.' There seems to be only a slight difference in wording. However, there is a very great difference in the effect." Sullivan, also in the interpersonal tradition, was, like Freud, very focused upon language. He (1956) noted, however, that people may grow up with a set of visual or auditory experiences that continue to influence other experiences. Several authors have differentiated the functioning of systems related to words, images, and behaviors. Horowitz (1970) had proposed that we store behavior along three dimensions, a verbal-lexicon dimension, an imagery dimension, and a motor-enactive dimension. Even before Paivio's (1971) influential book on the dual coding systems, *Imagery and Verbal Processes*, Balint wrote to Ahsen after Ahsen's (1968) work on eidetic therapy was published, "I must say your results are so remarkable that they are somewhat difficult to accept. . . . Having published one book will not be accepted as final proof of all your claims" (cited in Ahsen, 1977, 15).

Reyher (1963) investigated imagery association within a psychoanalytic framework likely much further than any other clinician and developed a method involving spontaneous visual imagery he called "emergent uncovering psychotherapy." He examined such processes both clinically and in the laboratory. Noting two separate information processing systems—the analogic-synthetic and the semantic-syntactic modes, Reyher (1978) viewed neither images nor perceptions as "cognitive." Reyher (1963), Ahsen, and Horowitz all think that visual images evoke less defensiveness than verbalizations because people have not learned to censor images the way they have words. Morishige and Reyher (1975) found that emotional arousal as measured by the galvanic skin response was greater during visual imagery than during verbalization. Reyher (1978) noted that spontaneous visual imagery does not usually occur in an interpersonal relationship, but instead is a private event. He suggested a number of cues indicating that such visual imagery may be taking place—motor activity—"Your cheeks are getting red", vague words such as "upset" or "bothered," cutoff sentences, or general appearance—"You appear to be nervous" (56). His method was to ask patients to close their eyes and to tell him what they saw. If they opened their eyes, he inquired what was going on, noting that there could be a great deal of resistance to doing so. Patients often reported symptoms they could not explain, such as their feeling scared or their hearts pounding. This is a slightly different instruction from that of instructing patients to say "whatever comes to mind."

I was relieved to be freed of saying whatever came to mind in my own analysis. Arriving at psychoanalysis early in the day just after reading the morning newspaper, I found that the idea of "free associating" brought forth many thoughts of political and economic concerns. Realizing this, I questioned what I should be doing. It was helpful that my analyst said I should talk about what I was "experiencing," not what I was thinking. Often, when patients get stuck, analysts say, "What's going through your mind?" The alternative—asking "What are you seeing in your mind's eye?"—is a useful one.

Singer (1974, 1978, 2006), an interpersonal psychoanalyst, has spent a large part of his career investigating the effects of imagery, but his work, widely referenced in psychology, is not widely cited in the psychoanalytic literature. His research (1974) found that, during the behavioral technique of systematic desensitization, the critical factor turns out to be the imagery used by the patient, not the hierarchy of frightening situations. Although Kazdin (1976) did not find a correlation with vividness in imagery and behavior change, he did not take controllability into consideration. Intensely vivid imagery that one cannot control is obviously not helpful. Richardson (1969) had found that high vividness and high controllability are related to change.

Horowitz (1970, 1978), who has written extensively about imagery and cognition, has described five sorts of interventions that can be used in place of interpretive interventions which he sees as sometimes leading patients to feel defensive. Interpretive interventions could be used, however, and would tell patients what they are afraid of and why. For example, when images are not associated with words, Horowitz suggests (1978, 45) saying, "Describe your images to me in words" or "Tell me what that image means" rather than the interpretive "You do not let yourself describe those images you are having because you are afraid to think clearly about and tell me about those ideas." When words are not connected with images, he suggests "Let yourself think in visual images and report whatever you experience to me." If images are vague, the therapist can say "Try and hold onto those images and 'tune them up.'" If there is no connection between primary and secondary process images, "Let yourself kind of dream about this right now," and if there is an enactive presentation not translated into images, "Try to picture yourself in your mind with that posture and expression on your face."

The examples above are all of requests by the therapist for images during verbalization. Another possibility is simply to ask patients to report freely any images they see. Other possibilities for using images come from images that the patient brings. This may occur when simply speaking or in reporting a dream.

Gestalt therapists ask patients to "be" each person or object in a dream by actually saying "I am. . . ." This brings about more immediate experiences than asking patients to provide associations. Associations often leave patients at an intellectual level. Being another person or object brings awareness of somatic and emotional experiences which are often disconnected. When one of my patients began treatment, I noticed how "sweet" she always was. She was a struggling singer, working at another part-time job to earn a living. She complained of a variety of problems including not being able to tell her parents that she was a lesbian, not being assertive in general, and not getting anywhere in her singing career. When I asked her if she ever felt angry, she told me "no." Inquiring how she managed never to get angry did not get very far. I suggested that it was very important for her to get in touch with any feelings that might lead to anger. In the fifth session, she came in with a dream of a man attempting to kill her lover. I asked her to be the man. She got into the role quite well. When I asked her later if she had ever felt like killing someone, she told me "no." Later in the session, however, she mentioned that if a man ever took her girlfriend away, she would want to kill him. I pointed out that she had told me she had never felt that way. She realized the contradiction and could feel herself wanting to kill such a man.

The next session she came in and reported that she had found a new voice. Her singing teacher and her lover had noticed it as well. She still had difficulty being assertive, however. She described an incident when a choir leader reprimanded her for not being on time (early enough before a church service). She said nothing, but was aware of angry feelings. When I asked if she had any thoughts about what she might want to tell him, she told me "no." I then asked her to imagine being another woman whom she admired and had described as very assertive arriving at the church. She had no difficulty saying what this woman would tell the choir leader—"I've never been late before and I won't be again." I suggested imagining being this woman the next time she had angry feelings. This technique worked. I had not seen any opportunities for getting at her fears of being assertive with me. I think it would have been unlikely that she would have told me much, as she had never told her previous therapist that she was a lesbian. I have no reason to think that she would have told me, either, except that I had asked directly about romantic experiences with women in getting her history. I would like to point out that her fears of being abandoned by her parents were not unrealistic. I did not encourage her to tell them about her sexual orientation, knowing about their religious beliefs and behaviors toward other relatives. When her mother finally inquired if she were a lesbian after the television show in which Ellen DeGeneres came out and my patient told her "yes," her father refused to speak to her for about a year, writing to her that she was living in sin and would be condemned to eternal damnation. She eventually sent him enough materials from the gay and lesbian center for parents who were of a fundamentalist religious persuasion that he changed his position.

The power of actually becoming the different characters in a dream was again brought home to me when a patient was discussing her annoyance at the lack of empathy she received from a friend who smokes marijuana. This young woman had been a pot smoker herself. I asked what had led her to stop. (I had learned of the extent of the marijuana smoking when I inquired again how much pot she was smoking after a dream in which she was in the clouds.) She said it wasn't our discussion—and mentioned I had said something about the effects being greater than people realized. It was when I asked her to play the characters in the bad dream, she said. Not remembering which dream she was referring to, I asked which character. She responded "the retarded boy"—an experience she related to her feelings after smoking marijuana.

Linda told me she had struggled with an exercise in her acting class in which the students were told to be with a comforting object—a doll or stuffed animal. I asked her to be the object she had focused upon in order to get the experience more alive and less intellectualized. Very lively experiencing being the doll, she vacillated from her feelings with the acting teacher, her mother, and me in a way so that I wasn't sure which of us she was talking about. Linda had been taken care of by a foster mother for two months after birth and then placed for adoption with a mother who was quite cruel and controlling. Linda hated dolls, other than a G.I. Joe doll. She did have one doll, though, that she had mixed feelings about—a Raggedy Ann doll. (Her brother had Raggedy Andy.) She could connect with its hair. It was half comforting. The doll's face looked sad—maybe she didn't treat it right, she said. She and her brother did mean things—they pulled the dolls' pants down and humiliated them. I asked her to be the doll. She said, "I feel abandoned" and began to cry. "I feel vulnerable."

I said, "Helpless and hopeless."

She continued, "I felt like this in acting class last week. It hasn't come up for me in awhile. . . . I felt rage at Susan [the acting teacher]. She was the enemy. I felt like fighting on many levels once I got vulnerable and she didn't hurt me. I thought of my mom—I didn't trust her." When I asked how I was the enemy, she said that she would cry and I would attack her, as her mother had done, slapping her hands to make her cry more. I told her that I would abandon her, too, at ten o'clock when our session was over. The end of the sessions had been an issue with us, with the patient even breaking my clock in what she thought was an accident and also dreaming about clocks. The exercise with the doll helped her get in touch with her own feelings of abandonment in a way she never had before, as she obviously had no memory of being abandoned by her first two mothers. Significantly, some time after this session, Linda finally contacted the adoption agency to try to find her birth mother. The two have been seeing each other since that time.

Bosnak (2003) has described the way patients discuss their dreams as "embodied imagination" and has differentiated this state from one with "mental imagery." Although he apparently does not suggest that patients "become" the different characters in their dreams, they seem to do so spontaneously in the sort of trance state they enter. Bosnak comments that these different subjectivities are present as a multiplicity of existences. Bromberg (2003) notes that this sort of dissociation is normal, not pathological. Behavior therapies have often used imagery in the technique of systematic desensitization before employing direct exposure for the treatment of phobias. Wachtel (1977) argued that this process was similar to what psychoanalysts did when asking patients to speak about anxiety-provoking situations in a safe, relaxed atmosphere. Feather and Rhoads (1972) extended this technique to work with patients' warded-off wishes and fears. One patient who had a driving phobia for ten years feared he would hit pedestrians. He was told to imagine deliberately running over someone. He imagined such scenes with increasing enjoyment and his anxiety diminished so that he was able to drive across state within two weeks. Another patient experienced a writing phobia related to revealing secret information. The patient was asked to imagine deliberately disclosing all the secrets of his company by emptying all the file cabinets into the street. The phobia disappeared. This patient had spent years in psychoanalysis without any improvement and may even have become worse. The technique seems consistent with Freudian theory. The only difference is that a request is made for the patient to imagine something.

Imagery is crucial in eye movement desensitization and reprocessing therapy (Shapiro 2001). In this therapy, the patient is asked to imagine a troubling scene, to give a level of disturbance rating, and the belief associated with the scene. The therapist then engages in a series of hand movements simulating rapid eye movements and the patient is asked visually to follow the movements. The patient is next asked to provide a positive belief associated with the scene, to rate how true it feels, and to scan the body for sensations. Further assessments and applications of the eye movement technique are applied until the patient is desensitized. Although some of its advocates have insisted that the rapid eye movements or other bilateral stimulation of the brain is crucial in this therapy, other clinicians have seen the value as lying in the process of imagining upsetting scenes, reducing the stress level while imagining them, connecting the images to words and meanings, focusing on the bodily sensations, and connecting a positive belief with the upsetting situation. Some of the statements of the therapist are remarkably similar to those that had been advocated by Ahsen: "Let's start with seeing this guy. . . . What emotion are you feeling: Where do you feel it in your body? Keep that picture and the feeling of danger," and so on.

The traction gained by the use of images may come from a principle similar to that underlying the use of transference—the power of immediacy. When patients are describing what they are seeing, as when they are discussing their feelings toward the analyst, they are experiencing in the present moment. In speaking, when people become emotionally involved, they switch to the present tense. Although they are describing something in the past and have been using the past tense, they move to using the present tense. The principle of immediacy will be discussed further in the next chapter. Perls (1976) emphasized this principle in his deviation from psychoanalytic technique. As a phenomenological therapy, Gestalt therapists replaced the free association of psychoanalysis with focused awareness. Gestalt technique encourages a focus upon "the now." When patients are talking about experiences in the past, emotions can become more intense if the therapist inquires "Can you be there right now?" and encourages the patient to describe the sensory elements of the situation.

There is a reluctance to focus upon visual imagery among some psychoanalysts, likely stemming from the tradition in the "talking cure" of verbal free association. Talking has become a sacred route to change. Even an emphasis on dreams (and their imagery) has diminished among some psychoanalysts (cf. Blechner 2001). It is okay if the patient imagines something and keeps talking, but, strangely, it seems unusual for analysts to inquire what patients might be seeing as opposed to what they are thinking. It seems infrequent for analysts to suggest that the patient image (as opposed to imagine) something, to explore the ramifications of the image, and to suggest that the patient relax while imagining it if it is anxiety provoking. Here we have encountered the psychoanalytic bugaboo—suggestion. Many psychoanalysts believe suggestion, especially suggesting behavior, is to be avoided if possible. I shall now turn to this topic.

THE PSYCHOANALYTIC BUGABOO: SUGGESTION AND SUGGESTING BEHAVIOR

With well-functioning patients, there are many reasons not to suggest behaviors. For example, patients can think of them on their own, and suggestions might well undermine their confidence. Suggesting fantasies, however, is another matter. Certainly, analysts ask for fantasies much of the time, especially in regard to transferential issues. The question, "What is your fantasy?" is undoubtedly quite common. Ferenczi (1985) used a technique called "forced fantasy." Although "forcing" is a strong word, suggesting a fantasy is likely not problematic for most analysts.

Ferenczi (1926), of course, also suggested behavior. He requested "the patient upon occasion, in addition to free association, to act or behave in a certain way in the hope of gaining thereby . . . mental material that lay buried in the unconscious" (37). He commented that "experience later taught me that one should never order or forbid any changes of behavior, but at most advise them, and that one should always be ready to withdraw one's advice if it turned out to be obstructive to the analysis or provocative of resistance" (1928, 96). He believed that "analysis is preparation for suggestion" (1932, 270).

Strachey (1934) had described, of course, the trance-like state which the psychoanalytic patient enters—akin to that in hypnosis—that allows the analyst to make suggestions altering the patient's superego by introjection of a kinder and gentler one. Although analysts came to eschew the notion of suggestion, Strachey quoted Freud's use of the term: Freud (1921) had previously defined suggestion as "a conviction which is not based upon perception and reasoning, but upon an erotic tie" (128), with an erotic tie referring simply to positive feeling. He was very concerned lest a cure be attributed to suggestion, a remnant of the hypnotic roots of psychoanalysis. As Gill (1993) noted, no concept in psychoanalysis remains unscathed from the hermeneutic, constructivist-interactional turn. It is acknowledged in contemporary relational/interpersonal, and intersubjective psychoanalysis that the patient and the analyst are coconstructing meaning and experience. It is acknowledged that the analyst suggests experiences the patient may be avoiding. Then it is only one step further for the analyst to suggest experiences in fantasy.

Suggestion is implicit in any verbalization that changes the words of the patient. Gill (1993), for example, concedes, "In this changed perspective one does not ask whether a suggestion is appropriate or not, if by that one means that there is a single appropriate thing to do according to some pre-determined theory or practice. One asks, rather, what this interaction means. Suggestions, witting or unwitting or otherwise put, direct or indirect, are intrinsic to the process" (112). Hoffman (1993) described a scene from a television show called *Sessions* starring an analyst or therapist played by Elliott Gould. The patient was about forty years old and estranged from his father who was scared about his wife's illness and his feelings of helplessness. The therapist said to the patient regarding the father: "Maybe he needs someone to talk to."

The patient asked, "You mean a shrink-type person like you?" The therapist responded, "Actually, I was thinking of a son-type person like you." The patient then became reconciled with his father. Hoffman argues in favor of the use of suggestion in light of the long-term consequences for the man if the father had died without reconciliation.

Although psychoanalysts may feel comfortable about influencing thoughts, feelings, and fantasies, there is still a taboo against directly influencing behaviors. It is as if once made conscious, some psychoanalysts seem to think behaviors change automatically. Recent distinctions regarding declarative and procedural memory make it clear, however, that some behaviors are learned through repetition and not changed simply by thinking about them. I cannot make my body move a tennis racket well simply by thinking about how it should move, although this may help. Practice is necessary. Once I move my mirror to a different wall, I know in my declarative memory where the mirror now hangs, but for a few days I catch my body having turned automatically to the wall where the mirror was previously hung when I wished to look in a mirror without focusing upon my intention. Similarly, as I am thinking how I need to buy a new microwave, I find myself putting my cup of coffee into the microwave that I have just learned is no longer working.

Psychoanalysts have always been intent on respecting the patient. This has meant not imposing one's own value system on the patient or subtly influencing the patient's values. Scientists in the twentieth century have acknowledged that phenomena cannot be measured without influencing them—we are influencing a process by the very fact of observing it. Sullivan (1953) had applied this principle to the psychoanalytic process. The observation-participatory model of interaction assumes that there is no way to be a completely objective observer—that we are influencing the therapy process by the very fact of observing it, even if that was all that therapists did.

The resistance by psychoanalysts to the use of behavioral techniques is puzzling, given, as stated earlier, that Freud himself recommended such an approach in treating phobics. Referring to agoraphobics, he (1919) stated, "One succeeds only when one can induce them . . . to go into the street and to struggle with their anxiety" (166). Freud held that "the pure gold of analysis might be freely alloyed with the copper of direct suggestion" and that the hypnotic means of influence "might find a place in [analysis] again (1919, 168). If we do not think that all phobias come from Oedipal issues or necessarily represent something symbolic, but think, in fact, that they might be learned from a traumatic experience, we cannot expect them to occur in the relationship with the analyst. Eissler (1953) reiterated Freud's point: "With phobics the analyst must often but not always deviate from the basic model technique to command the patient to expose himself to the feared situation" (104). He noted that in some treatments "it becomes evident that interpretation does not suffice as a therapeutic tool" (109). He goes on to say that "the analyst must impose on the patient a command: to expose himself to the dreaded situation despite his fear of it and regardless of any anxiety which might develop during that exposure" (110). Behaviors are part of the motor system, the bottom-up processes that affect emotions and emotional cognitions. Now that we think no longer just about the mind, but about the "bodymind," it makes sense to think about interventions that move the body.

SUMMARY

Thinking of top-down and bottom-up processes allows us to integrate thinking and research in psychology and psychoanalysis in a way to further the therapeutic process. Conscious processing (top-down) can be augmented by attempts to access sensory processes (bottom-up) that will bring about more possibilities for change. Visual imagery, accessing sensations in the body, and behavior change can improve the therapeutic endeavor.

Chapter 8

Toward Psychointegration: Going to Africa

Laura called me for an appointment having been given my name as someone who worked with people in the arts. We set a time and then she asked what floor my office was on. Fortunately, I had a few minutes to speak with her. (The facts are changed to preserve anonymity.)

Patient: I have an elevator phobia.

Therapist: Would it help if I came down and rode up with you?

P: Yes, I do better if there are other people on it. If I have trouble, I'll just walk up.

T: So you ride elevators?

P: Yes, sometimes.

T: What makes you able to ride them?

P: If they are open. Or at work where there are other people.

T: Have you had any treatment for the elevator phobia?

P: No.

T: Well, on your way here start some deep breathing. You know, long deep breaths like in yoga class. Can you visualize some place where you feel safe?

P: Yes, the beach.

T: Well, visualize the beach and think of being warm and relaxed. Let me tell you that I am not aware of there ever being a problem with anyone in the elevators in my building. I've never heard the alarm, and I've been here almost thirty years. New elevators were put in a few years ago, not because there was a problem but for aesthetic reasons, and there has been no problem with them. Why don't you call me a few minutes before you get to the building, and I'll come downstairs. If you can ride up, fine. If not, you can walk.

P: Okay.

When I made this arrangement, I was free the hour before the 4:30 appointment. The day before, however, I scheduled an appointment with someone back briefly from a remote country. I stopped at 4:25, but I could see my message light already blinking. I listened and Laura stated that she had arrived early and was waiting in the lobby. I went downstairs and went over to a young woman sitting on a bench. The postal carrier was putting the mail in beside her. I told Laura to take some deep breaths and did this along with her. We were standing in the lobby and she made constant eye contact. We stood there breathing slowly and I told her to tell me when she was ready to get on the elevator. I reminded her to visualize the beach. We kept taking long breaths and I said, "Just let me know when you are ready." She said, "I'll never be ready." I responded, "Well let's go then. If you don't want to do it, you can walk." We got in, but the elevator did not leave. (It does not leave when the outer door to the building is open, unless the doorman presses a release.) We got out, spoke to the doorman, who had been busy helping a woman inside with a baby carriage and a dog, and I asked her if she wanted to go again. She said "yes" and we got back in the elevator. The woman with the baby carriage and the dog got in and pressed the floor below. When she got off, I asked Laura:

T: Do you want to get off here?

P: No.

T: (When we got off at my floor) You seem to have done very well. I didn't see any shortness of breath.

P: I manage to look calm, but I'm not.

T: Well, you didn't panic.

P: No, I guess that's half of life. Just not letting people know how anxious you feel.

T: Well, I guess it does help in job interviews and many places. You certainly did not look anxious. How did you feel when the woman with the baby got in?

P: I like it when there are other people there.

T: (Handing her a piece of paper.) Let me get your name, phone numbers, address, and emergency contact information.

P: How many names do you want?

T: Two would be good. (She finishes and hands me the paper.) I'd like to take some notes. Is that okay?

P: Yes.

T: If it bothers you, just please ask me to stop.

P: I was given your name by [name], an MD at Wall Street Hospital. He is my psychiatrist. I haven't had any therapy for five years.

T: We've been talking about the elevator phobia, but when you called me you mentioned that you knew I was involved in the psychoanalysis and the arts group. I gather there was another reason for your coming to therapy.

P: Yes, whenever I went to therapy before, I always had another purpose. My family is heavy on depression—my father, my mother—alcohol, too. When I was eleven my mother was hospitalized for a nervous breakdown.

T: What exactly was wrong? Was she crying a lot?

P: We have never talked about it. I think she was suicidal and wouldn't go out of the house. I went to therapy in high school and in college to talk about her. I was the last to go on antidepressants in my family. I have a younger brother and he started taking them before me.

T: What are you taking?

P: I was taking Imipramine, but now I'm taking Lithium. I tried life without medication after college. I had my first solo performance at age sixteen. I had no idea how much work it would be. I didn't get much sleep right before it, trying to get ready. I stopped eating. Right after it, I had a manic episode. I had been practicing around the clock. I was kind of psychotic. I had delusions of grandeur.

T: Did you have any hallucinations?

P: No. I thought my music would change the world, though, that a message would be conveyed. I was high for two weeks. I went to [name of therapist] in the village. Then I crashed and went to the hospital.

T: How long were you there?

P: Two or three weeks.

T: Were you suicidal?

P: No.

T: How long ago was this?

P: Eleven years ago.

T: Have you been in the hospital since?

P: No. I started to become manic again before my next concert. But I made certain I slept. I was better prepared.

T: Better prepared for the concert?

P: Yes. I want more exposure now. I'm stifling myself. I'm working with my sister on (describes project). (She describes other work for money and I inquire about her parents' ethnicity which had seemed somewhat, albeit distantly, related to her art.)

T: Are you taking any other medications?

P: Centhroid and birth control pills. (She laughs.) I haven't had sex recently.

T: What other therapists have you seen?

P: I saw [x] and [y]. I stopped in 1999. I laughed about the birth control pills because I broke up with a man I had seen for eight years a few months ago.

T: What led you to stop seeing the other therapists?

P: The last one told me he had stopped being a professional artist. That bothered me. Then he came to one of my performances with a woman—I didn't expect to see him there—and later told me that it was his girlfriend, but that it didn't work out.

T: Where do your parents live now?

P: My mother lives in Queens and my father in Guttenberg. My sister lives in Seattle. My sister had a manic episode, too.

T: Tell me what kind of art you like to do the most. (I'm going to skip this part and her ethnic background to preserve confidentiality. She says she does not have any female role models in her field that she knows. I ask at one point, "What is your favorite piece of art?")

P: The Winged Victory of Samothrace [also known as the Nike of Samothrace]. I like fragments. She is human but not. She is incomplete. (She tells me a bit about her own work.) Your imagination fills the rest in.

T: Incomplete, you said. Is that a way you feel about yourself in any way?

P: Yes, I can see with my parents, how I might feel like that. I have a definition of myself as evolving—how I feel about myself as a woman, my role in relationships. I was in an all girls' school for twelve years.

T: At what age did you have your first crush or romantic involvement?

P: Fourteen. It began my pattern of relationships. I chose needy, depressed, alcoholic men.

T: Tell me about your father. What kind of work does he do?

P: He is in business.

T: And your mother?

P: She is unemployed now. She was later diagnosed as bipolar. She has beginning Alzheimer's.

T: What is your first memory?

P: I can remember lying on a table screaming. There was a bowl of hard-boiled eggs near me. There were women near me—my mom, my aunt. They were getting ready for something.

T: How old were you?

P: I was a baby.

T: And the first memory of your mother?

P: Singing me lullabies. I'd be lying in bed. I was three or four.

T: And of your father?

P: He was always in the background.

T: Were your parents affectionate?

P: My mother was.

T: Tell me about starting school.

P: I liked kindergarten. I went to [name of school]. I had trouble when I started first grade at [name of private girls' school]. It was more structured. I didn't have any choice. I just went where they sent me.

T: What kind of school would you have liked?

P: Just one with less structure.

T: Like what?

P: (Names two other private schools in Manhattan.)

T: Just keep telling me about your life growing up.

P: I finished high school in 1998—I moved out two years later. I had a roommate (also in the arts). She also worked in a store (says what kind).

T: Do you live with someone else now?

P: I have a roommate. She is also (in the arts).

T: Tell me about your friends.

P: They are mostly in the arts—all kinds. Most are filmmakers, but I have friends in all of the arts—painters, sculptors, photographers, musicians.

T: What exactly about elevators makes you feel scared?

P: The fear of getting stuck, of being powerless. I have all of these dreams—the bottom falling out, the elevator not having any buttons, the elevator moving from side to side.

T: Be an elevator. Say . . . I am an elevator. I am. . . .

P: (Laughs.)

T: What are you feeling?

P: I feel good. I'm an elevator, and I'm moving side to side. I'm going in an unexpected direction . . . (she begins to cry).

T: I don't have any control. . . .

P: I don't have any control. I don't know where I'm going.

T: You said you were concerned about being stifled. Being stifled—is that a feeling that is related to your fear of elevators?

P: Yes, if anything goes wrong. I can be around a lot of irrational behavior and put up with it. Two years ago, the guy I was involved with was a mess. All of them. I wonder what I'm doing. I guess with my mother I just learned to put up with a lot.

T: And you keep trying to master the difficult situation. You keep trying to cure someone.

P: Yes. I'm (describes work some more). I have a feeling of stagnating.

T: When did you first feel that feeling of stagnating?

P: Early grade school. Just not fitting in, it was not the right atmosphere. I should have been in a more diverse school.

T: How would you describe your school?

P: A tight-ass girls' school. You know, I grew up three blocks from here. I sometimes think about leaving. I've never left New York. I think about going to Europe or California. I just got my driver's license.

T: That's great. You know, you are talking about your desire to go some place else. Sometimes these fears, like elevator phobias, can be related to a fear of leaving. If you are afraid of leaving in some way, what would you be afraid of?

P: When I think about leaving, I get anxious about my mom. (She looks teary-eyed.)

T: You worry about her ending up in the hospital again.

P: Yes (teary-eyed). She's on Depakote and Xanax. She may have switched. I think she would be better off on Lithium. My mother and sister are both worried about the weight gain.

T: If you were successful in your work, what would happen?

P: My mother is needy. She is very concerned about money. She would be dependent on me.

T: So I guess you have some reasons for holding yourself back. Look, this elevator phobia is curable. Do you ever carry around a bag to breathe into—so you can breathe back the carbon dioxide and calm yourself down?

P: No, I've never done that. I could do that.

T: So, I can't meet this time next week. We had said we would meet usually on Tuesdays at six. But next week I could meet you on Wednesday at six. Is that okay?

P: That is fine.

T: Are you willing to ride down in the elevator by yourself or do you want me to go with you?

P: I want you to go.

On the way down in the elevator, I joked that we were going sideways to Europe. I said we were over the Atlantic Ocean and then about to land in Paris. Laura commented that I was "good at this."

This initial interview combines behavioral, psychoanalytic, and experiential (Gestalt) techniques. I think it makes clear what type of integrative possibilities I am suggesting. Although many therapists and analysts do not take a history during the first session (and some, never), I think it is crucial to know if someone has been hospitalized, suicidal, psychotic, and so on. I also think it is crucial to know why someone has stopped previous therapies. I know that Laura will have little difficulty speaking on her own in subsequent sessions. She is not highly defended and will make creative use of her time with me.

Some clinicians have advocated simply doing what works—a type of psychotherapy integration referred to as technical integration or eclecticism (Lazarus 1992). Other clinicians have advocated integration of various approaches from a theoretical point of view (Wachtel 1977; Messer 1983), assimilating other techniques into one's own already existing theoretical orientation. I am suggesting integrating various techniques into a psychoanalytic framework because contemporary psychoanalysis, when integrated theoretically with principles from learning theory, existential philosophy, and systems theories, potentially offers the most comprehensive understanding of human behavior due to its tradition of exploring unconscious processes and its wealth of freely emerged clinical data, although a cognitive theory integrating such processes would be similar.

Wachtel (1977, 1997) has been the foremost spokesperson for integration within psychoanalysis. Describing at length what psychoanalysis and learning theory have in common in the tradition of Dollard and Miller (1950), Wachtel has been in the forefront of the theory and organization of the movement toward psychotherapy integration (Goldfried and Norcross 1992; Stricker and Gold 1993a; Gold 1996). Insight is seen as facilitating therapeutic action in this model, as argued by Alexander (1930) and in interpersonal psychoanalysis, but believed to occur as a consequence of behavior change, as well as through exploration. Inquiry is given a major role, although interpretations just outside the patient's current state of awareness are also considered useful. Exposure is also critical—both through interpretation and confrontation of anxiety-provoking inner states and defenses, but also exposure to external sources of anxiety through systematic desensitization in imagination or in vivo. As in interpersonal and relational therapy, Wachtel (1984) has suggested that insight into the cyclical dynamics that are occurring with the patient and others, including the therapist, are a major route to change. In these vicious circles, "neither impulse nor defense, neither internal state nor external situation are primary but are continually determining each other in a series of repeated transactions" (48). The ways of avoiding anxiety by narrowing experience often result in self-fulfilling prophecies and vicious circles, with people enlisting accomplices in their neuroses.

Stricker and Gold (1988), working from a perspective of assimilating interventions into psychoanalytic treatment, have argued for interventions at three tiers—the behavioral, the cognitive-affective-interpersonal, and the intrapsychic. Gold and Stricker (2001) discussed three situations when integration is advantageous, if not absolutely necessary: (1) when work in the transference is insufficient to change ongoing relationships; (2) when deficits in internal structures prevent new experiences and representations; and (3) when a patient is preparing for an active episode of involvement in self-change, for example, asks specifically "How do I change this?" In discussing a patient with anxiety about her physical health and panic attacks, the therapist first explored her lack of comfort from her own parents. Having never been comforted by anyone, she was not able to trust the therapist who was not actively comforting either. The therapist saw her point and helped her to use relaxation exercises, self-soothing statements, and reviewed medical sites with her on the Internet. She then gained further insight into her somatic symptoms, and began to experience fully the rage, despair, and fear she had felt since childhood, mourned what she had not experienced from her parents, and showed an almost total cessation of her anxiety symptoms.

PARAMETERS FOR INTEGRATING OTHER TECHNIQUES OF INFLUENCING CONSCIOUS PROCESSES AND BEHAVIORS

Realizing that sometimes patients have not simply conflicts, but real deficits in knowledge, both Gedo (1988) and Basch (1988) argued for the introduction of educative techniques into psychoanalysis. Eissler (1953) had described three parameters: "(1) a parameter must be introduced only when it is proved that the basic technique does not suffice; (2) the parameter must never transgress the unavoidable minimum; (3) a parameter is to be used only when it finally leads to its self-elimination; that is to say, the final phase of the treatment must always proceed with a parameter of zero" (111). Frank (1991) went further and described seven guidelines for integrating active techniques into psychoanalytic treatment. The first overlaps with Eissler's but additionally he states (1) they should not be enactments and be done after consideration of the patient's overall therapeutic needs; (2) the analyst must monitor countertransferential reactions; (3) the gains and losses of using each approach must be weighed; (4) the analyst must not take initiative nor control away from the patient; (5) the analyst must not become overly invested in changing behavior; (6) active techniques can be modified and used in small doses to investigate the patient's reactions. Curtis (1996b) listed four guidelines: (1) they can be used to help reduce severe symptoms, with exploration of the meaning of any failures in the attempt; (2) they can be useful in inducing patients to emotionally understand events in their lives and to free inhibitions to awareness; (3) they should be used when the long-term benefits outweigh the costs; (4) they will be used to the extent the therapist values freeing inhibitions and trying out new experiences in comparison to analyzing the transference.

Analysts can incorporate techniques from other types of therapies if they are sincerely interested in helping the patient (Curtis, 1996a). As Wachtel, Frank, Stricker and Gold, and others have indicated when suggesting integrating nonanalytic techniques into psychoanalytic treatments, the effects of such interventions upon the therapeutic relationship and process can always be discussed later. Given the vast array of human problems and unconscious processes, it seems to be wishful thinking that knowing how to analyze transference and countertransference is the only major technical knowledge a psychoanalyst needs.

Philosophical Incompatibilities

Integrating therapeutic techniques has been referred to as "technical assimilation" (Lazarus 1992). At a theoretical level, is it possible to integrate the vastly different approaches of psychoanalysis and behavioral therapy? Philosophically, psychoanalysis is rooted in a belief that a reorganization of psychic structures occurs in an atmosphere in which everything is allowed to flow into consciousness and becomes integrated with existing processes. Psychoanalysis, as originally conceived, was a process in which the analyst interpreted the unconscious of the patient; the analyst, a neutral, objective observer, did not impose any influence upon the patient other than what was helpful in allowing the patient's unconscious unfold. Beginning with the free associations of the patient, the process was very much one from inside (the patient) out. When Alexander and French (1946) deliberately engaged in providing the patient alternative experiences, psychoanalysts rejected their technique. Still, the analyst is an influence outside the patient and, when seen five or six times per week, potentially has an enormous impact on a patient, just as a hypnotist might. As the analyst stops excluding from awareness sexual, aggressive, or other feelings toward the analyst, sexual and aggressive urges toward others also enter consciousness. In this model, the analyst's role is akin to that of a midwife. Psychoanalysis allows for outside influence, but it is only in the service of birthing what is present already unconsciously, or in the cocreation of meaning.

A similar conception of experience as emanating from the patient has also held for experiential therapies. The therapist did not impose meanings or directly try to influence the patient by manipulating the environment. Behavior therapy operated from a different model. Believing that environmental contingencies govern behaviors, behaviorists altered these external factors.

Over time psychoanalysts have recognized that the analyst has more influence than was believed in the days of the "blank screen." Beginning with Sullivan's (1953) notion of a participant observer, the role of the analyst's influence has received more and more attention. Recently, Fiscalini (2004) has argued for a third paradigm, "coparticipant psychoanalysis." Although interpersonal psychoanalysts recognized that culture plays a role in people's behaviors, thoughts, and feelings, the only outside influence allowed in the therapy has usually been the analyst or therapist. The tradition of attention to the therapeutic milieu advocated by interpersonalists at Sheppard-Enoch Pratt Hospital and Chestnut Lodge and the Eriksonian tradition at the Austen Riggs Center, represent exceptions. Still, the idea of controlling environmental influences, even at the request of the patient, has been counter to the value of personal responsibility. In contrast, in the behavioral model, the influence of outside forces is the path to change. With movement toward a nonlinear dynamical system model of change, the importance of both intrinsic organizing processes and external influences must be taken into account.

TOWARD INTEGRATED MODELS OF PSYCHOLOGICAL CHANGE

In 1994, Szalita published a paper called "The Dilemma of Therapeutic Changes in Psychotherapy: Psychointegration" in the *Israel Journal of Psychiatry and Related Sciences.* In it she described an approach that enabled the patient and the therapist to increase "responsible self-awareness, centered on steps leading to the development of an integrated, educated awareness" (106). Szalita backed off verbally from this intelligent man in a style that seems Rogerian, after hearing how each intervention from the previous analyst led to deterioration.

A dissociative model of mind requires a new look at the nature of therapeutic interaction. In a dissociative model it is assumed that there are many self-with-other states, many interpersonal patterns or vicious cycles in which the patient may engage. These are not necessarily unconscious, but may be conscious yet not integrated (Bromberg 1996). Using the principle that the patient requires a new experience, the analyst must engage the patient in an experience in the present. Certainly this activity may involve requesting that the patient recall another time when he or she was feeling quite differently with the analyst or elsewhere. Bromberg (1996) has described the necessity of helping the patient become aware of the conflicting nature of self-states by helping the patient hold them in awareness simultaneously. The shifts in self-with-other states as described by Bromberg, Goldberg (1999), and others can be hard to see clinically. Experiential process therapists have described therapy for assimilating "multiple voices" within patients by bringing these voices into awareness (Honos-Webb et al. 1999). Horowitz et al. (1993) has identified certain markers for the shifts in voices—what would traditionally be noted as defenses—efforts to retreat, contradict, minimize or obfuscate experience by using "weasel words" or frequent disavowals, negations, shifts of topics, and various nonverbal moves of the face, head, and hands.

There are many avenues to change—the model of interpretation-to-insight is only one model. The injunction to "only interpret" must be abandoned in order to have optimum therapeutic effectiveness unless psychoanalysts wish to disregard psychoanalysis as a theory of therapy and consider it only as a way to explore the mind. Consideration of top-down and bottom-up processes, desires for self-preservation and preservation of the meaning system, the dissociative nature of mental processes, and nonlinear dynamic processes lead us to think about the interaction of the self-system with all of the surrounding environmental influences.

Anthony Ryle (1990; Ryle and Low 1993) has introduced a number of cognitive therapy concepts and techniques into object relations theory, using more cognitive language. He believes that written formulations of the patient's sequences of responses are helpful and thinks that a visual representation of the conflicted aspects of personality appears to have an immediate containing effect. This formulation, which he calls the procedural sequence object relations model, includes events, the patient's perception, appraisal (beliefs, values, meanings), aim, possible consequences, choice of action, action, and the consequences of the action. The formulation resembles Luborsky's (1998) core conflictual relationship model to some extent. In this model, the part selves cannot make sense of the whole, and a visual representation of the "whole picture" is believed to be useful. Therapeutic change comes from an integration of partial reciprocal role procedures. The failures of integration "are seen as primarily due to failures of integration rather than as having a defensive function" (90).

For Ryle, children internalize adult "voices" related to these role procedures, drawing from Vygotsky's (1978) idea that internalization is the characteristic distinguishing humans from animals and the basis of our capacity for abstract thought. There may be "two or more quite recognizable, distinct patterns, occurring discontinuously" (Ryle and Law 1993, 90) that may be conscious. Although Ryle does not speak of dissociation, the model he is advocating is one of integrating dissociated self-with-other states, similar to what Bromberg (1996) has suggested.

Elsewhere I (Curtis 1991a) presented an integrated model of change that was alluded to in chapter 2. Starting with the version of Miller, Galanter, and Pribram's (1960) model of set-goals formulated by Carver and Scheier (1981), in more cognitive language, I described what happens when an individual encounters difficulty in fulfilling a desire. The person feels aroused and assesses the expectancy of fulfilling the desire. If the person is confident, the person remains engaged. If the person is not confident and the desire is not so important, the person disengages. If the desire is important, and avoiding lack of fulfillment is very important, the person becomes anxious. This arousal leads to automatic processing (Paulhus and Levitt 1987), to engaging in the dominant response—a pattern that was learned in an earlier situation that may or may not be the most adaptive in the current situation. A vicious circle may ensue if the pattern is not effective, with rumination, defenses, and excuses made for failure. If the desire is an important one, but lack of fulfillment is not felt to be crucial, that is, the person can tolerate failure to fulfill the desire, the person may either abandon attempts to fulfill the desire or engage in risk-taking behaviors, trying out patterns with uncertain outcomes, likely leading to failure. In order to do this, the person must tolerate the anxiety that comes with uncertainty and the probability of failure (Curtis 1991a) and the sadness that comes with failure. When attempts to fulfill the desire are abandoned or rendered not essential, the self-organization is open to change. The person is open to experiences that question the previous value system or disconfirm beliefs that were formerly important and new desires emerge.

An example of this occurs when some people receive information that they suffer from a life-threatening illness. If the person mourns the loss of life and accepts that death is inevitable, new values often emerge. Studies with patients suffering from AIDS and cancer (Taylor 1989) have found that people often report the happiest days of their lives after such reassessment of their value systems. Another example could be seen with a patient of mine to whom I said, "Your mother didn't love you. She did the best she could, but what she gave you was not love." My patient told me at the next session that she had cried and cried when she left. She had always told herself, "But she loves you" after every cruelty. She gave up the desire of being loved by her mother, now aware that her mother was not capable of loving her. After realizing there was nothing she could do to get her mother's love, she felt much better. Not too long afterwards, she found love from someone else for the first time.

Let me explicate the model being presented further (see Figure 8.1). First, there must be an awareness of a desire, or a wish, for those who prefer that term. This is important, as there are some people who have become so frightened of wanting anything or anything different from what their parents want, that they are not aware of their own desires. (Perhaps such a state also occurs in cultures where there is not an individualistic sense of identity, but I do not know personally anyone from such a culture.) In our culture, work may be required to help certain patients become aware of their own desires. (For example, one patient for whom ever wanting anything different from her parents was so anxiety-provoking that she did not even know what she preferred to eat.)

A reflective or metamonitoring state occurs when there is frustration in the attempt to fulfill a desire. An assessment is then made of the importance of fulfilling the desire. It either remains important and attended to or abandoned (although this is a continuum). The whole question of what is actually desired is a complicated one, embedded in a hierarchy of desires. A student may say that she doesn't want another student to work on the same research topic, for example. This desire, however, may be subsumed under the desire not to compete. A man may wish to leave his wife. This desire may be related to his desire to have a good sex life, and so forth. Psychoanalytic and experiential approaches to therapy provide ways of facilitating awareness of desires and where these desires fall in a person's overall meaning system. This complex web of associations has been a major focus of Lacanian (1988) thinking.

When fulfillment of the desire feels essential to the meaning system, the attempts to fulfill the desire continue and the person copes by either making excuses for the lack of fulfillment or finds ways of escaping the distress related to the lack of fulfillment. The person maintains a self-with-other state defending the importance of the fulfillment of this desire to the meaning system, staying in a vicious circle. There may be more than one such defensive self-with-other state or pattern of coping. These states have cognitive, affective, and behavioral (including interpersonal) aspects. The person may seek outside help at this point in order to fulfill the desire or cope better with its lack of fulfillment. The desires, or some derivatives of them, may then appear in relation to the therapist or may not. The vicious circle may involve only thought processes, moving into action (substance use, exercise, shopping, and so on), or avoiding anxiety-provoking situations (phobias, interpersonal contact, and so on).

Usually the help of a therapist is required to notice cognitive defenses. Both avoided situations and behaviors used defensively frequently have sufficient negative consequences that a person will notice them and seek to change the circle on his or her own. The person may obtain sufficient support to do this through religious experiences, friends or family, or seek outside help from a therapist or a support group such as Alcoholics Anonymous. Often another value system becomes apparent and a person is able to relinquish the old desires and move on without giving up an overarching desire. An example would be a person who desires to have a form of employment that is of value to others in the community. Although the person's identity may have been wrapped up in being a mechanic, for example, a friend's suggestion of moving on to plumbing may fulfill the desire. The inability to use the skills practiced for many years and the cost of learning new ones may be distressing, but tolerable. On the other hand, the prospect of being on welfare will not satisfy the overarching desire and may seem intolerable. Few people

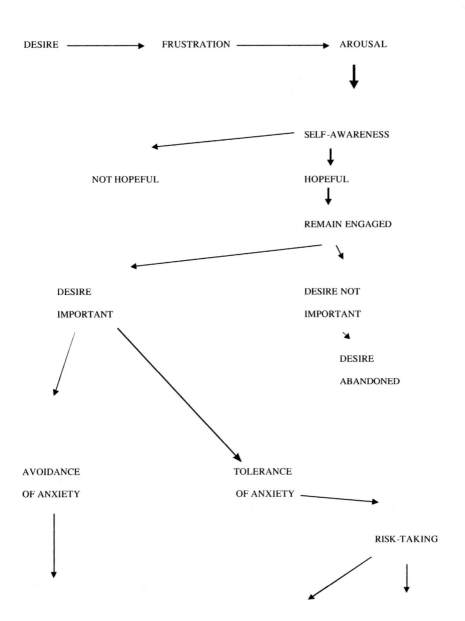

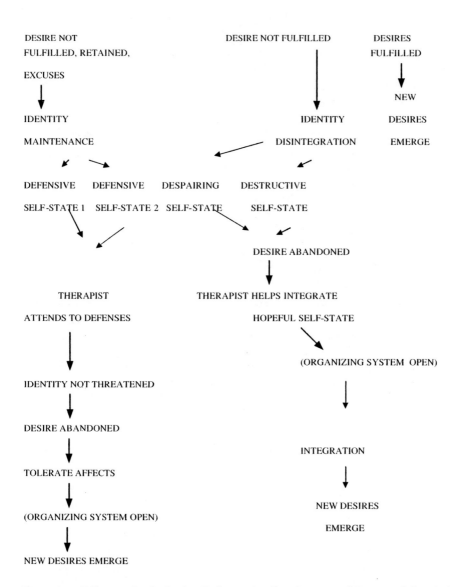

Figure 8.1 Failure to Attain Desire, Defense, the Abandonment of Hope, and the Work of the Therapist

are able to tolerate moving into the experience of having no meaning system without a sense of some relationship to another person—real or imagined—or a sense of being part of a larger whole (a religious sense). Simply being of meaning to at least one other person, or the hope that one will be of meaning, can suffice.

A clinical example will help clarify the change process being described. Susan, very lonely and isolated, often maintained a defensive state of feeling superior to others, mistrusting of them, feeling she would only be used by others or abandoned should she become more involved and that she will never get what she needs. In this state she felt smart, competent, and self-sufficient, but unattractive to men. Susan sometimes moved into another state where she felt undeserving of any relationships or happiness altogether because she failed to help her agoraphobic mother and did not go to the hospital the night she was dying. In this second state, her view of her mother was idealized, a wonderful mother whom all of her friends liked. She would never say the mother was agoraphobic, only "sick," and she was the bad daughter. In this state, it was very important for women to be attractive to men and find one who will take care of them, but she would fail because she was bad. In the first state she was competent and strong, but overweight, old, and unattractive. In the second state, she was pretty, but bad and dumb. She told me that women cannot be smart and attractive. One role of the therapist at a point like this is to help the patient attend to her defenses and to the shifts in her conscious, but dissociated self-states. The therapist must then help the patient tolerate the anxiety related to warded-off states. In order to tolerate such anxiety, the therapist might employ some of the techniques for "affect phobias" (McCullough et al. 2003).

When Susan would stop defending, she would become either despairing and paralyzed (she had stayed in her apartment for a year without going out before her father's death and feared going into this state again), or destructive—very cruel to others who were vulnerable and appearing as if she might become physically violent. These states were conscious ones that she felt and described, although for some people the warded-off states may not be conscious ones. These two particular self-with-other states are quite common and linked to the natural behavioral tendencies of flight and fight that aid in self-preservation (cf. Gray 1987). Although psychoanalysts may wish to work in the transference, such work is not possible with patients who are impulsive and will leave treatment when they become angry at the therapist. With some patients, it is possible to warn them in advance that they are going to feel angry and wish to leave and have them write down in advance what their good feelings are and instructions to themselves about what to do when the wish to leave begins (express the anger to the therapist). A lot of work is required to help some patients tolerate (sit with) their feelings without acting (moving into fight or flight) or becoming paralyzed. The difficulty working transferentially with patients who physically flee when a problem arises may explain to some extent why therapists like Linehan (1988) work successfully with such patients without working transferentially. Working with this whole process of defense, anxiety, and impulse is described in detail in recent works by Fosha (2000) and McCullough-Vaillant (1996).

Without either the beliefs that she had a good mother and is a bad daughter, or the beliefs that she is self-sufficient and others untrustworthy, the ways Susan had of making meaning out of her existence would disappear. Her meaning and identity would disintegrate. This was terrifying. There was no self-theory or what would formerly have been called ego. There is nothing in these moments except existence. This ego-less "no-self" state is what is aimed at in Zen Buddhism. It should be kept in mind, however, as Watts stated, "One must have a self to lose it." One will note the similarity of this process to Buddhist philosophy in general: "Life is suffering; the cause of all suffering is desire, and there is a way out of suffering."

The therapist must provide hope that there are possibilities—alternatives. With people who have other sources of social support, friends help maintain a sense of hope to take a person through the times of despair. This hopeful state in the other's presence must be integrated with the despairing and destructive states.

Patients are often reluctant to enter fully into the destructive self-with-other state. This fear is justified if a person is unable to control impulses or unable to differentiate clearly fantasy from reality. The therapist must help the patient with these abilities before encouraging the patient to become fully emerged in such a state. These are basic skills that should be part of any therapy early on when a patient comes in with either impulsive behaviors that must be addressed or failures in reality testing. With patients who become destructive to themselves or others, extreme caution is needed. The therapist must help the patient learn how to get herself out of such states before fully going into them. Patients who truly suffer from multiple personality or who claim they do are extreme examples of patients who require such work. There is considerable energy in this destructive state, and without a sense of the capability of hurting others in order to defend oneself, people cannot be fully assertive. These self-states—the urge to do nothing and die (a death instinct) and the urge to destroy others—come from feelings of helplessness and hopelessness.

When a sense of hope is totally lacking in the patient, it must come from interaction with the therapist. Hope accounts for 15 percent of the variance in therapy, according to Lambert and Barley (2002). The importance of optimism (Seligman 1975) and hope (Snyder 2004) in all aspects of life has been thoroughly investigated and documented. The patient's organizing system must be open to that of the therapist for any movement to take place. Some type of relaxation or desensitization is required in order for people to relax their defenses. Also, in my experience, unless I can enter fully into a sense of the patient's consciousness and figure some way to worm myself out of the ensuing despair, I cannot communicate hope to the patient. It is at these times that those words from Shakespeare's King Lear come to mind, "Expose thyself to feel what wretches feel that thou may'st shake the superflux to them and show the heavens more just." The energy required is felt as one truly of shaking the superflux. I have never accomplished this feat without tears and trembling. There is no question about an attempt to influence. I am attempting to have an influence toward life with all of the power I can muster. There is not a thought of "technical neutrality" in these moments of psychological life or death, unless by that phrase is meant a sense of the power of the instincts toward life and death, the power of consciousness and human ability, and the power of all that is protective and destructive that has gone before us and will follow after us—in other words, the convergence of desire, actuality, and possibility—perhaps something akin to the sense of the poet in the presence of his angel, not unlike an integration of id, ego, and superego into nonconflicted goal-directed behavior. When the patient's destructive energy is harnessed, it becomes a powerful form of assertiveness that we call "will." Most of us have seen this sort of determination in star athletes who somehow accomplish a feat that looks impossible. The emotional task is similar. We can identify these moments of emotional movement when we see them happen in life or on video. They have been referred to as "the transforming power of affect" (Fosha 2000). In our contemporary science, they are the moments when order begins to emerge out of the chaos and complexity that takes place upon the collision of two organizing systems.

For some people, there come times when everything to which they have been dedicated for their whole lives falls apart. Without providing the specifics, a patient's father was betrayed by friends and associates who made him appear responsible for wrongdoings and left him unemployed and largely unemployable, his wife unfaithful, his children not speaking to him because of his lifelong preoccupation with his work and neglect of them, and on the "black list" of all of his other friends. He took an overdose of drugs and died.

What is someone to do when all is lost? Religions provide helpful answers to people. Western religions have offered the possibility that bad things happen, but that these bad events are part of God's larger plan for a greater good. As was discussed earlier, finding something good in a horrible situation is an excellent way of coping. But what are people to do—people who try and, try they may, are unable to believe in a divine plan? Meditation traditions have offered another alternative: Focus consciousness on the immediate—the here-and-now of the senses, breathing, or thoughts as they come and go out of consciousness. It may work as long as a person has the means for physical survival without undue duress. A vast literature has now accumulated incorporating these mindfulness traditions into our understanding of psychoanalysis and psychotherapy, dating back at least to the interests of Horney and Fromm (Suzuki, Fromm, and DeMartino 1963). A new, consuming goal may emerge—exercise, gardening, becoming fluent in a foreign language and knowledgeable about its literature and culture, cooking, admiration of the beauty of nature, and so on.

Such pleasures are difficult to pursue, however, for people with no money. It is very hard, for example, to find anything to do for an inpatient in a place like New York City with no money and an afternoon pass when the weather is icy and stormy. Creativity is required. One is sometimes left to the pleasures inside found in the company of others, books, or creative activities, such as drawing or music. When such activities have never been a source of pleasure, as is the case for many deprived people, the task of the therapist is extremely difficult. This situation seems far removed from the writings in psychoanalysis where the patients always seem to have an education and a source of income. When external realities are grim, internal personality problems can pale in comparison.

Returning to Susan, extratherapeutic factors played a large role in her change, I think. Lambert and Barley (2002) report that 40 percent of change during therapy is accounted for by such factors. She was required to go for a diagnostic medical procedure and became convinced that she had cancer and would die. She delayed making the appointment for the procedure for months and missed the appointment, but eventually went. We discussed what she would do if she were told she had cancer. We faced the possibility of her death and what she would do in her last year of life. During this time, she stated that if she did not have cancer, she would begin to do what she needed to do to live—to really have a life. She did not have cancer and made up a list of what she would accomplish each week and each month in order to have the sort of life she really wanted. Thus far, she has kept to her goals.

EXAMPLES OF INTEGRATIONS OF "NONANALYTIC" TECHNIQUES WITH PSYCHOANALYTICALLY ORIENTED TREATMENTS

Rhoads (1988) has presented four types of integrations of behavior therapy with psychodynamic therapy: (1) behavioral therapy as an introduction to therapy; (2) behavior therapy as an adjunct to psychodynamic therapy; (3) psychodynamic therapy as an adjunct to behavior therapy; and (4) integrated approaches. Trained in psychoanalysis, Rhoads noted that the two types of therapies have in common aspects of cognitive learning, corrective experiences, modeling and identification with the therapist, working through, reinforcement, the use of fantasy, and the analysis of antecedents and consequences. Although behavioral methods usually may be inappropriate with higher-functioning patients, many, if not most, clinicians recognize their value with more disturbed patients. As an example of behavior therapy as an introduction to therapy, Rhoads gives the example of a man with a germ phobia so debilitating that he washed his hands thirty to forty times per day, with the morning shower lasting as long as four hours. He had been treated by talk therapy for a year without change. He was unable to work and had abandoned all social life. Arbitrary times for a number of hand washings equal to the daily baseline count were given, gloves taped to his wrists between washings, and the shower time reduced gradually. He eventually objected to the gloves and began to speak of his fears of dating "virtuous" women, his antagonism toward his family, and his guilt while the behavioral therapy continued. Another woman who had refused psychiatric help belched approximately four hundred times per day but allowed herself to be hospitalized and was required to belch five minutes at four times daily. Within a week her belches decreased to approximately twenty-five per day. At this point she learned to go to the bathroom prior to the belch. Within a week she began to discuss her difficulties. Once it was apparent that the therapist was able to help them with their behavioral problems, these patients were willing to look at other issues.

Rhoads also describes examples of referring patients for relaxation and assertiveness training. A man who was referred for relaxation training wasted many hours daily due to his anxiety and in his analytic therapy recounting his symptoms. Although when he returned to therapy with the analyst he complained about the authoritarian approach of the behavior therapist, he also stated "'you were wise to make a referral to someone for a specific technique which helped the therapy get under way'" (202). Predictably, he also complained about the analytic therapy being ineffectual, providing a further opening for discussion of his interpersonal difficulties. Assertiveness training helped the other patient voice specific complaints to her husband when individual and group therapies had not led to such a change. Using a psychodynamic understanding, Feather and Rhoads (1972) discussed the treatment of a woman with a cockroach phobia by desensitizing her to her husband and sex. Rhoads notes that all therapies have their limitations and that different types of therapies can be used to deal with various kinds of resistances.

Frank (1999) has described at length a case of integrating action-oriented techniques into an analytically oriented treatment. I shall only briefly summarize his presentation. In the case of Carrie, her anger and splitting mechanisms had become the major focus of the twice-a-week treatment during the fourth year. She was concerned that her anger would destroy her close relationships, but very little anger had been expressed, or, as far as Frank could tell, even felt, toward him. He was being preserved as a good object, as she had done with her father. The major problem at this point was that Carrie had become aggressive toward her two-year-old daughter, "roughing" her up and pushing her at times, in one instance so that she fell and was bruised. She understood that she acted as her own mother had and identified with this aggressive aspect of her mother, but her experience as a victim was felt as an unfamiliar part of herself over which she had little control.

Frank, familiar with a cognitive-behavioral anger management method, grappled with the decision of whether to offer this approach as a possibility to Carrie. Would the patient's shame and anger be addressed more productively through inquiry alone? How would it affect the analysis of the transference? From a behavioral perspective, would it work?

Frank was clear that an active technique should not be used instead of working analytically, colluding with the patient's resistance. Many other possibilities were considered, including that of an enactment because he felt "under fire" so to speak (he did not). The provision of practical help did seem to be actively responsive in exactly the way her parents had failed. Frank was not inspired by the goal of providing a new relational experience of the sort conceptualized by developmental-arrest theorists (Winnicott 1965) or by Alexander and French (1946) although he thinks some action techniques might be employed that way. When Frank explained the rationale and procedures for the action-oriented technique, Carrie was interested in engaging in the process. Frank also taught her relaxation skills, diaphragmatic breathing, and asked her to keep a diary regarding situations that provoked angry thought. She became aware of an automatic thought in these situations with her daughter. "She's just doing that to make me angry again" and that it was not rational. Carrie was able to relax herself and think, "What is it really I want to accomplish here?" The action-oriented technique was used to advance the analytic inquiry. Her wish to activate her ineffectual father to stop the abuse by her mother became apparent to her. Although anger toward Frank never became a significant element in the treatment, her conflictual feelings toward her father did. She realized that she had shielded both from anger in order to maintain a positive attachment. Carrie became able to handle her anger more effectively and to express her affection more openly to her child. She reported greater self-esteem and no longer equated maternal participation with destructiveness.

Westen (2000) discusses a case where he integrates the behavioral concept of conditioned emotional responses with the psychodynamic concepts of defense and resistance with a patient who was successful in his work life but was invisible in his social life. Westen realized that he had never heard the man discuss any of his successes for more than a few seconds. Having only received minimal praise from his parents, any feelings of pride were associated with aversive feelings of thwarted wished for admiration. Simply knowing about this connection did not break the association. With an exposure model in mind, Westen shared with him his understanding of why he was afraid to feel proud and suggested spending the next couple of sessions working their way though his history of accomplishments. Westen suggested he was a "pride phobic." Over the next couple of sessions, the patient ambivalently shared some of his accomplishments, with the resistance analyzed whenever he got off the topic. He experienced some pleasure having someone important in his life take an interest in his accomplishments. Although from a psychoanalytic self-psychological approach, this intervention could be conceptualized as mirroring what he never received as a child. Westen thought this point of view underscores the role of conflict in receiving this mirroring and the importance of actively structuring the situation in the behavioral tradition so that he was exposed to the feared experience.

Gold (1996) has described at length the treatment of James in his book on psychotherapy integration. Of note to the present discussion are the times that Gold introduces nonanalytic interventions. James was a machine-like workaholic who came to treatment feeling like "everything I touch turns to garbage" (66), in a precontemplation stage of change (Prochaska and Di Clementi 1982), attributing his problems to biological causes, and as someone who could not be influenced by another person.

James brought to treatment material about people's reactions to him at home and work. Gold commented on the theme of the impossibility of finding love and acceptance and "the ways in which he disavowed these wishes and the painful affect tied to them through his overinvolvement in his 'machine' ideal" (123). These interpretations met with "mild to moderate interest on James's part" (123). They "seemed to allow the occasional recall of previously forgotten events in his life when he had tried to reach his parents in some meaningful way or had tried to provoke a response in them through his academic successes. James approached interpretive work in an intellectualized machine-like way" (124), Gold continues. At this point Gold introduced experiential exercises, including the empty chair technique (Greenberg et al. 1993) with the purpose of deepening James's conscious access to his emotions. "These interventions worked as desired. James found himself confronting deep wells of grief, anger, rejection, and loss as he spoke to the images of his parents" (123–24). At a later point when James was slipping back to this pattern of overwork and avoidance of interpersonal involvement, an imagery exercise was designed in which James was asked to explain his absences from home to his children. This exercise yielded much guilt, shame, and sadness. James recreated with his children the relationship his own father had with him, and James wanted his boss to be the father he never had. A behavioral intervention that was used early on when James was anxious about not doing a perfect job or leaving the office at a reasonable hour was one referred to as "response cost." He became more aware of the pain of isolation. Gold incorporated experiential dialogues, social skills training, discussions of social behaviors, role-playing, assertiveness training, and behavioral rehearsal. Gold himself presents this case using the concept of "narrative" as the way of integrating different therapeutic modalities.

It is risky to advise action and have it not work out. For example, I inquired of a young woman who wanted to meet men if she ever spoke to any in whom she might be interested. (Although such a question does not explicitly represent the giving of advice, it implicitly does suggest action.) At the next session the young woman reported saying to an attractive man on the train from New Jersey to New York, "Are you married?" It had not occurred to me that she would begin a conversation in such a manner. Not surprisingly, the conversation did not go far.

The experiential tradition in psychotherapy and dynamic psychotherapy has emphasized the accessing of warded-off affect as the major route to change. According to this view, accessing emotional schemas leads to changes in cognitions and behaviors in the overall cognitive-emotional-behavioral representations or networks. Here the argument is that each emotion is associated with an adaptive action tendency (Fosha 2000). Damasio (1994, 139) notes that the word "emotion" means "movement out." Fosha (2000) states three additional postulates about the healing power of affect: (1) the experience of core affect is healing "in and of itself" (31), with an increase in the feeling of aliveness; (2) experiencing emotions confers a sense of mastery; and (3) affect is often a royal road to the unconscious. Whereas the affective route does not conflict with the psychoanalytic one (and is the one that Bucci [1997] and Spezzano [1993] have suggested), there has been less of an emphasis on the meanings of experience among experiential psychologists than among psychoanalysts. Concerns with the meaning system were even more neglected in the behavioral tradition in psychotherapy which focused upon altering directly the sensory-motor components of the survival system until its recent integration with the cognitive tradition, where meanings are also emphasized, although not unconscious ones. This absence will perhaps be rectified as the large role of unconscious (implicit) processes becomes more accepted by cognitive-behavioral clinicians.

PROBLEMS EMANATING FROM USING
ONLY ONE THEORETICAL APPROACH

Westen (2000) has presented some "horror stories" both from analytically oriented and cognitive-behavioral treatments. The first was a patient who was seen for five years in psychoanalysis by a prominent analyst. He had presented with a wide range of complaints, including depression and isolation. After five years, little had improved. He entered treatment with another clinician who discovered upon inquiry in the first session that the patient had a serious alcohol problem and had been intoxicated during much of his analysis. The analyst had never known because he did not believe in asking direct questions in the initial interview of the analysis, preferring for material to emerge at the patient's own pace. This was not simply the case of a bad analyst. He was a training analyst and had been selected by his peers as a master clinician.

I had a similar experience regarding the singer who found her "voice" described earlier. She had spent a year with an analyst without revealing that she was a lesbian. The analyst had not inquired about her history of romantic relationships initially and the fact that I did led her to reveal her orientation.

The second case Westen presented regards a patient who suffered from panic attacks and interpersonal problems. The clinician had addressed both problems psychodynamically and discovered a relation between the panic attack and an intense fear of being alone at night. The patient seemed preoccupied with her fear of panicking which had been interpreted as resistance against dealing with underlying issues. Westen points out that this hypothesis does not take into consideration the body of research showing that panic patients develop classically conditioned fear responses to their own interoceptive cues. Their fear of their fear and their own responses such as racing heart and shortness of breath contributes to triggering the attacks. The most effective treatment is desensitizing the person to the interoceptive cues. Talking someone out of a conditioned emotional response that occurs subcortically, via the thalamus to the amygdala is not easy. It would be simpler to have her run up and down the stairs and get desensitized.

Westen also describes a patient with a borderline personality organization and a history of lethal suicide attempts who saw a cognitive behavioral therapist who taught her relaxation techniques. After several sessions, she took an overdose. Another case regarded a man with a driving phobia and trouble getting along with people. The patient had a peculiar smirk on his face when he described watching his wife squirm. Westen asked, "What kind of pornography do you read?" He smiled and revealed that it was sadomasochistic. He had seen for a year a cognitive therapist who focused on his poor social skills. In the second session, Westen learned that the patient had experienced fantasies of raping and mutilating the previous therapist, but the therapist did not know because she had never asked about his fantasies regarding her. It seems unlikely that simple social skills training would overcome the effects on others of the patient's desire to hurt them. These examples all demonstrate the usefulness of knowledge from other therapeutic perspectives and literature.

RESEARCH REGARDING PSYCHOTHERAPY INTEGRATION

Shapiro and Morris (1978) argued that all gains in therapy could be due to modification of negative expectancies and development of positive perceptions of self and others. Shapiro and his colleagues at the Sheffield Psychotherapy Project (1981) actually examined the effects of combining different treatment modalities at different points in time. Llewelyn, Elliot, Shapiro, and Hardy (1988) studied anxious and depressed adults who received eight sessions of both cognitive-behavioral and insight-oriented therapy. They obtained self-reports from the patients regarding the helpful and hurtful aspects of the two treatments. Overall the experiences judged most helpful were increased awareness, obtaining problem solutions, reassurance, and personal contact. Reassurances and solutions to problems were more likely to be obtained during the cognitive-behavioral phase of the treatment and expansion of awareness and personal contact were most likely during the insight-oriented phase. Unwanted negative thoughts occurred about equally during both types of treatment and were negatively correlated with outcomes. They also found that the two phases were experienced most differently by patients when they received the cognitive-behavioral treatment first. This effect was found to be reduced in a study by Stiles, Barkham, Shapiro, and Firth-Cozens (1992) when the initial phase of cognitive-behavioral treatment included more attempts at expanded awareness and personal contact. Also when the presenting problems were vague, the cognitive interventions were less helpful.

Schottenbauer, Glass, and Arnkoff (2005) have reviewed the research on psychotherapy integration. A number of problems occur when trying to review this research: (1) it is hard to identify what constitutes integrative therapy; (2) it is hard to find studies with an appropriate control group; (3) it was difficult for the researchers to include research not published in English (much was published in Europe and South America where the integrative movement has taken hold); and (4) there are so many different types of integration — sequential, parallel, eclecticism, and so on, that it is difficult to separate such therapies from those that emphasize common factors. Most of the integrations do not include any interventions that appear psychoanalytic (I use this word because "psychodynamic" often connotes Freudian drive theory).

Research regarding therapies that integrate psychoanalytic understandings include Safran and his colleagues's (Muran and Safran 2002) "Brief Relational Therapy" (cf. Curtis 2001, for a review), Ryle's Cognitive-Analytic Therapy (1990), multimodal therapy (Lazarus 1981, 2005), Multisystemic Treatment of Antisocial Behavior in Children and Adolescents (Henggeler et al., 1998), and Treatment for Chronic Depression: Cognitive Behavioral Analysis System of Psychotherapy (McCullough 2000). Safran and Muran (2002) found that there were fewer drop-outs with brief relational therapy than with cognitive-behavioral therapy and that patients at a high risk for treatment failure did better with their brief relational therapy. Studies showing positive results for cognitive-analytic therapy did not have control groups (Garyfallos et al. 1998, 2002; Dunn et al. 1997; Pollock 2001), although a study comparing cognitive-analytic theory and cognitive-behavioral therapy for people with severe and complex difficulties in a day hospital is currently being conducted (Schottenbauer, Glass, and Arnkoff 2005). Many uncontrolled studies demonstrate the effectiveness of multimodal therapy (Kwee et al. 1986; Kwee and Kwee-Taams 1994). Two controlled studies, one with middle-school dropouts (Gerler, Drew, and Mohr 1990) and one with children with learning disabilities (Williams 1988), have found multimodal therapy to be superior to a control group. Many controlled studies demonstrate the effectiveness of multisystemic therapy with juvenile offenders. A number of studies examining McCullough's cognitive-behavioral analysis system of psychotherapy have found that this therapy in conjunction with medications results in greater decreases in depression and anxiety, and improved psychosocial functioning (Schottenbauer, Glass, and Arnkoff 2005). A variant of this therapy—short-term anxiety regulating therapy—was shown to reduce anxiety (McCullough and Andrews 2001).

Other research on integrative therapies includes research on Stiles et al.'s (1990) assimilation model and therapies for specific disorders, such as Allen's (2003) unified therapy for borderline personality disorder, Mennin's emotion regulation therapy for generalized anxiety disorder (Mennin, in press), Scaturo's (1994) integrative program for agoraphobia, Wolfe's (2005) integrative therapy for anxiety disorders, Johnson and Taylor's (1996) integrative treatment for eating disorders, as well as a number of common factors approaches (Schottenbauer, Glass, and Arnkoff 2005). Many other integrative treatments have control groups, but do not involve psychoanalytic approaches, such as Greenberg's (Greenberg and Watson 1998) comparison of "process-experiential" therapy with traditional client-centered therapy. These researchers found more improvement on most measures in a six-month follow-up with process-experiential therapy. Researchers now are focused upon what treatments work best for specific types of patients with particular types of problems. Hopefully, more research will include treatments where a psychoanalytic perspective is integrated. Most current research, however, is comparing specific types of therapies, but not integrative ones (cf. Knekt and Lindfors 2004). There is a small amount of funding for psychotherapy research in this country and a small number of psychoanalytically oriented therapists who conduct psychotherapy outcome research. Given these realities, it seems unlikely that empirical research will provide any answers in the near future about the extent to which the integration of techniques is superior to the use of one approach alone. Clinicians will likely continue to proceed using what seems to work best in the consulting room.

GOING TO AFRICA

Jennifer had been referred to me originally by a friend of hers. I had provided her with the name of another analyst at the time. She later came to see me when I had time, dissatisfied with the other analyst and not willing to go back to discuss her dissatisfactions. I saw her for approximately a year, and she had then moved out of New York City. She came back, saw me briefly again, and then went to live abroad. At one point she called me to get a referral in another city, which I gave her. When she returned to live in New York City again and finish an academic degree, she came back to treatment with me one time per week. Jennifer was well-functioning, very intelligent, well-educated, verbal, attractive, and witty. She did not know what she wanted to do with her life and had inherited enough money so that she did not have to work if she chose not to. Jennifer was finishing her degree in a month but did not have a clue as to what she was going to do next. A romantic relationship had also just ended a few months before. She had noticed that she was attracted to men who did all sorts of exciting, challenging things and wanted to be like them, but that she did not even have the courage to make phone calls at times to people who probably did not want to speak with her.

Jennifer did not believe she had much in common with her mother. Her mother did not work; had cooked the same meal each Monday, each Tuesday, and so on; and, according to the patient, did not dress very well. Jennifer believed they had little in common with each other. During the first treatment era, she had reported a dream in which her mother drank something to kill herself and gave the glass to her to drink, too. She refused. Her father was an outgoing, smart fellow whom she appeared to respect more. It was clear she respected me, as I had come highly recommended by a friend whose judgment she highly respected. She had at one point fantasized that I ran a school for little witches, teaching them how to conduct good magic (this was several years before the Broadway musical *Wicked*). She would often mention works of literature, and say, "You know, what's the title?" assuming from my many books that I read quite a lot.

I had cancelled the previous session due to a funeral. Although I had offered her another time, she did not call back to do so. Instead she said did not wish to leave her sick baby kitten and had thought about canceling the session, anyway.

Jennifer arrived five minutes early for the session. She said there was not much going, and she barely talked. She was taking care of her kitten, doing her school work, hadn't heard back from any job applications (having made five), and was thinking of going to another country for a month to work as an unpaid intern on a charitable project. Her mother had told her about a new dating service she thought she would try. I was rather bored and was about to ask her if she had had any dreams. The following transcript was begun a couple of hours after the session from session notes:

P: I've been having a lot of anxiety dreams. I had one that my kitten was locked out and there was a lion outside. (Stops.)

T: A lion?

P: Well, let me tell you the whole dream. I'm riding in a car with my father and a guy.

T: Who is driving?

P: I don't know. It was not me. It must have been my dad. We were driving and there was construction on the road. The car goes across a bridge—what do you call the kind that goes up? (She demonstrates with her hands.)

T: A drawbridge.

P: Yes, a drawbridge and the car starts rising. The car goes up and it connects to a Mobius strip, goes upside down and comes back down. I said, "Did you see that?" No one seemed to know what I was talking about. I told them and they didn't believe me. We then had a conversation about what to do if a bridge goes up. My dad says, "I'd put it in reverse." My dad had said to me one time, "Would you do what everyone else was doing?" I was about ten and my friends had all jumped into a bush. They just bounced out, but when I jumped into the bush, I landed there and stayed there. He said, "If everyone jumped out of a car, would you?" I said, "Yes." He didn't know I had the image of a car going around slowly in our little cul de sac. Of course, I wouldn't jump out if a car were going fast down the road! The light turns green and there is a lion on the side of the road. It is lost, like it left the zoo. No one seems to know or to be concerned and we're in a car so we are safe. We get home. I'm in the house. We know there's a lion outside. I'm scared. I want to make sure this lion can't get in. I realize it's not a rabid lion, though. I'm in a subdivision. There is no one else around. I realize my kitten is outside. The lion must have smelled him. I was worried the kitten had been eaten. But I think the lion is a block away. I open the window. He has never left the house without me. I hear him scratching outside the window. I pick him up. It makes me think of that Saul Bellow book. You know, the character goes to Africa. I remember that refrain, "I want, I want, I want." His face (the Bellow character) looks like a lion. (Stops.) There is also that ad, with the lion and other animals and the cat food. The lion has a nice face.

T: Yeah, you want to pet him. Be the lion. (At this point she said nothing for a long time.) (Coaxing her, being the lion) I'm strong. . . . I scare people sometimes.

P: "I'm in the wrong place. I should be in the zoo. Did I have a girlfriend in the zoo? I have nowhere to go. It was much better in the zoo. They try to make it like Africa. I'm fast. (Being herself, again.) I'm trying to make it back inside. I was outside. (Being the lion again.) I eat them up.

T: Human beings?

P: I have no idea about lions. I don't think they usually eat human beings. (Being herself again.) I see the lion. Scary. I'm standing out there and no one else is outside. I was having such a nice time outside. I hear Jennifer calling. I love Jennifer. I'm such a cute kitten. Strangers love me. Jennifer feeds me with her hand.

T: You know this part of yourself— the cute little Jennifer.

P: Yes.

T: What do you think this is all about?

P: I know. It's about this strong part of myself.

T: But Jennifer is afraid of the strong part of herself.

P: I know. He must be following me. It was a long drive.

T: The lion is a male lion?

P: Yes. Definitely. Female lions are not very attractive. They are sort of plain.

T: Be the lion again. You see Jennifer. How do you feel?

P: Indifferent. . . . He's always doing horrible things to gazelles.

T: Become the lion. Whom did you eat?

P: Harry [A past live-in boyfriend]. I've had a lot of dreams. I woke up dreaming he was on Match.com. He had broken up with his old girlfriend and come back to New York.

T: How did you feel?

P: I didn't even read it.

T: Be Harry.

P: I'm pretending I'm cheery. I have no idea what I'm doing with my life.
. . . Maybe I'll go to another country. . . . I'm trying to impress Ethan with
how happy I am, but I'm not. . . . I don't know what I'm doing. I see I'm like
Harry right now.

T: (Noting that the time is running out.) Yes, you hurt him. But who are
the other gazelles?

P: I don't know.

T: You used to have those revenge fantasies that we never understood.

P: I'd like to get revenge on Craig [the boyfriend who had just ended the
relationship with her two months ago].

T: Who else?

P: I don't know. (Gets up to leave.) My father, maybe.

T: And your mother.

P: Yes (with a sigh of recognition). Yes, my mother.

T: You have been talking about wanting to get in touch with this strong,
king of the jungle part of yourself.

P: I know. I know all of this.

T: Yes, but there are different ways of knowing. You know it intellectually,
but you don't know yet fully experiencing being the lion. It is important to
find out what is inside you.

P: I'll see you in two weeks.

T: You know, you are getting somewhere. I think you should come next
week and find out more about this lion within you.

P: I know. . . . I will (she says with certainty).

T: You could have come last week, but you were scared.

P: I know. This lion part is scary. I don't want to eat people up.

T: You don't have to. You are afraid of how competitive you might be.
How you might eat up the other animals. But you don't have to be. You can
integrate the lion part with the Jennifer part and the kitten part. That's what
you've been wanting to do.

All the while, I am aware that there is a Frommer's South Africa which has
been lying on the counter with a lot of other books for the past few weeks
(it has two elephants on the cover). I am wearing a necklace made in Africa.
(I had purchased it at a museum, though, and had never been to Africa. Had
I worn it before? In addition, I had just put out a new little monkey hanging
down over the edge of the counter within the last week.) Although I would
have preferred that Jennifer do more of the dream work on her own, I'm
aware of time running out, both in the session, and in our work. She will
go off to another country unless I can get her hooked on how important this

work is. She has it all planned out. We shall hopefully deal with her fears of staying with me before she leaves once again. The dream is very rich, and we have only begun to move, at last, into Jennifer's inner life and all of the many resources from which she has kept herself cut off. "I want, I want, I want," she states, capturing both the desire and the lack. Had I left out at some point the brochure from the Cape Town conference with a lion on the front? I don't think so. I shall ask her if she had noticed anything about Africa in my office. Of course, the couch has monkeys and parrots on it, the bathroom has towels with monkeys, towels with elks, and a photo entitled "Bathing the Elephants in Central Park." I think we'll go safely home to Africa together.

After the next session (in which Jennifer reported she had recalled that the lioness does the hunting), I remembered a dream I had soon after coming to New York. In the dream, there was a castle in Central Park. I went to the castle and inside to a room with black gold-trimmed, wrought-iron doors behind which the "ivories" were kept.

What are the "ivories"? I'm not sure, but I think they are related to Ahab's ivory leg, the "ungraspable phantom," and a voyage over uncharted waters to Africa—Africa representing the dark, unknown continent of unconscious processes. Before I return to such abstract subjects as the "ungraspable phantom" and the creative unconscious, however, I would like to discuss three elements that I think are central to effective therapeutic action that I would like to articulate now. These are immediacy, reinforcement of variations or perturbations (to use the language from nonlinear dynamic systems theory), and connecting warded off aspects of self. I think this fragment of a session with Jennifer illustrates these points.

THREE ELEMENTS IMPORTANT TO
EFFECTIVE THERAPEUTIC ACTION

Thinking in terms of the principles of immediacy, reinforcement of perturbations, and connecting allows us to avoid arguments related to traditional theoretical approaches. There are obviously other very important elements to effective therapeutic action, such as the therapeutic relationship, but I am trying to get beyond what has been routinely noted as common factors. I shall elaborate on these three elements a bit further.

Immediacy

When people tell stories about moments that are affectively charged, they switch into the present tense: "So here I am, standing on the pier with this. . . ." or "This fellow comes up and. . . ." Experiences in the present are alive. The language is vivid and connects the subsymbolic and symbolic systems that Bucci (1997) has discussed. Frequently, I say to patients when they are discussing their childhood or some event from the recent past, "Be there now" (Safran and Segal 1990). The patient then recalls and imagines the sensory environs and the emotions felt at the time. Asking patients to be "in the moment" helps them to get away from intellectual associations and to experience a moment with the sensory-emotional-bodily aspects connected to the cognitive ones. Stern (2004) recently has dedicated a whole book to the importance of "the present moment." Stern's major interest, however, is in regard to the moments of meeting between patient and analyst and experiences of intersubjective consciousness.

As discussed earlier, actors trained in method acting learn to become intensely aware of the sensory details in their surroundings so that they can communicate their feelings to their audience and hopefully, have the audience experience something similar. An example of this occurs in the film *About Schmidt* with Jack Nicholson. Nicholson sits down in a hot tub and the buoyant, relaxing water surrounds him. Somehow he conveys the bubbles all around so that the audience experiences this moment—the feeling of the hot tub—as well. It is possible, however, to ask patients to experience fully various parts of themselves they mention in passing. An example of this follows.

Sara was abusing cocaine, bingeing and purging, exercising compulsively, engaging in various dangerous activities, and although very talented, waiting on tables for a living. In one session she mentioned the devil inside her. When I asked her to be the devil, what was the devil saying; she said she couldn't do it—it was too dangerous. She did, however, go home, and spend the week thinking of herself as the devil, and writing a poem with herself as the devil. She gave up her compulsive and destructive behaviors after this activity and referred to it herself as a changing point afterwards. Now there was nothing "nonpsychoanalytic" about my intervention. My asking her to be the devil, however, came from experience with Gestalt techniques. These techniques seem like a powerful way to help someone integrate disavowed aspects of self—a goal of psychoanalysis, a central element of therapeutic action that I shall discuss momentarily.

Perturbations that Facilitate Patient Goals

A systems perspective suggests that there are many routes to change—that perturbations (variations) of any sort in a system may lead to other changes. Deviations in the patient's thoughts, feelings, and behaviors occur naturally, as in any living system. An aspect of the therapist's role is to provide some knowledge about which perturbations are more likely than others to be in a direction that might facilitate the patient's achieving a goal. For Jennifer, the experience of being a lion is a perturbation. The experience got reinforced as she spent time as the lion. Another example would be that of a patient who was usually late for appointments, class, work, social engagements—everything—who came on time for a change. I inquired how she managed to do it. We went over the morning step by step. I referred to her as a person who can be on time. I commented, "So you wanted to be on time today." The perturbation of being on time was reinforced.

Perturbations related to unconscious processes are the psychoanalyst's stock and trade. This is how one finds out the source of a patient's anxieties. For example, the free-floating anxiety of another patient—now centered on how she will be able to support herself in a manner not too removed from the upper-middle-class style in which she was reared and on not being lonely—is known to her as not realistic. The anxiety persists, nonetheless. When she finally started remembering her dreams, she dreamed that she was in a car that went under the water in the East River. There were alligators in the water. She then dreamed she had gone to a hair cutter who insisted on cutting her hair in the basement of the patient's own building. In the basement there were mice running around that might bite her. She didn't understand why the woman wanted to cut her hair in the basement.

Exploration of the feeling of mice gnawing gets at a memory of being picked on at camp and of not being liked by anyone in the cabin for eight weeks. This patient is nice to everyone in an attempt to be liked, an attempt that backfires. Only by becoming a "gnawing, biting mouse," however—perhaps even a rat—can the patient capture the potential for being aggressive that has long been disavowed in the desire to be liked by everyone, stand up for herself, and risk being disliked by others. Without the perturbation of gnawing mice provided in the dream, the disavowed aggression had not been apparent in this well-functioning patient, although such unconscious aggression was suggested by the anxiety.

Reinforcing perturbations has also been the major way of intervening in behavioral therapy. Behavioral and cognitive therapists have simply been more active in suggesting them. They have not utilized fully, however, the perturbations that provide an inkling into unconscious associations.

Connecting Warded-Off or Disavowed Aspects of Self

Jennifer had disavowed the aspect of herself that wished to be "king of the jungle." She had no difficulty connecting with the cute, "kitteny" part of herself. The ways of being that people find either most unpleasant or most inconsistent with their dominant self-theory or self-with-other state are often kept out of focal awareness much of the time. These states may be either conscious or unconscious. They may or may not conflict with the dominant self-with-other state. Given that psychoanalysts are especially interested in helping people become more aware of these warded-off or unconscious aspects of self, it is somewhat surprising that the powerful approaches to access such states developed by Gestalt therapists are not more broadly used. These approaches share the therapeutic traction that analysts find in analyzing the transference—the power of working in the here-and-now. Some examples of evoking various self-states can be found in the recent psychoanalytic literature, especially that of the current American relational group. These various self-states can often be accessed most easily through the characters in dreams, as has been discussed previously, because the patient can feel that this not fully integrated way of being belongs to another person and not the patient him or herself.

TOWARD PSYCHOINTEGRATION

Perhaps the word psychoanalysis should be reserved for a process of opening up new meanings, especially unconscious ones. Perhaps the broader process I'm describing should be called psychosynthesis or psychointegration. "Psychosynthesis," however, was a word used by Assagioli (1965) who departed from Freudianism, having been influenced by humanistic and experiential psychotherapies. He listed five differences with psychoanalysis, some of which are relevant to the current discussion. He placed greater emphasis upon (1) the will, deliberation, decisions, and so on; (2) the direct experience of the self; (3) recognition of positive, joyous experiences, loneliness not being considered essential; (4) the use of active techniques; and (5) conscious reconstruction of the personality. His ideas about the nature of what is unconscious, some of which are taken from Jungian psychoanalysis, imbue the word with too many specific meanings. "Psychointegration," as used previously only by Szalita (1994) to describe her version of psychoanalysis, is perhaps more appropriate. Psychology and psychoanalysis also must connect. If the adventure fails, we have, as Joyce put it, only "piers—disappointed bridges"—a passionless psychology and a wooly-mammoth psychoanalysis.

Chapter 9

The Affective Revolution and the Creative Unconscious: Two Areas of Convergence

The decade of the brain is just now ending and it is our view that the domain of emotion—affective science will be where new insights and improved understanding are most visible in this new century.

—Davidson, Jackson, and Kalin (2000, 904)

Other than banning the study of unconscious processes in psychology, the split between psychoanalysis and psychological science was most apparent in the neglect of affect in academic psychology and neuroscience. After the heydays of behaviorism and cognition, however, emotion has increasingly become a focus in psychological science, allowing for greater overlap with psychoanalytic understandings. The interest in emotion has even been called a revolution similar to the earilier "cognitive revolution" (Barsade, Brief, and Spataro 2003). And while emotion was always considered to be central to psychoanalytic theory, it was thought by many to be a missing aspect of Freud's theory (Spezzano 1993).

EMOTION IN PSYCHOLOGICAL SCIENCE

Between 1930 and 1960 there were relatively few books on emotion in scientific psychology. "Both neuroscience and cognitive science have neglected emotion until recently," Damasio wrote in 2000 (12). Tomkins and Plutchik published a book on emotions in 1962 and various other theories appeared in subsequent years (Barnard and Teasdale 1991; Bower 1981, 1992; Buck 1984, 1999; Frijda 1986, 2000; Izard and Bartlett 1972; Izard and Kobak 1991; Johnson and Multhaup 1992; Jones 1995; Lazarus and Folkman 1984, 1991; Leventhal and Scherer 1987; Oatley and Johnson-Laird 1987; Spezzano

1993). Cognitive researchers began to realize the necessity of examining the interplay between emotions and cognition (Clark and Fiske 1982). "Cognitive scientists are just beginning to pay attention to motivation and emotion, a long-neglected dimension of consciousness" (Ellis and Newton 2000, ix). Recently a number of books on cognition and emotion (e.g., Christianson 1992; Dalgleish and Power 1999; Moore and Oaksford 2002; Prinz 2004), many books on emotion (e.g., Despret 2004; Lewis and Haviland-Jones 1993, 2000; Mayne and Bonanno 2001; Turner 2004) and journals entitled *Cognition and Emotion* (1987), *Consciousness and Emotion*, and now *Emotion* (2001) have been published. Although cognitive neuroscience has become a hot topic, "affective neuroscience" (Davidson and Sutton 1995; Panksepp 1996, 1998), "affective science" (Davidson, Scherer, and Goldsmith 2003), and emotional cognition (Moore and Oaksford 2003; cf. also Cicchetti and Toth 1995; Eich et al. 2000; Ellis 1995; Lane and Nadel 2000) have now arrived, perhaps somewhat spurred on by the popular writings of Damasio (1994, 1999, 2003) and LeDoux (1994a, 1995, 1996) and also Goleman's (1995) work on "emotional intelligence" (see also Salovey and Mayer 1989–1990).

Damasio (2000) attributed the scientific neglect of emotion during the twentieth century to the belief that emotion was too subjective, too vague, and too irrational—being "at the opposite end of the finest human ability, reason" (12). He also attributed the neglect to three other factors: (1) the lack of an evolutionary perspective in the study of brain and mind in the twentieth century, noting certain exceptions, such as Edelman (1992); (2) the disregard for homeostatic regulation processes in shaping views about how the brain generated mental states; and (3) the absence of the notion of the organism in cognitive science and neuroscience, with the brain remaining consistently separated from the body.

Emotion likely did fall outside the domain of cognitive neuroscience due to the influence of Cartesian dualism (Lane, et al. 2000). In Descartes's model, reason was a manifestation of the soul whereas emotions were considered an expression of bodily phenomena that were shared with other animals. Reason and emotion could oppose each other and were antagonistic and separable. There has now been a reconciliation of cognition and emotion, with Damasio (1994) showing that emotional processes are required for certain types of decision making and Salovey and Mayer (1989–1990) demonstrating that emotional intelligence is an important predictor of success separate from purely cognitive intelligence. Lane, Nadel, Allen, and Kaszniak (2000) present the prevailing point of view when they state that "there may be no such thing as pure cognition without emotion, or pure emotion without cognition" (6). Contemporary researchers have adopted a model of affect infusing cognition and vice versa more akin to the view of Spinoza than to that of Descartes (Damasio 2003).

Now emotions are seen as organizing experience and linking biological and psychological systems (Levenson 1994). "Affect may well be the central organizing principle of individuals, groups, and society as a whole," state Mayne and Ramsey (2001, 31). Goal regulation is a function of relationships between cognitions and emotions (Gray and Braver 2002). Emotions are also seen as a signal to interrupt behavior (Simon 1967), as in Freudian theory.

The emotional-cognitive systems regulate behavioral activation and behavioral inhibition (Gray 2001). Emotions induce and constrain actions designed to alter the physical and social world (Lewis and Ferrari 2001) in ways that facilitate goal-attainment (Oatley and Johnson-Laird 1987; Stein and Trabasso 1992). Three levels of organization emerge (Lewis and Ferrari 2001). The organization that builds over seconds rapidly dissipates when desires are fulfilled. When action falls short of fulfilling desires, moods develop and action tendencies continually arise as long as an emotional organization remains in place. Recursive self-organizing processes leave some trace behind and personalities develop, such as those characterized by shyness, grumpiness, friendliness, and so on. Activation of connections in neural networks enhances the probability that the same patterns will recur. Cognitive-emotion-behavioral couplings are the source of personality structure.

Emotion in Psychoanalytic Theory

Affects, to many scholars, were not the centerpiece of Freud's work. Freud's theory emphasized more what was wished for than what was feared. Although his theory was one of both wishes and fears, the forbidden wishes that were repressed were of greater interest. As Fonagy, Gergely, Jurist, and Target (2002) have noted, Freud had two tendencies in the way he portrayed affects—one as manifestations of drives, the other as signals, as found in *Inhibitions, Symptoms, and Anxiety* (1926). By the time he elaborated the important concept of signal anxiety, his ideas about personality and the intervention of the psychoanalyst interpreting the repressed wishes had already been developed. Green (1999) has argued that only the first tendency represents a uniquely psychoanalytic perspective and that the second view places too much importance on conscious regulatory control, obscuring the effects of unconscious factors. Given all of the recent research indicating how unconscious signals affect regulation (Etkin et. al 2004; Ohman, Flykt, and Lundqvist 2000; Zajonc 1994) the idea of conscious signal anxiety is not inconsistent with a view of the overall importance of unconscious factors.

Emotion, especially anxiety, has been crucial in psychoanalytic theories since Freud (Shapiro and Emde 1992). Horney and Sullivan made anxiety central to their understanding of behavior, while preserving the role of unconscious and nonrational factors. Fenichel (1945) and Rapaport (1953) discussed the overwhelming effects of anxiety, especially after trauma, and the taming by the ego of the affects. Melanie Klein (1964, 1975) emphasized the role of feelings, and Kernberg (1982) saw affects as providing links between representations of self and others. Eagle (1984) has argued that modern dynamic therapies emphasize disavowed affect and disclaimed action tendencies as central to therapeutic change. Spezzano (1993) recently has put forth the view that affect was the foundation of Freud's theory of mental structures and documented his theory of affects—of mourning, melancholia, rage, anxiety, guilt, and so on. He argues that affect is the ontological ground of psychoanalysis, not drive, object representations, or the self. He also argues that affects are "preexperiential 'wired-in' capacities that constitute our fundamental categories of meaning" (113) and that later theories complement but do not contradict Freud's views.

Emotion in Other Psychotherapies

Dollard and Miller (1950) articulated how the reduction of anxiety is crucial for both psychoanalysts and behavioral therapists and how they both engage in systematic desensitization. Their view was that anxiety related to cues connected with attempts to gratify important interpersonal and other needs was what brought most people to therapy. Gray (1987) has more recently stated something similar although he has referred to "fear": The behaviors that lead to psychiatric hospitalization can for the "most part . . . be regarded as fear gone wrong, either because it is excessive, or because it is inappropriate". (332). In contemporary emotion-focused therapies that are dynamically oriented (Fosha 2000; McCullough-Vaillant 1996), the therapist conceptualizes primarily defenses, anxiety and painful affect in what is called the "triangle of defensive response" (Fosha, 107). Although operant behaviorists focus upon reinforcements as the major route to change, for escape and avoidance responses the absence of anxiety or safety is viewed as reinforcing (Seligman and Johnston 1973). Mahoney's (1991) constructivist approach in cognitive psychotherapy has incorporated emotion as a fundamental aspect of meaning construction in contrast to previous rational approaches in cognitive therapy where reason was elevated above emotion.

The physiological components of emotions are not necessarily conscious. Drawing from the work of Lang (1993), Ohman, Flykt, and Lundqvist (2000) state: "Conceptualizing emotion as composed of dissociable components implies that 'unconscious emotion' simply is a specific case of a dissociation—evidence of physiological or behavioral emotional activation in the absence of verbal reports of emotion or emotionally relevant stimulation" (297). As noted in an earlier chapter, Zajonc (1994) has argued that his research and that of others demonstrates that emotions can be unconscious. Etkin (Etkin et al. 2004) showed that the amygdala responds even when people are not conscious of the response. For Clore as well (1994), emotions inform the individual of the outcomes of "unconscious computations concerning the significance of events for one's concerns" so that "the individual can then allocate resources appropriately" (111).

Feelings guide behavior (Panksepp 1998). According to Dodge (1991), emotion is also "the energy that drives, organizes, amplifies, and attenuates cognitive activity" (159). They influence the tendency to avoid situations that threaten survival or survival of the meaning system and the tendency to seek out situations again. They reguide behavior, "first in very impulsive ways and then in more measured ways" through a "highly conserved subcortical train mechanism we still share with other species" (Panksepp 1994, 21). For Ekman, as well, emotions evolved for their adaptive value and prepare the organism for "quite different actions" (1994, 15). Ekman believes it is useful to think in terms of "emotion families" (15).

There seems to be little consensus about the use of the terms "feelings," "emotions," and "affect," although it appears that affect is the most general term, emotions more specific, and feelings the subjective sense of an emotion. When the emotion occurs frequently or continuously, it is a mood. Feelings are "desires satisfiable by actions that I can imagine performing" (Newton 2000, 101). Desires are associated with actions people can imagine performing. The image here is not a visual image but a motor image of what it would feel like to perform a certain action (Newton 2000). In voluntary action there is a motor image of the desired goal-state and this image plays a role in guiding the action (Blakemore et. al, 1998). There is no clear boundary between emotion and motivation (Ohman, Flykt, and Lundqvist 2000). Panksepp (2000b), noting that feeling states provide fundamental values for the guidance of behavior, argues that the neurobiological systems mediating the basic emotions are recruited to cope with a variety of survival needs.

According to Oatley and Johnson-Laird's (1987) theory, complementing Johnson-Laird's (1983) model of the mind, emotions impose a mode of operations consistent with the evolutionary function of that emotion. Processing is driven by goals. Fear and anxiety come from a background ensuring survival and safety. One of the important roles for emotion, then, is to provide a mechanism by which priorities can be assigned or altered. Emotions operate by the propagation of "emotion signals" originating as a function of obstacles to the attainment of important goals. Mathews and MacLeod (1994) think that this theory would predict the data they reviewed regarding the effects of anxiety on selective attention and memory. It also sounds quite similar to Freud's ideas about signal anxiety.

Centrality of Emotion Networks (or Schemas)

The current focus upon emotion is apparent in two major areas: the centrality of emotion networks and affect regulation. Neural network theories are very helpful in understanding emotional responses. The emotional system is composed of interconnected networks of structures in the brain including the thalamus, hypothalamus, hippocampus, amygdala, cingulate cortex, and prefrontal cortex (Davidson and Irwin 1999; Kolb and Whishaw 2001). Recently, a number of theorists in neuroscience (LeDoux 1993b; Panksepp 1998), psychoanalysis (Bucci 1997), cognitive science (Mathews and MacLeod 1994), cognitive therapy (Leahy 2002), and experiential therapy (Greenberg and Safran 1987; Greenberg 1993) have begun to write simply about emotion networks, emotion schemas, or mood networks (Bower 1981, 1992). (For a review of some of these theories, see Forgas 1999.) Ohman, Flykt, and Lundqvist (2000) understand their data regarding the preattentive bias to detect threatening information described in a previous chapter as being understood in terms of the neural network model for emotional activation presented by Damasio and colleagues and for fear as presented by LeDoux.

Bower (1981) had presented the earliest explicit "network theory" of emotion. In Bower's theory concepts, events, and emotions can all be represented as nodes within a representational network. Activation may spread to adjoining nodes—memory nodes or physiological or linguistic nodes. Emotional networks differ from other memory structures in that they directly involve the limbic circuits that drive behavior (Lang 1993). When expectations based upon preexisting schemas are not met, arousal occurs. Activation occurs from the concrete to the abstract in a bottom-up process, or vice versa in a top-down process, leading to arousal and preparation to cope with a changing environment (Mandler 1985). Comparison with preexisting patterns allows for rapid processing, but also for biases (Horowitz 1991). Activation of an emotional component of a network automatically leads to activation of other components, increasing the probability of the whole component becoming conscious (Lang 1984).

The other network theories have in common the postulating of at least two major networks—sensory network(s) and the other(s) more cognitive (Johnson and Multhaup 1992; Leventhal and Scherer 1987; Power and Dalgleish 1997; Teasdale and Barnard 1993). LeDoux (1996), similarly, as discussed earlier, described two routes to the amygdala—a "low" route where information goes directly to the amygdala from the sensory thalamus, and a "high" route where information goes from the thalamus to the amygdala via the neocortex for evaluation. LeDoux (2002) points out that this high route was often misunderstood as being conscious by readers of his earlier work, but it is not necessarily true. The direct route is faster and results in action that may be altered after assessment. Defense, food-seeking, and sex circuits all lead to such responses. Both systems operate simultaneously.

Affect Regulation and Its Failures

Emotions, or passions as they were often called, and their management have been a subject in philosophy since at least the time of the ancient Greeks. Fonagy, Gergely, Jurist, and Target (2002), in a review of Western philosophical perspectives on affect regulation point out that the ancient Greek virtue *sophrosune* concerned finding the right amount of pleasure, not restricting it. In most of both Asian and Western history, however, the theme has often been how to control emotions through reason.

In psychology Piaget and Inhelder (1971) stated that self-regulation seems to constitute one of the most "universal characteristics of life and the most general mechanisms to be found" (154). Research on emotion regulation began to flourish in the past three decades, initially in child development. Now emotion regulation is a subject of research in biological psychology and neuroscience, cognitive, social, personality, clinical, and health psychology (for a review and references, see Gross 1998). Although this research had its roots in psychoanalytic thinking, it is more focused on a concern with adaptive coping processes. The processes underlying emotion and emotion regulation appear to be the same (Campos, Frankel, and Camras 2004).

Freud (1926) was concerned with anxiety arising from both situational realities and strong impulses overwhelming the ego. The idea of repression and other defenses was that they protected against overwhelming anxiety. Managing drives and achieving pleasure through an optimal level of discharge can be thought of as a model of affect regulation. Hartmann and Lowenstein (1962) described how "regulations that have taken place in the outside world" become "replaced by inner regulations" (150). Although Spezzano (1993) argues persuasively that the concepts of affect and affect regulation have always been implicit in the major psychoanalytic theories, the term "affect regulation" has been used explicitly in many recent writings (Curtis 1991a; Fonagy, Gergely, Jurist, and Target 2002; Schore 1994), especially in reference to the mutual regulation of affect in dyadic systems, such as the infant-caretaker relation (Beebe and Lachmann 1994; Stern 1985; Stolorow and Atwood 1992). Perhaps because self-psychologists have used the concept most frequently, affect regulation has often been thought of as related to a deficit theory of psychic functioning. As Wilson, Passik, and Faude (1990) have argued, however, there is no reason for affect regulation to be associated with deficit more than conflict. For psychoanalysts, the concept of affect regulation is usually linked to the broader concept of self-regulation.

The concepts of affect regulation or emotion regulation have not been well defined (Bridges, Denham, and Ganiban 2004; Eisenberg and Spinrad 2004; Gross 1998, 1999; Magai 1999; Thompson 1994). Affect is usually, but not always, used as a broader term, encompassing both emotion and mood. Sroufe (1996) considers affect regulation to be the capacity to maintain organization in the face of tension. Therefore, affect regulation becomes essential to the maintenance of focused conscious activity. Gross (1999) defines affect regulation as "processes by which individuals influence which emotions they have, when they have them, and how they experience and express these emotions" (275). Fonagy, Gergely, Jurist, and Target explain that affect regulation has implications for the self, with self-regulation as a higher kind of affect regulation. Their psychoanalytic view emphasizes the role of mentalization and reflective functioning in the regulation process. Thompson (1994), a developmental theorist, also defines affect regulation as consisting of the "extrinsic and intrinsic processes responsible for monitoring, evaluating, and modifying emotional reactions, especially their intensive and temporal features, to accomplish one's goals" (27–28).

Events are appraised in terms of their significance for survival and well-being (Scherer 2000), which I have argued is related to the survival of a meaning system in human beings. Scherer specifies five "checks" (229) which are expected to always occur in the same order : (1) a novelty check—whether a novel event has occurred or is to be expected; (2) an intrinsic pleasantness check; (3) a goal/need significance check and an urgency subcheck; (4) a coping potential check with subchecks for control, power, and potential for adjustment to the final outcome; and (5) a norm/self compatibility check with subchecks for external and internal standards. Each evaluation check elicits a specific functional response pattern. Although Scherer acknowledges that there may be certain prototypical patterns that are hard-wired, as suggested by Ekman (1984), Izard (1971) and Tomkins (1962), he does not assume the whole pattern of response is hard-wired.

Westen (1994), who understands motivation in terms of affect regulation, specifically the attempt to maximize pleasure and minimize pain, proposes that feelings are the mechanism for the selection of behaviors, coping, and defensive strategies and has described affect regulation as central to behavioral, cognitive, psychodynamic, and evolutionary approaches to psychology. In behavioral theories the consequences of action—pleasure and pain—determine whether the behavior will be repeated again. In cognitive theories, affect regulation happens when discrepancies occur between desired and actual states and emotional feedback activates responses designed to minimize unpleasant feelings and maximize pleasant ones. In psychodynamic theories, wishes and fears relate to pleasure and pain. People distort information about themselves in order to avoid unpleasant emotions and to find compromise solutions (Brenner 1982) for regulating various affects simultaneously. In evolutionary theory, emotions and feeling states channel behavior in adaptive ways not rigidly controlled by instinct (Plutchik 1980; Tomkins 1980).

Verbal mediation may be helpful in that emotion regulation is superior in individuals showing left prefrontal cortex activity. Individuals with this activation are better able to suppress negative affect (Jackson, Burghy, Hanna, Larson, and Davidson, 2000). Redington and Reidbord (1992; Reidbord and Redington 1992; Reidbord 1993, 1995) have examined the affect regulation of patients and therapists. Schore (1994) has interpreted their findings (Redington and Reidbord, 1992; Reidbord and Redington, 1992) as demonstrating how nonverbal affect regulation occurs between therapist and patient. These researchers studied changes in the autonomic nervous system activity of patients—such as heart rate changes—during insight-oriented therapy.

Emotional regulation involves both conditions surrounding the generation of an emotion and responses to an emotion once it occurs (Gross 1999). Gross (1998) further differentiated among the strategies antecedent to an emotion in the following manner: (1) selecting or avoiding situations, such as flying on airplanes; (2) situation modification, such as asking a neighbor to lower the music at three in the morning; (3) attentional deployment, including distraction, concentration on work, for example, controlled starting of an emotion, as done by method actors, and rumination; and (4) cognitive changes, including classical defenses, downward social comparison, cognitive reframing, and reappraisal. Among response modulation strategies, he refers to drugs, alcohol, food, exercise, biofeedback, relaxation, expressive behavior, and suppression of emotions. If people are told that their mood is not changeable, they do not engage in various strategies they attempt when they believe their mood is changeable, such as eating fattening snacks, seeking immediate gratification, and engaging in frivolous procrastination (Tice, Bratslavsky, and Baumeister 2001). Psychopathology is considered to be related to failures in regulation strategies (Allen 2003). "Emotional self-regulation therapy" has now been created (Capafons 1999).

These regulation techniques noted in the experimental psychology literature all appear either to be conscious or readily accessible to consciousness. The traditional defenses from a psychoanalytic perspective need to be added to the strategies above, as they all help with emotional regulation. The rubric of emotional regulating strategies allows us to combine the research by experimental researchers on emotion with psychodynamically inspired work on personality, motivation, cognition, and memory (cf. Mikulincer and Shaver, in press).

EMOTION AND DESIRE

How does the focus upon affect and its regulation apply to the change process described previously and people's primary desires? It was argued that new experiences and new meanings of experience provide a comprehensive model of the change process. As we have now seen, these experiences are organized in affective/cognitive/behavioral networks.

Returning to the two major desires, survival and survival of the meaning system, when emotional regulation is made central, we see that affective/ cognitive networks signal an evaluation process regarding progress toward fulfillment of desires. Anxiety is then (a) regulated through defensive processes, including selective attention and memory; (b) tolerated by simultaneous activation of soothing, hopeful networks; or (c) becomes overwhelming and paralyzing. If the lack of fulfillment of important desires leads to a loss of the way of making meaning, sad and/or angry feelings will emerge that must be tolerated if new ways of making meaning are to be found or created. In this model of change, toleration of the lack of fulfillment of desires becomes central as opposed to awareness of unconscious desires in the Freudian model. In both models, experience must be reorganized. In the Freudian model, unconscious desires had to be integrated into the ego. In the current model, the painful lack of fulfillment of desire leads to reorganization of the way of making meaning—of views of the self and the world. The change process looks something like what was depicted in figure 8.1. Although this model should be acceptable to nonpsychoanalysts, psychoanalysts may react initially by thinking that it does not capture the analytic change process. It should be pointed out, however, that the whole process is potentially infused by unconscious experiences—the desires may be unconscious, their lack of fulfillment may be unconscious, and the whole scenario may be enacted transferentially with a therapist who helps make it conscious. On the other hand, the change process may sometimes be conscious and may occur outside psychotherapy.

Emotion researchers have investigated largely the effects of threats to physical survival in their studies—the effects of the perception of snakes or spiders upon subsequent responses. Threats to the meaning system—to the fundamental views of the self and the world—have rarely been investigated experimentally (with notable exceptions being Curtis, Pacell, and Garzsynski

[1991]; Shevrin [2000]; and Greenberg, Solomon, and Pyszczynski [1997]).
Future research should move into this area.

The Quantum Jitter of the Creative Unconscious

Having examined the ways in which psychology and psychoanalysis have
now focused on the organization of experience in emotional networks related
to the fulfillment of primary desires and the regulation of emotional experiences, it is now time to return to the other primary area of convergence — the
study of unconscious processes — the place where psychoanalysis has always
distinguished itself.

Although psychology and various forms of psychotherapy are increasingly
taking into account unconscious processes, there are still differences between
psychoanalysis and other therapies in the extent to which unconscious processes are valued.

Earlier I described a "social unconscious" in addition to what is unconscious intrapsychically. A concept of a "generative" unconscious in psychoanalysis has been discussed recently by Newirth (2003) and previously by
Curtis (1994). Newirth differentiated it from both the repressed unconscious
of Freudian psychoanalysis and the dissociative unconscious of relational
psychoanalysis, but did not include the unconscious of cognitive science.
Curtis's (1994) idea of a creative or "chthonic" unconscious was given a
name derived from Greek mythology ("chthonic" referring to spirits and dei-
ties living under the earth).

The idea of a creative unconscious provides a useful concept for unifying all unconscious experiences that have never reached awareness, both
those referred to as dynamic and those referred to as cognitive. The nature
of unconscious processes encompasses the whole world of what has been
known as "primary" processes — nonrational and nonlogical thinking — to
most clinicians. Matte-Blanco (1988) suggested that unconscious processes
have a logic of their own that effaces differences. Conscious processing, according to Matte-Blanco, follows Aristotelian logic, sharpens differences, and
moves between the concrete and the abstract. Newirth argued that the view
of unconscious processes as a repository of historical, irrational, or relational
schemas encouraged a view of the unconscious "simply as meanings outside
of awareness . . . [that are] a source of energy" (168).

Creative artists and scientists draw nonstop upon processes that are not
fully conscious. The vampires of Anne Rice and the madwoman in Stephen
King's attic are not emanations from the "clean" unconscious processes of
cognitive neuroscience. The extensive use of dreams by writers has been
documented by Epel (1993), for example. Scientists also draw from dreams,

as in the well-known example of Kachele's vision of the structure of benzene. One composer and teacher of music composition told me he directed his students to think about the musical problem they wanted to solve before they went to sleep at night so that they could work on the composition. Creative individuals have been found to fall asleep more quickly and to solve more problems through dreams than less creative individuals (Sladeczek and Domino 1985). As suggested by Matte-Blanco and Newirth, unconscious processes efface differences. For example, one person told me he had forgotten the name of a road he was supposed to turn on. All he could think of was "five milk pails." When he saw "Ive's Dairy Road," however, he knew it was the right turn.

A conceptualization of a creative unconscious precludes any benefit from separating the cognitive or adaptive unconscious from a psychoanalytic one. Speaking of a "cognitive unconscious" as distinct from a psychoanalytic unconscious does not help us understand Sirhan Siirhan or a serial killer. The creative unconscious can include the dark, murky, and soft of the arts and humanities as well as bright and clean of the "hard" sciences. A concept of a creative unconscious includes the dark and murky place from which all emanated and emanates. And, although unconscious processes can lead to quite adaptive functioning, they can also lead to deviant desires and fantasies—both experiences of genius and experiences of insane malevolence. There are not two or three "unconsciouses"—what is unconscious is simply unconscious.

Primary Process Thinking

Freud described the way primary process thinking showed up in symptoms, for example, jokes, slips of the tongue, and dreams. Holt (2002) has discussed how primary process thinking can be identified as well in free associations, other verbal tests, thematic apperception test stories, and Rorchach responses. He argues that art is resistant to reduction to secondary process thinking. As Isodora Duncan stated: "If I could tell you what it meant, there would be no point in dancing it" (Lewis 2007). The link between creativity and the controlled use of primary process holds for males, but not for females (Holt 2002; Russ 2002). Primary process thinking is considered to violate Aristotelian logic (Meloy 1986). It has been considered to be related to the satisfaction of desires (Spiro 1992), independent of feedback from reality (Noy 1969), and to be the "outcome of automatic mental routines triggering and distorting one another and the absence of intentional control" (Ochse 1989, 315). Fast (1983) considered primary process thinking to be linked to Piaget's sensorimotor intelligence and event-centered cognitions. Dorpat

(1994) has recently conceptualized the primary process system as organizing, evaluating, representing, and communicating the meanings of an individual's interactions with the external world. He (1991) has also suggested that the primary process system plays a role in both conscious and unconscious perception. Guided imagery therapy elicits more primary process (Stigler and Pokorny 2001). Developmentally, primary process organization is supplanted by secondary process organization around age seven (Brakel, Shevrin, and Villa 2002). As discussed earlier, Bucci (1997) has reconceptualized primary process thinking as subsymbolic processing.

The intentional loosening of controls allows for connections to be made that cannot when Aristotelian logic dominates. Opposites can coexist. Rothenberg (1996) has described this quality of thinking in creative people as Janusian thinking. Count Alfred Korzybski (1948) also emphasized the value of non-Aristotelian, nonlinear, non-Newtonian, and non-Euclidean (curved space) view of knowledge and epistemology, a precursor of Gestalt therapy's emphasis upon here-and-now experiences before they were seen as crucial by existentialists.

In recent years superstring theory has been offered as a way to unify relativity theory and quantum theory. This theory, acknowledging the limitations of the visible world, and seeking to recognize what is believed about the macroscopic universe and the microscopic underworld, suggests that the basic fabric of matter is not the different categories of particles that have been discovered in recent years, such as quarks and buons. Instead it proposes that the six basic particles are composed of the same basic fabric of matter—strings or loops formed into different patterns. Like these strings transforming themselves from circles to twists to many possibilities, and throbbing all the while in what Brian Greene (1999) has called a "quantum jitter," there is a microscopic underworld to our identities that is not simply old or young, masculine or feminine, black or white, but infinite in its array of patterns, like the basic fabric of reality itself. Becoming aware of our own chthonic underworlds expands our consciousness, our empathy for others, and awareness of our potentialities for existence—knowledge not only from where we have come, but also of possibilities for what we may become.

Embracing the Dark, Murky, Soft, and Wet: A Jungle Where Alligators May Bite

A broad view of unconscious processes, not simply as repressed, dissociated, or "cognitive" but instead as a source of infinite connections and unfoldings, akin in some ways to Fromm's (1992) idea of a life force, but with destructiveness an inherent part of any creative force, allows psychoanalysis, the study of unconscious processes, to be integrated with psychology, the scientific study of behavior, thoughts, and feelings, and for general principles to be integrated with the idiosyncrasies of specific cases.

Some people often make decisions, quickly or slowly, that are excellent, while others often make decisions that are disastrous. The regulation of experiences, including our emotional ones, often reflective of what is occurring unconsciously, is what helps some people make better decisions than others—those Salovey and Mayer (1989–1990) and Goleman (1995) called "emotionally intelligent." This ability marks the difference between knowledge and wisdom. Even Gladwell (2005) admits that those who make good decisions "owe success, at least in part, to the steps they have taken to shape and manage and educate their unconscious reactions" (16).

For many people, there are rats and alligators in the unconscious and people do not want to be bitten when they go down "under there." For others, who stay outside in the daylight on the open streets, unconscious processes function like ghosts, grabbing at passers-by unaware. Many of us who have endured the "dark and murky"—and many who simply fear those dark, murky unconscious desires and fantasies—stay "in control" so that unconscious processes— including experiences that would lead to creativity— are inhibited.

If we are to help people with our Western therapeutic interventions, we must go to the unknown, that space where creative life begins. We must go to that uncivilized, primitive jungle within us where the beasts still prowl and sometimes catch us unawares. We must draw from the not fully conscious— not always adaptive, but forever generative—resources within ourselves.

Chapter 10

Summary: Toward a Unifed Paradigm for a Psychoanalytically Informed Psychological Science

Two categories of human desires have been suggested as a useful rubric: (1) those related primarily to physical survival; and (2) those related to survival of the meaning system and the meaning-making system itself. These categories correspond to the two routes to emotional responses in the brain and to different routes to change in therapy that have differentiated the bottom-up behavioral and experiential therapies from often more top-down psychoanalytic and cognitive ones.

The Freudian division of ego, id and superego is now considered untenable and outdated by even Freudian analysts. Consistent with separating desires into both the physical and psychological, a new tri-partite theory of the self compatible with the major thinking in both psychology and psychoanalysis is suggested. Like Plato's charioteer with two horses, it is suggested that we think of the physical, experiencing self as the charioteer, and the actual and ideal selves — two facets of the meaning-making self — as the horses to be kept in balance. The differentiation of the actual from the ideal self is the major theme regarding the self cutting across both psychology and psychoanalysis. The ideal self is influenced to a large extent by the impact of visual stimuli in the media of which people are not fully conscious, creating a visible, social "unconscious," leaving many experiences in the environment not attended to, not only the intrapsychic feelings and desires prominent in Freud's theory.

Three views of the unconscious mind exist in psychology and psychoanalysis — the "repressed" unconscious of Freudian psychoanalysis, the "dissociated" unconscious of both interpersonal/relational psychoanalysis and neuroscience, and the "adaptive" unconscious of cognitive psychology. Thinking of all attention and memory as selective in nature renders these distinctions unnecessary. All attention and memory are influenced by the two major motivational systems. Until recently, cognitive psychologists only examined mental processes when participants were not made anxious by threats to the preservation of meaning and sanity itself. Psychoanalysts, however, have noted especially the processes of defense allowing for the preservation of the meaning-making system. Examination of mental processes in light of attention and inattention to threats to physical and psychological survival makes both normal and defensive processes understandable by the same principles.

Contemporary psychoanalysts have abandoned the interpretation-insight model of change. Instead, change is viewed as emanating from new experiences as well as from new meanings of experiences. A "new experiences" model suggests that some of the primacy given to verbal associations in psychoanalysis is outdated. A new experiences model of change allows for integration of the various models of psychotherapy and their techniques. All treatments need to consider the importance of unconscious factors, given the increasingly wide body of research findings on the role of nonconscious processes. Change occurs with the top-down processes of conscious attempts to alter thoughts, feelings, images, and behaviors interacting with bodily sensations and other bottom-up processes that are not fully conscious. Changes in the sensory-motor system through a more systematic focus upon the body, images, and behavior are consistent with the new experiences model of change. Such a model of change provides an umbrella for psychoanalysts, cognitive-behavioral, and experiential therapists. For a comprehensive theory of therapeutic action, either psychoanalysis must account more fully for other routes to change or else experiential and cognitive-behavioral theories must incorporate more thoroughly ways of helping patients gain more access to unconscious factors affecting behaviors, thoughts, and feelings, and almost everything interesting and passionate about human beings.

Psychoanalysis and psychology have converged in a greater focus upon emotional cognitions and affect regulation as a consequence of the "affective revolution," and with a greater recognition of the importance of unconscious processes. Crucial to these views of self, the mind, and change is a view of unconscious processes not as simply repressed, dissociated, or adaptive, but a cauldron of potential creations, a veritable "smithy of the soul," to quote James Joyce (1914–1915), forging for good or bad "the uncreated conscience" of our race.

References

Ablon, S. J. 2005. Is there a psychoanalytic process? What we can learn from empirical study of the analytic hour. Paper presented at the American Psychoanalytic Association Convention, January. New York, NY.

Ablon, J. S., and Jones, E. E. 2002. Validity of controlled clinical trials of psychotherapy: Findings from the NIMH treatment of depression collaborative research program. *American Journal of Psychiatry* 159, 775–783.

Abt, L. E. 1992. Clinical psychology and the emergence of psychotherapy. *Professional Psychology: Research and Practice* 23, 176–178.

Adams, H. E., Wright, L. W., Jr., and Lohr, B. A. 1996. Is homophobia associated with homosexual arousal? *Journal of Abnormal Psychology* 105, 440–446.

Adler, A. 1917. *Study of organ inferiority and its psychical compensation.* New York: Nervous and Mental Disease.

Ahsen, A. 1973. *Basic concepts in eidetic psychotherapy.* New York: Brandon House.

Ahsen, A. 1977. Eidetics: An overview. *Journal of Mental Imagery* 1, 5–38.

Ahsen, A. 1978. Eidetics: Neural experiential growth potential for the treatment of accident traumas, debilitating stress conditions, and chronic emotional blocking. *Journal of Mental Imagery* 2, 1–22.

Alexander, F. 1930. Concerning the genesis of the castration complex, trans. C. F. Menninger. *Psychoanalytic Review* 22, 49–52.

Alexander, F. 1963. The dynamics of psychotherapy in light of learning theory. *American Journal of Psychiatry* 120, 440–448.

Alexander, F. and French, T. M. 1946. *Psychoanalytic therapy, principles, and applications.* New York: Ronald Press.

Alford, C. F. 1991. *The self in social theory: A psychoanalytic account of its construction in Plato, Hobbes, Locke, Rawls, and Rousseau.* New Haven, CT: Yale University Press.

Allen, J. 2003. Affect regulation and the development of psychopathology. *Bulletin of the Menninger Clinic*, 67, 68–69.

Allport, D. A. 1989. Visual attention. In M.I. Posner, ed., *Foundations of cognitive science*, 631–682. Cambridge, MA: MIT Press.

Allport, G. W. 1940. The psychologist's frame of reference. *Psychological Bulletin* 37, 1–28.

Allport, G. W. 1955. *Becoming: Basic considerations for a psychology of personality.* New Haven, CT: Yale University Press.

Alphen, E. V. 1992. *Francis Bacon and the loss of self.* London: Reaktion Books.

Ambady, N., and Rosenthal, R. 1993. Half a minute: Predicting teacher evaluations from thin slices of nonverbal behavior and physical attraction. *Journal of Personality and Social Psychology* 64, 431–441.

Amir, N., Elias, J., Klumpp, H., and Przeworski, A. 2003. Attentional bias to threat in social phobia: Facilitated processing of threat difficulty disengaging attention from threat. *Behaviour Research and Therapy* 41, 1,325–1,335.

Amir, N., McNally, F. J., Rieman, B. C., Burns, J., Loenz, M., and Mullen, J. T. 1996. Suppression of the emotional Stroop effect by increased anxiety in patients with social phobia. *Behavior Research and Therapy* 34, 945–948.

Anderson, A. K., and Phelps, E. 2001. Lesions of the human amygdala impair enhanced perception of emotionally salient events. *Nature* 411, 305–309.

Anderson, J. R. 1982. Acquisition of cognitive skill. *Psychological Review* 8, 369–406.

Anderson, J. R. 1983. *The architecture of cognition.* Cambridge, MA: Harvard University Press.

Anderson, M. C. 2001. Active forgetting: Evidence for functional inhibition as a source of memory failure. *Journal of Aggression, Maltreatment and Trauma* 4, 185–211.

Anderson, M. C., and Green, C. 2001. Suppressing unwanted memories by executive control. *Nature* 410, 366–369.

Anderson, M. C., and Levy, B. 2002. Repression can and should be studied empirically. *Trends in Cognitive Sciences* 6, 502–503.

Anderson, R. C., and Pichert, J. W. 1978. Recall of previously unrecallable information following a shift in perspective. *Journal of Verbal Learning and Verbal Behavior* 17, 1–12.

Arkowitz, H. 1984. Historical perspective on the integration of psychoanalytic therapy and behavior therapy. In H. Arkowitz, and S. B. Messer, eds., *Psychoanalytic therapy and behavior therapy: Is integration possible?* 1–30. New York: Plenum.

Arkowitz, H., and Messer, S. B., eds. 1984. *Psychoanalytic therapy and behavior therapy: Is integration possible?* New York: Plenum.

Armony, J. L., and LeDoux, J. E. 2000. How danger is encoded: Toward a systems, cellular, and computational understanding of cognitive–emotional interactions in fear. 2nd ed. In M.S. Gazzaniga, ed., *The New Cognitive Neurosciences,* 1,067–1,079. Cambridge, MA: MIT Press.

Aron, L. 1996. *A meeting of minds: Mutuality in psychoanalysis.* Hillsdale, NJ: Analytic Press.

Aron, L., and Anderson, F. S., eds. 1998. *Relational perspectives on the body.* Hillsdale, NJ: Analytic Press.

Artaud, A. 1966. *The theatre and its double.* New York: Grove Press.

Assagioli, R. 1965. *Psychosynthesis: A manual of principles and techniques*. Oxford: Hobbs, Dorman.

Atkinson, J. W. 1957. Motivational determinants of risk-taking behavior. *Psychological Review* 64, 359–372.

Atwood, B., and Stolorow, R. 1984. *Structures of subjectivity*. Hillsdale, NJ: Analytic Press.

Baars, B. J. 1988. Momentary forgetting as a "resetting" of a conscious global workspace due to competition between incompatible contexts. In M. J. Horowitz, ed., *Psychodynamics and cognition*, 269–293. Chicago: University of Chicago.

Baars, B. J. 1997. *In the theater of consciousness: The workspace of the mind*. New York: Oxford University Press.

Bader, M. J. 1998. Postmodern epistemology: The problem of validation and the retreat from therapeutics in psychoanalysis. *Psychoanalytic Dialogues* 8, 1–32.

Bakan, D. 1966. *The duality of human existence: An essay on psychology and religion*. Oxford: Rand McNally.

Balint, M. 1952. Primary love and psychoanalytic technique. London: Hogarth Press.

Balint, M. 1968. The basic fault. Therapeutic aspects of regression. London: Tavistock Publications.

Balint, M., Ornstein, P. H., and Balint E. 1972. *Focal psychotherapy*. Philadelphia: J. B. Lipincott Co.

Banaji, M. R., and Greenwald, A. G. 1994. Implicit stereotyping and prejudice. In M. P. Zanna and J. M. Olson, eds., *The psychology of prejudice, The Ontario Symposium* Vol. 7, 55–76. Hillsdale, NJ: Erlbaum.

Bandura, A. 1973. *Aggression: A social learning analysis*. Englewood Cliffs, NJ: PrenticeHall.

Bandura, A. 1977. *Social learning theory*. New York: General Learning Press.

Bandura, A., Ross, D., and Ross, S. A. 1961. Transmission of aggression through imitation of aggressive models. *Journal of Abnormal and Social Psychology* 6, 575–582.

Bargh, J. A. 1989. Conditional automaticity: Varieties of automatic influence in social perception and cognition. In J. S. Uleman, and J. A. Bargh, eds., *Unintended thought*, 3–51. New York: Guilford Press.

Bargh, J. A. 1990. Auto-motives: Preconscious determinants of social interaction. In E.T. Higgins, and R. M. Sorrentino, eds., *Handbook of motivation and cognition*, vol. 2, 93–130. New York: Guilford Press.

Bargh, J. A. 1994. The four horsemen of automaticity: Awareness, intention, efficiency, and control in social cognition. In R. S. Wyer, Jr., and T. K. Srull, eds., *Handbook of social cognition*, 2nd ed., 1–40. Hillsdale, NJ: Lawrence Erlbaum Associates.

Bargh, J. A. 1997. The automaticity of everyday life. In R. Wyer, ed., *The automaticity of everyday life: Advances in social cognition*, vol. 10, 1–61. Hillsdale, NJ: Lawrence Erlbaum Associates.

Bargh, J. A. 2006. *Social psychology and the unconscious: The automaticity of higher mental processes*. Philadelphia: Psychology Press.

Bargh, J. A., and Chartran, T. L. 1999. The unbearable automaticity of being. *American Psychologist* 54, 462–479.

Bargh, J. A., and Gollwitzer, P. 1994. Environmental control of goal-directed action: Automatic and strategic contingencies between situations and behavior. In W. Spaulding, ed., *Integrative views of motivation, cognition, and emotion*, 71–124. Nebraska symposium on motivation. Lincoln: University of Nebraska Press.

Barlow, D. H. 2002. *Anxiety and its disorders: The nature and treatment of anxiety and panic*, 2nd ed. New York: Guilford Press.

Barnard, P. J., and Teasdale, J. D. 1991. Interacting cognitive subsystems: A systemic approach to cognitive-affective interaction and change. *Cognition and Emotion 5*, 1–39.

Baron, R. A., and Richardson, D. R. 1994. *Human aggression*, 2nd ed. New York: Plenum.

Barsade, S. G., Brief, A. P., and Spataro, S. 2003. The affective revolution in organizational behavior: The emergence of a paradigm. In J. Greenberg, ed., *Organizational behavior: The state of the science*, 3–52. Hillsdale, NJ: Laurence Erlbaum Associates.

Basch, M. 1988. *Understanding psychotherapy: The science behind the art*. New York: Basic Books.

Baudelaire, C. 1985. *Les fleurs du mal*. 1857. Reprint, Boston: David R. Godine.

Baumeister, R. F. 1991. *Meanings of life*. New York: Guilford Press.

Baumeister, R. F. 1996. Self-regulation and ego threat: Motivated cognition, self deception, and destructive goal setting. In P. M. Gollwitzer, and J. A. Bargh, eds., *The psychology of action: Linking cognition and motivation to behavior*, 27–47. New York: Guilford Press.

Baumeister, R. F., Bratslavsky, E., Finkenauer, C., and Vohs, K. D. 2001. Bad is stronger than good. *Review of General Psychology 5*, 323–370.

Baumeister, R. F., Heatherton, T. F., and Tice, D.M. 1994. *Losing control: How and why people fail at self-regulation*. San Diego, CA: Academic Press.

Baumgardner, A. H., and Brownlee, E. A. 1987. Strategic failure in social interaction: Evidence for expectancy disconfirmation processes. *Journal of Personality and Social Psychology 52*, 525–535.

Beck, A. T., Rush, A. J., Shaw, B. F., and Emery, G. 1979. *A cognitive therapy of depression*. New York: Guilford Press.

Becker, E. 1962. *The birth and death of meaning*. New York: Free Press.

Becker, E. 1969. *Angel in armor: A post–Freudian perspective on the nature of man*. New York: George Braziller.

Becker, E. 1973. *The denial of death*. New York: Free Press.

Becker, E. 1975. *Escape from evil*. New York: Free Press.

Beebe, B. 1998. A procedural theory for therapeutic action: Commentary on the symposium, "Interventions that effect change in psychotherapy." *Infant Mental Health Journal 19*, 333–340.

Beebe, B., Knoblauch, S. H., Rustin, J., and Sorter, D. 2003. Introduction: A systems view. *Psychoanalytic Dialogues 13*, 743–775.

Beebe, B., and Lachmann, F. M. 1994. Representation and internalization in infancy: Three principles of salience. *Psychoanalytic Psychology 11*, 127–165.

Belk, R. W. 1988. Possessions and the extended self. *Journal of Consumer Research 15*, 139–168.

Belk, R. W., and Pollay, R. W. 1985. Images of ourselves: The good life in twentieth century advertising. *Journal of Consumer Research* 11, 887–897.

Bellah, R. N. 1985. *Habits of the heart: Individualism and commitment in American life.* Berkeley: University of California Press.

Benjamin, J. 1990. *The bonds of love: Psychoanalysis, feminism and the problem of domination.* London: Virago.

Benjamin, W. 1931. A small history of photography. In *One-way street and other writings*, trans. E. Jephcott, and K. Shorter, 240–251. London: New Left Books.

Benjamin, W. 1969. The work of art in the age of mechanical reproduction. In H. Arendt, ed., *Illuminations*, trans. H. Zohn, 217–251. New York: Schocken.

Bergin, A. E. 1970. Cognitive therapy and behavior therapy: Foci for a multidimensional approach to treatment. *Behavior Therapy* 1, 205–212.

Berkowitz, L. 1993. *Aggression: Its causes, consequences, and control.* New York: McGraw-Hill.

Berliner, B. 1941. Short psychoanalytic psychotherapy: Its possibilities and its limitations. *Bulletin of the Menninger Clinic* 5, 204–213.

Bernstein, D. A., Roy, E. J., Srull, T. K., and Wickens, C. D. 1988. *Psychology.* Boston, Houghton Mifflin.

Bertalanffy, L. 1938. A quantitative theory of organic growth. *Human Biology* 10, 181–213.

Binswanger, H. 1991. Volition as cognitive self-regulation. *Organization Behavior and Human Decision Processes* 50, 154–178.

Bion, W. R. 1962. A theory of thinking. *International Journal of Psychoanalysis* 43, 4–5.

Bion, W. R. 1967. Notes on memory and desire. *Psychoanalytic Forum* 2, 271–280.

Bion, W. R. 1977. *Seven servants.* New York: Jason Aronson.

Bishop, S., Duncan, J., Brett, M., and Lawrence, A. 2004. Prefrontal cortical function and anxiety: Controlling attention to threat-related stimuli. *Nature Neuroscience* 7, 184–188.

Bjork, R. A. 1989. Retrieval inhibition as an adaptive mechanism in human memory. In H. L. Roediger III, and E I. Craik, eds., *Varieties of memory and consciousness: Essays in honor of Endel Tulving*, 195–210. Hillsdale, NJ: Erlbaum.

Blakemore, S. J., Goodbody, S. J., and Wolpert, D. M. 1998. Predicting the consequences of our own actions: The role of sensorimotor context estimation. *Journal of Neuroscience,* 18, 7,511–7,518.

Blechner, M. J. 1994. Projective identification and countertransference. Projective identification, countertransference, and the "maybe-me". *Contemporary Psychoanalysis* 30, 619–631. Panel presentation.

Blechner, M. J. 2001. *The dream frontier.* Hillsdale, NJ: Analytic Press.

Blum, H. P. 1992. Psychic change: The analytic relationships and agents of change. *International Journal of Psychoanalysis* 73, 255–265.

Bohart, A. 1993. Experiencing: The basis of psychotherapy. *Journal of Psychotherapy Integration* 3, 51–67.

Bohm, D. 1980. *Wholeness and the implicate order.* New York: Routledge.

Bohr, N. 1934. *Atomic theory and the description of nature*. Cambridge: Cambridge University Press.

Bollas, C. 1987. *The shadow of the object: Psychoanalysis of the unthought known*. New York: Columbia University Press.

Bolles, E. B. 1991. *A second way of knowing. The riddle of human perception*. New York: Prentice Hall.

Bonanno, G. A. 1988–1989. Sampling conscious thought: Influences of repression-sensitization and reporting conditions. *Imagination, Cognition and Personality* 8, 295–308.

Bonanno, G. A. 1990. Repression, accessibility, and the translation of private experience. *Psychoanalytic Psychology* 7, 453–473.

Bonanno, G. A. 2001. Emotion self-regulation. In T. J. Mayne and G. A. Bonanno, eds., *Emotions: Current issues and future directions*, 251–285. New York: Guilford Press.

Boorstin, D. J. 1961. *The image: A guide to pseudo-events in America*. New York: Vintage Books.

Borkovec, T. D., and Lyonfields, J. D. 1993. Worry: Thought suppression of emotional processing. In H. W. Krohne, ed., *Attention and avoidance: Strategies in coping with aversiveness*, 101–118. Seattle, WA: Hogrefe and Huber.

Bornstein, R. F. 2001. The impending death of psychoanalysis. *Psychoanalytic Psychology* 18, 3–20.

Bornstein, R., and Pittman, T., eds. 1992. *Perception without awareness*. New York: Guilford Press.

Bosnak, R. 2003. Embodied imagination. *Contemporary Psychoanalysis* 39, 683–695.

Bower, G. H. 1981. Mood and memory. *American Psychologist* 36, 129–148.

Bower, G. H. 1992. How might emotions affect learning? In S.A. Christianson, ed., *The handbook of emotion and memory: Research and theory*, 3–31. Hillsdale, NJ: Lawrence Erlbaum Associates.

Bowers, K. S. 1992. Imagination and dissociation in hypnotic responding. *International Journal of Clinical Experimental Hypnosis* 40, 253–275.

Bowers, K. S., and Davidson, T. M. 1991. A neo-dissociative critique of Spanos's social psychological model of hypnosis. In S. J. Lynn, and J. W. Rhue, eds., *Theories of hypnosis: Current models and perspectives*, 105–143. New York: Guilford Press.

Bowlby, J. 1973. Separation: Anxiety and anger. In *Attachment and Loss*, vol. 2, 415–437. New York: Basic Books.

Bradley, M. M., Codispoti, M., Cuthbert, B. N., and Lang, P. J. 2001. Emotion and motivation: I. Defensive and appetitive reactions in picture processing. *Emotion* 1, 276–298.

Brakel, L., Shevrin, H., and Villa, K. 2002. The priority of primary process categorizing: Experimental evidence supporting a psychoanalytic developmental hypothesis. *Journal of the American Psychoanalytic Association* 50, 483–505.

Brenner, C. 1982. The concept of the superego: A reformulation. *Psychoanalytic Quarterly* 51, 501–525.

Brenner, C. 1998. Beyond the ego and id revisited. *Journal of Clinical Psychoanalysis* 7, 165–180.

Breuer, J. and Freud., S. 1957. *Studies on hysteria.* In *The standard edition of the complete psychological works of Sigmund Freud,* vol. 2, London: Hogarth Press. (Original work published 1893–1895.)

Brewin, C. R., Dalgleish, T., and Joseph, S. 1996. A dual representation theory of posttraumatic stress disorder. *Psychological Review* 103, 670–686.

Brewin, C. R., and Power, M., eds. 1997. *The transformation of meaning.* Chichester, England: Wiley.

Bridges, L., Denham, S., and Ganiban, J. 2004. Definitional issues in emotion regulation research. *Child Development* 76, 340–346.

Brim, O. G. 1988. Losing and winning. *Psychology Today* 22, 48–52.

Broadbent, D. E. 1958. *Perception and communication.* London: Pergamon Press.

Broadbent, D. E. 1977. The hidden preattentive processes. *American Psychologist* 32, 109–118.

Broadbent, D. E., and Broadbent, M. 1988. Anxiety and attentional bias: State and trait. *Cognition and Emotion* 2, 165–183.

Bromberg, P. M. 1996. Standing in the spaces: The multiplicity of self and the psychoanalytic relationship. *Contemporary Psychoanalysis* 32, 509–535.

Bromberg, P. M. 2003. On being one's dream: Some reflections on Robert Bosnak's "Embodied Imagination." *Contemporary Psychoanalysis* 39, 697–710.

Brown, N. O. 1959. *Life against death.* New York: Vintage Books.

Brown, W. P. 1961. Conceptions of perceptual defense. *British Journal of Psychology, Monograph Supplement* 35, 1–107.

Bruner, J. S. 1957. Going beyond the information given. In J. S. Bruner, E. Brunswik, L. Festinger, F. Heider, K. F. Muenzinger, C. E. Osgood, and D. Rapaport, eds., *Contemporary approaches to cognition,* 41–69. Cambridge, MA: Harvard University Press.

Bruner, J. S., and Postman, L. 1949. On the perception of incongruity: A paradigm. *Journal of Personality* 18, 206–223.

Bucci, W. 1985. Dual coding: A cognitive model in psychoanalytic research. *Journal of American Psychoanalytic Association,* 33, 571–607.

Bucci, W. 1997. *Psychoanalysis and cognitive science: A multiple code theory.* New York: Guilford Press.

Buck, R. 1984. On the definition of emotion: Functional and structural considerations. *Cahiers de Psychologie Cognitive/Current Psychology of Cognition* 4, 44–47.

Buck, R. 1999. The biological affects: A typology. *Psychological Review* 106, 301–336.

Bulman, R. J., and Wortman, C. B. 1977. Attributions of blame and coping in the real world: Severe accident victims react to their lot. *Journal of Personality and Social Psychology* 35, 351–363.

Burgess, I. S., Jones, L. M., Robertson, S. A., Radcliffe, W. N., and Emerson, E. 1981. The degree of control exerted by phobic and nonphobic verbal stimuli over the recognition behaviour of phobic and nonphobic subjects. *Behaviour Research and Therapy* 19, 233–243.

Burns, D. D. 1989. *The feeling good handbook: Using the new mood therapy in everyday life.* New York: William Morrow.

Busch, F. 2004. A missing link in psychoanalytic technique: Psychoanalytic consciousness. *International Journal of Psychoanalysis* 85, 567–578.

Buss, D. 1995. Evolutionary psychology: A new paradigm for psychological science. *Psychological Inquiry* 6, 1–30.

Byrne, A., and Eysenck, M. W. 1995. Trait anxiety, anxious mood, and threat detection. *Cognition and Emotion* 9, 549–562.

Cahill, L., Babinsky, R., Markowitsch, H. J., and McGaugh, J. L. 1995. The amygdala and emotional memory. *Nature* 377, 295–296.

Campbell, C. 1987. *The romantic ethic and the spirit of modern consumerism.* Oxford: Basil Blackwell.

Campos, J. J., Frankel, C. B., and Camras, L. 2004. On the nature of emotion regulation. *Child Development* 75, 377–394.

Cantor, J. R., Zillmann, D., and Bryant, J. 1975. Enhancement of experienced sexual arousal in response to erotic stimuli through misattribution of unrelated residual excitation. *Journal of Personality and Social Psychology* 32, 69–75.

Cantor, N., and Mischel, W. 1977. Traits as prototypes: Effects on recognition memory. *Journal of Personality and Social Psychology* 35, 38–48.

Capafons, A. 1999. Applications of emotional self-regulation therapy. In I. Kirsch, A. Capafons, E. Cardena-Buelna, and S. Amigo, eds., *Clinical hypnosis and self-regulation: Cognitive–behavioral perspectives*, 331–349. Washington, DC: American Psychological Association.

Carlson, B. W. 1993. The accuracy of future forecasts and past judgments. *Organizational Behavior and Human Decision Processes* 54, 245–276.

Carlson, E. T. 1986. The history of dissociation until 1880. In J. M. Quen, ed., *Split minds, split brains*, 7–30. New York: New York University Press.

Carpenter, S. 1988. Self-relevance and goal-directed processing in the recall and weighting of information about others. *Journal of Experimental Social Psychology* 24, 310–332.

Carver, C. S., and Scheier, M. F. 1981. *Attention and self-regulation: A control-theory approach to human behavior.* Hillsdale, NJ: Lawrence Erlbaum Associates.

Carver, C. S. and Scheier, M. F. 1990. Principles of self-regulation: Action and emotion. In E. T. Higgins, and R. M. Sorrentino, eds., *Handbook of motivation and cognition: Foundations of social behavior*, vol. 2, 3–52. New York: Guilford Press.

Cassirer, E. 1946. *Language and myth.* New York: Harper Brothers.

Cattarin, J. A., Thompson, J. K., Thomas, C., and Williams, R. 2000. Body image, mood, and televised images of attractiveness. *Journal of Social and Clinical Psychology* 19, 220–239.

Chasseguet-Smirgel, J. 1992. Some thoughts on the psychoanalytic situation. *Journal of the American Psychoanalytic Association* 40, 3–25.

Chiagouris, L. and Mitchell, L. E. 1997. The new materialists. In L. Kahle, and L. Chiagouris, eds., *Values, lifestyles, and psychographics*, 263–282. A Volume in Advertising and Consumer Psychology Series: Backer Spielvogel Bates.

Choron, J. 1963. *Death and western thought.* New York: Collier.

Christianson, S. A., ed. 1992. *The handbook of emotion and memory: Research and theory.* Hillsdale, NJ: Lawrence Erlbaum Associates.

Christianson, S. A., Loftus, E., Hoffman, H., and Lofius, G. 1991. Eye fixations and memory for emotional events. *Journal of Experimental Psychology* 17, 690–701.

Chun, M. M., and Marois, R. 2002. The dark side of visual attention. *Current Opinion in Neurobiology* 12, 184–189.

Chun, M. M., and Potter, M. C. 1995. A two-stage model for multiple target detection in rapid serial visual presentation. *Journal of Experimental Psychology* 21, 109–127.

Cicchetti, D., and Toth, S. L., eds. 1995. *Emotion, cognition, and representation.* Rochester, NY: University of Rochester Press.

Clark, M., and Fiske, S. 1982. *Affect and cognition.* Hillsdale, NJ: Lawrence Erlbaum Associates.

Clayton, I. C., Richards, J. C., and Edwards, C. J. 1999. Selective attention in obsessive-compulsive disorder. *Journal of Abnormal Psychology* 108, 171–175.

Cloitre, M., Cancienne, J., Brodsky, B., Dulit, R., and Perry, S. W. 1996. Memory performance among women with parental abuse histories: Enhanced directed forgetting or directed remembering? *Journal of Abnormal Psychology* 105, 204–211.

Cloitre, M., and Liebowitz, M. R. 1991. Memory bias in panic disorder: An investigation of the cognitive avoidance hypothesis. *Cognitive Therapy and Research* 15, 371–386.

Clore, G. C. 1994. Why emotions are felt. In P. Ekman, and R. J. Davidson, eds., *The nature of emotion: Fundamental questions,* 103–111. New York: Oxford University Press.

Cocteau, J. 1947. *Le foyer des artistes.* Paris: Librarie Plon.

Cohen, G. A. 2000. *If you're egalitarian, how come you're so rich?* Cambridge, MA: Harvard University Press.

Cohen, J. D., Servan-Schreiber, D., and McClelland, J. L. 1992. A parallel distributed processing approach to automacity. *American Journal of Psychology* 105, 239–269.

Cohen, L. 2003. *A consumer's republic: The politics of mass consumption in postwar America.* New York: Alfred A. Knopf.

Comer, R., and Laird, J. D. 1975. Choosing to suffer as a consequence of expecting to suffer: Why do people do it? *Journal of Personality and Social Psychology* 32, 91–101.

Conant, J. 1948. *On understanding science: An historical approach.* New Haven, CT: Yale University Press.

Connolly, M. B., Crits-Christoph, P., Demorest, A., Azarian, K., Muenz, L., and Chittams, J. 1996. Varieties of transference patterns in psychotherapy. *Journal of Consulting and Clinical Psychology* 64, 1,213–1,221.

Connolly, M. B., Crits-Christoph, P., Shappell, S., Barber, J. P., Luborsky, L., and Shaffer, C. 1999.The relation of transference interpretations to outcome in the early sessions of brief supportive-expressive psychotherapy. *Psychotherapy Research 9,* 485–495.

Cook, J. R. 1985. Repression-sensitization and approach-avoidance as predictors of response to a laboratory stressor. *Journal of Personality and Social Psychology* 493, 759–773.

Cooper, A. 1995. The detailed inquiry. In M. Lionells, J. Fiscalini, C. H. Mann, and D. B. Stern, eds., *Handbook of interpersonal psychoanalysis*, 679–694. Hillsdale, NJ: Analytic Press.

Cooper, A. M. 1988. Our changing views of the therapeutic action of psychoanalysis: Comparing Strachey and Loewald. *Psychoanalytic Quarterly* 57, 15–27.

Cooper, S. H. 1993. The self construct in psychoanalytic theory: A comparative view. In Z. V. Segal, and S. J. Blatt, eds., *The self in emotional distress*, 41–67. New York: Guilford Press.

Corteen, R. S., and Wood, B. 1972. Autonomic responses to shock associated words in an unattended channel. *Journal of Experimental Psychology* 94, 308–313.

Cottle, T. J. 2001. *Mind fields: Adolescent consciousness in a culture of distraction.* New York: Peter Lang Publishing, Inc.

Crews, F. 1997. The legacy of Salem: Demonology for an age of science. *Skeptic 5,* 36–44.

Crits-Christoph, P., Cooper, A., and Luborsky, L. 1988. The accuracy of therapists' interpretations and the outcome of dynamic psychotherapy. *Journal of Consulting and Clinical Psychology 56*, 490–495.

Crits-Cristoph, P., and Luborsky, L. 1990. Changes in CCRT pervasiveness during psychotherapy. In L. Luborsky and P. Crits-Christoph, eds., *Understanding transference: The core-conflictual relationship theme method*, 133–146. New York: Basic Books.

Crocker, J., and Major, B. 1989. Social stigma and self-esteem: The self-protective properties of stigma. *Psychological Review 96*, 4, 608–630.

Crosby, F. 1976. A model of egoistical relative deprivation. *Psychological Review 83, 85–113.*

Curtis, R. C. 1989a. Choosing to suffer or to . . .?: Empirical studies and clinical theories of masochism. In R. Curtis, ed., *Self-defeating behaviors: Experimental research, clinical impressions, and practical implications*, 189–214. New York: Plenum.

Curtis, R. C. 1989b. Integration: Conditions under which self-defeating and self-enhancing behaviors develop. In R. Curtis, ed., *Self-defeating behaviors: Experimental research, clinical impressions, and practical implications*, 343–361. New York: Plenum Press.

Curtis, R. C. 1991a. Toward an integrative theory of psychological change in individuals and organizations: A cognitive-affective regulation model. In R. Curtis, and G. Stricker, eds., *How people change: Inside and outside therapy,* 191–210. New York: Plenum Press.

Curtis, R. C. 1991b. *How people change: Inside and outside therapy.* New York: Plenum.

Curtis, R. C. 1991c. *The relational self: Theoretical convergences in psychoanalysis and social psychology.* New York: Guilford Press.

Curtis, R. C. 1992a. Self-organizing processes, anxiety, and change. *Journal of Psychotherapy Integration 2,* 295–319.

Curtis, R. C. 1992b. A social-clinical model of conscious and unconscious processes. In R. C. Curtis Chair, Conscious and unconscious processes: Towards the second century. Symposium presented at the American Psychological Association, Washington, DC, August.

Curtis, R. C. 1992c. Effects of anxiety upon expectancy confirmation in perception of self and others. Paper presented at the European Society of Social Psychology. Leuven/Louvain, Belgium, July.

Curtis, R. C. 1994. Oedipus, Narcissus, and Gaia: Women's ambition, the battle with Nobodaddy, and the gestationally challenged. Paper-presented at the conference Psychoanalyses, Feminisms, Gainesville, Fla.

Curtis, R. C. 1996a. The "death" of Freud and the rebirth of free psychoanalytic inquiry. *Psychoanalytic Dialogues* 6, 563–589.

Curtis, R. C. 1996b. A new world symphony: Ferenczi and the integration of nonanalytic techniques into psychoanalytic practice. In P. L. Rudnytsky, A. Bokay, and P. Giampieri-Deutsch, eds., *Ferenczi's turn in psychoanalysis,* 248–265. New York: NYU Press.

Curtis, R. C. 2000. Loving the analysis of transference-countertransference or helping the patient? Paper presented at the meeting of the International Federation of Psychoanalytic Societies, Brooklyn, NY.

Curtis, R. C. 2001. Can we overuse our strengths? A review of J. Safran and J. C. Muran's *Negotiating the therapeutic alliance: A relational treatment guide. Contemporary Psychoanalysis* 37, 329–335.

Curtis, R. C., and Hirsch, I. 2004. Relational approaches to psychoanalytic psychotherapy. In A. S. Gurman, and S. Messer, eds., *Essential psychotherapies,* 69–106. New York: Guilford Press.

Curtis, R. C., Field, C., Knaan-Kostman, I., and Mannix, K. 2004. What 75 analysts found helpful and hurtful in their own analyses. *Psychoanalytic Psychology* 21, 183–202.

Curtis, R. C., Pacell, D., and Garzynski, J. 1991. Anxiety and self-confirming behavior. Paper presented at the annual meeting of the Eastern Psychological Association, New York, April.

Curtis, R. C., and Qaiser, M. 2005. Training analysis: Historical and empirical perspectives. In J. Geller, J. Norcross, and D. Orlinsky, eds., *The psychotherapists' own psychotherapy,* 345–378. New York: Oxford University Press.

Curtis, R. C., Rietdorf, P., and Ronell, D. 1980. "Appeasing the Gods?" Suffering to reduce probable future suffering. *Personality and Social Psychology Bulletin* 6, 234–241.

Curtis, R. C., Smith, P., and Moore, R. 1984. Suffering to improve outcomes determined by both chance and skill. *Journal of Social and Clinical Psychology* 2, 165–173.

Curtis, R. C., Velker, D., and Hillman, J. 1996. Anxiety, depression, and the recall of positive and negative statements consistent or inconsistent with the self-view. Paper presented at the annual meeting of the Eastern Psychological Association, Philadelphia.

Cushman, P. 1990. Why the self is empty: Toward a historically situated psychology. *American Psychologist* 45, 599–611.

Cushman, P. 1996. *Constructing the self, constructing America: A cultural history of psychotherapy.* Reading, MA: Addison-Wesley Longman.

Dalgleish, T., and Power, M. J., eds. 1999. *Handbook of cognition and emotion.* New York: John Wiley and Sons.

Damasio, A. R. 1994. *Descartes' error: Emotion, reason, and the human brain.* New York: G. P. Putnam.

Damasio, A. R. 1999. *The feeling of what happens: Body and emotion in the making of consciousness.* New York: Harcourt Brace.

Damasio, A. R. 2000. A second chance for emotion. In L. Nadel, and R. Lane, eds., *Cognitive neuroscience of emotion,* 12–23. London: Oxford University Press.

Damasio, A. R. 2001. The person within. *Nature,* 412, 685–686.

Damasio, A. R. 2003. Looking for Spinoza: Joy, sorrow, and the feeling brain. Orlando, FL: Harcourt.

Damasio, A. R., and Damasio, H. 1996. Making images and creating subjectivity. In R. Llinas, and P. S. Churchland, eds., *The mind–brain continuum: Sensory processes,* 19–27. Cambridge, MA: MIT Press.

Darwin, C. 1859. *On the origin of species.* London: John Murray.

Davanloo, H. 2000. *Intensive short-term dynamic psychotherapy: Selected papers of Habib Davanloo.* New York: John Wiley.

Davidson, R. J. 2000. Affective style, psychopathology, and resilience: Brain mechanisms and plasticity. *American Psychologist* 55, 1,196–1,214.

Davidson, R. J., and Irwin, W. 1999. The functional neuroanatomy of emotion and affective style. *Trends in Cognitive Science* 3, 11–21.

Davidson, R. J., Jackson, D., and Kalin, N. 2000. Emotion, plasticity, context, and regulation: Perspectives from affective neuroscience. *Psychological Bulletin* 126, 890–909.

Davidson, R. J., Scherer, K. R., and Goldsmith, H., eds. 2003. *Handbook of affective sciences.* London: Oxford University Press.

Davidson, R. J., and Sutton, S. K. 1995. Affective neuroscience: The emergence of a discipline. *Current Opinion in Neurobiology* 5, 217–224.

Davidson, T. M., and Bowers, K. S. 1991. Selective hypnotic amnesia: Is it a successful attempt to forget or an unsuccessful attempt to remember? *Journal of Abnormal Psychology* 100, 133–143.

Davies, J. M. 1996. Linking the "pre-analytic" with the postclassical: Integration, dissociation, and the multiplicity of unconscious process. *Contemporary Psychoanalysis* 32, 553–576.

Davies, J. M., and Frawley, M. G. 1992. Dissociative processes and transference-counter-transference paradigms in the psychoanalytically oriented treatment of adult survivors of childhood sexual abuse. *Psychoanalytic Dialogues* 2, 5–36.

Davies, J. M., and Frawley, M. G. 1994. *Treating the adult survivor of childhood sexual abuse: A psychoanalytic perspective.* New York: Basic Books.

Davis, J. A. 1959. A formal interpretation of the theory of relative deprivation. *Sociometry* 22, 289–296.

Davis, P. J. 1987. Repression and the inaccessibility of emotional memories. *Journal of Personality and Social Psychology* 53, 585–593.

Davis, P. J. 1990. Represssion and the inaccessibility of emotional memories. In J. L. Singer, ed., *Repression and dissociation: Implications for personality theory, psychopathology, and health,* 387–404. Chicago: University of Chicago Press.

Deaux, K. 1991. Social identities: Thoughts on structure and change. In R. C. Curtis, ed., *The relational self: Theoretical convergences in psychoanalysis and social psychology*, 77–93. NY: Guilford Press.

Deci, E. L., Koestner, R., and Ryan, R. M. 1999. A meta-analytic review of experiments examining the effects of extrinsic rewards on intrinsic motivation. *Psychological Bulletin* 125, 627–668.

De Gelder, B., de Haan, E., and Heywook, C. 2002. *Out of mind: Varieties of unconscious processes*. New York: Oxford University Press.

De Graff, J., Wann, D., and Naylor, T. 2001. *Affluenza*. San Francisco: Berrett-Koehler.

De Jonghe, R., Rijnierse, P., and Janssen, R. 1992. The role of support in psychoanalysis. *Journal of the American Psychoanalytic Association* 40, 475–499.

Derrida, J. 1967. La structure, le signe et le jeu dans le discours des sciences humaines. *L'écriture et la différence*, 409–428. Paris: Seuil.

Desoille, R. 1945. *Le rêve-éveillé en psychothérapie; essai sur la fonction de régulation de l'inconscient collectif*. Paris: Presses Universitaires de France.

Despret, V. 2004. Our emotional makeup: Ethnopsychology and selfhood. New York: Other Press.

Deutsch, F. 1949. Applied psychoanalysis. New York: Grune and Stratton.

Dimino, R. A. 2003. Early memories, attachment style, the role of peers, and adolescent substance use. *Dissertation Abstracts International: Section B: The Sciences and Engineering*, 6312-B, 6,091.

Dittmar, H. 1992. Perceived material wealth and first impressions. *British Journal of Social Psychology,* 31, 379–391.

Dixon, N. F. 1981. *Preconscious processing*. New York: John Wiley and Sons.

Dodge, K. A. 1991. Emotion and social information processing. In K. Dodge, and J. Garber, eds., *The development of emotion regulation and dysregulation*, 159–181. New York: Cambridge University Press.

Dollard, J., and Miller, N. E. 1950. *Personality and psychotherapy*. New York: McGraw-Hill.

Dorpat, T. L. 1994. On the double whammy and gaslighting. *Psychoanalysis and Psychotherapy* 11, 91–96.

Dozier, M., Stovall, K. C., and Albus, K. E. 1999. Attachment and psychopathology in adulthood. In J. Cassidy, and P. R. Shaver, eds., *Handbook of attachment: Theory, research, and clinical applications,* 497–519. New York: Guilford Press.

Dunn, M., Golynkina, K., Ryle, A., and Watson, J. P. 1997. A repeat audit of the cognitive analytic clinic at Guy's Hospital. *Psychiatric Bulletin* 21, 1–4.

Duval, S., and Wicklund, R. A. 1972. *A theory of objective self awareness*. Oxford: Academic Press.

Duval, T. S., Duval, V. H., and Mulilis, J. 1992. Effects of self-focus, discrepancy between self and standard, and outcome expectancy favorability on the tendency to match self to standard or to withdraw. *Journal of Personality and Social Psychology* 62, 340–348.

Eagle, M. N. 1984. *Recent developments in psychoanalysis: A critical evaluation*. New York: McGraw-Hill.

Eagle, M. N. 1987. The psychoanalytic and the cognitive unconscious. In R. Stern, ed., *Theories of the unconscious and theories of the self,* 155–189. Hillsdale, NJ: Analytic Press.

Eagle, M. N. 2000a. A critical evaluation of current conceptions of transference and countertransference. *Psychoanalytic Psychology* 17, 44–68.

Eagle, M. N. 2000b. A miniparadigm shift in psychoanalysis. Review of *Relational psychoanalysis: The emergence of a tradition,* ed. S. A. Mitchell and L. Aron. *Contemporary Psychology* 46, 673–676.

Eagle, M. N., and Wolitsky, D. 1980. Therapuetic influences in dynamic psychotherapy: A review and synthesis. In S. Slipp, ed., *Curative factors in dynamic psychotherapy,* 349–378. Northvale, NJ: Jason Aronson.

Easterlin, R. 1973. Does money buy happiness? *The Public Interest,* Winter, 3–10.

Easterlin, R. 1995. Will raising the incomes of all increase the happiness of all? *Journal of Economic Behavior and Organization* 2, 35–48.

Edelman, G. M. 1989. *The remembered present: A biological theory of consciousness.* New York: Basic Books.

Edelman, G. M. 1992. *Bright air, brilliant fire: On the matter of the mind.* New York: Basic Books.

Edwards, M. 2001. Jungian analytic art therapy. In J. A. Rubin, ed., *Approaches to art therapy: Theory and technique,* 2nd ed., 81–94. Philadelphia: Brunner-Routledge.

Egeth, H. 1977. Attention and preattention. In G. H. Bower, ed., *The psychology of learning and motivation,* vol. 11, 277–320. New York: Academic Press.

Eich, E., Kihlstrom, J. F., Bower, G. H., Forgas, J. P., and Niedenthal, P. M. 2000. *Cognition and emotion.* London: Oxford University Press.

Eigen, M. 1977. On breathing and identity. *Journal of Humanistic Psychology* 17, 35–39.

Eisenberg, N., and Spinrad, T. 2004. Emotion-related regulation: Sharpening the definition. *Child Development* 75, 334–339.

Eissler, K. R. 1953. The effect of the structure of the ego on psychoanalytic technique. *Journal of the American Psychoanalytic Association* 1, 104–143.

Eitinger, L. 1971. Organic and psychosomatic after effects of concentration camp imprisonment. *International Journal of Psychiatric Clinics* 8, 205–218.

Ekman, P. 1984. Expression and the nature of emotion. In K. Scherer, and P. Ekman, eds., *Approaches to emotion,* 319–343. Hillsdale, NJ: Lawrence Erlbaum Associates.

Ekman, P., and Davidson, R. J., eds. 1994. *The nature of emotion: Fundamental questions.* London: Oxford University Press.

Ekman, P., Friesen, W. V., and Hager, J. C. 2002. *The facial action coding system,* 2nd ed. Salt Lake City: Research Nexus eBook.

Eliade, M. 1978. *A history of religious ideas. Vol. 1: From the stone age to the Eleusinian mysteries,* trans. W. Trask. Chicago: University of Chicago Press.

Ellenberger, H. F. 1970. *The discovery of the unconscious: The history and evolution of dynamic psychiatry.* New York: Basic Books.

Ellenbogen, M. A., Schwartzman, A. E., Stewart, J., and Walker, C. 2002. Stress and selective attention: The interplay of mood, cortisol level and emotional information processing. *Psychophysiology* 39, 723–732.

Ellis, A. 1950. An introduction to the principles of scientific psychoanalysis. *Genetic Psychology Monograph* 41, 147–212.

Ellis, R. D. 1995. *Questioning consciousness: The interplay of imagery, cognition, and emotion in the human brain*. Amsterdam, Netherlands: John Benjamins Publishing Company.

Ellis, R. D., and Newton, N., eds. 2000. *The caldron of consciousness: Motivation, affect and self-organization—An anthology*. Amsterdam, Netherlands: John Benjamins Publishing Company.

Epel, N. 1993. *Writers dreaming: 26 writers talk about their dreams and the creative process*. New York: Vintage Books.

Epstein, M. 1996. *Thoughts without a thinker: Psychotherapy from a Buddhist perspective*. Cambridge, MA: Basic Books.

Epstein, S. E. 1991. Cognitive-experiential self theory: An integrative theory of personality. In R. C. Curtis, ed., *The relational self: Convergences in psychoanalysis and social psychology*, 111–137. New York: Guilford Press.

Erdelyi, M. H. 1974. A new look at the New Look: Perceptual defense and vigilance. *Psychological Review* 81, 1–25.

Erdelyi, M. H. 1985. *Psychoanalysis: Freud's cognitive psychology*. New York: Freeman.

Erdelyi, M. H. 1990. Repression, reconstruction, and defense: History and integration of the psychoanalytic and experimental frameworks. In J. L. Singer, ed., *Repression and Dissociation*, 1–31. Chicago: University of Chicago Press.

Erdelyi, M. H. 2001. Defense processes can be conscious or unconscious. *American Psychologist* 56, 761–762.

Erdelyi, M. H., and Becker, J. 1974. Hyperamnesia for pictures. Incremental memory for pictures but not words in multiple recall trials. *Cognitive Psychology* 6, 159–171.

Erdelyi, M. H., and Goldberg, B. 1979. Let's not sweep repression under the rug: Toward a cognitive psychology of repression. In J. F. Kihlstrom, and F. J. Evans, eds., *Functional disorders of memory*, 355–402. Hillsdale, NJ: Erlbaum.

Erikson, E. 1959. *Identity and the life cycle. Selected papers*. New York: International Universities Press.

Eriksen, C. W. 1960. Discrimination and learning without awareness: A methodological survey and evaluation. *Psychological Review* 67, 279–300.

Erikson, E. 1963. *Childhood and society*. New York: W. W. Norton.

Esteves, F., Dimberg, U., and Ohman, A. 1994. Automatically elicited fear: Conditioned skin conductance responses to masked facial expressions. *Cognition and Emotion*, 8, 393–413.

Etkin, A., Klemenhagen, K. C., Dudman, J. T., Rogan, M. T., Hen, R., Kandel, E. R., and Hirsch, J. 2004. Individual differences in trait anxiety predict the response of the basolateral amygdala to unconsciously processed fearful faces. *Neuron* 44, 1,043–1,055.

Ewen, S., and Ewen E. 1992. *Channels of desire: Mass images and the shaping of American consciousness*. Minneapolis: University of Minnesota Press.

Eysenck, H. 1952. The effects of psychotherapy: An evaluation. *Journal of Consulting Psychology* 16, 319–324.

Eysenck, H. 1966. Personality and extra-sensory perception. *Journal of the Society for Psychical Research* 44, 55–71.

Eysenck, H. 1990. *The decline and fall of the Freudian empire.* Washington, DC: Scott-Townsend Publishers.

Eysenck, H., and Wilson, G. C. 1973. *The experimental study of Freudian theories.* London: Methuen.

Fair, C. M. 1992. *Cortical memory functions.* Birkhäuser.

Fairbairn, W. R. D. 1929. Dissociation and repression. In E. F. Birtles, and D. E. Scharff, eds., *From instinct to self: Selected papers of W. R. D. Fairbairn,* 13–79. Northvale, NJ: Jason Aronson, 1994.

Fairbairn, W. R. D. 1944. Endopsychic structure considered in terms of object-relationships. *International Journal of Psycho-Analysis* 25, 70–93.

Fairbairn, W. R. D. 1952. *Psychological studies of the personality.* London: Routledge and Kegan Paul.

Fairbairn, W. R. D. 1954. *An object-relations theory of the personality.* New York: Basic Books.

Fanselow, M. S. 2000. Contextual fear, gestalt memories, and the hippocampus. *Behavioral Brain Research* 110, 73–81.

Fast, I. 1983. Primary-process cognition: A reformulation. *Annual of Psychoanalysis,* 11, 199–225.

Fast, I. 1998. *Selving: A relational theory of self organization.* Hillsdale, NJ: Analytic Press.

Feather, B. W., and Rhoads, J. M. 1972. Psychoanalytic behavior therapy—II. Clinical aspects. *Archives of General Psychiatry* 26, 503–511.

Feather, N. T. 1982. *Expectations and actions: Expectancy–value models in psychology.* Hillsdale, NJ: Lawrence Erlbaum Associates.

Featherstone, M. 1991. The body in consumer culture. In M. Featherstone, ed., *The Body: Social Process and Cultural Theory,* 170–196. London: Sage Publications.

Fenichel, O. 1945. *The psychoanalytic theory of neurosis.* Oxford: Norton and Co.

Fensterheim, H. 1994. Hyperventilation and psychopathology: A clinical perspective. In B. H. Timmons, and R. Ley, eds., *Behavioral and psychological approaches to breathing disorders,* 139–148. New York: Plenum Press.

Ferenczi, S. 1926. *Further contributions to the theory and technique of psychoanalysis.* London: Hogarth Press.

Ferenczi, S. 1928. The elasticity of psychoanalytic technique. In S. Ferenczi, ed. 1955, 87–101. London: Maresfield Reprints.

Ferenczi, S. 1932. Notes and fragments. In S. Ferenczi, ed., *Final contributions to the problems and methods of psycho-analysis,* 216–279 New York: Basic Books.

Ferenczi, S. 1955. *Final contributions to the problems and methods of psychoanalysis,* ed. M. Balint, trans. E. Mosbacher, ed. New York: Bruner/Mazel.

Ferenczi, S. 1985. *The clinical diary of Sandor Ferenczi,* ed. J. Dupont, trans. M. Balint, and N. Z. Jackson, ed., Cambridge, MA: Harvard University Press.

Ferenczi, S., and Rank, O. 1923. *The development of psycho-analysis,* trans. C. Newton. Madison, CT: International Universities Press.

Finagarette, H. 1969. *Self-deception*. London: Routledge and Kegan-Paul.

Fiscalini, J. 2004. *Coparticipant psychoanalysis: Toward a new theory of clinical inquiry*. New York: Columbia University Press.

Fischer, C. 2007. What wealth–happiness paradox? A short note on the American case. *Journal of Happiness Studies, DOI* 10, 1007/s10902-0079047-4.

Fisher, S., and Greenberg, R. P. 1977. *Scientific credibility of Freud's theory and therapy*. New York: Basic Books.

Flax, J. 1981. Psychoanalysis and the philosophy of science: Critique or resistance. *Journal of Philosophy* 78, 561–569.

Foa, E. B., and Kozak, M. J. 1986. Emotional processing of fear: Exposure to corrective information. *Psychological Bulletin,* 99, 20–35.

Foa, E. B., and McNally, R. J. 1986. Sensitivity to feared stimuli in obsessive-compulsives: A dichotic listening analysis. *Cognitive Therapy and Research* 10, 477–485.

Fonagy, P. 1998. Moments of change in psychoanalytic theory: Discussion of a new theory of psychic change. *Infant Mental Health Journal* 19, 346–353.

Fonagy, P. 1999. Moments of change in psychoanalytic theory: Discussion of a new theory of psychic change. *Infant Mental Health Journal* 19, 346–353.

Fonagy, P. 2000. Memory and therapeutic action: Response. *International Journal of Psycho-Analysis* 81, 594–595.

Fonagy, P, Gergely, G., Jurist, E. L., and Target, M. 2002. *Affect regulation, mentalization, and the development of the self*. New York: Other Press.

Fonagy, P, and Target, M. 1997. Attachment and reflective function: Their role in self-organization. *Development and Psychopathology* 9, 679–700.

Forgas, J. P. 1999. Network theories and beyond. In T. Dalgleish, and M. J. Power, eds., *Handbook of cognition and emotion*, 591–611. New York: John Wiley and Sons.

Fosha, D. 2000. *The transforming power of affect: A model for accelerated change*. New York: Basic Books.

Foucault, M. 1970. *The order of things: An archeology of the human sciences*, trans. anonymous. London: Tavistock.

Fox, E., Russo, R., and Dutton, K. 2002. Attentional bias for threat: Evidence for delayed disengagement from emotional faces. *Cognition and Emotion* 16, 355–379.

Fox, W. S., and Philliber, W. W. 1978. Television viewing and the perception of affluence. *Sociological Quarterly* 19, 103–112.

Frank, J. 1961. *Persuasion and healing*. Baltimore: Johns Hopkins University Press.

Frank, K. A. 1991. *Action techniques in psychoanalysis. Contemporary Psychoanalysis* 26, 732–736.

Frank, K. A. 1999. *Psychoanalytic participation: Action, interaction, and integration*. Hillsdale, NJ: Analytic Press.

Frankl, V. E. 1959. *Man's search for meaning*. New York: Washington Square Press/Pocket Books.

Frankl, V. E. 1984. *Man's search for meaning: An introduction to logotherapy*, trans. I. Lasch. New York: Simon and Schuster.

Freedberg, D. 1989. *The power of images: Studies in the history and theory of response*. Chicago: University of Chicago Press.

Freeman, R. 1994. *The concept of transference: An introduction to its role in the psychoanalytic process*. London: Kornac Books.

Freiwald, W. A., and Kanwisher, N. G. 2004. Visual selective attention: Insights from brain imaging and neurophysiology. In M. S. Gazzaniga, ed., *The cognitive neurosciences*, 3rd ed, 575–588. Cambridge, MA: MIT Press.

French, T. M. 1933. Interrelations between psychoanalysis and the experimental work of Pavlov. *American Journal of Psychiatry* 89, 1165–1203.

Fretigny, R., and Virel, A. 1968. *L'imagerie mentale*. Geneva: Mont-Blanc.

Fretter, P. B., Bucci, W., Broitman, J., Silberschatz, G. et al. 1994. How the patient's plan relates to the concept of transference. *Psychotherapy Research* 4, 58–72.

Freud, S. 1892–1893. A case of successful treatment by hypnotism with some remarks on the origin of hysterical symptoms through 'counterwill.' *Standard Edition of the Complete Psychological Works of Sigmund Freud*, 1:115–128. London: Hogarth Press, 1958.

Freud, S. [1894] 1963. The defense neuron-psychoses. In P. Rieff, ed., *Sigmund Freud: Early psychoanalytic writings*, trans. J. Rickman. New York: Collier.

Freud, S. 1895. On the grounds for detaching a particular syndrome from neurasthenia under the description 'anxiety neurosis.' *Standard Edition* 3: 85–117.

Freud, S. 1900. The interpretation of dreams. *Standard Edition* 4–5.

Freud, S. 1901. On dreams. *Standard Edition* 5: 633–685.

Freud, S. 1904. Psychopathology of everyday life. *Standard Edition* 6 whole volume.

Freud, S. 1905. Three essays on the theory of sexuality. *Standard Edition* 7: 125–245.

Freud, S. 1914. On the history of the psychoanalytic movement. *Standard Edition* 14: 1–66.

Freud, S. 1915a. Instincts and their vicissitudes. *Standard Edition* 14: 111–140.

Freud, S. 1915b. Repression. *Standard Edition* 14: 143–158.

Freud, S. 1915c. The unconscious. *Standard Edition* 14: 159–215.

Freud, S. 1916. Introductory lectures on psycho-analysis, part III: General theory of the neurosis. *Standard Edition* 16:243–448.

Freud, S. 1919. Lines of advance in psychoanalytic therapy. *Standard Edition* 27: 157–168.

Freud, S. 1921. Group psychology and the analysis of the ego. *Standard Edition* 18: 69–143.

Freud, S. 1923. *The ego and the id*. New York: Norton.

Freud, S. 1926. *Inhibitions, symptoms and anxiety*. New York: Norton.

Freud, S. 1933. New introductory lectures on psycho–analysis. *Standard Edition* 22: 3–182.

Freud, S. 1956. Memorandum on the electrical treatment of war neurotics. *Standard Edition* 17: 211. Originally published 1920, *International Journal of Psychoanalysis* 37, 16–18.

Freud, S. 1961. *Civilization and its discontents*. In J. Strachey, ed. New York: W.W. Norton.

Freud, S., and Breuer, J. 1893. On the psychical mechanism of hysterical phenomena. *Standard Edition* 2: 3–17.

Freyd, J. L. 1996. *Betrayal trauma: The logic of forgetting childhood abuse.* Cambridge, MA: Harvard University Press.

Friedman, M., Charney, D., and Deutch, Y., eds. 1995. *Neurobiological and clinical consequences of stress.* Philadelphia, PA: Lippincott-Raven.

Frijda, N. H. 1986. *The emotions.* New York: Cambridge University Press.

Frijda, N. 2000. *Emotions.* In K. Pawlik, and M. Rosenzweig, eds., *Identity and emotion: Development through self-organization.* Studies in emotion and social interaction, 207–222. International handbook of psychology 33. London, England: Sage Publications Ltd.

Fromm, E. 1941. *Escape from freedom.* New York: Avon.

Fromm, E. 1947. *Man for himself, an inquiry into the psychology of ethics.* New York: Holt, Rinehart and Winston.

Fromm, E. 1955. *The sane society.* New York: Rinehart.

Fromm, E. 1986. *For the love of life.* New York: Free Press.

Fromm, E. 1990. *Beyond the chains of illusion: My encounter with Marx and Freud.* New York: Continuum.

Fromm, E. 1992. *The revision of psychoanalysis.* Boulder: Westview Press.

Frontline/World. Episode no. 204, Bhutan: The Last Place. www.pbs.org/Frontlineworld/about/episodeguide.html.

Frosh, S. 1989. *Psychoanalysis and psychology: Minding the gap.* New York: NYU Press.

Fuller, B. A. G., and McMurrin, S. M. 1955. *A history of philosophy*, 3rd ed. New York: Holt, Rinehart and Winston.

Funder, D. C. 1997. *The personality puzzle.* New York: Norton.

Gabbard, G. O., Horwitz, L., Allen J.G., Frieswyk, S., Newsom, G., Colson, D. B., and Coyne, L. 1994. Transference interpretation in the psychotherapy of borderline patients: A high-risk, high-gain phenomenon. *Harvard Review of Psychiatry* 2, 59–69.

Gabbard, G. O., and Westen, D. 2003. Rethinking therapeutic action. *International Journal of Psychoanalysis* 84, 823–841.

Galatzer-Levy, R. M. 2004. Chaotic possibilities: Toward a new model of development. *International Journal of Psychoanalysis* 85, 419–441.

Galbraith, J. K. 1969. *The affluent society.* Boston: Houghton Mifflin.

Garyfallos, G., Adamopoulous, A., Mastrogianni, A., Voikli, M., Saitis, M., Alektoridis, P. 1998. Evaluation of cognitive analytic therapy CAT outcome in Greek psychiatric outpatients. *European Journal of Psychiatry* 12, 167–179.

Garyfallos, G., Adamopoulous, A., Karastergious, A., Voikli, M., Zlatanos, D., and Tsifida, S. 2002. Evaluation of cognitive-analytic therapy CAT outcome: A 4-8 year follow up. *European Journal of Psychiatry* 16, 197–209.

Gazzaniga, M. S. 1967. The split brain in man. *Scientific American* 217, 24–29.

Gazzaniga, M. S. 1998. The split brain revisited. *Scientific American,* 279, 50–55.

Gedo, J. E. 1988. *The mind in disorder: Psychoanalytic models of pathology.* Hillsdale, NJ: Analytic Press.

Geen, R. G. 1990. *Human aggression*. Belmont, CA: Brooks/Cole Publishing.

Gendlin, E. T. 1962. *Experiencing and the creation of meaning: A philosophical and psychological approach to the subjective*. Oxford: Free Press Glencoe.

Gendlin, E. T. 1981. *Focusing*, 2nd ed. New York: Bantam Books.

Gendlin, E. T. 1996. *Focusing-oriented psychotherapy: A manual of the experiential method*. New York: Guilford Press.

Gentile, D. A., and Walsh, D. A. 2002. A normative study of family media habits. *Journal of Applied Developmental Psychology* 23, 157–178.

Gergen, K. J. 1991. *The saturated self: Dilemmas of identity in contemporary life*. New York: Basic Books.

Gerler, E. R., Drew, N. S., and Mohr, P. 1990. Succeeding in middle school: A multimodal approach. *Elementary School Guidance and Counseling* 24, 263–271.

Gill, M. M. 1976. Metapsychology is not psychology. *Psychological Issues* 9, 71–105.

Gill, M. M. 1979. The analysis of the transference. *Journal of the American Psychoanalytic Association* 27 (Suppl.), 263–288.

Gill, M. M. 1982. *Analysis of transference*, vol. 1. New York: International Universities Press.

Gill, M. M. 1984. Psychoanalysis and psychotherapy: A revision. *The International Review of Psychoanalysis* 11, 161–179.

Gill, M. M. 1993. Interaction and interpretation: Commentary on Morris Eagle's "Enactments, transference, and symptomatic cure." *Psychoanalytic Dialogues* 3, 111–122.

Gill, M. M. 1994. *Psychoanalysis in transition: A personal view*. Hillsdale, NJ: Analytic Press.

Gill, M. M., and Holzman, P. 1976. *Psychological issues monograph*, no 36, 91–105. New York: International Universities Press.

Gilligan, J. 1996. *Violence: Reflections on a national epidemic*. New York: Vintage Books.

Gitelson, M. 1962. The curative factors in psychoanalysis. Part 1. *International Journal of Psychoanalysis* 43, 194–205.

Gladwell, M. 2004. *The tipping point*. New York: Little, Brown.

Gladwell, M. 2005. *Blink: The power of thinking without thinking*. New York: Little, Brown.

Glaser, J., and Banaji, M. R. 1999. When fair is foul and foul is fair: Reverse priming in automatic evaluation. *Journal of Personality and Social Psychology* 7, 669–687.

Glaser, J., and Kihlstrom, J. F. 2005. Compensatory automaticity: Unconscious volition is not an oxymoron. In R. R. Hassin, J. S. Uleman, S. James, and J. A. Bargh, eds., *The new unconscious*, 171–195. Cambridge: Oxford University Press.

Gleick, J. 1987. *Chaos: Making a new science*. New York: Viking.

Glover, E. 1955. *The technique of psychoanalysis*. New York: International Universities Press.

Gold, J. W. 1993. The sociocultural context of psychotherapy integration. In G. Stricker, and J. R. Gold, eds., *Comprehensive handbook of psychotherapy integration*, 3–8. New York: Plenum.

Gold, J. R. 1996. *Key concepts in psychotherapy integration.* New York: Plenum.

Gold, J., and Stricker, G. 2001. A relational psychodynamic perspective on assimilative integration. *Journal of Psychotherapy Integration* 11, 43–58.

Goldapple, K., Segal, Z., Garson, C., Lau, M., Bieling, P., Kennedy, S., and Mayberg, H. 2004. Treatment-specific effects of cognitive behavior therapy. *Archives of General Psychiatry* 61, 34–41.

Goldberg, A. 1999a. *Being of two minds: The vertical split in psychoanalysis and psychotherapy.* Hillsdale, NJ: Analytic Press.

Goldberg, A., ed. 1999b. *Pluralism in self psychology: Progress in self psychology,* vol. 15. Hillsdale, NJ: Analytic Press.

Goldensohn, S. S. 1977. Graduates' evaluation of their psychoanalytic training. *Journal of the American Academy of Psychoanalysis* 5, 51–64.

Goldfried, M. R. 1980. Toward a delineation of psychological change principles. *American Psychologist* 35, 991–999.

Goldfried, M. R., and Newman, C. F. 1992. A history of psychotherapy integration. In J. C. Norcross, and M. R. Goldfried, eds., *Handbook of psychotherapy integration,* 46–93. New York: Basic Books.

Goldfried, M. R., and Norcross, J. C., eds. 1992. *Handbook of psychotherapy integration.* New York: Basic Books.

Goldfried, M. R., Raue, P. J., and Castonguay, L. G. 1998. The therapeutic focus in significant sessions of master therapists: A comparison of cognitive-behavioral and psychodynamic-interpersonal interventions. *Journal of Consulting and Clinical Psychology* 66, 803–810.

Goldfried, M. R., and Robins, C. 1983. Self-schemata, cognitive bias, and the processing of therapeutic experiences. In P. C. Kendall, ed., *Advances in cognitive-behavioral research and therapy,* 33–80. San Diego, CA: Academic Press.

Goleman, D. 1995. *Emotional intelligence.* New York, England: Bantam Books.

Goleman, D. 2003. *Destructive emotions: A scientific dialogue with the Dalai Lama.* New York: Bantam Books.

Gollwitzer, P. M. 1999. Implementation intentions: Strong effects of simple plans. *American Psychologist* 54, 493–503.

Gòrnik-Durose, M. 2001. Mass–mediated influences on patterns of consumption in Polish youth. In W. Wosinska, R. B. Cialdini, D. W. Barrett, and J. Reykowski, eds., *The practice of social influence in multiple cultures, applied social research,* 223–234. Hillsdale, NJ. Lawrence Erlbaum Associates.

Gosling, S. D., Ko, S. J., Mannarelli, T., and Morris, M. E. 2002. A room with a cue: Personality judgments based on offices and bedrooms. *Journal of Personality and Social Psychology* 82, 379–398.

Gould, S. J. 1977. *Ontogeny and phylogeny.* Cambridge, MA: Harvard University Press.

Gould, W. B. 1993. *Victor E. Frankl: Life with meaning.* Belmont: Brooks/Cole.

Gray, J. R. 1987. *The psychology of fear and stress,* 2nd ed. New York: Cambridge University Press.

Gray, J. R. 2001. Emotional modulation of cognitive control: Approach-withdrawal states double-dissociate spatial from verbal two-back task performance. *Journal of Experimental Psychology: General* 130, 436–452.

Gray, J. R., and Braver, T. S. 2002. Integration of emotion and cognitive control: A neurocomputational hypothesis of dynamic goal regulation. In S. C. Moore, and M. Oaksford, eds., *Emotional cognition: From brain to behaviour*, 289–316. Amsterdam, Netherlands: John Benjamins Publishing Company.

Green, A. 1999. On discrimination and non-discrimination between affect and representation. *Revista Chilena de Psicoanalisis* 16, 26–62.

Green, J. D., Pinter, B., and Sedikides, C. 2005. Mnemic neglect and self-threat: Trait modifiability moderates self–protection. *European Journal of Social Psychology* 35, 225–235.

Green, J. D., and Sedikides, C. 2004. Retrieval selectivity in the processing of self-referent information: Testing the boundaries of self–protection. *Self and Identity* 3, 69–80.

Greenberg, J. 1986. Theoretical models and the analyst's neutrality. *Contemporary Psychoanalysis* 22, 87–106.

Greenberg, J. 1991. *Oedipus and beyond*. Cambridge, MA: Harvard University Press.

Greenberg, J., and Mitchell, S. A. 1983. *Object relations in psychoanalytic theory*. Cambridge, MA: Harvard University Press.

Greenberg, J., Solomon, S., and Pyszczynski, T. 1997. Terror management theory of self-esteem and cultural worldviews: Empirical assessments and conceptual refinements. In M. P. Zanna, ed., *Advances in experimental social psychology*, vol. 29, 61–139. San Diego, CA: Academic Press.

Greenberg, L. S. 1991. Research on the process of change. *Psychotherapy Research* 1, 3–16.

Greenberg, L. S. 1993. Emotional change processes in psychotherapy. In M. Lewis, and J. Haviland, eds., *Handbook of emotion*, 499–510. New York: Guilford Press.

Greenberg, L. S. 1995. The self is flexibly various and requires an integrative approach. *Journal of Psychotherapy Integration* 5, 323–329.

Greenberg, L. S., and Pascual-Leone, J. 1997. Emotion in the creation of personal meaning. In M. J. Power, J. Michael, and C. R. Brewin, eds., *The transformation of meaning in psychological therapies: Integrating theory and practice*, 157–173. New York: John Wiley.

Greenberg, L. S., Rice, L. N., and Elliott, R. K. 1993. *Facilitating emotional change: The moment-by-moment process*. New York: Guilford Press.

Greenberg, L. S., and Safran, J. D. 1984. Integrating affect and cognition: A perspective on therapeutic change. *Cognitive Therapy and Research* 8, 559–578.

Greenberg, L. S., and Safran, J. D. 1987. *Emotion in psychotherapy: Affect, cognition, and the process of change*. New York: Guilford Press.

Greenberg, L. S., and Watson, J. C. 1998. Experiential therapy in the treatment of depression: Differential effects of the client-centered relationship conditions and active experiential interventions. *Psychotherapy Research* 2, 210–224.

Greene, B. R. 1999. *The elegant universe: Superstrings, hidden dimensions, and the quest for the ultimate theory*. New York: W. W. Norton.

Greenwald, A. G. 1980. The totalitarian ego: Fabrication and revision of personal history. *American Psychologist*, 35, 603–618.

Greenwald, A. G. 1992. New look 3: Unconscious cognition reclaimed. *American Psychologist* 47, 766–779.

Greenwald, A. G. 1997. Self-knowledge and self-deception: Further consideration. In M. Myslobodsky, ed., *The mythomanias: The nature of deception and self-deception,* 51–72. England: Lawrence Erlbaum Associates.

Greenwald, A. G., and Banaji, M. R. 1995. Implicit social cognition: Attitudes, self-esteem, and stereotypes. *Psychological Review* 102, 4–27.

Grinker, R. R. 1976. Discussion of Strupp's "Some critical comments on the future of psychoanalytic therapy." *Bulletin of the Menninger Clinic* 40, 247–254.

Gross, J. 1998. The emerging field of emotion regulation: An integrative review. *Review of General Psychology* 2, 271–299.

Gross, J. 1999. Emotion regulation: Past, present, future. *Cognition and Emotion* 13, 551–573.

Grunbaum, A. 1983. Is object-relations theory better founded than orthodox psychoanalysis? A reply to Jane Flax. *Journal of Philosophy,* 80, 46–51.

Grunbaum, A. 1984. *The foundations of psychoanalysis: A philosophical critique.* Berkeley: University of California Press.

Guidano, V. F. 1991. *The self in process: Toward a post-rationalist cognitive therapy.* New York: Guilford Press.

Guntrip, H. 1969. *Schizoid phenomena, object relations and the self.* New York: International Universities Press.

Guntrip, H. 1975. My experience of analysis with Fairbairn and Winnicott. *International Review of Psycho-Analysis* 2, 145–156.

Gurman, A. S., and Messer, S. B. 1997. *Essential psychotherapies: Theory and practice.* New York: Guilford Press.

Gurr, T. R. 1970. *Why men rebel.* Princeton, NJ: Princeton University Press.

Hagerty, M. R., and Veenhoven, R. 2003. Wealth and happiness revisited—Growing national income does go with greater happiness. *Social Indicators Research* 64, 1–27.

Hall, G. S. 1915. Thanatopia and immortality. *American Journal of Psychology* 26, 550–613.

Halpern, P. M. 2004. *Great beyond: Higher dimension, parallel universes, and the extraordinary search for a theory of everything.* New York: Doubleday.

Hammer, E. F., ed. 1968. *Use of interpretation in treatment: Technique and art.* New York: Grune and Stratton.

Hansen, C. H., and Hansen, R. D. 1988. Finding the face in the crowd: An anger superiority effect. *Journal of Personality and Social Psychology* 54, 917–924.

Hare, R. D. 1966. Denial of threat and emotional response to impending painful stimulation. *Journal of Consulting Psychology* 30, 359–361.

Hargreaves, D., and Tiggermann, M. 2002. The effect of television commercials on mood and body dissatisfaction. *Journal of Social and Clinical Psychology* 21, 287–308.

Harris, A. 1996. False memory? False memory syndrome? The so-called false memory syndrome? *Psychoanalytic Dialogues* 6, 155–187.

Harris, A., and Gold, B. H. 2001. The fog rolled in: Induced dissociative states in clinical process. *Psychoanalytic Dialogues* 11, 357–384.

Harris, J. R. 1995. Where is the child's environment? A group socialization theory of development. *Psychological Review* 102, 458–489.

Harris, J. R. 1998. *The nurture assumption: Why children turn out the way they do.* NY: Free Press.

Harris, J. R. 2000. Socialization, personality development, and the child's environments: Comment on Vandell 2000, *Developmental Psychology* 36, 711–723.

Harter, S. 1983. To smile or not to smile: Issues in the examination of cross-cultural differences and similarities. *Monographs of the Society for Research in Child Development* 48, 80–87.

Hartmann, H. 1950. Comments on the psychoanalytic theory of the ego. *Psychoanalytic Study of the Child* 5, 74–96.

Hartmann, H., and Lowenstein, R. M. 1962. Notes on the superego. *The Psychoanalytic Study of the Child* 17, 42–81.

Hassin, R., Uleman, J., and Bargh, J., eds. 2005. *The new unconscious.* New York: Oxford University Press.

Haviland-Jones, J. M., and Lewis, M., eds. 2000. *Handbook of emotions*, 2nd ed. New York: Guilford Press.

Hayek, F. A. 1952. *Counter-revolution of science: Studies on the abuse of reason.* Indianapolis: Liberty Press.

Head H., and Holmes, G. 1911. Sensory disturbances from cerebral lesions. *Brain* 34, 102–254.

Heatherton, T. F., Baumeister, R. F., and Tice, D. M. 1994. *Losing control: How and why people fail at self-regulation.* San Diego, CA: Academic Press.

Hebb, D. O., 1946. On the nature of fear. *Psychological Review* 53, 259–276.

Heisenberg, W. 1958a. The representation of nature in contemporary physics. *Daedalus* (summer), 95–108.

Heisenberg, W. 1958b. *The physicist's conception of nature*, trans. A. J. Pomerans. New York: Harcourt Brace.

Henggeler, S. W., Schoenwald, S. K., Borduin, C. M., Rowland, M. D., and Cunningham, P.B. 1998. *Multisystemic treatment of antisocial behavior in children and adolescents.* New York: Guilford Press.

Henry, W. P., Strupp, H. H., Schacht, T. E., and Gaston, L. 1994. Psychodynamic approaches. In A. E. Bergin, and S. L. Garfield, eds., *Handbook of psychotherapy and behavior change*, 4th ed., 467–508). Oxford: John Wiley and Sons.

Herbart, J. F. 1896. *Herbart's ABC of sense-perception, and minor pedagogical works*, trans.W. J. Eckoff. New York: D. Appleton. In C. DeGarmo, ed., *Herbart and the Herbartians,* 130–140. Folcroft, PA: Folcroft Library Editions.

Herman, J. 1992. *Trauma and recovery.* New York: Basic Books.

Herzberg, A. 1945. *Active psychotherapy.* New York: Grune and Stratton.

Hickey, D. 1997. *Air guitar: Essays on art and democracy.* Los Angeles: Art Issues Press.

Higgins, E. T. 1987. Self-discrepancy: A theory relating self and affect. *Psychological Review* 94, 319–340.

Higgins, E. T. 1989. Knowledge accessibility and activation: Subjectivity and suffering from unconscious sources. In J. S. Uleman, and J. A. Bargh, eds., *Unintended thought,* 75–123. New York: Guilford Press.

Higgins, E. T., and Tykocinski, O. 1992. Self-discrepancies and biographical memory: Personality and cognition at the level of psychological situation. *Personality and Social Psychology Bulletin* 18, 527–535.

Hilgard, E. R. 1977. Controversies over consciousness and the rise of cognitive psychology. *Australian Psychologist* 12, 7–26.

Hilsenroth, M. J., Blagys, M. D., Ackerman, S. J., Bonge, D. R., and Blais, M. A. 2005. Measuring psychodynamic–interpersonal and cognitive–behavioral techniques: Development of the comparative psychotherapy process scale. *Psychotherapy: Theory, Research, Practice, Training* 42, 340–356.

Hobbs, N. 1968. Sources of gain in psychotherapy. In E. F. Hammer, ed., *Use of interpretation in treatment,* 13–21. New York: Grune and Stratton.

Hoffman, D. D. 1998. *Visual intelligence: How we create what we see.* New York: W. W. Norton.

Hoffman, I. Z. 1993. The intimate authority of the psychoanalyst's presence. *Psychologist/ Psychoanalyst* 13, 15–23.

Hoffman, I. Z. 1996. Merton M. Gill: A study in theory development in psychoanalysis. *Psychoanalytic Dialogues* 6, 5–53.

Hoffman, M. L. 1987. The contribution of empathy to justice and moral judgment. In N. Eisenberg, and J. Stayer, eds., *Empathy and its development. Cambridge studies in social and emotional development,* 47–80. New York: Cambridge University Press.

Hoffman, R. R., ed. 1992. *The psychology of expertise: Cognitive research and empirical AI.* New York: Springer-Verlag Publishing.

Hoglend, P. 1996. Long-term effects of transference interpretations: Comparing results from a quasi-experimental and a naturalistic long-term follow-up study of brief dynamic psychotherapy. *Acta Psychiatrica Scandinavica* 93, 205–211.

Hoglend, P. 2004. Analysis of transference in psychodynamic psychotherapy: A review of empirical research. *Canadian Journal of Psychoanalysis* 12, 280–300.

Hollander, E., and Stein, D. J. 1995. *Impulsivity and aggression.* Oxford: John Wiley.

Holmes, D. S. 1990. The evidence for repression: An examination of sixty years of research. In J. L. Singer, ed., *Repression and dissociation,* 85–102. Chicago: University of Chicago Press.

Holmes, J. 1998. The changing aims of psychoanalytic psychotherapy: An integrative perspective. *International Journal of Psycho-Analysis* 79, 227–240.

Holmqvist, R. 2001. Patterns of consistency and deviation in therapists' countertransference feelings. *Journal of Psychotherapy Practice and Research* 10, 104–116.

Holt, R. R. 1976. Drive or wish? A reconsideration of the psychoanalytic theory of motivation. In M. M. Gill, and P. S. Holzman, eds., *Psychology versus metapsychology: Psychoanalytic essays in memory of George S. Klein, Psychological Issues* 9: Monograph No. 36: 158–197. New York: International Universities Press.

Holt, R. R. 1985. The current status of psychoanalytic theory. *Psychoanalytic Psychology* 2, 289–315.

Holt, R. R. 2002. Quantitative research on the primary process: Method and findings. *Journal of the American Psychoanalytic Association* 50, 457–482.

Holzman, P. S. 1985. Psychoanalysis: Is the therapy destroying the science? *Journal of the American Psychoanalytic Association* 33, 735–770.

Honos-Webb, L., Surko, M., Stiles, W. B., and Greenberg, L. S. 1999. Assimilation of voices in psychotherapy: The case of Jan. *Journal of Counseling Psychology* 46, 448–460.

Hopenwasser, K. 1998. Listening to the body: Somatic representations of dissociated memory. In L. Aron, and F. S. Anderson, eds., *Relational perspectives on the body*, 215–236. Hillsdale, NJ: Analytic Press.

Horney, K. 1950. *Neurosis and human growth: The struggle toward self-realization*. New York: Norton.

Hornstein, G. A. 1992. The return of the repressed. *American Psychologist* 47, 254–263.

Horowitz, M. J. 1970. *Image formation and cognition*. New York: Appleton-Century-Crofts.

Horowitz, M. J. 1978. *Image formation and cognition*, 2nd ed. New York: Appleton-Century-Crofts.

Horowitz, M. J. 1983. *Image formation and psychotherapy*. New York: Jason Aronson.

Horowitz, M. J. 1991. *Person schemas and maladaptive interpersonal patterns*. Chicago: University of Chicago Press.

Horowitz, M. J., ed. 1999. *Essential papers on posttraumatic stress disorder*. New York: NYU Press.

Horowitz, M. J., Stinson, C., Curtis, D., Ewert, M., Redington, D., Singer, J., Bucci, W., Mergenthaler, E., Milbrath, C., and Hartley, D. 1993. Topics and signs: Defensive control of emotional expression. *Journal of Consulting and Clinical Psychology* 61, 421–430.

Horvath, A. O., and Bedi, R. P. 2002. The alliance. In J. C. Norcross, ed., *Psychotherapy relationships that work*, 37–70. New York: Oxford University Press.

Hoyt, I. P. 1987. Dissociation, repression, disconnections: Toward a "neo-repression" theory of affect without awareness. University of Wisconsin. Unpublished manuscript.

Huber, J. 1965. *Through an eastern window*. New York: Bantam.

Hughes, L. 1951. Dream boogie. In *Montage of a dream deferred*. New York: Holt.

Huizinga, J. 1954. *The waning of the middle ages*. New York: Doubleday.

Hull, C. L. 1952. *A behavioral system*. New Haven, CT: Yale University Press.

Ingle, D. 1975. Focal attention in the frog: behavior and physiological correlates. *Science* 188, 1,033–1,035.

Ischlondy, N. E. 1930. Neuropsyche und hirnride: Physiologische grundlagen der tiefenpsychologie unter besonder berucksichting der psychoanalyse. Berlin: Urban und Schwarzenberg. Cited in Arkowitz, 1984.

Izard, C. 1971. *The face of emotion*. East Norwalk, CT: Appleton-Century-Crofts.

Izard, C., and Bartlett, E. 1972. *Patterns of emotions: A new analysis of anxiety and depression*. Oxford, England: Academic Press.

Izard, C., and Kobak, R. 1991. Emotions system functioning and emotion regulation. In J. Garber, and K. Dodge, eds., *The development of emotion regulation and dysregulation. Cambridge studies in social and emotional development*, 303–321. New York: Cambridge University Press.

Jackson, D. C., Burghy, C. J., Hanna, A. J., Larson, C. L., and Davidson, R. J. 2000. Resting frontal and anterior temporal EEG asymmetry predicts ability to regulate negative emotion. *Psychophysiology* 37, S50.

Jacobs, T. J. 1990. The corrective emotional experience—Its place in current technique. *Psychoanalytic Inquiry* 10, 433–454.

Jacobson, J. J. 1994. Signal affects and our psychoanalytic confusion of tongues. *Journal of the American Psychoanalytic Association* 42, 15–42.

Jacoby, L., and Kelley, C. 1992. A process–dissociation framework for investigating unconscious influences: Freudian slips, projective tests, subliminal perception, and signal detection theory. *Current Directions in Psychological Science* 1, 174–179.

Jacoby, L., Lindsay, S., and Toth, J. P. 1992. Unconscious influences revealed: Attention, awareness, and control. *American Psychologist* 47, 802–809.

James, W. 1890. *The principles of psychology*. New York: Henry Holt.

James, W. 1892/1963. *Psychology*. Oxford: Fawcett.

James, W. 1958. *The varieties of religious experience*. New York: Penguin Books. (Original work published 1849.)

James, W. 1968. The self. In C. Gordon, and K. S. Gergen, eds., *The self in interaction*, vol. 1, 41–50. New York: John Wiley.

Janet, P. 1889. *Psychological automatisms*. Paris: Alcan.

Janet, P. 1907. *The major symptoms of hysteria*. London and New York: Macmillan.

Janoff-Bulman, R. J. 1985. The aftermath of victimization: Rebuilding shattered assumptions. In C. R. Figley, ed., *Trauma and its wake*, 15–35. New York: Bruner/Mazel.

Jastrow, J. 1906. *The subconscious*. Boston: Houghton Mifflin.

Jastrow, J. 1932. *The house that Freud built*. Oxford: Greenberg.

Joffe, W. and Sandler, J. 1968. *From safety to superego*. New York: Guilford Press.

Johnson, C. L., and Taylor, C. 1996. Working with difficult-to-treat eating disorders using an integration of twelve-step and traditional psychotherapies. *Psychiatric Clinics of North America* 19, 829–841.

Johnson, M., and Multhaup, K. 1992. Emotion and MEM. In S. A. Christianson, ed., *The Handbook of Emotion and Memory*, 33–66. Hillsdale, NJ: Lawrence Erlbaum Associates.

Johnson-Laird, P. N. 1983. A computational analysis of consciousness. *Cognition and Brain Theory* 6, 499–508.

Johnston, W. A., and Dark, V. J. 1986. Selective attention. *Annual Review of Psychology* 37, 43–75.

Jones, E. 1935. Artistic form and the unconscious. *Mind* 44, 496–498.

Jones, J. 1995. *Affects as process*. Hillsdale, NJ: Analytic Press.

Jones, J. V., Jr. 1995. Constructivism and individual psychology: Common ground for dialogue. *Individual Psychology: Journal of Adlerian Theory, Research and Practice* 51, 231–243.

Joseph, R. 1996. *Neuropsychiatry, neuropsychology, and clinical neuroscience*. Baltimore: Williams and Wilkins.

Josephs, L. 1995. *Balancing empathy and interpretation*. Northvale, NJ: Aronson.

Josephs, L. 2004. Seduced by affluence: How material envy strains the analytic relationship. *Contemporary Psychoanalysis* 40, 389–408.

Joyce, J. 2003. *A portrait of the artist as a young man.* New York: Penguin. (Original work published 1914–15.)

Judd, C. M., Blair, I. V., and Chapleau, K. M. 2004. Automatic stereotypes vs. automatic prejudice: Sorting out the possibilities in the Payne 2001 weapon paradigm. *Journal of Experimental Social Psychology* 40, 75–81.

Jung, C. G., 1916. Long, C. E. Trans. *Collected papers on analytical psychology,* Oxford: Balliere, Tindall and Cox .

Kagan, J. 1979. Family experience and the child's development. *American Psychologist* 34, 886–891.

Kagan, J., and Klein, R. E. 1973. Cross-cultural perspectives on early development. *American Psychologist* 28, 947–961.

Kahneman, D. 1973. *Attention and effort.* Englewood Cliffs, NJ: Prentice Hall.

Kahneman, D., and Treisman, A. 1984. Changing views of attention and automaticity. In R. Parasuraman, D. R. Davies, and J. Beatty, eds., *Variants of attention,* 29–61. New York: Academic Press.

Kaku, M. 2004. *Parallel worlds.* New York: Doubleday.

Kanwisher, N. G. 2004. MRI investigations of human extrastriate cortex: People, places, and things. Paper presented at Brain and Mind, Columbia 250th anniversary symposium, New York, May.

Kasser, T., and Kanner, A. D. 2003. *Psychology and consumer culture: The struggle for a good life in a materialistic society.* Washington, DC: American Psychological Society.

Kavanaugh, G. 1995. The nature of therapeutic action. In M. Lionels, D. B. Stern, C. Mann, and J. Fiscalini, eds. *Handbook of interpersonal psychoanalysis.* Hillsdale, NJ: Analytic Press.

Kazdin, A. E. 1976. Effects of covert modeling, multiple models, and model reinforcement on assertive behavior. *Behavior Therapy* 7, 211–222.

Kennedy, J. L. 1938. The visual cues from the backs of the ESP cards. *Journal of Psychology: Interdisciplinary and Applied* 6, 149–153.

Kent. E. 1981. *The brains of men and machines.* Peterborough, NH: BYTE.

Kernberg, O. F. 1976. Technical considerations in the treatment of borderline personality organization. *Journal of the American Psychoanalytic Association* 24, 795–829.

Kernberg, O. F. 1982. Self, ego, affects, and drives. *Journal of the American Psychoanalytic Association* 30, 893–917.

Kernberg, O. F., Koeningsberg, A. C., Carr, A. C., and Appelbaum, A. H. 1989. *Psychodynamic psychotherapy of borderline patients.* New York: Basic Books.

Kihlstrom, J. F. 1987. The cognitive unconscious. *Science* 237, 1,445–1,452.

Kihlstrom, J. F. 1990. The psychological unconscious. In L. A. Pervin, ed., *Handbook of personality theory and research,* 445–464. New York: Guilford Press.

Kihlstrom, J. F. and Hoyt, I. 1990. Repression, dissociation, and hypnosis. In J. L. Singer, ed., *Repression and dissociation: Implications for personality theory, psychopathology, and health,* 181–208. Chicago: University of Chicago Press.

Kihlstrom, J. F., Barnhardt, T. M., and Tataryn, D. J. 1992. Implicit perception. In R. Bornstein, and T. Pittman, eds., *Perception without awareness: Cognitive, clinical, and social perspectives,* 17–54. New York: Guilford Press.

Kihlstrom, J. F., Mulvaney, S., Tobias, B. A., and Tobis, I. P. 2000. The emotional unconscious. In E. Eich, J. F. Kihlstrom, G. H. Bower, J. P. Forags, and P. M. Niedenthal, eds., *Cognition and emotion*, 30–86. New York: Oxford University Press.

Kindt, M., and Brosschot, J. F. 1998. Cognitive inhibition in phobia. *British Journal of Clinical Psychology* 37, 103–106.

Klein, G. S. 1967. Peremptory ideation: Structure and force in motivated ideas. In R. R. Holt, ed., Motives and thought: Psychoanalytic essays in honor of David Rapaport, 80–128. *Psychological Issues* 5 Monograph No. 18/19. New York: International Universities Press.

Klein, G. S. 1976. *Psychoanalytic theory: An exploration of essentials.* New York: International Universities Press.

Klein, M. 1964. *Contributions to psychoanalysis* 1921–1945. New York: McGraw-Hill.

Klein, M. 1975. *Envy and gratitude and other works.* New York: Delacorte Press.

Knekt, P., and Lindfors, O. 2004. A randomized trial of the effect of four forms of psychotherapy on depressive and anxiety disorders. Design, methods, and results on the effectiveness of short-term psychodynamic psychotherapy and solution-focused therapy during a one-year follow-up. Helsinki: The Social Security Institution, Finland, *Studies in Social Security and Health* 77.

Knoblauch, S. H. 2000. *The musical edge of therapeutic dialogue.* Hillsdale, NJ: Analytic Press, Inc. 2000.

Kohut, H. 1971. *The analysis of the self.* New York: International Universities Press.

Kohut, H. 1977. *The restoration of the self.* New York: International Universities Press.

Kohut, H. 1984. Introspection, empathy, and semicircle of mental health. *Emotions and Behavior Monographs* 3, 345–375.

Kolb, B., and Whishaw, I. Q. 2001. *An introduction to brain and behavior.* New York: Worth Publishers.

Koltko-Rivera, M. E. 2004. The psychology of worldviews. *Review of General Psychology* 8, 3–58.

Korzybski, A. 1948. *Science and sanity: An introduction to non-Aristotelian systems and general semantics*, 3rd ed. Oxford: The International Non-Aristotelian.

Kosbab, F. P. 1974. Imagery techniques in psychiatry. *Archives of General Psychiatry* 31, 283–290.

Koutstaal, W., and Schacter, D. 1997. Intentional forgetting and voluntary thought suppression: Two potential methods for coping with childhood trauma. In L. Dickstein, and M. Riba et al., eds., *American Psychiatric Press Review of Psychiatry*, vol. 16, 79–121. Washington, DC: American Psychiatric Association.

Krohne, H. W., and Hindel, C. 1988. Trait anxiety, state anxiety, and coping behavior as predictors of athletic performance. *Anxiety Research* 1, 225–234.

Krohne, H. W. 1993. Vigilance and cognitive avoidance as concepts in coping research. In H. W. Krohne, ed., *Attention and avoidance. Strategies in coping with aversiveness*, 19–50. Seattle: Hogrefe and Huber.

Krugman, P. 2002. The end of middle-class America. *The New York Times Magazine*, October 20, 63–67.

Kubie, L. S. 1934. Relation of the conditioned reflex to psychoanalytic technique. *Archives of Neurology and Psychiatry* 32, 1,137–1,142.

Kubler-Ross, E. 1969. *On death and dying.* New York: Macmillan.

Kulas, J. F., Conger, J. C., and Smolin, J. M. 2003. The effect of emotion on memory: An investigation of attentional bias. *Journal of Anxiety Disorders* 17, 103–113.

Kvarnes, R., and Parloff, G. 1976. *A Harry Stack Sullivan case seminar.* New York: W. W. Norton.

Kwee, M. G. T., Duivenvoorden, H. J., Trijsburg, R. W., and Thiel, J. H. 1986. Multimodal therapy in an inpatient setting. *Current Psychological Research and Reviews* 5, 344–357.

Kwee, M. G. T., and Kwee-Taams, M. K. 1994. *Klinishegedragstherapie in Nederland and vlaanderen.* Delft, Holland, Netherlands: Eubron.

LaBar, K. S., and Phelps, E. A. 1998. Arousal-mediated memory consolidation: Role of the medial temporal lobe in humans. *Psychological Science* 9, 490–493.

Lacan, J. 1978. Four fundamental concepts of psycho-analysis, ed. J. Miller, trans. A. Sheridan. 1964. Reprint, New York: W.W. Norton.

Lacan, J. 1988. *The seminar, Book II: The ego in Freud's theory and in the technique of psychoanalysis* 1954–1955, ed. J. Miller, trans. S. Tomaselli. New York. W.W. Norton.

Lachman, R., Lachman, J. L., and Butterfield, E. C. 1979. *Cognitive psychology and information processing: An introduction.* Mahway, NJ: Lawrence Erlbaum Associates.

Lambert, M. J., Shapiro, D. A., and Bergin, A. E. 1986. The effectiveness of psychotherapy. In S. L. Garfield, and A. E. Bergin, eds., *Handbook of psychotherapy and behavior change*, 3rd ed., 157–211. New York: Wiley.

Lambert, M. J., and Barley, D. E. 2002. Research summary on the therapeutic relationship and psychotherapy outcome. In J. C. Norcross, ed., *Psychotherapy relationships that work,* 17–32. Oxford: Oxford University Press.

Lane, R. D., and Nadel, L., eds. 2000. *Cognitive neuroscience of emotion.* London: Oxford University Press.

Lane, R. D., Nadel, L., Allen, J. J. B., and Kaszniak, A. W. 2000. The study of emotion from the perspective of cognitive neuroscience. In R. D. Lane, L. Nadel, G. Ahern, J. J. B. Allen, A. W. Kaszniak, S. Rapcsak, and G. E. Schwartz, eds., *Cognitive neuroscience of emotion,* 3–11. New York: Oxford University Press.

Lang, P. J. 1984. *Cognition in emotion: Concept and action.* In C. Izard, J. Kagan, and R. Zajonc, eds., *Emotions, cognition and behavior*, 192–228. New York: Cambridge University Press.

Lang, P. J. 1985. The cognitive psychophysiology of emotion: Fear and anxiety. In A. H. Tuma, and J. D. Maser, eds., *Anxiety and the anxiety disorders,* 131–170. Hillsdale, NJ: Lawrence Erlbaum Associates.

Lang, P. J. 1993. The network model of emotion: Motivational connections. In R. Wyer, and T. Srull, eds., *Perspectives on anger and emotion. Advances in social cognition*, vol. 6, 109–133. England: Lawrence Erlbaum Associates.

Lang, P. J., Bradley, M. M., and Cuthbert, B. N. 1997. Motivated attention: Affect, activation, and action. In P. Lang, R. F. Simons, and M. Balaban, eds., *Attention and orienting: Sensory and motivational processes*, 97–136. Hillsdale, NJ: Lawrence Erlbaum Associates.

Larsen, R. J., Chan, P. Y., and Lambert, A. 2004. Perceptual consequences of threat and prejudice: Misperceiving weapons and other dangerous objects. Unpublished manuscript, Washington University.

Larsen, R. J., and Yarkoni, T. 2004. Negative stimuli cause more interference than positive stimuli in the affective Simon task. Unpublished manuscript, Washington University.

Latane, B., and Darley, J. M. 1968. Group inhibition of bystander intervention in emergencies. *Journal of Personality and Social Psychology* 10, 215–221.

Lavie, N. 1995. Perceptual load as a necessary condition for selective attention. *Journal of Experimental Psychology: Human Perception and Performance* 21, 451–468.

Lazarus, A. A. 1967. In support of technical eclecticism. *Psychological Reports,* 21, 415–416.

Lazarus, A. A. 1981. *The practice of multimodal therapy.* New York: McGraw-Hill.

Lazarus, A. A. 1992. Multimodal therapy: Technical eclecticism with minimal integration. In M. R. Goldfried, and J. C. Norcross, eds., *Handbook of psychotherapy integration,* 231–263. New York: Basic Books.

Lazarus, A. A. 2005. Mutimodal therapy. In M. R. Goldfried, and J. C. Norcross, eds., *Handbook of psychotherapy integration,* 2nd ed., 105–120. New York: Oxford University Press.

Lazarus, R. S. 1991. *Emotion and adaptation.* London: Oxford University Press.

Lazarus, R. S., and Alfert, E. 1964. Short-circuiting of threat by experimentally altering cognitive appraisal. *Journal of Abnormal and Social Psychology* 69, 195–205.

Lazarus, R. S., and Folkman, S. 1984. *Stress, appraisal, and coping.* New York: Springer.

Leahy, R. 2002. A model of emotional schemas. *Cognitive and Behavioral Practice* 9, 177–190.

Leahey, T. H., and Harris, R. J. 2001. *Learning and cognition,* 5th ed. Upper Saddle River, NJ: Prentice Hall.

Leaton, R. N., and Borszcz, G. S. 1985. Potentiated startle: Its relation to freezing and shock intensity in rats. *Journal of Experimental Psychology: Animal Behavior Processes* 11, 421–428.

LeDoux, J. E. 1990. Information flow from sensation to emotion: Plasticity in the neural computation of stimulus values. In M. Gabriel and J. Moore, eds., *Learning and computational neuroscience: Foundations of adaptive networks.* Cambridge, MA: MIT Press.

LeDoux, J. E. 1993a. Emotional memory systems in the brain. *Behavioural Brain Research* 58, 69–79.

LeDoux, J. E. 1993b. Emotional networks in the brain. In M. Lewis, ed., *Handbook of emotions,* 109–118. New York, NY: Guilford Press.

LeDoux, J. E. 1993c. Emotional memory: In search of systems and synapses. In F. M. Crinella, and J. Yu, eds., *Brain mechanisms: Papers in memory of Robert Thompson,* 149–157. New York: New York Academy of Sciences.

LeDoux, J. E. 1994a. Cognitive–emotional interactions in the brain. In P. Ekman, and R. Davidson, eds., *The nature of emotion*, 216–223. Oxford: Oxford University Press.

LeDoux, J. E. 1994b. The degree of emotional control depends on the kind of personal system involved. In P. Ekman, and R. Davidson, eds., *The nature of emotion*, 270–272. Oxford: Oxford University Press.

LeDoux, J. E. 1995. Setting "stress" into motion: Brain mechanisms of stimulus evaluation. In M. J. Friedman, D. S. Charney, and A. Y. Deutch, eds., *Neurobiological and clinical consequences of stress: From normal adaptation to post-traumatic stress disorder*, 125–134. Philadelphia: Lippincott Williams and Wilkins.

LeDoux, J. E. 1996. *The emotional brain: The mysterious underpinnings of emotional life*. New York: Simon and Schuster.

LeDoux, J. E. 1999. Cognition and emotion: Listen to the brain. In R. Lane, ed., *Emotion and Cognitive Neuroscience*, 129–155. Oxford University Press: New York.

LeDoux, J. E. 2002. *Synaptic self: How our brains become who we are*. New York: Viking Penguin Books.

Lerner, M. J. 1980. *The belief in a just world: A fundamental delusion*. New York: Plenum.

Leuner, H. 1975. The role of imagery in psychotherapy. In S. Arieti, and G. Chrzanowski, eds., *New dimensions in psychiatry: A world view*. New York: John Wiley and Sons.

Leuzinger-Bohleber, M., and Pfeifer, R. 2002. Remembering a depressive primary object. *International Journal of Psycho-Analysis* 83, 3–33.

Levenson, E. A. 1972. *The fallacy of understanding: An inquiry into the changing structure of psychoanalysis*. New York: Basic Books.

Levenson, E. A. 2003. On seeing what is said: Visual aids to the psychoanalytic process. *Contemporary Psychoanalysis* 39, 233–249.

Levenson, R. W. 1994. I. Human emotion: A functional view. II. The search for autonomic specificity. III. Emotional control: Variation and consequences. In P. Ekman, and R. Davidson, eds., *The nature of emotion: Fundamental questions*, 123–126. New York: Oxford University Press.

Leventhal, H., and Scherer, K. R. 1987. The relationship of emotion and cognition: A functional approach to a semantic controversy. *Cognition and Emotion, 1,* 3–28.

Levin, F. M. 1991. *Mapping the mind: The intersection of psychoanalysis and neuroscience*. Hillsdale, NJ: Analytic Press.

Levine, W. B. 1997. The capacity for countertransference. *Psychoanalytic Inquiry* 17, 44–68.

Levitt, J. T., Hoffman, E. C., Grisham, J. R., and Barlow, D. H. 2001. Empirically supported treatments for panic disorder. *Psychiatric Annals* 31, 478–487.

Levy, B. J., and Anderson, M. C. 2002. Inhibitory processes and the control of memory retrieval. *Trends in Cognitive Science, 6,* 299–305.

Lewicki, P. 1986. *Nonconscious social information processing*. San Diego, CA: Academic Press.

Lewicki, P., Czyzewska, M., and Hoffman, H. 1987. Unconscious acquisition of complex procedural knowledge. *Journal of Experimental Psychology: Learning, Memory, and Cognition* 13, 523–530.

Lewin, R. 1992. *Complexity: Life at the edge of chaos*. New York: MacMillan.

Lewis, J. J. 2007. Isadora Duncan quotes. www.WomensHistory.about.com. Retrieved Jan. 30, 2007.

Lewis, M. and Ferrari, M. 2001. Cognitive–emotional self-organization in personality development and personal identity. In E. S. Kunnen, and H. A. Bosma, eds., *Identity and emotion: Development through self-organization*, 177–201. New York: Cambridge University Press.

Lewis, M., and Haviland-Jones, J. M., eds. 1993. *Handbook of emotions*. New York: Guilford Press.

Lewis, M., and Haviland-Jones, J. M., eds. 2000. *Handbook of emotions*, 2nd. ed. New York: Guilford Press.

Libet, B., Gleason, C. A., Wright, E. W., and Pearl, D. K. 1983. Time of conscious intention to act in relation to onset of cerebral activity readiness-potential. The unconscious initiation of a freely voluntary act. *Brain* 106, 623–642.

Lichtenberg, J. D. 1989. *Psychoanalysis and motivation*. Hillsdale, NJ: Analytic Press.

Lichtenberg, J. D., Lachmann, F. M., and Fosshage, J. M. 1992. *Self and motivational systems: Toward a theory of psychoanalytic technique*. Hillsdale, NJ: Analytic Press.

Lichtenberg, J. D., Lachmann, F. M., and Fosshage, J. L. 2002. *A spirit of inquiry: Communication in psychoanalysis*. Hillsdale, NJ: Analytic Press.

Lieberman, J. S. 2000. Panel report: The search for meaning in the affective expressions of the adolescent patient. *International Journal of Psycho–Analysis* 81, 324–327.

Linehan, M. 1988. Perspectives on the interpersonal relationship in behavior therapy. *Journal of Integrative and Eclectic Psychotherapy* 7, 278–290.

Linehan, M. 1993. *Cognitive–behavioral treatment of borderline personality disorder*. New York: Guilford Press.

Linehan, M., and Heard, H. L. 1992. Dialectical behavior therapy for borderline personality disorder. In E. Marziali, and J. F. Clarkin, eds., *Borderline personality disorder: Clinical and empirical perspectives*, 248–267. New York: Guilford Press.

Linehan, M., and Koerner, K. 2002. Dialectical behavior therapy for borderline personality disorder. In M. C. Tompson, and S. G. Hofmann, eds., *Treating chronic and severe mental disorders: A handbook of empirically supported interventions*, 317–342. New York: Guilford Press.

Lionells, M., J. Fiscalini, C. Mann, and D. Stern, eds., *Handbook of interpersonal psychoanalysis*. Hillsdale, NJ: Analytic Press.

Lipp, O. V., and Edwards, M. S. 2002. Effect of instructed extinction on verbal and autonomic indices of Pavlovian learning with fear–relevant and fear–irrelevant conditional stimuli. *Journal of Psychophysiology* 16, 176–186.

Llewelyn, S. P., Elliot, R., Shapiro, D. A., Hardy, G., et al. 1988. Client perceptions of significant events in prescriptive and exploratory periods of individual therapy. *British Journal of Clinical Psychology* 27, 105–114.

Locke, E. A., and Latham, G. P. 1994. Goal setting theory. In H. F. O'Neil. Jr., and M. Drillings, eds., *Motivation: Theory and research*, 13–29. Hillsdale, NJ: Lawrence Erlbaum Associates.

Loewald, H. W. 1960. On the therapeutic action of psycho-analysis. *International Journal of Psychoanalysis* 41, 16–33.

Loewald, H. W. 1970. Psychoanalytic theory and psychoanalytic process. *Psychoanalytic Study of the Child* 25, 45–68.

Loewald, H. W. 1980. *Papers on psychoanalysis.* New Haven: Yale University Press.

Loewald, H. W. 1988. Termination analyzable and unanalyzable. *Psychoanalytic Study of the Child* 43, 155–166.

Loftus, E. F., Loftus, G. R., and Messo, J. 1987. Some facts about "weapon focus." *Law and Human Behavior* 11, 55–62.

London, P. 1964. *The modes and morals of psychotherapy.* New York: Holt, Rinehart and Winston.

Lowen, A. 1971. *The language of the body.* New York: Collier.

Luborsky, L. 1984. *Principles of psychoanalytic psychology: A manual for supportive-expressive treatment.* New York: Basic Books.

Luborsky, L. 1998. A guide to the CCRT method. In L. P. Luborsky and P. Crits-Christoph, eds., *Understanding transference: The core conflictual relationship theme method,* 2nd ed., 15–42. Washington, DC: American Psychological Association.

Luborsky, L., and Crits-Christoph, P. 1990. *Understanding transference: The core conflictual relationship theme method.* New York: Basic Books.

Luck, S. J., and Hillyard, S. A. 2000. The operation of selective attention at multiple stages of processing: Evidence from human and monkey electrophysiology. In M. S. Gazzaniga, ed., *The new cognitive neurosciences,* 2nd ed., 687–700. Cambridge, MA: MIT Press.

Lyddon, W. J., and Jones, J. V., eds. 2001. *Empirically supported cognitive therapies: Current and future applications.* New York: Springer Publishing.

Lyons-Ruth, K. 1998. Implicit relational knowing: Its role in development and psychoanalytic treatment. *Infant Mental Health Journal* 19, 282–289.

MacKay, D. G., Shafto, M., Taylor, J. K., Marian, D., Abrams, L., and Dyer, J. R. 2004. Relations between emotion, memory, and attention: Evidence from taboo Stroop, lexical decision, and immediate memory tasks. *Memory and Cognition* 32, 474–488.

MacLean, P. D. 1973. *A triune concept of the brain and behaviour: Hincks memorial lecture.* Toronto: University of Toronto Press.

MacLeod, C. M. 1975. Long-term recognition and recall following directed forgetting. *Journal of Experimental Psychology: Human Learning and Memory* 1, 271–279.

MacLeod, C. M. 1989. Directed forgetting affects both direct and indirect tests of memory. *Journal of Experimental Psychology: Learning, Memory, and Cognition* 15, 13–21.

MacLeod, C. M., and Mathews, A. 1988. Anxiety and the allocation of attention to threat. *Quarterly Journal of Experimental Psychology. A Human Experimental Psychology* 40, 653–670.

Magai, C. 1999. Affect, imagery, and attachment: Working models of interpersonal affect and the socialization of emotion. In J. Cassidy and P. Shaver, eds., *Handbook of attachment: Theory, research, and clinical applications,* 787–802. New York: Guilford Press.

Mahoney, M. J. 1991. *Human change processes: The scientific foundations of psychotherapy.* New York: Basic Books.

Malan, D. H. 1976. *The frontier of brief psychotherapy.* New York: Plenum Press.

Mandler, G. 1985. From association to structure. *Journal of Experimental Psychology: Learning, Memory, and Cognition* 11, 464–468.

Maner, J. K., Becker, D. V., Kenrick, D. T., Becker, D. V., Robertson, T. E., Hofer, B., Neuberg, S. L., Delton, A. W., Butner, J., and Schaller, M. 2005. Functional projection: How fundamental social motives can bias interpersonal perception. *Journal of Personality and Social Psychology 88, 63–78.*

Mann, C. 1995. The goals of interpersonal psychoanalysis. In M. Lionells, J. Fiscalini, C. Mann, and D. Stern, eds., *Handbook of interpersonal psychoanalysis,* 555–568. Hillsdale, NJ: Analytic Press.

Mann, J. 1992. *Time-limited psychotherapy: A psychodynamic approach.* Cambridge, MA: Harvard University Press.

Marcel, A. 1983. Conscious and unconscious perception: An approach to the relations between phenomenal experience and perceptual processes. *Cognitive Psychology* 15, 238–300.

Marks, I. M., and Gelder, M. G. 1966. Common ground between behavior therapy and psychodynamic methods. *British Journal of Medical Psychology* 39, 11–23.

Markus, H., and Wurf, E. 1987. The dynamic self-concept: A social psychological perspective. In M. R. Rosenzweig, and L. W. Porter, eds., *Annual review of psychology,* vol. 38, 299–337. Palo Alto, CA: Annual Reviews.

Marmor, J. 1964. Psychoanalytic therapy and theories of learning. In J. Masserman, ed., *Science and psychoanalysis,* vol. 7, 265–279. New York: Grune and Stratton.

Martin, J. P. 1997. Mindfulness: A proposed common factor. *Journal of Psychotherapy Integration* 7, 291–312.

Marziali, E. A. 1984. Prediction of outcome of brief psychotherapy from therapist interpretive interventions. *Archives of General Psychiatry* 41, 301–304.

Marziali, E. A., and Sullivan, J. M. 1980. Methodological issues in the content analysis of brief psychotherapy. *British Journal of Medical Psychology* 53, 19–27.

Maslow, A. H. 1962. *Toward a psychology of being.* Princeton, NJ: Van Nostrand.

Maslow, A. H. 1970. *Motivation and personality,* 2nd ed. New York: Harper and Row.

Mason, W. 2006. Alone in the dark: The philosopher Colin McGinn examines why movies have power over us. *New York Times Book Review,* Jan. 22, 2006, 6.

Mathews, A., and Klug, F. 1993. Emotionality and interference with color-naming in anxiety. *Behaviour Research and Therapy* 31, 57–62.

Mathews, A., and MacLeod, C. M. 1994. Cognitive approaches to emotion and emotional disorders. *Annual Review of Psychology* 45, 25–50.

Matthews, R., and Matthews, A. M. 1986. Infertility and involuntary childlessness: The transition to nonparenthood. *The Journal of Marriage and the Family* 48, 641–649.

Matte-Blanco, I. 1988. *Thinking, feeling and being: Clinical reflections on the fundamental antinomy of human beings and world.* Florence, KY: Taylor and Frances/Routledge.

Mayer, J. D., Salovey, P., and Caruso, D. R. 2002. MSCEIT User's Manual. North Tonawanda, NY: Multi-Health Systems.

Mayne, T., and Bonanno, G., eds. 2001. *Emotions: Currrent issues and future directions*. New York: Guilford Press.

Mayne, T., and Ramsey, J. 2001. The structure of emotions: A nonlinear dynamic systems approach. In T. Mayne, and G. Bonanno, eds., *Emotions: Currrent issues and future directions. Emotions and social behavior*, 1–37. New York: Guilford Press.

McClelland, D. C., Atkinson, J. W., Clark R. A., and Lowell, E. L. 1953. *The achievement motive*. New York: Appleton-Century-Crofts.

McClelland, D. C., Koestner, R., and Weinberger, J. 1989. How do self-attributed and implicit motives differ? *Psychological Review* 96, 690–702.

McCracken, G. 1986. Culture and consumption: A theoretical account of the structure and movement of the cultural meaning of consumer goods. *Journal of Consumer Research* 13, 71–84.

McCullough, J. P., Jr. 2000. *Treatment for chronic depression: Cognitive behavioral analysis system of psychotherapy*. New York: Guilford Press.

McCullough, L., Kuhn, N., Andrews, S., Kaplan, A., Wolf, J., and Hurley, C. L. 2003. *Treating affect phobia: A manual for short-term dynamic psychotherapy*. New York: Guilford Press.

McCullough, L. and Andrews, S. 2001. Assimilative integration: Short-term dynamic psychotherapy for treating affect phobias. *Clinical Psychology Science and Practice* 8, 82–97.

McCullough, L., Winston, A., Farber, B. A., Porter, F., et al. 1991. The relationship of patient-therapist interaction to outcome in brief psychotherapy. *Psychotherapy: Theory, Research, Practice, Training* 28, 525–533.

McCullough-Vaillant, L. 1996. *Changing character: Short-term anxiety-regulating psychotherapy for restructuring defenses, affects, and attachment*. New York: Basic Books.

McDougall, J. 1989. *Theaters of the body: A psychoanalytic approach to psychosomatic illness*. New York: W. W. Norton.

McGinn, C. 2005. *The power of movies: How screen and mind interact*. New York: Pantheon.

McGinnies, E. 1949. Emotionality and perceptual defense. *Psychological Review* 56, 244–251.

McKenna, F. P., and Sharma, D. 2004. Reversing the emotional Stroop effect: The role of fast and slow components. *Journal of Experimental Psychology: Learning Memory and Cognition* 30, 382–392.

McLuhan, M., and Fiore, Q. 1967. *Medium is the massage*. New York: Random House.

McNally, R. J., Richard, J., Riemann, B. C., and Kim, E. 1990. Selective processing of threat cues in panic disorder. *Behaviour Research and Therapy* 28, 407–412.

McNally, R. J. 2003. Human evolutionary psychology. *American Journal of Psychiatry*, 160, 1,368–1,369.

Meissner, W. W. 1991. *What is effective in psychoanalytic therapy: The move from interpretation to relation*. Northvale, NJ: Jason Aronson.

Meissner, W. W. 2000. The self-as-person in psychoanalysis. *Psychoanalysis and Contemporary Thought* 23, 479–523.

Meloy, J. R. 1986. On the relationship between primary process and thought disorder. *Journal of the American Academy of Psychoanalysis and Dynamic Psychiatry* 14, 47–56.

Menaker, E. 1991. Questioning the sacred cow of the transference. In R. C. Curtis, and G. Stricker, eds., *How people change: Inside and outside therapy,* 13–20. New York: Plenum Press.

Mendes, E. R. P., and Drummond, S. B. 2002. Contemporary adolescence and the crisis of ideals. *International Forum of Psychoanalysis* 11, 125–134.

Mennin, D. S. 2006. Emotion regulation therapy: An integrative approach to treatment-resistant anxiety disorders. *Journal of Contemporary Psychotherapy* 36, 95–105.

Merikle, P. M. 1982. Unconscious perception revisited. *Perception and Psychophysics* 31, 298–301.

Messer, S. 1983. Integrating psychoanalytic and behaviour therapy: Limitations, possibilities and trade-offs. *British Journal of Clinical Psychology* 22, 131–132.

Migone, P., and Liotti, G. 1998. Psychoanalysis and cognitive-evolutionary psychology: An attempt at integration. *International Journal of Psycho-Analysis* 79, 1,071–1,095.

Mikail, S. F., Henderson, P. R., Tasca, G. A. 1994. An interpersonally based model of chronic pain: An application of attachment theory. *Clinical Psychology Review* 14, 1–16.

Mikulas, W. L. 1978. Four noble truths of Buddhism related to behavior therapy. *Psychological Record* 28, 59–67.

Miller, G. A., Galanter, E., and Pribram, K. H. 1960. *Plans and the structure of behavior.* New York: Holt, Rinehart, and Winston.

Millon, T. 1996. *Major theories of personality disorder.* New York: Guilford Press.

Milton, J. 2001. Psychoanalysis and cognitive behaviour therapy—Rival paradigms or . . . *International Journal of Psycho-Analysis* 82, 431–447.

Mischel, W., Ebbesen, E. B., and Zeiss, A. R. 1973. Selective attention to the self: Situational and dispositional determinants. *Journal of Personality and Social Psychology* 27, 129–142.

Mitchell, S. A. 1988. *Relational concepts in psychoanalysis.* New York: Basic Books.

Mitchell, S. A. 1997. *Influence and autonomy in psychoanalysis.* Hillsdale, NJ: Analytic Press.

Mitchell, S. A., and Aron, L. 1999. *Relational psychoanalysis: The emergence of a tradition.* Hillsdale, NJ: Analytic Press.

Modell, A. H. 2003. *Imagination and the meaningful brain.* Cambridge, MA: MIT Press.

Mogg, K., Mathews, A., and Eysenck, M. 1992. Attentional bias to threat in clinical anxiety states. *Cognition and Emotion* 6, 149–159.

Moore, S., and Oaksford, M., eds. 2002. *Emotional cognition: From brain to behaviour.* Amsterdam: John Benjamins Publishing Company.

Moray, N. 1959. Attention in dichotic listening: Affective cues and the influence of instructions. *Quarterly Journal of Experimental Psychology* 11, 56–60.

Morgan, A. 1998. Moving along to things left undone. *Infant Mental Health Journal* 19, 324–332.

Morishige, H., and Reyher, J. 1975. Alpha rhythm during three conditions of visual imagery and emergent uncovering psychotherapy: The critical role of anxiety. *Journal of Abnormal Psychology* 84, 531–538.

Morokoff, P. J. 1985. Effects of sex guilt, repression, sexual "arousability," and sexual experience on female sexual arousal during erotica and fantasy. *Journal of Personality and Social Psychology* 49, 177–187.

Morris, J. S., Ohman, A., and Dolan, R. J. 1998. Conscious and unconscious emotional learning in the human amygdala. *Nature* 393, 467–470.

Muran, J. C., and Safran, J. D. 2002. Brief relational psychotherapy. In J. J. Magnavita, ed., *The comprehensive handbook of psychotherapy. Psychodynamic/object relations approaches*, vol. 1, 253–281. New York: John Wiley.

Myers, L. B., Brewin, C. R., and Power, M. J. 1998. Repressive coping and the directed forgetting of emotional material. *Journal of Abnormal Psychology* 107, 141–148.

Myers, P. N., and Biocca, F. A. 1992. The elastic body image. *Journal of Communication* 42, 108–133.

Nathanson, D. L. 2001. Parents versus peers: Exploring the significance of peer mediation of antisocial television. *Communication Research* 28, 251–274.

Natsoulas, F. 2000. Freud and consciousness: X. The place of consciousness in Freud's science. *Psychoanalysis and Contemporary Thought* 23, 525–561.

Neisser, U. 1967. *Cognitive psychology*. New York: Appleton-Century-Crofts.

Newirth, J. 2003. *Between emotion and cognition: The generative unconscious*. New York: Other Press.

Newman, L. S., Duff, K. J. and Baumeister, R. F. 1997. A new look at defensive projection: Thought suppression, accessibility, and biased person perception. *Journal of Personality and Social Psychology* 72, 980–1001.

Newton, N. 2000. Conscious emotion in a dynamic system: How can I know how I feel? In N. Newton, and R. Ellis, eds., *The caldron of consciousness: Motivation, affect and self-organization—An anthologogy*, 91–105. Amsterdam: John Benjamins Publishing Company.

New York Times. God (or not), physics and of course, love: Scientists take a leap. January 4, 2005, F3.

Nisbett, R. E., and Ross, L. 1980. *Human inference: Strategies and shortcomings of social judgment*. Englewood Cliffs, NJ: Prentice Hall.

Nisbett, R. E., and Wilson, T. 1977. Telling more than we can know: Verbal reports on mental processes. *Psychological Review* 84, 231–259.

Norcross, J. C., ed. 2002. *Psychotherapy relationships that work: Therapist contributions and responsiveness to patients*. New York: Oxford University Press.

Noy, P. 1969. A revision of the psychoanalytic theory of the primary process. *International Journal of Psycho-Analysis* 50, 155–178.

Oatley, K., and Johnson-Laird, P. 1987. Towards a cognitive theory of emotions. *Cognition and Emotion* 1, 29–50.

Ochse, R. 1989. A new look at primary process thinking and its relation to inspiration. *New Ideas in Psychology* 7, 315–330.

Ochsner, K. N., and Lieberman, M. D. 2001. The emergence of social cognitive neuroscience. *American Psychologist* 56, 717–734.

Ogrodniczuk, J. S., and Piper, W. E. 1999. Use of transference interpretations in dynamically oriented individual psychotherapy for patients with personality disorders. *Journal of Personality Disorders* 13, 297–311.

Ogrodniczuk, J. S., Piper, W. E., Joyce, A. S., and McCallum, M. 1999. Transference interpretations in short-term dynamic psychotherapy. *Journal of Nervous and Mental Disease* 187, 571–578.

Ohman, A. 1979. The orienting response, attention, and learning: an information processing perspective. In H. D. Kimmel, E. H. van Olst, and J. F. Orlebeke, eds., *The orienting reflex in humans,* 443–472. Hillsdale, NJ: Lawrence Erlbaum Associates.

Ohman, A. 1992. Orienting and attention: Preferred preattentive processing of potentially phobic stimuli. In B. A. Campbell, R. Richardson, and H. Haynes, eds., *Attention and information processing in infants and adults: Perspectives from human and animal research,* 263–295. Hillsdale, NJ: Lawrence Erlbaum Associates.

Ohman, A. 1993. Fear and anxiety as emotional phenomena: Clinical phenomenology, evolutionary perspectives, and information processing mechanisms. In M. Lewis, and J. M. Haviland, eds., *Handbook of emotions,* 511–536. New York: Guilford Press.

Ohman, A. 1997. As fast as the blink of an eye: Preattentive processing and evolutionary facilitation of attention. In P. J. Lang, M. Balaban, and R. F. Simons, eds., *Attention and motivation: Cognitive perspectives from psychophysiology, reflexology, and neuroscience,* 165–184. Hillsdale, NJ: Erlbaum.

Ohman, A., Flykt, A., and Esteves, F. 2001. Emotion drives attention: Detecting the snake in the grass. *Journal of Experimental Psychology: General,* 130, 466–478.

Ohman, A., Flykt, A. and Lundqvist, D. 2000. Unconscious emotion: Evolutionary perspectives, psychophysiological data and neuropsychological mechanisms. In L. Nadel, and R. D. Lang, eds., *Cognitive neuroscience of emotion,* 296–327. London: Oxford University Press.

Ohman, A., and Soares, J. J. F. 1994. "Unconscious anxiety": Phobic responses to masked stimuli. *Journal of Abnormal Psychology* 103, 231–240.

Olson, J. M., and Zanna, M. P. 1979. A new look at selective exposure. *Journal of Experimental Social Psychology* 15, 1–15.

Orlinsky, D.E., and Howard, K.J. 1986. Process and outcome of psychotherapy. In S.L. Garfield, and A.E. Bergin, eds., *Handbook of psychotherapy and behavior change,* 311–381. New York: Wiley.

Ostow, M., and Bates, G. C. 2000. Affect regulation. *International Journal of Psychoanalysis* 81, 317–318.

Packard, V. O. 1957. *The hidden persuaders.* New York: D. McKay Co.

Paetzold, H. 1996. The status of the image. In J. Thompson, ed., *Towards a theory of the image,* 94–107. Maasticht: Jan Van Eyck Akademe.

Paivio, A. 1971. *Imagery and verbal processes.* Oxford: Holt, Rinehart and Winston.

Paivio, A. 1986. *Mental representations: A dual coding approach.* Oxford: Oxford University Press.

Paller, K. A. 1990. Recall and stem-completion priming have different electrophysiological correlates and are modified differentially by directed forgetting. *Journal of Experimental Psychology: Learning, Memory, and Cognition* 16, 1,021–1,032.

Pally, R. 1998. Emotional processing: The mind-body connection. *International Journal of Psycho-Analysis* 79, 349–362.

Pally, R., and Olds, D. 1998. Consciousness: a neuroscience perspective. *International Journal of Psycho-analysis* 79, 971–989.

Palumbo, R. and Gillman, I. 1984. Effects of subliminal activation of oedipal fantasies on competitive performance: A replication and extension. *Journal of Nervous and Mental Disease* 172, 737–741.

Panksepp, J. 1994. Six short essays on various emotion topics. In R. Davidson and P. Ekman, eds., *Questions about Emotions,* 86–88. New York: Oxford University Press.

Panksepp, J. 1996. Modern approaches to understanding fear: From laboratory to clinical practice. *Advances in Biological Psychiatry* 2, 209–230.

Panksepp, J. 1998. *Affective neuroscience, the foundations of human and animal emotions.* New York: Oxford University Press.

Panksepp, J. 2000a. On preventing another century of misunderstanding: Toward a psychoethology of human experience and a psychoneurology of affect. *Neuro-psychoanalysis* 2, 240–255.

Panksepp, J. 2000b. The neuro-evolutionary cusp between emotions and cognitions: Implications for understanding consciousness and the emergence of a unified mind science. *Consciousness and Emotion* 1, 15–54.

Parkes, C. M., and Weiss, R. S. 1995. *Recovery from bereavement.* New York: Basic Books.

Parsons, D. A., Fulgenzi, L. B., and Edelberg, R. 1969. Aggressiveness and psychophysiological responsivity in groups of repressors and sensitizers. *Journal of Personality and Social Psychology* 12, 235–244.

Paulhus, D. L., and Levitt, K. 1987. Desirable responding triggered by affect: Automatic egotism? *Journal of Personality and Social Psychology* 52, 245–259.

Payne, B. K. 2001. Prejudice and perception: The role of automatic and controlled processes in misperceiving a weapon. *Journal of Personality and Social Psychology* 81, 181–192.

Payne, B. K., Lambert, A. J., and Jacoby, L. L. 2002. Best laid plans: Effects of goals on accessibility bias and cognitive control in race-based misperceptions of weapons. *Journal of Experimental Social Psychology* 38, 384–396.

Perls, F. 1976. *The Gestalt approach and eye witness to therapy.* New York: Bantam.

Perse, E. 2001. *Media effects and society.* Hillsdale, NJ: Lawrence Erlbaum Associates.

Person, E. S. 1993. Introduction. In E. S. Person, A. Hagelin, and P. Fongay, eds., *On Freud's observations on transference-love,* 1–14. New Haven, CT: Yale University Press.

Phelps, E. A. 2005. The interaction of emotion and cognition: The relation between the human amygdala and cognitive awareness. In R. R. Hassin, J. S. Uleman, and

J. A. Bargh, eds., *The new unconscious*, 61–76. New York: Oxford University Press.

Phillips, D. P. 1974. The influence of suggestion on suicide: Substantive and theoretical implications of the Werther effect. *American Sociological Review* 39, 340–354

Phillips, D. P. 1979. Suicide, motor vehicle fatalities, and the mass media: Evidence toward a theory of suggestion. *American Journal of Sociology* 84, 1150–1174.

Piaget, J. and Inhelder, B. 1971. *Mental imagery in the child; a study of the development of imaginal representation* P. A. Chilton, trans. New York: Basic Books.

Pierce, C. S., and Jastrow, J. 1884. On small differences in sensation. *Memoirs of the National Academy of Science* 3, 75–83.

Piers, C. 2000. Character as self-organizing complexity. *Psychoanalysis and Contemporary Thought* 23, 3–34.

Piper, W. E., Azim, H. F., Joyce, A. S., and McCallum, M. 1991. Transference interpretations, therapeutic alliance, and outcome in short-term individual psychotherapy. *Archives of General Psychiatry* 48, 946–953.

Piper, W. E., Debbane, E. G., Bienvenu, J. P., and Garant, J. 1986. Relationships between the object focus of therapist interpretations and outcome in short-term, individual psychotherapy. *British Journal of Medical Psychology* 59, 1–11.

Piper, W. E., McCallum, M., Azim, H. F., and Joyce, A. S. 1993. Understanding the relationship between transference interpretation and outcome in the context of other variables. *American Journal of Psychotherapy* 47, 479–493.

Plato. 1996. *Protagoras, Philebus and Gorgias (Great Books in Philosophy).* Amherst, NY: Prometheus.

Plutchik, R. 1962. *The emotions: Facts, theories and a new model.* New York: Random House.

Plutchik, R. 1980. A general psychoevolutionary theory of emotion. In R. Plutchik and H. Kellerman, eds., *Emotion: Theory, research, and experience: Theories of emotion,* vol. 1, 3–33. New York: Academic Press.

Pollak, S. D., and Tolley-Schell, S. A. 2003. Selective attention to facial emotion in physically abused children. *Journal of Abnormal Psychology* 112, 323–338.

Pollock, P. H. 2001. *Cognitive analytic therapy for adult survivors of childhood abuse.* Chichester, England: Wiley.

Popper, K. R. 1983. *Realism and the aim of science.* Totowa, NJ: Rowman and Littlefield.

Popper, K. R., and Eccles, J. C. 1977. *Self and its brain.* New York: Springer-Verlag.

Posner, M. I. 2004. *Cognitive neuroscience of attention.* New York: Guilford Press.

Posner, M. I., and Snyder, C. R. 1975. Facilitation and inhibition in the processing of signals. In P. M. Rabbitt, and S. Dornic, eds., *Attention and performance,* vol. 5, 669–682. New York: Academic Press.

Postman, N. 1985. *Amusing ourselves to death: public discourse in the age of show business.* New York: Penguin Books.

Postman, N. 1992. *Technopoly: the surrender of culture to technology.* New York: Basic Books.

Power, M. 1999. Two routes to emotion: Some implications of multi-level theories of emotion for therapeutic practice. *Behavioural and Cognitive Psychotherapy* 27, 129–141.

Power, M., and Dalgleish, T. 1997. *Cognition and emotion: From order to disorder.* East Sussex, UK: Psychology Press Publishers.

Powers, W. T. 1973. *Behavior: The control of perception.* Chicago: Aldine.

Prigogine, I. and Strengers, J. 1984. O*rder out of chaos: Man's new dialogue with nature.* New York: Bantam.

Prince, M. 1906. *The dissociation of a personality.* Oxford: Longmans, Green and Co.

Prince, M. 1910. The mechanism and interpretation of dreams—A reply to Dr. Jones. *Journal of Abnormal Psychology* 5, 337–353.

Prince, M. 1914. *The unconscious.* New York: Macmillan.

Prince, R. M. 1999. *The death of psychoanalysis: Murder? Suicide? Or rumor greatly exaggerated?* Northvale, NJ: Jason Aronson.

Prinz, J. 2004. *Gut reactions: A perceptual theory of emotion.* New York: Oxford University Press.

Prochaska, J. O. and DiClemente, C. C. 1982. Transtheoretical therapy: Toward a more integrative model of change. *Psychotherapy: Theory, Research and Practice* 19, 276–288.

Pulver, S. E. 1992. Psychic change: Insight or relationship? *International Journal of Psychoanalysis* 73, 199–208.

Pumpian-Mindlin, E. 1953. Considerations in the selection of patients for short-term therapy. *American Journal of Psychotherapy* 7, 641–653.

Putnam, F. W. 1996. Posttraumatic stress disorder in children and adolescents. *American Psychiatric Press Review of Psychiatry* 15, 447–467.

Putnam, J. J. 1906. Recent experiments in the study and treatment of hysteria at the Massachusetts General Hospital with remarks on Freud's method of treatment by "psycho-analysis." *Journal of Abnormal Psychology* 1, 26–41.

Racker, H. 1968. *Transference and countertransference.* Madison: International Universities Press.

Ramachandran, B. S. 1996. Illusions of body image: what they reveal about human nautre. In R. Llinás, and P. S. Churchland, eds., *The mind-brain continuum: Sensory processes,* 29–60. Cambridge, MA: MIT Press.

Ramachandran, V. S. 2005. Mirror neurons and imitation learning as the driving force behind human evolution. Retrieved from www.edge.org/3rd_culture/ramachandran/ramachandran_p1.html

Rand, N. 2004. The hidden soul: The growth of the unconscious in philosophy, psychology, medicine, and literature 1950–1900. *American Imago* 61, 257–289.

Rank, O. 1931. *The analysis of the analyst and its role in the general situation. The technique of psychoanalysis: III.* Oxford: Deuticke.

Rank, O. 1961. *Psychology and the soul.* New York: Perpetua Books.

Rank, O. 1968a. *Art and artist: Creative urge and personality development.* New York: Agathon Press.

Rank, O. 1968b. Le traumatisme de la naissance Payot, Paris 1e éd. 1924.

Rapaport, D. 1953. On the psycho-analytic theory of affects. *International Journal of Psycho-Analysis* 34, 177–198.

Rassuli, K. and Hollander, S. 1986. Desire—Induced, innate, insatiable? *Journal of Macromarketing* 6, 4–24.

Rauch, S., van der Kolk, B., Fisler, R., Alper, N., Scott, O., Savage, C., Fischman, A., Jenike, M. T., and Pitman, R. 1996. A symptom provocation study of posttraumatic stress disorder using positron emission tomography and script-driven imagery. *Archives of General Psychiatry* 53, 380–387.

Rawls, J. 1971. *A theory of justice*. Cambridge, MA: Harvard University Press.

Raymond, J. E., Fenske, M. J., and Tavassoli, N. T. 2003. Selective attention determines emotional responses to novel visual stimuli. *Psychological Science* 14, 537–542.

Raymond, J.E., Shapiro, K. L., and Arnell, K.M. 1992. Temporary suppression of visual processing in an RSVP task: An attentional blink? *Journal of Experimental Psychology: Human Perception and Performance* 18, 849–860.

Redington, D. J., and Reidbord, S. P. 1992. Chaotic dynamics in autonomic nervous system activity of a patient during a psychotherapy session. *Biological Psychiatry* 31, 993–1,007.

Reich, W. 1949. *Character-analysis*, 3rd ed. Oxford: Orgone Institute Press.

Reidbord, S. P. 1993. Nonlinear analysis of autonomic responses in a therapist during psychotherapy. *Journal of Nervous and Mental Disease* 181, 428–435.

Reidbord, S. P. 1995. The dynamics of mind and body during clinical interviews: Research trends, potential, and future directions. In R. F. Port, and T. van Gelder, eds., *Mind as motion: Explorations in the dynamics of cognition*, 527–547. Cambridge, MA: MIT Press.

Reidbord, S. P., and Redington, D. J. 1992. Psychophysiological processes during insight-oriented therapy: Further investigation into nonlinear psychodynamics. *Journal of Nervous and Mental Disease* 180, 649–657.

Reinecke, M. A., and Freeman, A. 2003. Cognitive therapy. In A. S. Gurman, and S. B. Messer, eds., *Essential psychotherapies: Theory and practice*, 2nd ed., 224–271. New York: Guilford Press.

Reiner, A. 1990. An explanation of behavior. *Science* 250, 303–305.

Reyher, J. 1963. Free imagery: An uncovering procedure. *Journal of Clinical Psychology* 19, 454–459.

Reyher, J. 1978. Emergent uncovering psychotherapy: The use of imagoic and linguistic vehicles in objectifying psychodynamic processes. In J. L. Singer, and K. S. Pope, eds., *The power of human imagination: New methods in psychotherapy*, 51–93. New York: Plenum Press.

Rhoads, J. 1988. Combinations and synthesis of psychotherapies. *Psychiatric Annals* 18, 280–287.

Richardson, A. 1969. *Mental imagery*. London: Routledge and Kegan Paul.

Richins, M. L. 1991. Social comparison and the idealized images of advertising. *Journal of Consumer Research* 18, 71–83.

Richins, M. L. 1995. Social comparison, advertising, and consumer discontent. *American Behavioral Scientist* 38, 593–607.

Richins, M. L. 1996. Materialism, desire, and discontent: Contributions of idealized advertising images and social comparison. In R. P. Hill, ed., *Marketing and consumer research in the public interest,* 109–132. Thousand Oaks, CA: Sage Publications.

Rieman, B. C., and McNally, R. J. 1995. Cognitive processing of personally relevant information. *Cognition and Emotion* 9, 325–340.

Rogers, C. R. 1942. *Counseling and psychotherapy: Newer concepts in practice.* Oxford, England: Houghton Mifflin.

Rogers, C. R. 1951. *Client-centered therapy: Its current practice, implications, and theory.* Boston: Houghton Mifflin.

Rogers, C. R. 1961. *On becoming a person: A therapist's view of psychotherapy.* Boston: Houghton Mifflin.

Rogers, C. R. 1963. Psychotherapy today or where do we go from here? *American Journal of Psychotherapy,* 17, 5–15.

Rogers, T. B. 1981. A model of the self as an aspect of the human information processing system. In N. Cantor and J. F. Kihlstrom, eds., *Personality, cognition, and social interaction,* 193–214. Hillsdale, NJ: Lawrence Erlbaum Associates.

Rosenblatt, A. 2004. Insight, working through, and practice: The role of procedural knowledge. *Journal of the American Psychoanalytic Association* 52, 189–207.

Rosenzweig, S. 1936. Some implicit common factors in diverse methods in psychotherapy. *Amercian Journal of Orthopsychiatry* 6, 412–415.

Rothenberg, A. 1996. The Janusian process in scientific creativity. *Creativity Research Journal* 9, 207–231.

Routh, D. K. 2000. Clinical psychology training: A history of ideas and practices prior to 1946. *American Psychologist* 55, 236–241.

Rowe, D. C. 1994. *The limits of family influence: Genes, experience, and behavior.* New York: Guilford Press.

Rubinstein, D. H. 1983. Epidemic suicide among Micronesian adolescents. *Social Science and Medicine* 17, 657–665.

Rubinstein, D. H. 1995. Love and suffering: Adolescent socialization and suicide in Micronesia. *The Contemporary Pacific* 7, 21–53.

Ruiz-Caballero, J. A., and Bermudez, J. 1997. Anxiety and attention: Is there an attentional bias for positive emotional stimuli? *Journal of General Psychology* 124, 194–210.

Runciman, W. G. 1966. *Relative deprivation and social justice: A study of attitudes to social inequality in twentieth century England.* Berkeley: University of California Press.

Russ, S. W. 2002. Gender differences in primary process thinking and creativity. In J. Masling, and R. Bornstein, eds., *The psychodynamics of gender and gender role,* 53–80. Washington, DC: American Psychological Association.

Rutherford, E. M., MacLeod, C., and Campbell, L. W. 2004. Negative selectivity effects and emotional selectivity effects in anxiety: Differential attentional correlates of state and trait variables. *Cognition and emotion* 18, 711–720.

Ryle, A. 1990. *Cognitive–analytic therapy: Active participation in change. A new integration in brief psychotherapy.* Chichester, England: John Wiley and Sons.

Ryle, A. and Low, J. 1993. Cognitive analytic therapy. In G. Stricker, and J. R. Gold, eds., *Comprehensive handbook of psychotherapy integration*, 87–100. New York: Plenum Press.

Ryle, G. 1949. *The concept of mind*. London: Hutchinson.

Safran, J. D. 1991. Affective change processes: A synthesis and critical analysis. In J. D. Safran, and L. S. Greenberg, eds., *Emotion, psychotherapy and change*, 339–362. New York: Guilford Press.

Safran, J.D., ed. 2003. *Psychoanalysis and Buddhism: An unfolding dialogue*. Boston: Wisdom Publications.

Safran, J. D., and Greenberg, L.S. 1991. Emotion in human functioning: Theory and therapeutic implications. In J. D. Safran, and L. S. Greenberg, eds., *Emotion, psychotherapy and change*, 3–15. New York: Guilford Press.

Safran, J. D., and Muran, J. C. 2001. The therapeutic alliance as a process of intersubjective negotiation. In J.C. Muran, ed., *Self-relations in the psychotherapy process*, 165–192. Washington, DC: American Psychological Association.

Safran, J. D., and Segal, Z.V. 1990. Interpersonal process in cognitive therapy. New York: Basic Books.

Salovey, P., and Mayer, J.D. 1989–1990. Emotional intelligence. *Imagination, cognition, and personality* 9, 185–211.

Salovey, P., and Rodin, J. 1984. Some antecedents and consequences of social-comparison jealousy. *Journal of Personality and Social Psychology* 47, 780–792.

Salter, A. 1952. *The case against psychoanalysis*. New York: Henry Holt.

Sandell, R., Blomberg, J., Lazar, A., Carlsson, J., Broberg, J., and Schubert, J. 2000. Varieties of long-term outcome among patients in psychoanalysis and long-term psychotherapy: A review of findings in the Stockholm Outcome of Psychoanalysis and Psychotherapy Project STOPP. *International Journal of Psychoanalysis* 8, 921–942.

Sander, L. 1998. Interventions that effect change in psychotherapy: A model based on infant research. *Infant Mental Health Journal* 19, 280–281.

Sanderson, W. C., and Rego, S. A. 2002. Empirically supported treatment for panic disorder: Research, theory, and application of cognitive behavioral therapy. In R. L. Leahy, and T. E. Dowd, eds., *Clinical advances in cognitive psychotherapy: Theory and application of cognitive behavioral therapy*, 211–239. New York: Springer Publishing.

Sandler, J. 1985. Towards a reconsideration of the psychoanalytic theory of motivation. *Bulletin of the Anna Freud Centre* 8, 223–244.

Sass, L. A. 1988. The self and its vicissitudes: An archaeological study of the psychoanalytic avant-garde. *Social Research* 55, 551–607.

Scaturo, D. J. 1994. Integrative psychotherapy for panic disorder and agoraphobia in clinical practice. *Journal of Integrative Psychotherapy* 4, 253–272.

Schacter, D. 1987. Implicit expressions of memory in organic amnesia: Learning of new facts and associations. *Human Neurobiology* 6, 107–118.

Schacter, J. 2002. *Transference: Shibboleth or albatross?* Hillsdale, NJ: Analytic Press.

Schachter, S., and Singer, J. E. 1962. Cognitive, social and physiological determinants of emotional states. *Psychological Review* 69, 379–399.

Schafer, R. 1967. Ideals, the ego ideal, and the ideal self. In R. R. Holt, ed., *Motives and thought: Psychoanalytic essays in honor of David Rapaport*, 131–174. New York: International Universities Press.

Schafer, R. 1976. *A new language for psycho-analysis*. New Haven, CT: Yale University Press.

Schafer, R. 1992. *Retelling a life: Narration and dialogue in psychoanalysis*. New York: Basic Books.

Scherer, K. 2000. Emotions as episodes of subsystems synchronization driven by nonlinear appraisal processes. In M. Lewis, and I. Granic, eds., *Emotion, development, and self-organization: Dynamic systems approaches to emotional development. Cambridge studies in social and emotional development*, 70–99. New York: Cambridge University Press.

Schneider, W., and Shiffrin, R. 1977. Controlled and automatic human information processing: I. Detection, search, and attention. *Psychological Review 84,* 1–66.

Schooler, J. W. 2002. Verbalization produces a transfer inappropriate processing shift. *Applied Cognitive Psychology 16,* 989–997.

Schor, J. B. 1998. *The overspent American*. New York: Basic Books.

Schore, A. N. 1994. *Affect regulation and the origin of the self: The neurobiology of emotional development*. Hillsdale, NJ: Lawrence Erlbaum Associates.

Schorr, J. E. 1971. *Psycho-Imagination therapy*. New York: Intercontinental Medical.

Schottenbauer, M. A., Glass, C. R., and Arnkoff, D. B. 2005. Outcome research on psychotherapy integration. In J. C. Norcross, and M. R. Goldfried, eds., *Handbook of psychotherapy integration*, 2nd ed., 459–493. New York: Oxford University Press.

Schupp, H. T., Cuthbert, B. N., Bradley, M. M., Hillman, C. H., Hamm, A. O., and Lang, P. J. 2004. Brain processes in emotional perception: Motivated attention. *Cognition and Emotion 18,* 593–611.

Scott, W. D. 1908. An interpretation of the psycho-analytic method in psychotherapy with a report of a case so treated. *Journal of Abnormal Psychology 3,* 371–379.

Seligman, M. E. 1975. *Helplessness: On depression, development, and death*. San Francisco: Freeman.

Seligman, M. E. and Johnston, J. C. 1973. A cognitive theory of avoidance learning. In D.B. Lumsden, and F.J. McGuigan, eds., *Contemporary approaches to conditioning and learning,* 69–110. Oxford: V. H. Winston and Sons.

Sennett, R. 2003. *Respect in a world of inequality*. New York: Norton.

Sennett, R., and Cobb, J. 1972. *The hidden injuries of class*. New York: Vintage Books.

Shakespeare, W. 2004. *King Lear*. 1608. Reprint, New York: Washington Square Press.

Shakow, D., and Rapaport, D. 1964. *The influence of Freud on American psychology*. New York: International Universities Press.

Shapiro, A. K. and Morris, L. A. 1978. The placebo effect in medical and psychological therapies. In S. L. Bergin, and A. E. Garfield, eds., *Handbook of psychotherapy and behavior change*, 369–410. New York: Wiley.

Shapiro, D. 1976. The analyst's own analysis. *Journal of the American Psychoanalytic Association* 24, 5–42.

Shapiro, D. 1987. Implications of psychotherapy research for the study of meditation. In M. A. West, ed., *The psychology of meditation*, 173–188. New York: Clarendon Press/Oxford University Press.

Shapiro, F. 2001. *Eye movement desensitization and reprocessing: Basic principles, protocols, and procedures*, 2nd ed. New York: Guilford Press.

Shapiro, T. and Emde, R. N.,, eds. 1992. *Affect: Psychoanalytic perspectives*. Madison, CT: International Universities Press.

Shiffrin, R., and Schneider, W. 1977. Controlled and automatic human information processing: II. Perceptual learning, automatic attending and a general theory. *Psychological Review* 84, 127–190.

Shevrin, H. 1992. The Freudian unconscious and the cognitive unconscious: Identical or fraternal twins? In J. W. Barron, M. N. Eagle, and D. L. Wolitzky, eds., *Interface of psychoanalysis and psychology*, 313–326. Washington, DC: American Psychological Association.

Shevrin, H. 1995a. Is psychoanalysis one science, two sciences, or no science at all? A discourse among friendly antagonists. *Journal of the American Psychoanalytic Association* 43, 963–986.

Shevrin, H. 1995b. Is psychoanalysis one science, two sciences, or no science at all? A discourse among friendly anatagonists: Commentary reply. *Journal of the American Psychoanalytic Association* 43, 1,035–1,049.

Shevrin, H. 2000. The experimental investigation of unconscious conflict, unconscious affect, and unconscious signal anxiety. In M. Velmans, ed., *Investigating phenomenal consciousness: New methodologies and maps. Advances in consciousness research*, vol. 13, 33–65. Amsterdam, Netherlands: John Benjamins Publishing Company.

Shevrin, H., Bond, J. A., Brakel, L. A., Hertel, R. K., and Williams, W. J. 1996. *Conscious and unconscious processes: Psychodynamic, cognitive, and neurophysiological convergences*. New York: Guilford Press.

Shevrin, H., and Dickman, S. 1980. The psychological unconscious: A necessary assumption for all psychological theory? *American Psychologist* 35,421–434.

Shrum, L. J., O'Guinn, T. C., Semenik, R. J., and Faber, R. J. 1991. Processes and effects in the construction of normative consumer beliefs: The role of television. In R. H. Holman, and M. R. Solomon, eds., *Advances in consumer research*, vol. 18, 755–763. Provo, UT: Association for Consumer Research.

Sidis, B. 1902. Mental dissociation in depressive delusional states. In B. Sidis, W. A. White, and G. M. Parker, eds., *Psychopathological researches: Studies in mental dissociation*, 159–219. London: Stechert.

Sifneos, P. E. 1987. Short-term dynamic psychotherapy, 2nd ed. New York: Plenum.

Silver, R. L., Boon, C., and Stones, M. H. 1983. Searching for a meaning in misfortune: Making sense of incest. *Journal of Social Issues* 39, 81–102.

Silverman, L. H. 1983. The subliminal psychodynamic method. Overview and comprehensive listing of studies. In J. Masling, ed., *Empirical studies of psychoanalytic theory*, vol. 1, 69–103. Hillsdale, NJ: Erlbaum.

Simon, H.A. 1967. Motivational and emotional controls of cognition. *Psychological Review,* 74, 29–39.

Singer, J. L. 1974. *Imagery and daydreaming methods in psychotherapy and behavior modification.* New York: Academic Press.

Singer, J. L. 1978. The constructive potential of imagery and fantasy processes: Implications for child development, psychotherapy, and personal growth. In E. G. Witenberg, ed. *Interpersonal psychoanalysis: New directions,* 105–150. New York: Gardner Press.

Singer, J. L. 1988. Psychoanalytic theory in the context of contemporary psychology: The Helen Block Lewis memorial Address. *Psychoanalytic Psychology* 5, 95–125.

Singer, J. L. 1990. *Repression and dissociation: Implications for personality theory, psychopathology, and health.* Chicago: University of Chicago Press.

Singer, J. L. 2006. *Imagery in psychotherapy.* Washington, DC: American Psychological Association.

Skinner, B. F. 1953. *Science and human behavior.* New York: Macmillan.

Sladeczek, J., and Domino, J. 1985. Creativity, sleep, and primary process thinking in dreams. *Journal of Creative Behaviour* 19, 38–47.

Slipp, S. 1982. *Curative factors in dynamic psychotherapy.* Northvale, NJ: Jason Aronson.

Sloane, R. B. Staples, F. R., Cristol, A. H., Yorkstan, N. J., and Whipple, K. 1975. *Psychotherapy vs. behavior therapy.* Cambridge, MA: Harvard University Press.

Slochower, J. A. 1996. *Holding and psychoanalysis: A relational perspective.* Hillsdale, NJ: Analytic Press.

Sloman, S. A. 1996. The empirical case for two systems of reasoning. *Psychological Bulletin* 119, 3–22.

Smith, D. 2002. The theory heard 'round the world. *Monitor on Psychology* 33, 30–32.

Smith, E. R. 1998. Mental representation and memory. In D. Gilbert, S. Fiske, and G. Lindzey, eds., *Handbook of social psychology,* 4th ed., vol. 1, 391–445. New York: McGraw-Hill.

Smith, E. W. L. 1985. *The body in psychotherapy.* New York: McFarland and Company.

Smith, R. H., Diener, E., and Garonzik, R. 1990. The roles of outcome satisfaction and comparison alternatives in envy. *British Journal of Social Psychology* 29, 247–255

Smolensky, P. 1988. On the proper treatment of connectionism. *Behavioral and Brain Sciences* 11, 1–74.

Snyder, C. 2004. Hope and depression: A light in the darkness. *Journal of Social and Clinical Psychology* 23, 47–351.

Solms, M. 1997. What Is Consciousness? *Journal of the American Psychoanalytic Association* 45, 681–703.

Solms, M. 2000. A psychoanalytic perspective on confabulation. *Neuro-psychoanalysis* 2, 133–138.

Sorrentino, R. M., and Roney, C. J. 2000. *The uncertain mind: Individual differences in facing the unknown.* Philadelphia: Psychology Press.

Spence, D. P. 1992. Interpretation: A critical perspective. In J. W. Barron, M. N. Eagle, and D. L. Wolitzky, eds., *Interface of psychoanalysis and psychology*, 558–572. Washington, DC: American Psychological Association.

Spence, D. P. 1993. Beneath the analytic surface: The analysand's theory of mind. *International Journal of Psycho-Analysis* 74, 729–738.

Spence, D. P., Dahl, H., and Jones, E. E. 1993. Impact of interpretation on associative freedom. *Journal of Consulting and Clinical Psychology* 61, 395–402.

Sperry, R. W. 1964. The great cerebral commissure. *Scientific American* 210, 42–52.

Spezzano, C. 1993. *Affect in psychoanalysis: A clinical synthesis.* Hillsdale, NJ: Analytic Press.

Spiller, R. E., Thorp, W., Johnson, T. H., Canby, H. S., and Ludwig, R. M. 1963. *Literary history of the United States,* 3rd ed., New York: Macmillan.

Spiro, M. E. 1992. The "primary process" revisited. In R. M. Boyer, and L. B. Boyer, eds., *The psychoanalytic study of society, vol.* 17, *Essays in honor of George D. and Louise A. Spindler*, 171–180. Hillsdale, NJ: Analytic Press.

Spitz, R. A. 1945. Hospitalism: An inquiry into the genesis of psychiatry conditions in early childhood: *Psychoanalytic Study of the Child,* 1, 53–74.

Squire, L. R. 1987. *Memory and brain.* Oxford: Oxford University Press.

Squire, L. R., and Kandel, E. R. 1999. *Memory: From mind to molecules.* New York: W. H. Freeman Scientific American Library.

Squire, L. R., and Zola-Morgan, S. 1991. The medial temporal lobe memory system. *Science* 253, 1,380–1,386.

Sroufe, L. 1996. *Emotional development: The organization of emotional life in the early years.* New York: Cambridge University Press.

Staats, A. W. 1983a. Need for a new philosophy: A call for the revolution to unity. Symposium paper, World Congress on Behavior Therapy, Washington, DC.

Staats, A. W. 1983b. Psychology's disunity: Anachronistic crisis before the revolution to unity. Symposium paper, American Psychological Association Convention, Anaheim, California.

Staats, A. W. 1991. Unified positivism and unification psychology: Fad or new field? *American Psychologist* 46, 899–912.

Stamenov, M., and V. Gallese, eds. 2002. *Mirror neurons and the evolution of brain and language.* Philadelphia: John Benjamins Publishing Company.

Stark, M. 1999. *Modes of therapeutic action: Enhancement of knowledge, provision of experience, and engagement in relationship.* Northvale, NJ: Jason Aronson.

Stark, R., and Bainbridge, W. S. 1985. *The future of religion: Secularization, revival, and cult formation.* Berkeley: University of California Press.

Stein, N., and Trabasso, T. 1992. The organization of emotional experience: Creating links among thinking, language, and intentional action. *Cognition and Emotion,* 6, 225–244.

Stephan, W. G., and Stephan, C. 1985. Intergroup anxiety. *Journal of Social Issues* 41, 157–176.

Sterba, R. 1934. The fate of the ego in analytic therapy. *The International Journal of Psycho-Analysis* 15, 117–126.

Stern, D. B. 1997. *Unformulated experience: From dissociation to imagination in psychoanalysis*. Hillsdale, NJ: Analytic Press.

Stern, D. N. 1983. The role and structure of mother/infant play. *Psychiatrie de l'Enfant*, 26, 193–216.

Stern, D. N. 1998. The process of therapeutic change involving implicit knowledge: Some implications of developmental observations for adult psychotherapy. *Infant Mental Health Journal* 19, 300–308.

Stern, D. N. 1985. *The interpersonal world of the infant: A view from psychoanalysis and developmental psychology*. New York: Basic.

Stern, D. N. 2004. *The present moment in psychotherapy and everyday life*. New York: W.W. Norton and Company.

Stern, D. N. Sander, L., Nahum, J., Harrison, A., Lyons-Ruth, K., Morgan, A., Bruschweiler-Stern, N., and Tronick, E. 1998. Non-interpretive mechanisms in psychoanalytic therapy: the 'something more' than interpretations. *International Journal of Psycho-analysis* 79, 903–921.

Stern, S. 2002. The self as a relational structure: A dialogue with multiple self theory. *Psychoanalytic Dialogues* 12, 693–714.

Sternberg, R. J., and Grigorenko, E. L. 2001. Unified psychology. *American Psychologist* 56, 1,069–1,079.

Stigler, M., and Pokorny, D. 2001. Emotions and primary process in guided imagery psychotherapy: Computerized text-analytic measures. *Psychotherapy Research* 11, 415–431.

Stiles, W. B., Barkham, M., Shapiro, D.A., and Firth-Cozens, J. 1992. Treatment order and thematic continuity between contrasting psychotherapies: Exploring an implication of the assimilation model. *Psychotherapy Research*, 2, 112–124.

Stiles, W. B., Elliott, R., Llewelyn, S. P., Firth-Cozens, J. A., Margison, F. R., Shapiro, D. A., and Hardy, G. 1990. Assimilation of problematic experiences by clients in psychotherapy. *Psychotherapy*, 27, 411–420.

Stolorow, R. 1994. Kohut, Gill, and the new psychoanalytic paradigm. In A. Goldberg, ed., *A decade of progress: Progress in self psychology,* vol. 10, 221–226. Hillsdale, NJ: Analytic Press.

Stolorow, R. D., and Atwood, G. E. 1992. *Contexts of being: The Intersubjective foundations of psychological life*. Hillsdale, NJ: Analytic Press.

Stone, L. 1954. The widening scope of indications for psychoanalysis. *Journal of the American Psychoanalytic Association* 2, 567–594.

Stone, L. 1967. The psychoanalytic situation and transference: Post-script to an earlier communication. *Journal of the American Psychoanalytic Association* 15, 3–58.

Storrs, A. 1988. *Solitude: A Return to the Self*. New York: New York Free Press.

Stouffer, S. A., Lumsdaine, A. A., Lumsdaine, M. H., Williams, R. M., Smith, M. B., Janis, I. L., Star, S. A., and Cottrell, L. S. 1949. *The American soldier: combat and its aftermath. Studies in social psychology in World War II,* vol. 2. Princeton, NJ: Princeton University Press.

Strachey, J. 1934. The nature of the therapeutic action of psychoanalysis. *International Journal of Psycho-analysis* 15, 127–159.

Strasberg, L. 1991. Strasberg at the Actors Studio: Tape-recorded sessions. R. Nethman, ed. New York: Theater Communication Group.

Strenger, C. 1991. *Between Hermeneutics and Science*. Madison: International Universities Press.

Stricker, G., and Gold, J. 1988. A psychodynamic approach to personality disorders. *Journal of Personality Disorders* 2, 350–359.

Stricker, G., and Gold, J. 1993. *Comprehensive handbook of psychotherapy integration*. New York: Plenum.

Strupp, H. 1976. Some critical comments on the future of psychoanalytic therapy. *Bulletin of the Menninger Clinic* 40, 238–254.

Strupp, H., and Binder, J. 1984. *Psychotherapy in a new key*. New York: Basic Books.

Sullivan, H. S. 1940. *Conceptions of modern psychiatry*, New York: Norton.

Sullivan, H. S. 1948. The meaning of anxiety in psychiatry and life. *Psychiatry: Journal for the Study of Interpersonal Processes* 11, 1–13.

Sullivan, H. S. 1953. *The interpersonal theory of psychiatry*. New York: Norton.

Sullivan, H. S. 1956. Selective inattention. In H. S. Perry, M. L. Gawel, and M. Gibbon, eds., *Clinical studies in psychiatry*, 38–76. New York: Norton.

Summers, F. 2003. It's more than interpreting an interpretation: Response to Stolorow 2002. *Psychoanalytic Psychology* 20, 393–394.

Suttie, I. D. 1935. *The origins of love and hate*. Oxford: Kegan Paul.

Suzuki, D., Fromm, E., and De Martino, R. 1963. *Zen Buddhism and psychoanalysis*. Oxford: Grove.

Swann, W. B. 1987. Identity negotiation: Where two roads meet. *Journal of Personality and Social Psychology* 53, 1,038–1,051.

Szalita, A. B. 1994. The dilemma of therapeutic changes in psychotherapy: Psychointegration. *Israel Journal of Psychiatry and Related Sciences* 32, 106–114.

Taylor, C. 1985. What is human agency? *In Human Agency and Language, Philosophical Papers*, vol. 1, 15–44. Cambridge: Cambridge University Press.

Taylor, S. E. 1983. Adjustment to threatening events: A theory of cognitive adaptation. *American Psychologist* 38, 1,161–1,173.

Taylor, S. E. 1989. *Positive illusions: Creative self-deception and the healthy mind*. New York: Basic Books.

Taylor, S. E., Lichtman, R. R., and Wood, J. V. 1984. Attributions, beliefs about control, and adjustment to breast cancer. *Journal of Personality and Social Psychology*, 46, 489–502.

Teasdale, J. D. 1997. The transformation of meaning: The interacting cognitive subsystems approach. In M. J. Power, C. R. Brewin, eds., *The transformation of meaning in psychological therapies: Integrating theory and practice*, 141–156. New York: John Wiley and Sons.

Teasdale, J. D., and Barnard, P. J. 1993. *Affect, cognition and change: Re-modelling depressive thought*. Hove: Lawrence Erlbaum Associates.

Thomä, H., and Kächele, H. 1988. *Psychoanalytic practice*. Berlin: Springer-Verlag.

Thomä, H., and Kächele, H. 1994. *Psychoanalytic practice: Vol 2—Clinical studies*. Northvale, NJ: Jason Aronson.

Thompson, C. 1950. *Psychoanalysis: evolution and development*. Oxford: Hermitagehouse.

Thompson, C. 1953. Transference and character analysis. *Samiksa* 7, 260–270.

Thompson, R. A. 1994. Emotion regulation:A theme in search for definition. *Monographs of the Society for Research in Child Development* 59, 25–52.

Tice, D., Bratslavsky, E., and Baumeister, R. 2001. Emotional distress regulation takes precedence over impulse control: If you feel bad, do it! *Journal of Personality and Social Psychology* 80, 53–67.

Tillich, P. 1952. *The Courage to be.* New Haven: Yale University Press.

Tomkins, S. 1962. *Affect, imagery, consciousness,* vol. 1, vol. 2. New York: Springer.

Tomkins, S. 1980. Affect as amplification: Some modifications in theory. In R. Plutchik and H. Kellerman, eds., *Emotion: Theory, research, and experience. Vol. 1: Theories of emotion,* 141–164. New York: Academic Press.

Triesman, A. 1960. Contextual cues in selective listening. *Quarterly Journal of Experimental Psychology* 12, 242–8.

Tronick, E. Z. 1998. Non-interpretive mechanisms in psychoanalytic therapy: The "something more" than interpretation. *International Journal of Psychoanalysis* 79, 903–921.

Turner, J. H. 2004. *Theory and research on human emotions advances in group processes.* Connecticut: JAI Press.

Tuttman, S. 1982. The impact of the analyst's personality on treatment. *Issues in Ego Psychology* 5, 25–31.

Tversky, A., and Kahneman, D. 1973a. *Judgment under uncertainty: Heuristics and biases,* vol. 13. Oxford, England: Oregon Research Institute.

Tversky, A., and Kahneman, D. 1973b. Availability: A heuristic for judging frequency and probability. *Cognitive Psychology* 5, 207–232

Vaillant, G. 2004. Adult maturation: Keystone of mental health. Paper presented at the William Alanson White Institute Convention, New York, October.

Valenstein, A. 1983. Working through and resistance to change: Insight and the action system. *Journal of the American Psychoanalytic Association* 31 (Suppl.), 353–373.

Van Alphen, E. 1992. *Francis Bacon and the loss of self.* London: Reaktion Books.

Vandell, D. L. 2000. Parents, peer groups, and other socializing influences. *Developmental Psychology* 36, 699–710.

van der Kolk, B. A. 1987. *Psychological trauma.* Washington, DC: American Psychiatric Press.

van der Kolk, B. A. 1994. The body keeps the score. *Harvard Review of Psychiatry* 1, 253–265.

van der Kolk, B. A. 1999. The body keeps the score: Memory and the evolving psychobiology of posttraumatic stress. In M. J. Horowitz, ed., *Essential papers on posttraumatic stress disorder: Essential papers in psychoanalysis,* 301–326. New York: New York University Press.

van der Kolk, B. A., McFarlane, A. C., and Weisaeth, L., eds., 1996. *Traumatic stress.* New York: Guilford Press.

Veblen, T. 1931. *Theory of the leisure class: an economic study of institutions,* New York: Viking Press, 1931.

Velmanns M., 1991. Is human information processing conscious? *Behavioral and Brain Sciences* 14, 651–726.

Volkan, V. D. 1982. *Linking objects and linking phenomena*. Madison, CT: International Universties Press.

Volkan, V. D. 2001. Transgenerational transmissions and chosen traumas: an aspect of large-group identity. *Group Analysis* 34, 561–569.

Vygotsky, L. S. 1978. *Mind in society: The development of higher psychological processes*. Cambridge, MA: Harvard University Press.

Wachtel, P. L. 1967. Conceptions of broad and narrow attention. *Psychological Bulletin* 68, 417–429.

Wachtel, P. L. 1975. Behavior therapy and the facilitation of psychoanalytic exploration. *Psychotherapy: Theory, Research, and Practice* 12, 68–72.

Wachtel, P. L. 1977. *Psychoanalysis and behavior therapy: Toward an integration.* New York: Basic Books.

Wachtel, P. L. 1983. *The poverty of affluence.* New York: The Free Press.

Wachtel, P. L. 1984. On theory, practice, and the nature of integration. In H. Arkowitz, and S. B. Messer, eds., *Psychoanalytic therapy and behavior therapy: Is integration possible?* 31–52. New York: Plenum.

Wachtel, P. L. 1992. On theory, practice, and the nature of integration. In R. B. Miller, ed., *The restoration of dialogue: Readings in the philosophy of clinical psychology,* 418–432. Washington, DC: American Psychological Association.

Wachtel, P. L. 1996. *Therapeutic communication: Principles and effective practice.* New York: Guilford Press.

Wachtel, P. L. 1997. *Psychoanalysis, behavior therapy, and the relational world.* Washington, DC: American Psychological Association.

Wachtel, P. L. 2003. Revisioning the inner world. Paper given at the W. A. White Institute. New York, April.

Waldrop, M. A. 1992. *Complexity: The emerging science at the edge of order and chaos.* New York: Simon and Schuster.

Wallerstein, R. S. 1986. *Forty-two lives in treatment: A study of psychoanalysis and psychotherapy.* New York: Guilford Press.

Wallerstein, R. S. 1989. Follow-up psychoanalysis: Clinical and research values. *Journal of the American Psychoanalytic Association* 37, 921–941.

Wallerstein, R. S. 1995a. *The effectiveness of psychotherapy and psychoanalysis: Conceptual issues and empirical work.* Madison, WI: International Universities Press.

Wallerstein, R. S. 1995b. *The talking cures: The psychoanalyses and the psychotherapies.* New Haven, CT: Yale University Press.

Wallerstein, R. S., Blum, H. P., and Weinshel, E. M. 1989. *The psychoanalytic core: Essays in honor of Leo Rangell, M.D.* Madison, WI: International Universities Press.

Walster, E., Walster, G. W., and Berscheid, E. 1978. *Equity: Theory and research.* Boston: Allyn and Bacon.

Watkins, Mary M. 1976. *Waking dreams.* Gordon and Breach.

Watson, G. 1940. Areas of agreement in psychotherapy. *American Journal of Orthopsychiatry* 10, 698–709.

Watson, J. B. 1927. The myth of the unconscious. *Harpers* 155, 502–508.

Weber, M. 1930. *The Protestant Ethic and the Spirit of Capitalism,* trans. Talcott Parson. New York: Charles Scribner's Sons.

Wegner, D. 1992. You can't always think what you want: Problems in the suppression of unwanted thoughts. In M. P. Zanna, ed., *Advances in Experimental Social Psychology* 25, 193–225.

Wegner, D. 1994. Ironic processes of mental control. *Psychological Review* 101, 34–52.

Wegner, D. 2002. *The illusion of conscious will.* Cambridge, MA: MIT Press.

Wegner, D., and Bargh, J. A. 1998. Control and automaticity in social life. In D. T. Gilbert, S. T. Fiske, and G. Lindzey, eds., *The handbook of social psychology,* vol. 1, 446–496. Boston: McGraw-Hill.

Wegner, D., Schneider, D., Carter, S., and White, T. 1987. Paradoxical effects of thought suppression. *Journal of Personality and Social Psychology* 53, 5–13.

Wegner, D., and Wenzlaff, R. M. 1996. Mental control. In E. T. Higgins, and A. W. Kruglanski, eds. *Social psychology: Handbook of basic principles*, 466–492. New York: Guilford Press.

Weinberger, D. 1990. The construct validity of the repressive coping style. In J. L. Singer, ed., *Repression and dissociation: Implications for personality theory, psychopathology and health,* 337–386. Chicago: University of Chicago Press.

Weinberger, J., and Hardaway, R. 1990. Separating science from myth in subliminal psychodynamic activation. *Clinical Psychology Review* 10, 727–756.

Weinberger, J., Kelner, S., and McClelland, D. 1997. The effects of subliminalsymbiotic stimulation on free-response and self-report mood. *Journal of Nervous and Mental Disease* 185, 599–605.

Weiner, B., and Kukla, A. 1970. An attributional analysis of achievement motivation. *Journal of Personality and Social Psychology* 15, 1–20.

Weiskrantz, L. 1986. Some aspects of memory functions and the temporal lobes. *Acta Neurologica Scandinavica* 74, 69–74.

Weiss, J., Sampson, H., and the Mount Zion Psychotherapy Research Group. 1986. *The psychoanalytic process: Theory, clinical observation, and empirical research.* New York: Guilford Press.

Westen, D. 1992. The cognitive self and the psychoanalytic self: Can we put ourselves together? *Psychological Inquiry* 3, 1–13.

Westen, D. 1994. Toward an integrative model of affect regulation: Applications to social-psychological research. *Journal of Personality* 62, 641–667.

Westen, D. 1997. Towards a clinically and empirically sound theory of motivation. *International Journal of Psycho-analysis* 78, 521–548.

Westen, D. 1998. The scientific legacy of Sigmund Freud: Toward a psychodynamically informed psychological science. *Psychological Bulletin* 124, 333–371.

Westen, D. 2000. Integrative psychotherapy: Integrating psychodynamic and cognitive-behavioral theory and technique. In C. R. Snyder and R. E. Ingram, eds., *Handbook of psychological change: Psychotherapy processes and practices for the 21st century,* 217–242. New York: Wiley.

Westen, D. 2002a. The language of psychoanalytic discourse. *Psychoanalytic Dialogues* 12, 857–898.

Westen, D. 2002b. The search for objectivity in the study of subjectivity. *Psychoanalytic Dialogues* 12, 915–92

Westen, D., and Morrison, K. 2001. A multidimensional meta-analysis of treatments for depression, panic, and generalized anxiety disorder: An empirical examination of the status of empirically supported therapies. *Journal of Consulting and Clinical Psychology* 69, 875–899.

Wetzel, C. D. 1975. Effect of orienting tasks and cue timing on the free recall of remember- and forget-cued words. *Journal of Experimental Psychology: Human Learning and Memory* 104, 556–566.

Whalen, P. J., Rauch, S. L., Etcoff, N. L., McInerney, S. C., Lee, M. B., and Jenike, M. A. 1998. Masked presentations of emotional facial expressions modulate amygdala activity without explicit knowledge. *Journal of Neuroscience* 18, 411–418.

Whittle, P. 1999. Experimental psychology and psychoanalysis: What we can learn from a century of misunderstanding. *Neuro-psychoanalysis* 1, 233–245.

Whyte, L. 1978. *The unconscious before Freud.* New York: St. Martin.

Wiener, N. 1948. *Cybernetics.* New York: Wiley.

Wilcox, K., and Laird, J. D. 2000. The impact of media images of super-slender women on women's self-esteem. *Journal of Research in Personality* 34, 278–286.

Williams, J. M. G., Mathews, A., and MacLeod, C. 1996. The emotional Stroop task and psychopathology. *Psychological Bulletin* 120, 3–24.

Williams, J. M. G., Watts, F. N., MacLeod, C., and Mathews, A. 1997. *Cognitive Psychology and Emotional Disorders.* Chichester, England: Wiley.

Williams, T. A. 1988. *A multimodal approach to assessment and intervention with children with learning disabilities.* Unpublished doctoral dissertation, Department of Psychology, University of Glasgow, Scotland.

Wilson, A., Passik, S. D., and Faude, J. P. 1990. Self-regulation and its failures. In Masling, J., ed., 1990. *Empirical studies of psychoanalytic theories,* vol. 3., 149–213. Hillsdale, NJ: Analytic Press.

Wilson, E., and MacLeod, C. 2003. Contrasting two accounts of anxiety-linked attentional bias: Selective attention to varying levels of stimulus threat intensity. *Journal of Abnormal Psychology* 112, 212–218.

Wilson, E. O. 1998. *Consilience: The unity of knowledge.* New York: Knopf.

Wilson T. D. 2002. *Strangers to ourselves: Discovering the adaptive unconscious.* Cambridge, MA: The Belknap Press of Harvard University Press.

Winnicott, D. W. 1954. Mind and its relation to the psyche-soma. *British Journal of Medical Psychology* 27, 201–209.

Winnicott, D. W. 1958. The capacity to be alone. *International Journal of Psychoanalysis* 39, 416–420.

Winnicott, D. W. 1965. *The maturational process and the facilitating environment.* New York: International Universities Press.

Witenberg, E. G. 1987. Clinical innovations and theoretical controversy. *Contemporary Psychoanalysis* 23, 183–198.

Wolf, E. 1966. Learning theory and psychoanalysis. *British Journal of Medical Psychology* 39, 1–10.

Wolfe, B. E. 1995. Self pathology and psychotherapy integration. *Journal of Psychotherapy Integration* 5, 293–312.

Wolfe, B. E. 2005. Integrative psychotherapy for anxiety disorders. In J. C. Norcross, and M. R. Goldfried, eds., *Handbook of psychotherapy integration*, 2nd ed. New York: Oxford University Press.

Woodward, A. E., Bjork, R. A., and Jongeward, R. H. 1973. Recall and recognition as a function of primary rehearsal. *Journal of Verbal Learning and Verbal Behavior* 12, 608–617.

Woodworth, R. S. 1916. Letter to the editor. *The Nation* 103, 396.

Woodworth, R. S. 1917. Some criticisms of the Freudian psychology. *Journal of Abnormal Psychology* 12, 174–194.

Woodworth, R. S. 1948. *Contemporary Schools of Psychology*. New York: Ronald.

Zajonc, R. B. 1965. Social Facilitation. *Science* 149, 269–274.

Zajonc, R. B. 1980. Feeling and thinking: Preferences need no inferences. *American Psychologist* 35, 151–175.

Zajonc, R. B. 1994. Evidence for nonconscious emotions. In P. Ekman, and R. J. Davidson, eds., *The nature of emotion: Fundamental questions,* 293–297. New York: Oxford University Press.

Zeman, A. 2003. *Consciousness: A user's guide.* New Haven: Yale University Press.

Zillman, D., and Bryant, J. 1974. Retaliatory equity as a factor in humor appreciation. *Journal of Experimental Social Psychology* 10, 480–488.

Index

About the Author

Rebecca Coleman Curtis, Ph.D., is professor of psychology at the Derner Institute of Advances Psychological Studies at Adelphi University in Garden City, New York, where she is currently director of research. She is also faculty and supervisor at the W. A. White Institute of Psychiatry, Psychology, and Psychoanalysis and a supervisor at the National Institute for the Psychotherapies in Manhattan. Editor of *Self-Defeating Behaviors* and *The Relational Self*, she is author of numerous research articles and chapters and coeditor of *How People Change* and *On Deaths and Endings: Psychoanalysts' Reflections on Finality, Transformations and New Beginnings.* Dr. Curtis has a practice in psychology and psychoanalysis in Manhattan where she lives with her husband, an attorney.